IT'S A BEAUTIFUL
DAY FOR BASEBALL

THE NATIONAL PASTIME
IN THE 1960'S

DOUG KURKUL

Publisher: K Executive Group
ISBN: 978-1629672724
Library of Congress Control Number: 2024908686

Doug Kurkul, K Executive Group, 869 E. Schaumburg Rd, STE 221, Schaumburg, IL 60194, douglaskurkul@gmail.com.

Cover Design: Tatiana Fernandez
Interior Formatting: Brian Schwartz

ALSO AVAILABLE FROM THE AUTHOR

Portrait of a Franchise: An Intimate Look at Cleveland Indians Baseball during the Rockin' Sixties

v24-0428

ACKNOWLEDGEMENTS

The author thanks the Baseball Hall of Fame Library and Research Center and the Society for American Baseball Research for their indispensable assistance.

Thanks also go out to the following former players, coaches and executives – including 11 all-stars -- for sharing their memories from the 1960s: Max Alvis, Bob Aspromonte, Ken Aspromonte, Steve Bailey, Ken Berry, Dick Bosman, Ted Bowsfield, Ron Brand, Jackie Brandt, Bruce Brubaker, Larry Burright, Dr. Pete Charton, George Culver, Johnny Edwards, Chuck Essegian, Eddie Fisher, James French, Esq., Vern Fuller, Jake Gibbs, Gus Gil, Pat Gillick, Tom Gramly, Billy Harris, Sonny Jackson, Charlie James, Larry Jaster, Lou Klimchock, Darold Knowles, Don Lee, Jim Lonborg, Jeoff Long, Ken McBride, Tom McCraw, Sam McDowell, Jim Merritt, Joe Moeller, Joe Nossek, Dr. Rich Nye, Nate Oliver, Claude Osteen, Phil Regan, Merv Rettenmund, Tom Reynolds, Branch Rickey III, Ken Rudolph, Roland Sheldon, Bart Shirley, Sonny Siebert, Dick Simpson, Duke Sims, Al Spangler, Jack Spring, George Strickland, Ron Stone, Ken Suarez, Dick Tomanek, Del Unser, Dr. Dave Watkins, and Stan Williams.

PREFACE

Baseball has long been referred to as the national pastime and 60 years ago, the sport still enjoyed an undisputed claim on that title. A 1964 Harris poll found 48 percent of Americans named baseball as their favorite sport. No other game was close.

Millions of people played baseball in that era. Kids emulated their heroes while playing baseball on city alleys, suburban backyards and rural fields. Adults in huge numbers played in manicured sandlot leagues that were so competitive that the games drew large crowds and the scores were reported in the next morning's newspapers. Some of the best amateur players gathered in Wichita every summer to compete in the National Baseball Congress World Series. Little League and Pony League boomed in popularity. In the eastern states, the Babe Ruth League was attracting teen ballplayers like a young Bruce Springsteen in New Jersey. If Americans weren't playing hardball, they were playing softball or wiffle ball.

The Sixties were one of the most memorable eras in the 150-year history of major league baseball (MLB) and radio was the media that linked millions of Americans to the national pastime. Most homes lacked central air conditioning so on sultry summer evenings, folks relaxed on front porches and back patios with a cold beverage, up and down the block, street after street, listening to a ballgame on transistor radios that had become commercially available only a few years earlier. Often, the beverage at their side was brewed by the same company sponsoring the broadcast. The best of the radio voices – the likes of Red Barber in New York, Vin Scully in Los Angeles, Ray Scott in Minnesota, Jimmy Dudley in Cleveland, Bob Prince in Pittsburgh, Ernie Harwell in Detroit and others -- wove descriptions so rich and compelling that listeners awaited the call of every pitch.

On the field, it was seemingly an endless series of beautiful days for baseball. The quality of play had never been better up to that point, thanks to integration (since 1947) and the arrival of the first wave of Latino talent. Fueled by these changes, the talent on the diamond was exceptional. No fewer than 53 of the era's players have made their way to Cooperstown.

The period's top MLB players were just as famous as Hollywood's most glamorous stars, Washington's most powerful politicos, or the guitar heroes from the emerging British and American rock and roll bands. That level of recognition and notoriety far exceeded today's game of baseball, where many all-stars are largely unknown outside of the city in which they currently play. As pitcher Sam McDowell, one of the top strikeout artists of the Sixties, wrote in *The Saga of Sudden Sam,* "It has been contended correctly that Mike Trout, the greatest player in the game today, could walk down most streets in America and not be recognized. Can one imagine Willie Mays or Mickey Mantle not being mobbed in the same scenario in the 1950s or 1960s?"

The story lines captured the nation's imagination then and still resonate today. Mazeroski's walk-off homer. Mantle and Maris chasing Ruth's record. Wills surpassing Cobb for the most steals in a season. Koufax's unprecedented dominance and sudden retirement. Back-to-back triple crowns. The year of the pitcher. The miracle Mets.

Comparisons of eras are inevitable. Hall of Fame pitcher Jim Kaat describes the differences as well as anyone, writing in 2022, "Baseball has changed so much. And in my opinion, not for the better. The appeal of the game is still the ability of the players – at a higher level than ever before. There's more power and greater skill, agility and speed. But it has decreased, in my opinion, in executing the fundamentals and in exhibiting in many cases a lower baseball IQ. Today," he continued, "a higher percent of at bats result in a walk, strikeout or home run. Is that what fans want to see? There is a lot more to baseball than titanic home runs."

Today, a pitcher who survives for six innings allowing only three runs is credited with a "quality start." Bob Gibson, one of the most intimidating fireballers of all time, countered, "In my day, a quality start was a complete game victory." Hurlers then pitched inside to gain a strategic advantage. Hitters skillfully dropped bunts and hit behind runners. On the base paths, players went into second based hard, intent on breaking up double plays. Fielders crashed into fences making seemingly impossible catches. Unlike today, players took infield practice on a daily basis.

Concurrently, America was changing and baseball as an industry was evolving – slowly -- along with it. The civil rights movement, the labor movement, the drug culture, suburbanization and the demographic growth of the West and the South all touched the game as the decade progressed.

With fewer teams and less roster shuffling, it was incredibly difficult to scale the minor leagues and become a major leaguer. For those who made it, it was often the fulfillment of a long-held dream.

Now, six decades later, these former players and their careers are worth remembering. Their own memories are compelling.

One of the Hall of Famers, outfielder Billy Williams, still calls the era "the golden age of baseball." His former teammate, pitcher Rich Nye, reflects, "I think baseball in the Sixties was more about having fun, not about money. Those players were passionate about the game and many would have played for almost nothing, only to have the chance and opportunity."

Phil Regan, the longtime pitcher, coach and manager, concurs, reflecting, "That was the greatest era for baseball. Games played with sound fundamentals." Another former pitcher, Pete Charton of the Red Sox, reflects, "It is important to note how the players absolutely loved baseball, how fiercely competitive it was, and how the arrival of the players union forever changed player-management relationships, players, and fan loyalties, and eventually, I believe, to the declining popularity of baseball." Numerous other former players share similar sentiments in the pages that follow.

So what was it like to be a professional ballplayer in the Sixties? *It's a Beautiful Day for Baseball* provides an inside look at the national pastime – on and off the field – and the men who played the game during that monumental decade. The book is organized as follows:

- Section One provides a loving look at the sport, noting how much it has evolved on and off the diamond.

- Section Two highlights the experiences and memories of a mix of dozens of superstars, journeymen and short-term major leaguers, providing a 360-degree perspective.

- Until the advent of the designated hitter, every ballplayer wore a glove as he made his living. The Appendix provides original research into the leather of choice worn by more than 300 players of that era.

We now go back to an epoch when the White House was occupied by men named Eisenhower, Kennedy, Johnson and Nixon; a time when televisions purchased at Sears were beginning to show color images; and when The Andy Griffith Show and Gunsmoke were near the top of the ratings. A time when radio stations were phasing out the Mills Brothers, Frankie Avalon and Frank Sinatra from the playlists so as to transition to the Beach Boys, the Beatles, the Rolling Stones, Jimi Hendrix and the Doors. And to a time when the great game of baseball, for a short time longer, blessed with some of the most memorable stars to ever don a uniform, was still the country's undisputed favorite sport. Here we go…

CONTENTS

SECTION I:
THE NATIONAL PASTIME IN A MEMORABLE DECADE

It was the bottom of the ninth inning in game seven of the 1960 World Series and to the surprise of baseball insiders, the underdog, blue-collar Pittsburgh Pirates had pushed the Series against the heavily favored New York Yankees to a seventh and final game.

On this Thursday afternoon at Forbes Field in the nation's greatest steel-manufacturing center, the Pirates jumped out to a 4-0 lead, only to watch New York's explosive hitters give their club a 7-4 advantage. Not to be deterred, Pittsburgh clawed back with five runs in the bottom of the eighth frame to retake a 9-7 lead. In turn, the Yankees scored twice in the top of the ninth to tie the game at 9.

At that moment, 36,683 attendees in the ballpark were at the edge of their seats, as were hundreds of thousands more watching on television. It was 4:00 a.m. in Vietnam, where some of the U.S. troops were tuned in live on Armed Forces Radio. Richard Nixon and John Kennedy, preparing for their third presential debate that evening, were both said to be following the game. Singer Bing Crosby, one of the Pirates' owners, was listening to the game from Paris, confident that the crew he had hired to record a kinescope film of the game was capturing it for posterity.

With Ralph Terry, the Yankees' fifth pitcher of the game, toeing the rubber, all eyes were on Pirates second baseman Bill Mazeroski, who stepped to the plate. On a 1-0 delivery, Maz took a swing that would be remembered for the ages. He drilled a home run to give the Pirates a dramatic 10-9 victory and the world championship, concluding what is often called the greatest baseball game of all time. The moment is so compelling that its black-and-white video is replayed on YouTube thousands of times every year.

That was a different era and baseball was a different industry. There were 16 MLB teams, compared to 30 today. All of the qualification activity to get into the World Series until 1969 occurred during the regular season. (In 1960, the Yankees had won 97 games, the Pirates 95 contests, and there was no question that they were the two best teams in the sport that year.) Conversely, in 2023, 12 MLB teams went to the post-season, all with at least a theoretical chance to land in the fall classic.

MLB began emulating hockey and basketball by instituting playoff series in 1969, when each league was split into two divisions. By 1973, when the NL Eastern Division champ Mets with their pedestrian 82-79 record reached the World Series, it was crystal clear: The fall classic would come to feature the hottest teams, not necessarily the best ones.

Pennant races as baseball knew them became a thing of the past. Pre-1969, not every year featured a pennant chase; sometimes, the top team ran away with the title. But in seasons such as 1964 when both leagues had ultra-competitive races involving several contenders, baseball was the talk of the nation, with team members competing for pride and World Series bonus money. For some players, a World Series bonus could equal a 50 percent boost in their annual compensation, creating an incredible incentive to win. Author Doug Wilson described it well, writing, "September during a pennant race is when legends are made." These days, there are still battles to win a division title or a wild-card slot, but players and fans alike know it's not the same thing.

Steve Blass, the former pitcher for the Pirates, spoke for many when he wrote, "Personally, I have always felt that the playoffs are a crapshoot, anyway, and a team's true value is what it does over 162 games, not a best-of-five or best-of-seven series."

Extending the post-season generates more revenue for the sport but lengthens the season. Whereas the 1960 Series ended on October 13, the 2022 World Series, which lasted six games, was not completed until November 5. When it's more than half-way into football season and there's frost on the leftover pumpkins, it's hard for the World Series to command the passionate interest it once did.

This book does not assert whether the quality of play was better or worse in the 1960s, only that the game itself was very different, on and off the field.

Former players from that epoch often comment on the greater emphasis then on fundamentals. Notes all-star outfielder Ken Berry, who played for four teams over 14 years and then remained in the game for decades in a variety of capacities, "The Sixties was pure baseball. Contact on double plays. Players staying with the same team. Poor salaries. Now, it's too far the other way."

Former 20-game winner Claude Osteen, who logged years of duty with the Senators and Dodgers, agrees. In 2022, he recalled the Sixties as a time when "The game was played the way it was meant to be played. Offense, pitching, defense, all with correct fundamentals."

The late Stan Williams, who pitched for several clubs including the Dodgers, Yankees, Indians and Twins, emphasized that pitching inside was an integral part of the sport in those days. Bill Wakefield, a hurler on the 1964 Mets, said he never deliberately threw at a hitter, but frequently pitched inside on the first pitch of each at bat to ensure the hitter wasn't comfortable. These days, brushback pitches seem less common.

Today, many hitters go an entire season without laying down a sacrifice bunt. Bunting used to be a bigger part of the game. In the AL in 1963, the average team delivered 71.6 sacrifice hits. By comparison, in 2021, the average AL team laid down only 15.3 sacrifices. Pat Gillick, a minor-league player in the Sixties who later became a Hall-of-Fame team executive, emphasizes that clubs used to manufacture runs little by little, whereas now they wait for home runs and a big inning.

Another of the sport's fundamentals is making contact with the pitch. Today's batters routinely chase high pitches and strike out with alarming frequency. The late Bob Hale, a first baseman who played from 1955 to 1961, spoke for many in declaring that he hated to strike out. And he rarely did. The two squads in the 1960 World Series together fanned a combined 9.4 times per game. Even in the year of the pitcher, the 1968 World Series saw only 14.1 K's per contest. In the 2022 World Series, there was an astounding 21.3 whiffs per night.

The same pattern existed in regular-season action. In the NL in 1965, the average team struck out 965 times. In the NL in 2021, the average club whiffed 1,418 times – about a 50 percent increase. Fewer strikeouts meant more balls in play and more action. Strikeouts are exciting when they are relatively rare and when a true ace is baffling the competition, like when Bob Gibson fanned 17 Tigers in game one of the 1968 World Series. When they become commonplace, strikeouts deaden the experience of playing or watching a game.

In comparing the eras, players from the 1960s are quick to bring up the pace of play. Games had become so slow that in 2023, MLB adopted a pitch clock, a move supported by former outfielder Del Unser, who like many believe that baseball should be a fast-paced game.

Former hurler Tommy John, like many former stars, was not a fan of the slower game, with batters stepping out, pitchers laboring slowly, constant pitching changes and long commercial breaks. "The thing about that era [the Sixties], there was no BS on the field," he told an online interviewer. "You played the game, you played it hard. You won or you lost."

In the Sixties, the swift pace made for exciting play and allowed fans to get home at a reasonable hour. In the 2022 fall classic, every contest lasted well over three hours, clear evidence that something had to change.

Mid-inning pitching changes were less common. "They didn't count pitches then or restrict innings," noted Jim Kaat. "They counted outs. The goal was to get 27 of them and pitch nine innings."

Whereas teams these days carry 12 to 13 pitchers and always seem to have fresh arms, MLB clubs then typically had only nine or 10 pitchers, and managers were judicious in going to the pen. In 1965, the NL had only four pitchers appear in 65 or more games. By 2021, despite having more pitchers on every roster to split the load, 26 NL hurlers reached that level.

Even with that swift pace of yesteryear, some thought the game should be even quicker. In 1963, the Double-A Texas League experimented with a clock, manufactured by General Indicator Company, the scoreboard division of Sherrill-Gibbes Company of New York. Likened to a 24-second clock in basketball, a buzzer would sound if a pitcher failed to deliver his pitch within the prescribed time, and the umpire would add a ball to the count. The concept was debated but not adopted by MLB until 60 years later. Likewise, with relatively quick games, there was no need for contrived schemes like starting a runner at second base in extra innings.

Today, clubs adhere to strict pitch count limits, so much so that a hurler will be lifted upon reaching the target even if he is working on a no-hitter. In the Sixties, starting pitchers were expected to go deep into games. Being called a "seven-inning pitcher" was an insult.

A prime example was Ron Taylor, whose MLB debut was a start at Fenway Park for the Indians in April 1962. It was so cold that only 2,466 Boston fans braved the elements. Taylor pitched brilliantly and lost the game when he yielded a grand-slam homer in the 12th inning. Today, no manager would dream of letting a rookie hurler pitch into the 12th frame in his first start on a blustery afternoon.

In the years before MLB adopted a money-saving central scouting bureau, and before an amateur draft was introduced, talent scouts played a greater role. With prospects able, for the one and only time in their lives, to consider all bids and sign with the team making the most attractive offer, it was truly a free-market system.

Teams employed a staff of full-time scouts and maintained relationships with part-time bird-dog scouts around the country. As Skip Lockwood, one of the largest bonus-recipients described them, "These men were tobacco-chewing hangers on. Some had been fringe players, others just liked going to games with a stopwatch around their necks. They followed high school and college teams like a pack of mad dogs, hoping to sniff out some warm meat they called talent. Most could justify their Lincoln Town Cars and well-padded expense accounts." The best scouts were not only superb judges of talent, but also skilled in the art of persuasion, advising front offices where to allocate their funds, and then talking eager prospects and their parents into choosing their organization.

The scouts freely compared notes among themselves but did so with the guile of skilled poker players, for they were in keen competition to build a resume of successful signings. A scout who signed one of the game's cherished stars would find his own services in high demand for years to come.

Sportswriters traveled with the players from city to city, allowing ample time for them to develop relationships and an element of trust with one another. That practice was phased out in the 1990s when teams began excluding the media from team travel.

Nearly every team had one or more nationally known stars. Even casual fans could recite many players on each team's roster. While the MLB product on the field was spectacular, American society was changing and baseball as an industry was struggling to keep up.

The NL and AL were separate legal entities under the umbrella of MLB, with their own league president and front office. Warren Giles, a former Reds executive, was the NL president for the entire decade, with Joe Cronin, a former Hall of Fame infielder, holding the same post in the junior circuit. Each league office performed certain functions, such as hiring and evaluating umpires (in the mid-Sixties, the NL officials were unionized whereas the AL umpires were just starting to move in that direction).

The league offices were thinly staffed and the standards of operation were inconsistent. When two AL umpires, Lou Salerno and Bill Valentine were fired (probably for a combination of anger management issues and union organizing activity), a reason cited by Cronin was that they "lacked class at any time." Yet, when the matter went to the courts and the league president was asked if he would recommend the former umps for employment in the NL, he replied that he would. Cronin implied either that the AL had higher standards than the NL or that the reasons for terminating the pair were on shaky legal ground. These days, MLB would have a tighter legal strategy.

Another implication concerned where controversial matters were decided. Until the 1969 arrival of Commissioner Bowie Kuhn, who seemed to relish stepping into controversies, recent commissioners were reluctant to wade into white-hot quagmires, and it was convenient to pass the buck by saying it was "a league matter."

There was even an anti-fraternization policy between the league operations. A mid-Sixties proposal to locate the commissioner's office and both league offices in the same building in New York was shot down because it was argued that co-location might diminish competition between the two leagues (even though the only on-field competition occurred during exhibition games, the all-star game, and the World Series).

Another role of the league office was scheduling, and it was common for teams to play double-headers on Sundays. It made for a long day for the ballplayers but was a true BOGO deal for the fans. Some teams carried a pitcher on the roster primarily to start the second games of Sunday twin-bills. These days, on the rare occasions that a team plays two games in one day, the fans usually pay twice.

Eventually, the league offices were eliminated, with their functions consolidated under MLB. From the players' viewpoint, the presence of two largely independent leagues meant more than just who hired umps and approved schedules. With less player movement and no interleague play, there was pride in one's own league, and constant bantering about which loop was superior. Players who had spent their entire careers in the AL sometimes resented the "arrogance" of certain NL players and this carried into the early Seventies. When Vida Blue of the A's went into the 1971 all-star break with a 17-3 record, NL all-stars joked, "Sure he has 17 wins – in the American League!"

For a time, it looked like there might be a third major league, the Continental League. As the Sixties commenced, the two leagues had eight teams each, as there had been no expansion since the AL became the second of the major leagues in 1901.

There was growing pressure to place new teams in key locales. The fastest-growing state, California, had only two teams in 1960. Texas, another large state, had none. New York had gone from three teams to just one, and attorney William Shea was leading the charge for MLB to provide another team in the Big Apple. MLB formed an Expansion Committee in December 1958, with owners Philip Wrigley of the Cubs and Walter O'Malley of the Dodgers representing the NL, plus the less influential A's owner Arnold Johnson and Indians minority shareholder George Medinger representing the AL.

Shea and Branch Rickey (the legendary general manager who played a key role in integrating baseball and developing the modern farm system), contemplated creating a third major league with franchises in Atlanta, Buffalo, Dallas-Fort Worth, Denver, Houston, Minneapolis, New York and Toronto. Rickey lined up wealthy, influential leaders to back the proposed new franchises.

The MLB club owners did not welcome the unpredictability of a new third league, so even though some were ambivalent about expansion, they were motivated to prevent the new league from seeing the light of day.

Ultimately, the NL announced in the autumn of 1960 that it would methodically move to provide Shea and New York with a team, and add a club in Houston, in 1962. Weeks later, the AL tried to one-up the NL with its own hastily planned announcements. It would add one team in southern California and one in the nation's capital -- to replace the original Senators who were moving to the Twin Cities – in time for spring training just a few months later in 1961. Together, these developments took the steam out of the Continental League's momentum.

In the AL, the new Senators predictably struggled, while the Angels, managed by former Giants skipper Bill Rigney, surged to a surprising third place in 1962, their second season. But it would be many years before either squad made the post-season. Among the NL expansion squads, 1969 was an important year for both, as Houston reached the .500 mark for the first time and the Mets staged their memorable championship run.

Expansion worked well enough that owners added two more teams in each league in 1969. From the players' perspective, expansion equaled opportunity. MLB went from 400 roster spots in 1960 to 600 by the close of the decade. It was still incredibly competitive, but scores of ballplayers who would have been confined to the bushes now got to play in the big leagues and some did quite well (see the entries on Nate Colbert and Lou Piniella).

Nowadays, there are 30 teams with 750 roster spots. Constant shuffling of players to and from the minor leagues, and onto and off of the injured list, means that more than 1,000 players now see action in any season.

In the Sixties, with the relatively smaller number of jobs available, it was remarkable how many brother combinations occupied those positions – as witnessed with the Aaron, Allen, Alou, Bennett, Boyer, Brown, Conigliaro, Freese, Gagliano, Keough, Klaus, Lary, Locke, May, Niekro, Olivo, O'Toole, Perry, Sherry, and Torre brothers.

Expansion watered down the pitching. In 1961, baseball's top subplot was the historic chase of Babe Ruth's single-season home run record waged by Roger Maris and Mickey Mantle of the Yankees. They weren't the only ones to feast on thinner pitching depth. Norm Cash and Rocky Colavito of the Tigers also had monster seasons, and it was a lesser-remembered, fun-loving slugger, Jim Gentile of the Orioles, who bested all of them with a league-high 141 RBI. When the NL expanded the next year, there was a similar but less pronounced effect, as runs scored rose modestly from 700 to 728 per club (skewed by expansion Houston scoring only 592 runs and the Mets 617 times).

Despite the initial increase in offense, pitchers steadily reclaimed the upper hand, and scoring became so scarce that by 1968, one attending a game had a significant likelihood of seeing a shutout. Stolen bases, hit-and-run plays, sacrifice bunts and sacrifice flies all took on importance.

Rule changes were implemented for the 1969 season to lower the pitcher's mound by five inches and downsize the strike zone. Some people blamed Bob Gibson of the Cardinals, who recorded a historic 1.12 ERA in 1968, for making the rule changes necessary.

Baseball men debated why the scoring was down. Ted Williams and Stan Musial, who knew hitting as well as anyone, speculated it was because more pitchers were mastering the slider, then a relatively new pitch. That trend, in turn, yielded concerns about pitchers' arms.

In 1968, the A's pitching coach, Barnacle Bill Posedel, forbade all but one of his pitchers (Catfish Hunter) from throwing the pitch. "The way the slider is thrown, it hurts the arm. It hurts the elbow," the aging coach posited. Yet in retrospect, the screwball may have been a greater risk for pitchers' arms than the slider. Medicine in that era offered few solutions for arm injuries beyond rubdowns, ice treatments and cortisone shots. Ligament replacement (Tommy John) surgery was not introduced until 1974.

Another difference was access to statistics. Printed box scores did not include batting averages until the early 1990s. Players and fans alike looked forward to the Sunday newspapers to see the league leaders.

Leon Wagner, an outfielder who played primarily for the Angels and Indians, said he drew his motivation from seeing his name listed among league leaders. Journeyman outfielder Don Lock reflected years later in an interview on radio station KFH, "All I ever read was the Sunday paper. That's how you knew what was going on. Back in those days, they didn't even put the batting averages up on the scoreboards. So, on Sunday mornings you'd get up, get a newspaper, have breakfast, look at the statistics, and go to the ballpark."

Players sometimes had access to a copy of *The Sporting News*, either in the clubhouse or by purchasing a copy themselves. *TSN* called itself the Bible of Baseball but it really was more of a "hometown newspaper" for the industry, providing not only statistics and game accounts, but also reams of information about baseball players, their families, managers, front office staff and even the minor leagues. Only the most avid of fans read *TSN* each week, but it was required reading for front office honchos, team managers and scouts.

Statistics like slugging percentage and on-base percentage were readily available. Pitch counts were not tracked carefully by most teams, which explains why starting pitchers were sometimes still in the game in the 15th inning. Modern statistics like WAR ratings, range factor and the velocity of the ball coming off the bat were decades away. The scarcity of radar guns meant that players could only estimate how fast pitches were traveling, but scouts with stopwatches had a good read on how fast batters could make it to first base.

As MLB expanded, more minor league affiliates were needed. In 1962, there were 145 farm teams for an average of better than seven per franchise. The Dodgers, Braves and Giants – all based in the NL -- topped out the list with 10 minor-league teams apiece that year, while the newly established Angels of the AL had the fewest affiliates.

Nowadays, a minor-league team will have a manager, pitching coach, hitting coach and quite often an assistant coach and a development coach, along with a trainer. In the Sixties, the minor-league manager worked solo, wearing all hats, and sometimes even driving the team bus.

The Triple-A level in the summer of 1962 had three circuits – the Pacific Coast League, the International League, and the American Association. At the Double-A level, there was just one loop, the Texas League (the Eastern League and South Atlantic League became Double-A entries in 1963). The Single-A level featured two leagues.

Beneath A-ball was a bevy of other circuits, now mostly extinct, with names like Northern, Midwest, Appalachian, New-York Penn, Carolina, Western Carolina, Florida State, Alabama-Florida, Georgia-Florida, Midwest, Pioneer, California, and Northwest leagues. These were supplemented by the Peninsula Winter League, plus Instructional Leagues in Arizona and Florida. The plethora of minor circuits brought the genuine joys of pro baseball to small and midsize towns to see teams like the Gastonia Rippers, Bakersfield Bears, Burlington Bees, Idaho Falls Chukars, Appleton Foxes, Aberdeen Pheasants, Knoxville Smokies, Dubuque Packers and Moultrie Colt .22s. The larger number of minor leagues and teams provided hope and opportunity to about 3,625 minor-league players in a given year.

Each of the minor leagues was individually administered, providing a semblance of independence and an ability to focus on the needs of the club owners and the region's fans. Each league paid dues to an umbrella group, the National Association of Professional Baseball Leagues (NABPL). In the early 1960s, the NABPL was based in Columbus, Ohio, the hometown of George Trautman, who ran the organization until his death in 1963. Phil Piton, a lifelong baseball man, succeeded him and held the post through 1971. The NAPBL was in operation from 1902 until 2021, when

MLB executed a hostile takeover of the minor leagues, slashed the number of teams, and began running everything from New York City.

Life in the lower rungs of the minor leagues was not luxurious. Food allowances were stingy, and married players like future A's pitcher Paul Lindblad often skimped on meals to send extra money to their families. Steve Bailey, who later pitched for the Indians, recalled a team motel in Keokuk, Iowa, infested with bedbugs. Travel in the lower levels was by bus. The trip from Mobile to Charlotte, for example, was 13 hours. Long rides on buses that lacked air conditioning were an ordeal; players did their best to pass the time by playing cards, telling tall tales about baseball and women, or trying to catch 40 winks. Pitcher Bob Heffner recalled drying out his shirts by laying them over the open bus windows. "I lost a shirt or two that way," he joked.

While conditions were challenging, players' memories are often fond. Ken Harrelson wrote of his class-D ball experience, "We were overcrowded, not making much money to play in tiny ballparks in front of few fans, running to catch our bus after taking a pee, all while sleeping and eating in boarding houses – and we loved every minute of it."

At the Triple-A level, conditions were often better. Former Dodgers hurler Bruce Brubaker recalled in 2022, "I pitched for five years in the Pacific Coast League. We traveled by jet and the hotel accommodations were good."

Getting called up to the major leagues for the first time often was a magical moment, notwithstanding that it often required players to catch the first available flight (not infrequently the red-eye), hurriedly check into a hotel, and then rush to the ballpark. These players typically had no idea how long they would be with the parent club.

Young Steve Blass learned the news of his first call-up when his pregnant wife Karen fielded a phone call from the Pirates' general manager early one morning. Waking her husband up, she yelled, "Get your ass out of bed, we're going to the big leagues!" They drove from Columbus to Pittsburgh the same day in the pouring rain.

Another case in point was the late Billy Harris, an infielder with the Indians and Royals, who was called up for the first time in 1968 to replace an injured player. Harris learned of his call-up while standing on third base. Manager Red Davis broke the exciting news, saying they had to get the game over with so Harris could get to an airport. Harris played well upon his recall and was heartened several weeks later when the Indians flew his wife to Cleveland, and had a driver bring their car all the way from Portland, Oregon. "Holy shit, I've got a chance to stay with the team the rest of the season," he recalled thinking.

The story of how pitcher Jim Nash reported for his first MLB call-up in 1966 is one that would never happen today, in the age of credits cards, cash dispensers, and Uber rides. Nash's Triple-A team had just arrived by bus in Charlotte when he learned that he was to catch the first flight to Detroit to join the A's (to replace Chuck Dobson who had been placed on the injured list). The team pre-purchased his flight but when it landed, he had only $8 in his wallet. He picked up a taxi at the airport but when the meter started approaching $8, he exited the taxi and took a bus the rest of the way to the team's downtown hotel.

The baseball lifestyle had more than its share of advantages as well as perks, and often represented a dream come true, but it could be very tough on wives and children, as exemplified by the family of Sammy Taylor, who caught for the Cubs and the Mets.

Early in the 1962 season, he rented a small apartment in Chicago to share with his wife Polly and young daughter. Several weeks into the season, he told the Cubs he was contemplating quitting baseball because his salary wasn't enough to afford housing both in Chicago and back home in South Carolina. The Cubs responded that he was receiving a competitive wage. To make matters worse, newspapers began carrying stories that Polly was not happy in Chicago, where she lacked the support system that a young mother should have, and that their marriage might be on the rocks. Unhappy with the Cubs' response, he left the team, was suspended, and then was traded to the Mets, who improved his salary. Happily, the couple prospered in marriage for decades to come.

As players' and managers' children grew older, there were wonderful adventures. Future big-leaguer Terry Francona had the run of ballparks when his dad (Tito Francona) was an active player. Manager Birdie Tebbetts always selected an apartment complex with a swimming pool to keep his children active all summer. (When he took a minor-league managerial job in 1967 in Marion, Virginia, the roughest adjustment was the change in lifestyle for his family summering in a small town.) Debbie Menke, daughter of former Braves, Astros and Reds infielder Denis Menke, said in a 2015 online post, "While my friends got to play all summer, we had to go to a ballgame every night. I knew every nook and cranny of the Astrodome. And my first date was with a bat boy."

Baseball careers were often interrupted with military service, as the nation did not adopt an all-volunteer military until 1973. Until then, players could be called away for a couple of weeks or a couple of years. Service in the armed forces could interrupt players' career progression, and occasionally affect the MLB standings.

Moreover, there was always the risk of non-baseball injury. Dave Dowling, a promising NL pitcher, tore his rotator cuff while moving some metal lockers on Army Reserve duty. He went on to become an orthodontist –much sooner than he expected. Gary Sanossian was a minor-league pitching prospect stationed in Vietnam when his base was attacked, sirens activated, and everyone scampered for the bunker. Gary tripped over his commanding officer and landed hard on his pitching elbow, ending his hopes for an MLB career.

Military service sometimes reinforced players' sense of patriotism. Former Yankees pitcher Roland Sheldon reflected in 2022, "Everyone should spend some time in the service of their country. It builds character and a pure love for our country. It is a way to mature and make something of yourself."

Spring training was also different. The training facilities and exhibition fields were more primitive, providing less comfort for the players, and greater access to players for snowbirds, local fans and autograph hunters. Newer training facilities have reduced public access to the players.

In 1964, 15 of the 20 MLB teams trained in Florida, whereas today, a majority of squads trains in Arizona. One consequence of having an odd number of teams in Florida and Arizona was the use of split-squads, so that every club could be in action on any given day. Split-squad games were not popular with fans, who sprung for tickets only to find that half of a club's players were not even with the team that day.

While today's MLB players have the benefits of better training regimens, year-around access to fitness centers and nutrition counseling, many of them have concentrated on baseball from an early age. Yesteryear's players usually competed in several high school sports, be it football, basketball, track and field, or hockey. Because each sport develops different muscle systems, youngsters who compete in multiple sports often have a more completely developed body. Steve Hamilton, Cotton Nash, Dick Groat, Daryl Sutherland and Dave DeBusschere had sufficient conditioning to play in MLB and the NBA.

Suburbanization resulted in families living further from the ballpark. Coupled with rising crime in certain inner cities, the result was disappointing attendance in some markets, though teams such as the Dodgers in the early-to-mid decade, were setting attendance records. In 1969, the Mets topped two million fans. Five others (Red Sox, Dodgers, Cardinals, Cubs, Tigers) enjoyed strong support and eclipsed 1.5 million. Six more topped one million admissions (Braves, Astros, Twins, Expos, Yankees, Orioles). The others were below one million.

Teams staged promotions and some of them were highly effective at driving attendance. Bat Day, Ball Day, Straight A Student Day, Ladies Day, Senior Citizens Day, Grandstand Managers Night, Fireworks Night, and Camera Day, where players were stationed near the stands before the game so that fans could take photographs, were common promotions. A's owner Charles O. Finley staged less conventional promotions like cow-milking contests and mule-riding exhibitions.

Old-Timer games were another popular promotion, especially the Yankees, who could trot out an impressive lineup of former greats. Not to be outdone, the 1968 A's lined up all three DiMaggio brothers to play the outfield together in an exhibition contest. But as the Sixties progressed, teams began relying more on media contracts for revenue, and were less dependent on ticket and concession sales.

Baseball was not immune from the era's other social issues. The civil rights movement was in full force, and black players, whether hailing from the U.S. or Latin America, endured horrendous discrimination and abuse, both during spring training in the South and sometimes during the regular season. Numerous examples are presented in this book (see entries on Earl Battey, Ed Charles, Mudcat Grant, Joe Morgan, Blue Moon Odom, John Roseboro, and Billy Williams).

Blatant examples pertained to restaurant access and hotel accommodations. Gus Gil, a future infielder for the Indians, Pilots and Brewers, recalled spring training in the Reds organization. When the team bus stopped and the players filed into a restaurant, Gil was forced to remain on the bus. He was grateful to teammates Tommy Helms and Pete Rose for bringing him food, but long remembered the indignity.

Before the passage of the Civil Rights Act, young pitcher Rudy May experienced discrimination during training camp for the first time. As he told interviewer Jeff Pearlman, "I got into a little bit of trouble because I was the only black player from the West Coast. I didn't know that I was not conducting myself as I should have been. For instance, the clubhouse was segregated. The whites were on one side and the blacks were on the other … and I was there a whole week before I realized that. I didn't know. One of my teammates told me, 'Why are you going in the front door of the clubhouse? Why are you drinking out of the fountain—you're not supposed to do that. There's a bucket in the back for us to drink out of.'"

On the day the Civil Rights Act passed, May and his black teammates walked across Kinston, North Carolina from a black-owned motel and integrated a formerly white-only hotel. It was a moment of justice, though the black players were afraid for their safety as they made the walk. Even after the adoption of the 1963 Civil Rights Act, black players encountered more subtle forms of bias including housing discrimination. And some teams, including the Red Sox, seemed to keep an informal cap on the number of black players on their roster.

White players sometimes took a stand against racism. For example, in 1959, Red Sox coach Del Baker harassed a black player on an opposing team, using the "n word." Baker's involvement in baseball went back to the dead ball era and he was now in his mid-sixties. Pitcher Bill Monbouquette, just 22 years old, confronted Baker, telling him his conduct was inappropriate. "I'll knock you right on your ass. I don't care if you're the coach or not," he warned.

When riots tore apart urban areas between 1965 and 1968, players were well aware of what was happening. In Los Angeles, John Roseboro, Lou Johnson and Willie Crawford of the Dodgers were living not far from the riot zone and were cautious as they traveled. Teammate Jeff Torborg said he and a number of other Dodgers carried guns in case they had to defend themselves. Others recalled riding on a team bus viewing burned-out commercial and residential buildings in Washington, D.C. and Detroit, or assisting police in calming neighborhoods. Baseball also played a role of unification and healing in some communities. The 1968 Tigers' success had a positive influence on reuniting riot-torn Detroit.

Meanwhile, Latin American players were beginning to join the pantheon of stars. But they faced transitions, including language, culture and customs, even before the need to scale the minor leagues and get to the majors. Many of them wore a cross necklace around their neck, perhaps to remind them of their faith.

In 1964, Roberto Clemente was asked why some Latino players underperformed MLB expectations. His response as published in *The Sporting News* was revealing. "Maybe this is puzzling to Americans, but it isn't puzzling to any of us from Latin America or Cuba who have gone through this ordeal," he explained. "It takes all of us some time to get adjusted. We lead different lives in America. We're always meeting new people, seeing new faces. The language barrier is great at first and we have trouble ordering food in restaurants. Even segregation baffles us."

Behind the scenes, drugs were becoming more common. Jim Bouton's 1970 book, *Ball Four,* revealed that some Yankees players used readily available amphetamines (or greenies) to amp up for games (MLB finally banned them in 2006.) Marijuana use among players was not common in the early Sixties but increased as the decade progressed. Use of cocaine was rarer, but not unheard of around the game. A legal drug being used extensively was cortisone, shot into injured players by trainers. The shots could dull the pain of a sore arm for a while, but was usually no cure, and over time, multiple shots were not conducive to long-term health.

Many MLB players were cigarette smokers. It wasn't until 1964 that the Surgeon General offered definitive evidence that smoking was a cause of serious lung disease. Lacking the knowledge that we have today, many players smoked in the dugout, the locker room, the team bus, the airplane, and wherever they went.

Chewing tobacco was also far more common then. Look at any picture of Hall of Fame second basemen Nellie Fox and Bill Mazeroski, for example, and inevitably you'll see a bulge in one cheek. Only in the last 25 years has MLB instituted intensive educational programs aimed at preventing young players from developing the chewing tobacco habit.

Drinking alcohol, especially beer, was engrained in the game's culture. Nearly every team had a brewery as a sponsor, be it Anheuser-Busch, Schlitz, Pabst, Ballantine, Stroh's, Carling Black Label and several others. The breweries were all too happy to distribute free cases of their product to team members. Some players (see entry on Steve Bilko) were content to down beers in the hotel room after contests. Players with a more adventurous spirit -- and often their managers and coaches -- convened at dance clubs, American Legion halls, corner saloons, or hotel bars to consume their beverage of choice.

The lax attitudes about alcohol were in many cases harmless, allowing young men to unwind together, taking the edge off an extraordinarily competitive line of work. But sometimes those lax attitudes led to drinking problems and team officials rarely intervened unless a player's on-field performance declined.

Pitcher Ryne Duren later recalled being "addicted to booze the way a junkie is addicted to heroin." Outfielder Gary Geiger, who played for four teams between 1958 and 1970, used alcohol to dull his terrible fear of flying. His flight-related anxiety would flare up the day before each flight. Over time, he developed serious health problems as a result of the hooch. Bo Belinsky, John Blanchard, Curt Blefary, Vic Davalillo, Chuck Dobson, Mickey Mantle, Billy Martin, Don Newcombe, Ray Oyler, Sam McDowell and others also paid a price for their overindulgence, though some such as McDowell successfully entered recovery and then helped others overcome their addiction.

Unlike today, where baseball teams offer excellent sports psychology resources, players in the Sixties were on their own, young men navigating the path of a high-profile career while traveling from city to city in an ultra-competitive field.

On the Dodgers, an informal Sunday chapel allowed Don Sutton, Joe Moeller and Jeff Torborg to worship together. With the Yankees, once broadcaster Red Barber heard the story of three Yankees players arriving late for an afternoon game because they were surrounded by autograph-seekers at a Sunday morning church service, Barber began leading Sunday morning prayer meetings. Writer Watson Spoelstra founded the Baseball Chapel in 1973. A number of other ballplayers were known to be devout Christians – Don Demeter, Jerry Kindall, Lou Klimchock, Lindy McDaniel, Albie Pearson, Bobby Richardson, Dave Wickersham, and Al Worthington among them, but they were exceptions to the rule. Jewish players were likewise mostly on their own to practice their religion. Faith was for the most part a very quiet part of the game.

Equipment has also evolved over the years. Catchers masks are now lighter and more comfortable, made from new composite materials, offering strong protection. Chest protector designs have also improved. Uniforms have come a long way and are more breathable.

Massachusetts-based Spalding had been supplying the baseballs used in the NL since 1876 and in the AL since 1901. The price of their baseballs depended on who was asking. In 1960, the AL paid $3.74 per dozen and the NL paid $4.48 per dozen. If you ran a sporting goods store, your cost was just over $21 for 12 balls. If you were purchasing for a college or youth league, you would pay even more.

This sweetheart arrangement for MLB eventually backfired on Spalding. College and amateur leagues, where Spalding used to make their profits, began procuring lower-cost balls from other sources. Spalding, which asked MLB for a renegotiation of terms, became a branch of Toledo-based Questor Corp. in 1970 and produced MLB's official balls only until 1977, when Rawlings assumed that role.

What mattered to MLB players, of course, was the consistency of the balls, not the manufacturer or the price. Complaints periodically surfaced from pitchers about balls being "juiced" and from hitters about balls being "deadened." MLB and Spalding maintained that the composition remained consistent. The White Sox, who relied on superb pitching, were suspected of storing balls in a damp location to deaden them. The team's grounds crew also maintained a wet infield to slow down the pace of ground balls.

Young players, after signing their first pro contract, typically signed with one of the four major glovemakers – Spalding, Rawlings, MacGregor and Wilson. They received a couple of free gloves and baseball shoes each year (sometimes with a set of golf clubs thrown in as a signing bonus) in exchange for a lifetime endorsement deal. The four competed to sign promising prospects, and once players became stars, their names were featured in print ads (or on the gloves themselves under separate royalty deals).

The gloves of choice for more than 300 players are listed in the Appendix. While nearly all major leaguers used gloves from one of the "big four," Sears made a splash in 1960 when it signed Ted Williams to an endorsement deal for all of its baseball, fishing, hunting and camping gear, replacing its JC Higgins brand. Other more obscure glove options included Nocona (commonly expressed as Nokona), Hollander and Sonnet.

Spalding's promotions manager Duke Zilber, who previously was the general manager of the Reading Indians and a minor-league umpire, would visit minor league parks with trunks full of gloves and cleats to distribute to grateful young players. Spalding, which was the parent company of Rawlings from 1955 until the FTC and a court decision forced a divestiture in 1963, had a cadre of stars that included Yogi Berra, Rocky Colavito, Don Drysdale, Roger Maris, and Tracy Stallard. (That was not the only time that Maris and Stallard's name would appear in the same paragraph. Stallard served up Maris' 61st home run in 1961.)

Rawlings, founded in 1898, proudly boasted that some of the game's greatest fielders – Ken Boyer, Roberto Clemente, Dick Groat, Randy Hundley, Mickey Mantle, and Brooks Robinson among them – used their rawhides. The company scored a public relations coup as sponsor of gold glove awards (and silver glove awards for minor leaguers) for defensive excellence, gaining valuable branding.

Rawlings in St. Louis employed Harry Latina, known as "the glove doctor," along with his son Roland, to oversee glove design. At one time, Harry and Roland claimed 90 percent of the patents for baseball gloves and mitts. Rawlings had about 2,000 employees and did its manufacturing in five facilities in Missouri and three in Puerto Rico, producing equipment for a variety of sports.

Cincinnati-based MacGregor was a division of Brunswick Corp, the folks best known at the time for bowling alley equipment. Their client list was as impressive as anyone's including Hank Aaron, Richie Ashburn, Del Crandall, Willie Mays, Bill Mazeroski, Tony Oliva, Pete Rose, and Bobby Richardson.

Wilson traced its roots to a Chicago meatpacking operation in 1913 that used animal byproducts to make tennis racket strings. Under the leadership of Thomas Wilson, the sports operation was spun off and moved into a full line of sporting goods. It remained privately owned until acquired by an equity group in 1967. Wilson had its own cadre of endorsers, such as Luis Aparicio, Ernie Banks, Nellie Fox, Gil Hodges, Al Kaline, Harmon Killebrew, Willie McCovey, Juan Marichal, Hoyt Wilhelm, and Early Wynn.

Whereas most hitters back in the 1920s had swung bats weighing 36 or more ounces, by the 1950s, 32-ounce bats were common. Ted Williams popularized the notion that a hitter could generate more bat speed and exit velocity with a lighter bat. According to a SABR article by Steven Bratkovich, several 1960s hitters went with heavier bats, notably Orlando Cepeda, Dick (Richie) Allen, and Roberto Clemente, but most favored lighter models. Batting gloves came into vogue in the Sixties (see entry on Ken Harrelson). The practice became so widespread that by the 1980s, an entrepreneur named Irving Franklin won the contract to provide the official batting glove of MLB.

Wearing eyeglasses on the field was common. Frank Howard, a home run champion with the Senators, may have been the most prominent. Players started to wear contact lenses in the early Seventies.

Until 1965 when MLB established an amateur player draft, prospects could negotiate for the best possible offer. The draft limited the player to the team that selected him. This major change had enormous implications for the game (see entry on Rick Reichardt). Scouting evolved, as clubs prepared for the draft, deciding whether to select college or high-school players, and gauging whether they would be able to sign the player. In many cases, teams miscalculated by drafting players who opted for another year in college. The A's selected outfielder Rick Monday as the first player chosen in the 1965 draft. Hall of Famer Johnny Bench was the 36th player overall, selected by the Reds.

In 1967, the minimum MLB salary was $6,000. In 2022, the minimum MLB salary was $700,000. Because player salaries were more comparable to the compensation earned by the folks in the grandstands in the Sixties, there was an element of affinity with players that has long since been lost.

Many players resented their lack of bargaining clout every winter. The imbalance of negotiating power began to chip away in 1966 when labor economist Marvin Miller visited every team in spring training, hoping to be elected president of the players' association. He received a chilly welcome from some in management, such as Indians manager Birdie Tebbetts who asked him if he was a communist. Despite the skepticism of some players, such as Ken Harrelson who feared losing income if there was a strike, and Wes Parker who felt the Dodgers ownership treated players well, Miller was elected on a 489-136 vote.

It was not until the mid-1970s, with the end of the reserve clause and the advent of free agency, that player salaries skyrocketed and multi-year contracts became common. For many of the players from the Sixties, those changes came too late to make a difference.

Since baseball salaries were modest, most players took winter jobs. Norm Siebern and Hank Fischer sold mutual funds. Moe Drabowsky was a runner for a stock brokerage. Denny McLain gave organ concerts and taught music lessons. Dwight Siebler worked at his family's HVAC business. Steve Blass drove a delivery truck. Vern Fuller worked in hotel and restaurant management. Bob Locker worked for a fishing-supply company. Rich Rollins sold insurance and snowmobiles. Bill Stafford was a deputy sheriff. Danny Cater worked several winters at the Little League International headquarters.

For a time, Jim Bunning officiated basketball games. Ray Herbert worked at a Montgomery Ward store. Pete Magrini sold cars. Steve Ridzik worked for a food distributor. Carl Willey sold men's clothes. Bo Belinsky did a nightclub act. Ken Berry worked in a grocery store, sandblasted headstones, worked in a state office building and offered hitting lessons – "whatever it took" as he put it. Others played winter ball offshore or took classes during the winter to prepare for their post-baseball careers.

While the likes of Brooks Robinson, Pete Rose, Norm Cash and Gates Brown earned money as speakers on the winter banquet circuit, there were only so many of those gigs to go around. Some stars, like Bob Gibson, worked the banquet circuit initially, only to grow tired of the routine.

Today, by contrast, most players make enough from their baseball salary that they can focus on their fitness and their family, without worrying about a winter job.

Spring training was a time of sweating off excess weight, training bodies into game-ready condition, and getting one's timing back. Happily, most players were in fine shape by the time Opening Day rolled around.

Weight management was a challenge for dozens of players. When Dick Bosman of the Senators discussed his offseason wedding plans, manager Ted Williams made a friendly wager over how much weight Dick would gain as a married man. Bosman won the wager, but some players struggled mightily. Third baseman Bob Bailey's wife loved to bake desserts, which may have been counter-productive to his fitness. Pirates slugger Willie Stargell often reported heavier than the team-set goal, and club officials worked with him every spring on experimental diets to shed the extra pounds.

Stargell was a star performer, but teams were less forgiving of marginal players who reported plump. Utility infielder Mike de la Hoz was reportedly out of shape when he reported to the Indians camp in 1962. The new manager, Mel McGaha, demoted him for virtually the entire season, and the player always felt the skipper had something against him personally. But when De la Hoz arrived home in Miami after the season, the scout who signed him, Monchy De Arco, read him the riot act about the need to stay in better shape. The infielder did so and was back in MLB until the end of the decade.

Pitcher Sparky Lyle began gaining weight early in his career. He was driving to Winter Haven for the 1970 spring training when he was pulled over for speeding. Lyle explained that he was rushing to training camp in Florida, to which the officer asked if he was a football player. "No, I'm a baseball player," Lyle responded. The officer, looking at Lyle's poor physique, replied, "With that stomach?" Indeed, Lyle's ERA ballooned along with his weight that season and the front office pressured him to shed some pounds.

MLB in those days had longer service requirements for qualifying for a pension. Pitcher Rich Nye called the league office to confirm he had sufficient service time before finalizing his retirement plans. Many other players were demoted back to the minor leagues just before qualifying and never made it back. An example was Jack Spring, who pitched for five MLB clubs. He was with Cleveland and pitching well in 1965 when demoted to the minors. Upon asking manager Birdie Tebbetts why he was being sent down, he was told, "You drew the short straw." Spring pitched four and a half more seasons in the minors, but never again got activated, even though his former Angels teammate Dean Chance was lobbying on his behalf. Spring went into teaching, coaching (one of his young players was future actor Kurt Russell) and later enjoyed a comfortable retirement, but not as carefree as it could have been with a baseball pension.

Although very few players were earning six-figure salaries, those who had regular MLB roles for a number of years earned respectable money. When pitcher Dave Wickersham retired after 10 years in the majors, he said, "I want the young people to know that playing professional baseball…was an excellent way to make a livelihood." Dave's salary in 1969 was $25,000 (the median American family income was $9,400.) When the alternative was working in a coal mine or on an assembly line, playing professional baseball for as long as possible was an easy choice.

The next section of the book will examine the careers and experiences of more than 200 athletes who made their living as ballplayers during the Sixties. Space did not permit profiling all of the players and no slight is meant to those not covered here. Our goal has been to spotlight a broad array of player experiences and to share some of the era's greatest baseball stories.

SECTION II:
PLAYERS AND EXPERIENCES

ERNIE BANKS

Ernie Banks was that rarest of breeds, the power-hitting shortstop. He cleared the 40-homer mark five times at that position, yet his Cubs never finished higher than fifth place during that juncture. But the star never demanded a trade, criticized his manager, or showed up his sometimes-hapless teammates.

At times, there were second-guessers, even in the Cubs organization, who said he should be playing another position. Writer Edgar Munzel in the October 28, 1959 issue of *The Sporting News* wrote, "Another accolade is certain to be paid him next spring…Banks finally will be acclaimed a top-flight shortstop by the brass of his own club. For the first time in five years they won't be trying to shift him elsewhere. Ernie is like the prophet who is without honor in his own land. Virtually every other club rated him a sound shortstop, but Wrigley officials never seemed to be quite satisfied."

Banks quieted those critics in 1959 when he committed only 12 errors, breaking the previous record of 14 held by glove wizards Phil Rizzuto and Roy McMillan. While Banks lacked the range of a Luis Aparicio, who played across town for the White Sox, Ernie made nearly all of the routine plays and then some -- while driving in a league-best 143 RBI and winning another MVP trophy.

An iron man in his own right, he played in 717 consecutive games from the late Fifties through 1961. Managers could count on him being in the lineup, and being enthusiastic, as exemplified in his "Let's play two!" mantra.

The streak ended in June 1961. Banks, who had knee trouble dating back to his days in the Army, was having his knees drained with some regularity, and played through the pain. But by that June, with floating cartilage in the left knee, he finally took himself out of the lineup for a time.

Raised in a rough Dallas neighborhood, Banks later played Negro League baseball for the Kansas City Monarchs. That team's owner, T.Y. Baird, supplemented his income over time by selling a total of 38 player contracts to major-league organizations; 29 of those players, including Banks, made it to the majors.

At that time, Cubs general manager Wid Matthews had a keen interest in Banks. He met with Baird at the Conrad Hilton Hotel in late summer 1953 and agreed to Baird's price of $15,000. It was the biggest of Baird's transactions. Banks got into 10 games before the Cubs' season was over and hit .314. His first two home runs, coming six days apart, were both against Gerry Staley.

The Cubs' star held down the shortstop job from 1954 until 1962, when at the age of 31 he shifted to first base. Banks continued to provide big-time production from his new position. In fact, there were 43 games in which he and Ron Santo both homered, and 42 in which he and Billy Williams both left the yard. As late as 1969, at the age of 38, he produced 106 RBI. In total, Banks was an all-star in 11 seasons.

"There will never be another Mister Cub," teammate Don Kessinger said. "He loved being at the ballpark." Rich Nye, another teammate, called Banks "Mister Sunshine," noting that he was always checking up to make sure Cubs players were doing alright.

Ken Holtzman remembered the serious side of Banks. "Ernie and I had several long and extended conversations during road trips which were very revealing about his inner goodness, intelligence, and strength of character. Although most people associate him with being perpetually upbeat, I got to see his serious side as well as his honesty and knowledge."

Indeed, Banks' upbeat public persona was balanced by a somber orientation at home. His family learned to give him space, and he not infrequently spent time in the back yard by himself. Banks married and divorced four times. He tried his hand briefly at politics, running without success for Chicago alderman as a Republican in 1962.

Banks' closest friend on the Cubs during the early years was second baseman Gene Baker, who roomed with him on road trips until early in the 1957 season. (Baker managed the Pirates for two innings in 1963, making him the first African American to manage in MLB.) Later, Banks developed close relationships with Billy Williams, Ferguson Jenkins and Randy Hundley – bonds that endured long past his playing days.

For Banks, the hiring of Leo Durocher as Cubs manager in 1966 marked a turning point. Ernie was a legend in his own time, but Durocher nitpicked and ridiculed Banks, and called him names like "Gramps." It was Durocher's way of signaling that he was in charge, and nobody was going to be a more recognized personality. Durocher openly tried to replace Banks at first base numerous times – with Dick Nen, Lee Thomas, Norm Gigon, Jim Hickman, Clarence Jones and others – but repeatedly none could deliver like Ernie. Banks would play six more years, all under Durocher.

The Cubs' best shot at a pennant during the Banks years was in 1969. The season was a month too long, and the upstart Mets surpassed the Bruins in the standings, despite big years from several players. Many baseball observers blamed Durocher for failing to give the key players a day off now and again; by late August, many of them were banged up and exhausted, while the young Mets team was kicking into high gear.

In 1970, injuries limited Banks' availability, and the Cubs were no match for other contenders. He retired after an injury-plagued 1971 season with 512 home runs and was a proud member of the 2,500-hit club. Six years later, he was elected to the Hall of Fame.

Revered in Chicago, he was welcomed back to Wrigley Field after his retirement on countless special occasions. Yet, he could sometimes go unrecognized in other markets. In the early 2000s, Herb Smith, a friend of Banks who ran an executive search firm in Ohio, recalled playing basketball with Banks and several other men in their sixties on the driveway of his home in Shaker Heights, Ohio. "The neighborhood kids just looked and thought we were a bunch of old guys shooting hoops, never realizing there was a Hall of Famer in their neighborhood."

Sadly, Banks missed the chance to see his team win the world championship in 2016; he passed away from heart failure at age 83 in 2015. A lifetime Cubs fan, he would have been proud. As writer Jack Bungart wrote, "The transcendent Banks, with his inimitable style and grace, touched so many lives, with such profound depth, that the sabermetrics geeks of today's baseball possibly couldn't begin to measure it."

George Altman

The Kansas City Monarchs sent many ballplayers to the major leagues. One of the last to arrive was George Altman, who came to MLB after serving in the Army. An outfielder with speed, power and a good arm, Altman spent nine years with the Cubs, Cards, and Mets. He was a two-time all-star with a lifetime batting average of .269. One of his career highlights was blasting two home runs in the same game against Sandy Koufax. He also led the league in triples in 1961.

In the book *My Baseball Journey from the Negro Leagues to the Majors,* Altman and co-author Lew Freedman wrote, "The most frustrating aspect of my career was how often I got hurt. Most of my injuries were smaller ones, not things that knocked you out for the season, but I had illnesses and sprains, things like that. I tried not to get discouraged and always tried to get back into the lineup as quickly as I could."

Altman's days as a big leaguer ended on his own terms. After playing well for Triple-A Tacoma in 1967, Altman received a Cubs invitation to spring training. But after contemplating how disrespectfully Cubs manager Leo Durocher was treating Altman's friend, Ernie Banks, George opted for guaranteed money in Japan. He extended his career there, where he hit another 205 homers, from 1968 to 1975, and became the first to qualify for a pension from both American and Japanese baseball.

When he got to Japan, he found that the baseball customs were very different. Players had to provide their own bats and shower towels. Practice sessions could last for five hours. Night games had curfews based on the closing time for the nearby subway. Fans tossed foul balls back onto the field. The loudspeakers were staffed by female public-address announcers. Umpires seemed to employ a larger strike zone when American hitters were at the plate. Players who disagreed with umpires' calls did not hesitate to make physical contact with them.

Despite the differences, Altman welcomed the generous Japanese salary and the fact that his first $20,000 of income was exempt from U.S. income taxes.

What George didn't appreciate about Japanese baseball was the practice of cutting off every throw from the outfield. He told writer Wells Twombley, "I don't know why they do it, but they do. I guess they feel that they all don't have great arms, so they do it. It is now a custom, so what can you do? I enjoy the money they pay me, so I don't complain. My wife hates it over there, but it beats being a has-been over here."

These days, Altman resides in Missouri, but remains a loyal Cubs fan. In 2014, he returned to Wrigley Field to lead the crowd in "Take Me Out to the Ballgame." When the Cubs won the World Series in 2016, few were any happier than George Altman.

MIKE MCCORMICK

By most measures, the senior circuit was the stronger of the two leagues in the Sixties. The NL performed better in World Series action (six to four) and all-star games (nine to one). It had slightly more parity (six pennant-winning clubs compared to five in the AL). During the seven years in the decade when only one Cy Young award was presented, it went five times to an NL pitcher.

Another comparison concerns each league's ERA champions. Nine different hurlers led the AL in ERA during the decade, and none so far have been elected to join the game's immortals. In the NL, Hall of Famer Sandy Koufax won the ERA title five times. Four other enshrined hurlers led the league once each – Warren Spahn, Phil Niekro, Bob Gibson and Juan Marichal. Only in 1960 was the NL title won by someone – Mike McCormick -- not enshrined in Cooperstown.

Mike pitched in MLB for 16 years, becoming the Giants' number-three starter while still a teenager in 1958. He was a cog in their staff until 1962 when a sore shoulder limited him to five victories. His blazing fastball never returned and instead he turned to the true art of pitching, changing speeds, spotting locations and mixing in a screwball. Cortisone and pain pills fueled his comeback.

After four years in the AL with Baltimore and Washington, he was thrilled to be traded back to the Giants for the 1967 season. Along with his wife Carolyn and four children, Mike had retained their home in Mountain View, California, where they were surrounded by his dazzling collection of antique schoolhouse and railroad station clocks, most dating back to the 1860s to 1880s.

Mike won 22 contests and the Cy Young Award in 1967. He hung out all season with his road roommate, pitcher Ray Sadecki, as teammates called the fun-loving pair "Frick and Frack." The only disappointment was a second-place Giants finish behind the Cardinals. Roger Maris was quoted that season in *The Sporting News* saying, "I've always had trouble with McCormick. He's always on the borderline with his pitches."

At his original hometown of Alhambra, a banquet was held that winter with 600 in attendance, all in honor of McCormick. The speakers ranged from his high school baseball coach Maynard Hoarst to USC running back O.J. Simpson.

Teammates selected McCormick to be their player representative to management. He was with the Giants through 1970, followed by short stints with the Yankees and Royals. An attempted comeback with the Giants in spring training in 1972 was short-lived, but he did pitch in the minor leagues for a couple more years. He retired with a record of 134-128 with a 3.73 ERA and 23 shutouts.

McCormick later worked in equipment sales and as a goodwill ambassador for the Giants. He passed away in 2020 in Cornelius, North Carolina.

DUKE SIMS

Catcher Duke Sims was only the 16th person born in Utah to make the show. Factor in that he grew up in Idaho, where winter lasts almost half the year, and only Las Vegas could determine the odds Sims overcame by becoming a big leaguer.

Sims played three sports in high school but loved baseball the most. "I got to watch a ton of baseball players coming through Pocatello, Idaho and all I wanted to do was to play in the big leagues," he recalled. "The man who signed me with the Indians is the only man who ever killed anybody in baseball – Carl Mays. He was of course a teammate of Babe Ruth." Mays was a scout for the Indians at the time.

"The Yankees were hot after me and had agreed to terms that would allow me to play ball and go to the University of California," Sim said. "Their scout was Tony Robello who held the minor league record for most home runs in a season. One night," Sims continued, "he was supposed to come to the house, but when he didn't show up that night, my mother got mad and said, 'You're not going to sign with the Yankees!'"

"Several other teams were scouting me. I was working up in Boise, cutting sheet metal, to save money for college, getting up at four in the morning so I could be at work at five, and then get off at 1:30 so I could go home and get my baseball stuff together to play semi-pro baseball. I think I was making a buck sixty an hour. My hands were all cut up from the sheet metal, and it was kind of hard to play. So, Carl kept calling, and the money kept growing. And so I signed a contract. The Indians actually put the most money on the table."

As a young catcher, he benefited from spring training instructors. Coach John Schulte, who had played with the 1927 Cardinals, was one of them. "His philosophy in catching was unlike anything I had ever seen, because he was a more vertical and upright guy. He helped with my positioning."

Another who helped was a coach named Bill Lobe. "My elbow always hurt. Lobe took me out and taught me how to throw, and it took about 30 days, and one day it all came together and the ball just exploded, and everyone else just saw it. Once he got my wrist straight, my elbow quit hurting."

Bright, articulate, handsome and clever, Sims enjoyed life to the fullest. "Duke Sims was an anomaly in baseball," recalled pitcher Steve Bailey. "He did everything the way he wanted to do it. And it cost him. But he's the kind of guy the fans loved because he was an independent thinker and a bit of a rebel." Teammate Vern Fuller recalled him as a ladies man. Hurler Larry Burchart recalled Sims getting on a pitcher's case if he lost focus.

The challenge of catching knuckleballs prompted one of Sims' clever ideas. "We had an oversized catcher's mitt and I never liked using it," he recalled. "I got to the point where I was catching the knuckleballers with a first baseman's glove. To my knowledge, I might be the only one ever to do it. I pulled the rulebook out one night, and the rulebook said there can only be one first baseman's glove on the playing field. But it defines the playing field as the area in fair territory. And it's like a light bulb went on in my head. I work in foul territory."

"I thought, shit, I'm going to use my first baseman's glove. First, it's lighter. Second, I can get the ball out quicker, so if a runner tries to steal, at least I can make a throw." From that point on, Sims did so, catching knuckleball specialists like Bob Tiefenauer and Eddie Fisher in Cleveland, Hoyt Wilhelm in Los Angles, and Joe Niekro in Detroit.

"I did this one game in Chicago," he remembered. "Back then, Eddie Stanky and all the managers carried the rulebook in their hip pocket. So, we're ahead like 6 to 2, and our knuckleballer is getting ready to come in, and I glanced over at the bench, and Stanky can't wait to get on the field to protest. He's like a little butterfly, hollering, 'You can't use that glove.' The umpire was standing right there, and I told him, 'I'm standing in foul territory,' and he said, 'you sure are.' So, after the pitch is thrown, here comes Eddie and he protests the ballgame. I said, 'Mr. Stanky, you're going to lose this one.' And we went on to win the game."

Former teammate George Culver reflected in 2022, "Sims is still one of my all-time favorite guys. We played together in Triple-A at Portland and again with the Indians. If you were in the bullpen with him during the games, you had to be ready for anything. He could get pretty gross, but in a comical way."

Looking back, Sims marvels at the quality of pitchers he caught during the Cleveland years, including Sam McDowell, Luis Tiant, Gary Bell, Sonny Siebert, Ralph Terry, Steve Hargan, Stan Williams, and Dean Chance. Sims was one of Cleveland's top three home run hitters four straight years, from 1967 to 1970. He could also play first base and left field, but missed time periodically with back trouble. From 1971 to 1974, he played with the Dodgers, Tigers, Yankees and Rangers. He closed his career with a .239 batting average and 100 home runs.

Since retiring from the game, Sims, who lives in a golf community in Las Vegas, has engaged in a variety of entrepreneurial and charitable endeavors.

KEN BERRY

A gold-glove outfielder and AL all-star, Ken Berry enjoyed an 11-year career with the White Sox, Angels, Brewers, and Indians. The Kansas native's stories illustrate how the 1960s playing experience could vary based on who was managing the team.

"Al Lopez was my first manager and he was one of those guys who didn't say much to anybody," Berry recalled on a 2021 podcast. The Sox were a winning team with strong pitching. "When I was there, we didn't do anything except try to get one run. When we got one run, we'd try to get one more. And that was it. We didn't hit and run. We didn't delayed-steal."

"Lopez got sick and they brought in Eddie Stanky. Eddie said, 'We get 27 outs. We're not going to waste them.' He was very difficult to play for but he also taught me more about the game than any manager I had."

"One time I was in Boston. We were in the pennant race…I couldn't get out and take infield because my back was hurting so I went in to the trainer for a quick rub and some hot stuff on my back so I could play the game. Stanky came in and looked at me laying on the table and said, 'You're a dog.' Now here's a guy I've been busting my tail for all year, running into fences and jumping on fences, stealing bases and breaking up double plays, and he comes in and says that. But I understood where he was coming from. He was old school."

Berry's third manager with the ChiSox was Don Gutteridge in 1970. "He was from Kansas and I loved him because he was a great guy, but he was not what you would call a good manager," Berry recalled. "He did nothing. The phone would ring in the dugout and it would be the general manager, who was an alcoholic…and he would call down and tell Gutteridge what to do. It was the worst team I ever played on. We were 56 and 106."

Chuck Tanner came in as manager late in the season, and Berry recalled him as "the most positive, upbeat manager I ever played for."

"From there, I was traded to California where I had Bobby Winkles and Lefty Phillips, who spit on his shirt. Whenever you talked to Lefty," Berry recalled, "you had to stand back a bit because he spit and it was all over the front of his shirt. So, he wasn't the most impressive manager I had." Winkles was respected for his record as a college coach, but the Angels floundered under both skippers.

Berry spent the 1974 season with Milwaukee, where manager Del Crandall was an advocate of the delayed steal. Berry later emphasized that play as a minor-league skipper. His final manager was Frank Robinson during Berry's brief stay with the 1975 Indians.

Reflecting on his career as a premier defensive outfielder, Berry in 2022 stated, "I used a 'trapeze' glove by Rawlings. It was a six-fingered glove with a great pocket and easy to break in." The trapeze glove – first introduced in 1960 -- has a leather strap with lacing on each side, in lieu of a traditional pocket.

On the road, Berry's roommates included catcher Jerry McNertney and infielder Ron Hansen with the White Sox, as well as catcher John Stephenson and pitcher Jim Maloney with the Angels. When time permits, Ken has enjoyed golf and fishing.

Berry was a lifetime .255 hitter with 58 home runs, five of which came against Mickey Lolich. More than anything, pitchers loved having him in the outfield, where he often robbed batters of hits. A longtime resident of Topeka, Kansas, Berry recently wrote a baseball novel titled, *Comeback*.

HANK AARON

One of baseball's remarkable trivia points was that for many years, Hank Aaron topped both the list of all players in alphabetical order; and the all-time home run list. Eventually, David Aardsma supplanted Aaron on the first list, and the controversial Barry Bonds on the second one.

Aaron still is atop at least two other lists, holding a pair of cherished records. His 2,297 RBI is 79 higher than the second-place Albert Pujols. Aaron also holds the record for the most total bases with 6,856 – miles ahead of Pujols in second place with 6,211. Moreover, his 3,771 hits trail only Pete Rose and Ty Cobb.

Of course, Aaron is most famous for eclipsing Ruth's longstanding title as the all-time home run king. Aaron retired with 755 circuit shots – 41 more than the Babe. (Bonds later hit 762.)

Aaron was a complete ballplayer. He won batting titles, hit for power, stole bases, gunned down opposing baserunners, and won gold glove awards. He performed well when the spotlight shined brightest. In three trips to the post-season with the Braves, Aaron hit .362 with six homers in 69 at bats.

In 1957, the 23-year-old Aaron played a crucial role in powering manager Fred Haney's Braves to the pennant and world championship. It was their fifth year after relocating from Boston to Milwaukee, and Aaron hit .322 with 44 home runs, and 132 RBI. The Braves outlasted the Yankees in a seven-game fall classic. When the Braves repeated as pennant winners in 1958, Aaron was again instrumental. Haney said Aaron was both the best fastball-hitter and best curveball-hitter he had ever seen.

Broadcaster Joe Garagiola once asked Aaron if he was "a guess hitter," meaning a batter who anticipates what pitch the hurler will throw next. Aaron quipped in response, "Yeah, when they go 2-and-0 on me, I guess they're going to throw a strike." Garagiola, who had a sensational sense of humor, could only laugh and concede that Aaron had a good point.

After Aaron hit .355 in 1959, an article in the January 1960 issue of *Baseball Digest* speculated on whether Aaron would ever hit .400. Six-time batting champion Stan Musial was quoted as saying he doubted there would ever be another .400 hitter, but if so, Aaron had as good a chance as anyone.

"What Aaron has," said three-time .400 hitter Rogers Hornsby in the same article, "is a smooth pivot that gives him power. He makes use of what the good Lord gave him – the eyes, arms, legs and coordination of a natural hitter." Hornsby said Aaron was the only hitter with a shot at the .400 mark. Aaron had a good quote for this topic, as well, saying batting averages "are for the men with the pencils to worry about."

After placing second in both 1959 and 1960, the Braves drifted to fourth place in 1961. The love affair between Milwaukee residents and the team showed signs of strain, and owner Lou Perini sold the club to a syndicate headed by Chicago insurance magnate William Bartholomay in 1962. After finishing fifth and sixth the next two seasons, Milwaukee placed ninth out of the league's 10 teams in attendance in 1963 and there was rampant speculation that the franchise would relocate.

As the Braves contemplated a move from Milwaukee to Atlanta, Aaron and teammate Lee Maye voiced concerns about playing in a then-segregated city. After two more fifth-place seasons in Milwaukee in 1964 and 1965, the relocation was consummated and the team moved to Atlanta. More than 1.5 million fans rocked the turnstiles to see the club in 1966 and while the team placed fifth, Aaron enjoyed another fine season with 44 home runs and 127 RBI. By then, the great civil rights legislation of the Sixties was beginning to provide more protection of the rights of African Americans. Aaron found Atlanta to his liking, enough to make it his permanent home.

Like all black players of his generation, he experienced inexcusable discrimination, but refused to allow bitterness to define his life view. As time went on, he became more outspoken in denouncing discriminatory policies, within and outside the national pastime.

Aaron was from Mobile, Alabama, and divided his time as a youth between school, working odd jobs like picking cotton, and playing baseball. By age 14, the talented youngster was playing semi-pro ball with the Pritchett Athletics; he later joined the Mobile Black Bears. The next step in his progression came in 1951, at age 17, when he signed with the Negro American League champion Indianapolis Clowns. Aaron never understood the team's name since it didn't play a single game in Indiana that season.

After the Clowns repeated as champions in 1952, Aaron received contract offers from the Giants and Braves. For a mere $50 per month difference, Aaron chose the Braves – one of the best investments in the history of the sport. He rocketed through the farm system, and by 1954, at the age of 20, Aaron was already a sterling MLB performer.

Aaron won six straight match-ups on the 1959 television show, *Home Run Derby,* adding another $13,000 of income to support his wife and children.

During the Sixties, Aaron won three more home run titles and made every all-star team. In 1969, under manager Luman Harris, Aaron helped the Braves win the first-ever NL West title, delivering 44 home runs. The Braves' season ended when they faced the red-hot Mets in the NLCS.

Aaron was mild-tempered and generally got along well with teammates. After he and teammate Rico Carty got into a physical altercation on a chartered flight, he called it "the most embarrassing thing that ever happened to me." (Teammates Tony Cloninger, Clay Carroll, Gary Geiger and Pat Jarvis stepped in to separate the fist-throwing combatants.) Aaron and Carty had been road roommates for a couple of seasons until the Braves offered Aaron a private room. That seemed to change their relationship, and a remark on the flight by the sharp-tongued Carty angered Aaron, leading to the fracas. After the plane landed, Aaron and teammate Bob Uecker took a taxi to the hotel, while Carty traveled with the rest of the team by bus. Aaron and Carty never were close thereafter, though Carty remained with the Braves for several more years.

Hank also made a point of being accessible and open with reporters, knowing that they too had a job to do. He also enjoyed playing alongside his younger brother Tommie, who was with the Braves on and off from 1962 to 1971. But it was tough on Tommie. "The media was always comparing us. I'm sure, by me being successful, it put a lot of pressure on him," Hank recalled. "He couldn't play up to his potential."

Hank aged well as a slugger. He passed Mickey Mantle on the all-time home run list on July 30, 1969. In 1971, at age 37, he delivered a monster season with 47 home runs and a league-best .669 slugging percentage. He surpassed Willie Mays, who was still active, on the career homer list on August 6, 1972. On the personal front, after years of marital difficulty, Aaron and his first wife divorced in 1971 and he married a former Atlanta television personality in 1973.

Aaron was on fire at the plate in 1973 and finished the season with 713 career home runs, just one shy of Ruth's record. That provided the sport with a full winter of anticipation and publicity, though Aaron personally endured racial antagonism, nasty letters, and threats that drained the joy from the experience. When the 1974 season commenced, he delivered homer number 714 against Jack Billingham and number 715, to set the new record, against Al Downing before the home crowd in Atlanta.

The Braves traded him to the Milwaukee Brewers to allow Aaron to finish his career where it started. In two final seasons with the Brewers, he set the all-time RBI record.

Throughout his career, he was respected for his humility as much as for his ability and accomplishments. "Hank was a quiet man because he lacked the bravado often associated with a star player," remembers teammate Bob Aspromonte. "He was respected by all of the major-league players and was a close friend to me."

After his playing career, Aaron headed up player development for the Braves, became a multiple-franchise owner with Church's Fried Chicken, operated several auto dealerships, and served on numerous charitable boards. He was just shy of his 87th birthday when he passed away in 2021.

AL DOWNING

This hurler is often remembered as the pitcher who surrendered Hank Aaron's 715th homer, but his career had no shortages of accomplishments. The pride of Trenton, New Jersey, Al Downing won in double figures for the Yankees each year from 1963 to 1967 and later became a 20-game winner for the Dodgers. Over 17 years, he compiled a record of 123-107 with a 3.22 ERA.

Downing was a big part of the Yankees' success in 1963, when several pitchers went down with injuries or ineffectiveness. The 22-year-old posted a 13-5 record and led the AL in strikeouts-per-inning. In one game against Cleveland, he fanned 14 hitters. A year later, he won 13 games again, pacing the loop in both strikeouts and walks. In one 1967 game, he struck out three straight batters on just nine pitches.

A lefty pitcher who batted righty, Downing was a flame-thrower who delivered a good change-up with an identical motion. His road roommate, catcher Elston Howard, said, "He's got fire in his arm." Yogi Berra commented, "This guy can throw it by you and he can break your back with the curve ball." For trivia fans, Downing attended the same high school as pitcher Bo Belinsky and was born on the same day as pitcher Fred Talbot, who was briefly a teammate.

Downing also had leadership skills and maturity, demonstrated as early as high school when he was a three-time class president. Ever inquisitive, he peppered teammate Whitey Ford with questions about pitching, and Ford answered as many as he could. During the off-seasons, Downing pursued studies at Rider College.

Regarding the record-breaking 715th home run in 1974, "There was no book on Aaron," Downing later reflected. "He had the book on you. There was no one way to pitch to him."

FRITZ PETERSON

Fritz Peterson aptly referred to himself as a good number-two pitcher. He was number two behind Mel Stottlemyre in the Bronx, and behind Gaylord Perry in Cleveland. At his peak from 1966 to 1972, he had six winning seasons in seven years, including a 20-win campaign in 1970. The lefty had a couple of losing seasons in 1973-1974 but bounced back with a 14-8 record in 1975.

Peterson, who was a White Sox fan growing up in the suburbs of Chicago, was even the number two pitcher at his prep school, the old Arlington High School, which was just steps from the Arlington Park horseracing facility. Gene Dahlquist was the top pitcher but pursued a career in football. The high school's venerable baseball program later produced major leaguers Paul Splittorff and George Vukovich before the school was shut down due to enrollment shortfalls during the Eighties.

In 1963, three years after completing high school, Peterson tried out with the A's in Kansas City. His tryout did not lead to a signing, but Fritz became friends with another auditioning player, Dave Duncan, who later became his battery mate in Cleveland. Peterson ultimately signed with the Yankees, began his pro career pitching for the Harlan (Kentucky) Yankees in the Appalachian League, and made his debut in the Bronx three years later.

In 1970, both Peterson and Stottlemyre were all-stars. Peterson not only notched 20 victories, but led the league in WHIP and strikeout-to-walk ratio, surrendering just 40 free passes. The Yankees won 93 games that year, but were no match for the Orioles, who captured not only the division crown but the world championship.

One teammate whose play Fritz was not enamored with was outfielder Roy White. He wrote, "I was fairly open about my relationship with Roy White. It was not always great. For many years, I blamed Roy for costing us dozens of runs for playing too deep in left field. I never said anything, letting the situation simmer while it hovered over the team like some voodoo curse."

Peterson was with Cleveland from 1973 to 1976, then joined the Rangers. During spring training of 1977, he signed with the White Sox, but failed to make their roster. He retired rather than accept a minor-league assignment, concluding his career with a 133-131 record and a 3.30 ERA.

Peterson said the most fearsome hitters he ever faced were Frank Howard and Dick Allen, always a threat to crush a homer. But the best hitter over the course of his career, he reflected, was Al Kaline, for his consistency and refusal to ever give in.

As most readers of this book know, Peterson and Yankee teammate Mike Kekich made national news in 1973 when they held separate press conferences to announce that they were trading families. Peterson quipped that it was actually the wives who were trading their husbands. Peterson authored the books, *Mickey Mantle is Going to Heaven* and *When the Yankees were on the Fritz: The Horace Clarke Years.* He also brought joy to many fans by posting his baseball reflections on Facebook. Peterson passed away in 2024.

JIM DAVENPORT

Imagine the excitement in the spring of 1958 when MLB first arrived in San Francisco. Grand celebrations and lavish parties marked the occasion. A downtown parade attracted revelers on both sides of the city blocks, as convertibles drove by carrying owner Horace Stoneham, mayor George Christopher, and celebrities like actress Shirley Temple Black. Stars Willie Mays and Hank Sauer rode together in one car, while Felipe Alou and Orlando Cepeda were in another. The parade began at Seals Stadium and wound its way to the Sheraton Palace Hotel, where a grand luncheon was held.

Giants manager Bill Rigney was all smiles as he rode in the back of one of the convertibles, waving to the crowds, but he also had some decisions to make, hoping to improve upon his team's third-place finish from 1957. In a surprise, he handed the leadoff spot in the batting order to rookie third baseman Jim Davenport. The youngster went on to help the Giants to victories in two of their first three home games against the Dodgers. The two teams then flew to Los Angeles, and Davenport registered the first hit in the major league history of that city. After his first four games as a major leaguer, Jim's batting average was .556.

His fast start at the plate notwithstanding, it was Jim's fielding skills that kept him with the Giants for 13 years. To this day, the "Frisco Flash" has one of the 20 best all-time fielding percentages for a third baseman. He was versatile enough to swing over to shortstop or second base as needed. Writers said he possessed "the fastest hands in the West."

Small but tough, he battled constant injuries and illnesses. In 1958, he pulled a rib-cage muscle and later lost three games after fouling a pitch off his ankle. The following year, Jim missed almost a month following a collision at home plate with catcher Ed Bailey and a couple of games with eye problems. In 1960, he lost a week after taking a Larry Jackson pitch to the collar bone and then had to adopt a milk-heavy diet after developing ulcers.

His best season was 1962, the year that Alvin Dark guided the Giants to the pennant. Davenport batted .297 with 14 home runs, made the all-star team, and was awarded a gold glove. He struggled at the plate in the World Series, batting .136 in seven games, as the Giants lost to the Yankees.

Willie McCovey later said that although Davenport looked up to him and Willie Mays, they, in turn, respected Davenport. So did Maury Wills of the Dodgers, who considered Davenport the game's most underrated third sacker. "Davenport could do everything but run the bases and steal," Wills wrote. "He was an outstanding hitter, an excellent third baseman and a smart baseball player. He hurt us as much as anybody on the Giants."

In the late Sixties, Jim was used as a late-game defensive replacement for Jim Ray Hart. Teammate Willie Mays said, "He played third base the best of anybody in the league." He remained with the Giants until July 1970, when he was released at age 36.

Jim was from a tiny Birmingham suburb called Siluria, Alabama, as was outfielder Willie Kirkland, who was a 1958 teammate. Siluria was so small, Jim used to jest, that even people in Birmingham were unfamiliar with it. He played quarterback at Southern Miss, but said pro football wasn't for him. "A guy my size could get killed" in the NFL, he stated, only half-jokingly.

Davenport later coached with the Padres, Phillies, and Indians, and was an advance scout for the Tigers. But most of the time he worked in the Giants' organization. "Jimmy's a pillar of that organization," said former player Joe Amalfitano. "If you cut his veins, red wouldn't come out. It would be orange and black." Jim was still affiliated with the Giants when he died of heart failure in Redwood City, California at age 82 in 2016.

JUAN PIZARRO

The cover story of the May 1959 issue of *Baseball Digest* was titled, "The Mystery of Juan Pizarro." Praising his fastball, curve and screwball, the article compared the 22-year-old southpaw, then pitching for the Braves, to Lefty Grove and Carl Hubbell, and labeled him "the ultimate successor to Warren Spahn." Those were lofty expectations for a young pitcher with just 11 career wins.

The Braves had signed Pizarro at the recommendation of Luis Olmo, a former Dodgers and Braves outfielder who was from Puerto Rico. Eventually, the Braves lost patience, but Pizarro became a dominant hurler with the White Sox.

After a lengthy contract holdout, he was 16-8 in 1963, with only his teammate Gary Peters notching a lower ERA. Pizarro was equally dominant the next season, going 19-8 with the fifth-best ERA in the circuit. Juan made the all-star team both seasons.

Manager Al Lopez commented that he had "overpowering speed and a rubber arm to go with it." Lopez noted that Pizarro had added a slow curve and a hard slider to his warchest, as well. "When he mixes them up good, he's mighty tough to hit," Lopez said. "We hate to hit against that guy," added Mickey Mantle. "We'd rather face anybody else on the White Sox staff."

In 1965, Pizarro was plagued by a torn triceps tendon in his shoulder, which cost him half the season. He finished with a 6-3 record, followed by an 8-6 mark mostly as a reliever in 1966. The White Sox then traded him to Pittsburgh in the swap that sent Wilbur Wood to the Windy City.

Thereafter, Pizarro remained a serviceable but no longer extraordinary pitcher, living a nomadic existence. Before retiring in 1974, he pitched for the Pirates, Red Sox, Indians, A's, Cubs and Astros, as well as four minor league clubs. His 1968 season included an arrest when he and third baseman Joe Foy got into a 4:00 a.m. auto accident just nine hours before a double-header. When Juan arrived in Cleveland in 1969 as part of the Hawk Harrelson trade, he shrugged his shoulders and said, "It's just another jump, that's all." He did enjoy a partial resurgence with the Cubs in 1971, posting a 7-6 record with three shutouts.

Over the course of 18 years in the majors, Pizarro posted a record of 131-105, a solid .555 winning percentage and a 3.43 ERA. Today, he resides in San Juan, Puerto Rico.

BOB ALLISON

Any list of the 10 most feared AL sluggers in the Sixties might include Bob Allison, who was so muscular that he was sometimes called Mister Atlas. A former University of Kansas fullback, Allison combined a golden work ethic with such supreme intensity that he was checked out at the Mayo Clinic for a possible ulcer. No ulcer, docs concluded, just a nervous stomach, characteristic of a competitor who found it impossible to relax. Since he had played more football than baseball before turning pro, he still had to learn the art of hitting, which he called "the hardest thing I've had to learn how to do."

The outfielder's MLB career began with a bang in 1959, when he led the AL in triples and slugged 30 home runs (including two grand-slams) en route to the top rookie award. From that genesis, Allison played a pivotal role as the last-place 1959 Senators evolved into the 1965 AL champion Minnesota Twins.

In 1961, the year the franchise relocated, Allison enjoyed the first of two 100-RBI seasons. In one memorable game in 1962, both Allison and teammate Harmon Killebrew hit grand slam home runs in the first inning against the Indians. In 1963, he led the league in OPS and runs scored, and delivered a three-homer game against Cleveland.

Highlights of his 1964 season included tying a big-league record with two doubles in one inning, batting a career-best .287, and making the all-star team for the third and final time. In 1965, he hit 23 home runs in the regular season and one more in the World Series, despite a serious wrist injury.

Although his batting averages later tailed off, he again eclipsed the 20-homer mark in 1967 and 1968. He was so popular in the Twin Cities that he co-hosted a 30-minute television sports show with broadcaster Herb Carneal on WCTN.

Compared to teammate Harmon Killebrew, whose big swing delivered tape-measure homers, Allison was more of a line-drive hitter – but strong enough to clear the fences with regularity.

Speaking of swings, Allison was quick to engage his dukes. On June 18, 1961, at Comiskey Park, Allison was playing first base and approached the mound to urge teammate Camilo Pascual to keep an eye on the runner at first base, Minnie Minoso. Pascual waved his glove and essentially told Allison to leave the pitcher's work to him. Minoso got a big jump on the next pitch and swiped second base. Back in the dugout at the end of the inning, the pair traded barbs, Allison shoved Pascual into a steel post, and Pascual grabbed a bat to defend himself. The pitcher heaved the bat toward Allison, but it instead struck coach Clyde McCullough, who himself was trying to recover from an ulcer at the time. Allison threw a couple more punches before teammates broke up the fracas.

Allison was also involved in the 1969 incident outside the Lindell AC on Cass Avenue in Detroit in which Twins manager Billy Martin beat up pitcher Dave Boswell, who was Allison's roommate. Lindell's AC – the AC stood for "Athletic Club" -- was well known in sports and entertainment circles. NFL star Alex Karras was forced to sell his one-third stake in the saloon during his one-year suspension from football for gambling. Karras and wrestler Dick the Bruiser had gotten into a brawl at the bar in 1963 that reportedly sent several police officers to a hospital for medical treatment. (Lindell's was just one of Martin's favorite watering holes in Detroit. Another was Reedy's Tavern, just a block from Tiger Stadium. Decades later, Martin was in the car of tavern owner Bill Reedy at the time of the Christmas Day crash that killed Martin. Hawk Harrelson once won bets with several NFL players at Lindell's by beating them in arm wrestling.)

Boswell's fistfight with his own manager was the talk of baseball, and the pitcher clearly got the worst of it, requiring several dozen stitches on his hand and face. Accounts differ over Allison's role in that ruckus, which likely contributed to Martin's eventual dismissal as manager.

By 1968, Allison was getting periodic cortisone shots for an ailing knee. In 1970, he retired with a .255 career average, 1,281hits, and 256 home runs.

After baseball, Bob worked in public relations for Coca-Cola and enjoyed golf and hunting. He was 60 when he died in Arizona of a rare brain disease called ataxia. As of 2024, he was still third on the Senators-Twins all-time home run list, trailing only Killebrew and Kent Hrbek.

Denny McLain

Baseball is a young man's game and when young men experience success, one of their greatest challenges can be managing the opportunities that come their way. By his 26th birthday, Denny McLain seemingly had it all. The Tigers hurler was a three-time 20-game winner with 114 wins to his credit. He drove a Thunderbird presented to him by Ford Motor Company in honor of his stunning 1968 season, owned a personal aircraft, and was married to Sharon Boudreau, daughter of an all-time great shortstop. An acclaimed organist and nightclub entertainer, he seemed like an athletic renaissance man. Viewed from afar, his future looked bright.

Baseball insiders and beat reporters knew otherwise. McLain was addicted to caffeine, drinking up to a case of Pepsi each day as his teeth were rotting. His aching shoulder needed frequent cortisone shots. Even worse, he got involved in gambling. Initially, it seemed harmless. During the winter of 1964-1965 in Puerto Rico, Denny and pitcher Jack Hamilton ran a small-time gambling operation in the basement of their apartment building. Later, he and a partner (the merchandising director for Pepsi of Michigan) got involved in big-time bookmaking which brought McLain into contact with organized crime figures and evidently led to an off-the-field injury late in the 1967 pennant race.

McLain posted a 31-6 record in 1968 and won the Cy Young Award, helping the Tigers to the world championship. In 1969, he won 24 games and shared the Cy Young honors with Mike Cuellar of the Orioles. His blazing fastball and killer instinct came naturally. Former Tigers manager Charlie Dressen had taught him the curve and the change-up.

Yet, problems festered. He was often away between starts. Teammates became resentful even when McLain was pitching well. As Bill Freehan wrote in *Behind the Mask,* "Denny's a tough guy to understand. His concentration wanders a lot when he's on the mound, and off the mound *he* wanders a lot, running off after games to play the organ in nightclubs, flying around in his plane, looking after all his businesses. I've never had real good rapport with Denny. He likes to fight with me about strategy, and when things aren't going well for him, he likes to break things and yell at the fans and the other players. I've never had as much trouble communicating with any other pitcher as I've had with Denny. But, at the same time, I've never caught a better pitcher in my life." Mickey Lolich was also vocal about McLain being afforded unequal treatment from management.

Not all of his teammates were alienated. Outfielder Jim Northrup remained close with Denny and brainstormed with him on how to make extra income. Bill Campbell, the reserve infielder on the 1969 team (and future broadcaster), roomed with him on road trips and said decades later that the star pitcher always treated him well.

But a contemporary report in 1970 by George Vecsey in *The New York Times* elaborated, "In the last two years he would perform [music] in one city, then fly to another city to pitch on the same day. He usually appeared haggard at the ballpark after his troubles with air traffic delays or traffic jams on the road. But the image also emerged of a young man falling into debt. Now there are rumors of deeper troubles...."

By the time the article appeared, Commissioner Bowie Kuhn had investigated his 1967 gambling associations and suspended him for half of the 1970 season. It was the sport's first gambling-related suspension since the 1920s. Some teammates were relieved the penalty was not even worse.

McLain was back on the mound on July 1, 1970, with more than 53,000 fans in the stands, but was no longer the same pitcher. He struggled to a 3-5 record with a 4.63 ERA during the second half, losing time to a second suspension for dumping ice water on two baseball writers, and a third one for carrying a firearm on a team flight.

The Tigers cut their losses by sending McLain to DC in an eight-player deal. McLain had a dreadful year in 1971, losing 22 games and clashing with Senators' manager Ted Williams, who had opposed the trade. Denny unsuccessfully attempted to recapture his magic formula in 1972 with Oakland and Atlanta, and in 1973 in the minor leagues.

It was a swift downfall from the halcyon days of 1968, when McLain was the AL MVP. The Tigers had a 103-59 record that year, capped off by winning the World Series in seven games. According to McLain, they achieved that success despite manager Mayo Smith, who "drank so much that it usually took him three or four innings to sober up and get his head in the game." Denny credited coaches Wally Moses and Johnny Sain as being top-rate.

Having needed dozens of cortisone shots, McLain received $31,500 as a workers comp settlement in 1977. Once his pitching days were behind him, McLain entered into a variety of endeavors, from owning businesses, to broadcasting and bookmaking. He was convicted of a series of white-collar crimes in the Eighties and again in the Nineties. In recent years he has been a sports analyst, still respected for his opinions. An amazing talent in his prime, his record was 131-91 with a 3.39 ERA and 19 shutouts.

FRANK ROBINSON

Frank Robinson was a man of firsts. He was the first member of the Reds selected as rookie of the year...the first player to win the MVP award in both leagues...and eventually the first African American manager in baseball. He also placed first in his league in slugging percentage four years and hit by pitches seven times.

Robby was born in Texas and grew up in Oakland. His father left the family when Frank was just four years old. Asked later how he developed such quick reflexes, he noted that he had nine siblings, and had to be quick at the dinner table if he hoped to get any food. He played high school and American Legion ball with Vada Pinson, and the pair wound up as teammates on the Reds, close friends spending time together on and off the field.

When he slugged 38 home runs in 1956, that set a record (since broken) for most homers by a rookie. Five years later came his banner 1961 season, when he earned the first of the MVP awards. He hit .323 with 37 home runs and 124 RBI, and even swiped 22 bases. Armed with six sluggers in double figures for home runs, the Reds powered their way to the pennant with a 93-61 record in the NL's final season with a 154-game schedule, four games ahead of the second-place Dodgers.

Going into the World Series, the Yankees were heavily favored. The Reds managed to win game two in the Bronx to even the Series but dropped the next three games. Frank hit only .200 over the five games.

Statistically, Robinson's 1962 season was even stronger, but the Reds settled for third place, and Frank placed fourth in the MVP balloting, with Maury Wills of the Dodgers receiving the award. Robby's offensive production sagged in 1963 but rebounded the next two seasons. Oddly, no matter how well he hit, the Cincy fans were quick to boo if he didn't come through. He told Associated Press in 1965, "I am more relaxed on the road because there is no booing."

Frank was a muscular specimen who played the game with a combination of sound fundamentals and high intensity. He crowded the plate and slid hard into second base to break up double plays. He likely was on few of his opponents' Christmas card lists.

The Reds saw Robinson at age 30 and concluded that a further decline in production was imminent. They were also eager to boost their pitching corps. One scenario the Reds proposed involved trading their slugger to Houston for outfielder Jim Wynn and hurler Larry Dierker, but Houston felt the price tag was too high. Houston countered with utility man Bob Aspromonte and pitcher Turk Farrell, which didn't interest the Reds.

The Orioles were also interested. The Birds had recorded winning records in five of the previous six seasons but needed a catalyst to put them over the top. They also knew Robinson could help mightily at the gate (home attendance averaged less than 10,000 per game in 1965). The final deal sent Frank to Baltimore for starting pitcher Milt Pappas, reliever Jack Baldschun, and outfield prospect Dick Simpson.

The Orioles' front office was ecstatic. They already had Boog Powell at first base, Brooks Robinson at third, and Curt Blefary in left. Landing Robby gave them what Harry Dalton, the general-manager designee, called "cannons at the corners."

After 10 years in Cincinnati, Robinson was not eager to leave, despite the booing. He had friends in the city and enjoyed attending Cincinnati Royals NBA games. The trade also cost him some pocket change, as he had been slated to represent the NL in a celebrity bowling tournament in Phoenix and was suddenly an AL player. Participants were to receive $400 to $600 apiece.

Robby took the trade news as a challenge to up his performance. The intense competitor delivered a triple crown for the 1966 Orioles, pacing the league in batting clip, home runs and RBI. In the World Series, he helped the Birds sweep Los Angeles four straight. "Frank took us from being a good team in 1965 to a great team in 1966," remembered teammate Jim Palmer.

Always playing hard, he collided with Al Weis on the basepath in 1967 and missed 28 games to double vision, but he still turned in a sterling season. After an offensive downturn in 1968, he bounced back strong from 1969 to 1971, helping the O's to pennants each year. Robby also served as judge in a "kangaroo court," imposing small fines after team victories for a variety of transgressions. The sessions were fun, fostered teamwork, and reminded younger players of the need for sound fundamentals.

The Orioles traded Frank to the Dodgers after the 1971 season and missed the slugger mightily the following season. Meanwhile, Frank clashed with Dodgers manager Walt Alston and lasted only one season. He played for the Angels in 1973, his last season with 30 home runs.

Robinson was named Indians manager for the 1975 season. When Frank debuted as Indians manager, Jackie Robinson's widow was in attendance and in dramatic fashion, Robby slugged a first-inning home run to key an Indians victory. (Interestingly, the first black head coach in the NBA was Frank's high school teammate, Bill Russell.)

Frank also managed the Giants, Orioles, Expos and Nationals. He was elected to the Hall of Fame in 1982 and although he had played more games with the Reds, he chose to go into Cooperstown with an Orioles cap on his plaque. A lifetime .294 hitter with 586 home runs, Robinson was 83 years old when he died in Los Angeles in 2019.

ANDY ETCHEBARREN

At a 1966 pool party, catcher Andy Etchebarren noticed Orioles teammate Frank Robinson, who did not know how to swim, was at the bottom of the deep end. Andy dived in and rescued his teammate, possibly saving his life. Though he made many contributions to the Orioles, none were quite so personal as that one.

Andy starred at La Puente High School in California and signed with the Orioles for an $80,000 bonus. In 1962, his second pro season, he played at Single-A Elmira in the Eastern League where his manager was Earl Weaver. Pat Gillick, the future Hall of Fame executive, was a pitcher on that squad. Looking back, Gillick wrote "Andy was the best defensive catcher in my five-year minor-league pitching career."

The backstop joined the starting lineup in 1966 and repaid manager Hank Bauer's confidence by handling the pitching staff with aplomb. Bauer observed a flaw in how Andy gripped the bat and suggested a change that seemed to help. Though he batted only .221, he set what would be career highs in homers (11) and RBI (50). He also caught all four games in the World Series, as the Orioles swept the Dodgers.

Bauer also helped Andy improve his skills at blocking bad pitches. As described by Phil Jackman in the March 25, 1967 issue of *The Sporting News,* "Bauer stands about 20 feet away from the catcher gunning baseballs at his feet and well in front of him as simulated potential wild pitches. It is Etchebarren's task to block, knock down or smother these bullets, a job that can become painful at times."

Over time, the Orioles moved to a platoon, with Etchebarren playing against lefties and Elrod Hendricks against righties. Andy remained with the Orioles through 1975, allowing him to collect two championship rings. The two-time all-star closed out with the Angels and Brewers with a lifetime batting average of .235 with 49 home runs and 625 hits.

As affable as he was knowledgeable, Andy managed in the minor leagues for 16 years. He was also the Orioles bench coach for two years under manager Davey Johnson and a first base coach for the Brewers. He was 76 years old when he died in 2019.

BROOKS ROBINSON

Brooks Robinson was one of the most popular ballplayers of his era, known for being friendly and polite as well as being a clutch hitter and a phenomenal fielder.

The story begins in 1955, when Orioles manager Paul Richards received a letter from his former Atlanta Crackers teammate, Lindsay Deal, commending an Arkansas high school athlete. Brooks Robinson, Deal wrote, was being scouted by the White Sox, Red Sox, Cardinals, Phillies, A's, Tigers and Yankees. The Orioles, Deal argued, would do well to make an aggressive play for this soon-to-graduate prospect.

Richards, a native Texan with a profane vocabulary who was nicknamed "the Wizard of Waxahachie," was in the process of rebuilding the Orioles, who had recently relocated from St. Louis where they were known as the Browns. Richards sent two Orioles scouts; he was a pioneer in using both a scout and cross-checker to evaluate talent.

The scouts liked what they saw and in speaking with Brooks and his parents, they realized that Brooks' father had a profoundly positive impact on his son, instilling a love for the game –

Brooks grew up listening to Cardinals games on KMOX-AM – along with sound baseball fundamentals and personal discipline. (Brooks returned the favor a few years later by helping his dad get a part-time scouting job with the Houston Colt .45s. Since his dad worked as a fireman, he had several free days per week to scout talent.)

Richards placed a phone call to the youngster. With several offers from which to choose, the Robinson family decided to insist on a big-league contract, which would limit the number of times Brooks could be bounced between the major and minor leagues. The Orioles offered satisfactory terms and Brooks quickly boarded a plane to Baltimore. Richards invited him to travel with the team for a week before reporting to the Class B team in York, Pennsylvania. Brooks made his MLB debut the same season, overwhelmed at the plate but already showing poise at the hot corner. After the season, he joined fellow prospects Tito Francona, Wayne Causey, Bob Hale and Marv Breeding in a 66-game winter ball season in Columbia.

It was not until 1959 that Brooks became more proficient at the plate, hitting .284 in 88 games, while enjoying rooming on road trips with Jerry Walker, a young pitcher from Oklahoma. In 1960, Brooks made his first AL all-star team, captured his first gold glove, and placed third in the AL MVP voting. He also established himself as the leader on the young Orioles team.

Defensively, he made spectacular plays going to his right, his left and vertically. He practiced fielding grounders for hours, concentrating on establishing perfect footwork and knowing when to throw to second for a force-out and when to throw to first base. Nobody questioned where his nicknames – "The Vacuum Cleaner" and "Mr. Impossible" – came from.

Writer Red Smith commented at the time, "I can't recall any player in any sport who ever had such a knack for always being in the right place at the right time." Though naturally left-handed, he played baseball right-handed, which allowed him to perform his dazzling glovework with his dominant hand. George Kell, a fellow Arkansan, later wrote, "There never was a finer fielding third baseman than Brooks." Teammate Milt Pappas later said, "Brooks made so many great plays, he just amazed me."

That 1960 season was one of the most joyful of Brooks's career. He drove in 88 RBI and helped the Orioles to a surprising second-place finish behind New York. Up-and-comers like Robinson, Ron Hansen, Jim Gentile and Jackie Brandt provided the offense while an even younger kiddie corps manned the rotation. After the season, Brooks married flight attendant Constance Louise Butcher of Windsor Canada. After a leisurely car trip across much of North America, they moved into a rowhouse just 10 blocks from Memorial Stadium that Brooks had purchased from a member of the Colts football team, LG Dupre.

The Orioles were a close-knit team. Many of the players had progressed through the minor leagues together and they socialized off the field. One by one, as the players tied the knot, their wives became friends, as well. As Doug Wilson wrote in *Brooks: The Biography of Brooks Robinson,* "Athletes, who were not making much more money than most of the city's workers, were full-time members of the community – friends and neighbors – not secluded away in gated, guarded mansions in the suburbs."

Proving that his breakout season was no fluke, Brooks hit .287 in 1961, placing second in the AL in hits. The biggest surprise that summer was when Richards unexpectedly stepped away from the manager's role to take a front-office position with the expansion Houston club. Then in 1962, Brooks hit .303 with 23 home runs and led the AL in sacrifice flies. He became only the sixth player to hit grand-slams in successive games, though the Orioles placed a disappointing seventh under new manager Billy Hitchcock. The new skipper ran a looser ship with no team curfew, and some of his young players took advantage of his leniency. Baltimore improved to fourth in 1963, Brooks retrogressed to just a .251 batting average, attendance declined, and Hitchcock lost his job at season's end.

The Orioles hired Hank Bauer, a Purple Heart military hero and former Yankees slugger, to manage the team in 1964. Hank's former teammate, Gene Woodling, was on the coaching staff and convinced Robby to use a heavier bat. That led to a great year, as he batted .317 with 28 home runs and a league-leading 118 RBI. All would prove to be career highs. Though the Orioles fell short in their attempt to outlast the Yankees, it had been one hell of a pennant race, and Brooks was rewarded with the regular-season MVP award. Several weeks later, the Orioles made him their first-ever $50,000 per year player.

The Orioles were again a strong contender in 1965 but settled for third place with 94 wins. Brooks had a banner year, and placed third in the MVP derby, but it was clear that the team needed another power bat. Larry McPhail was on his way out as general manager, but helped engineer the trade that brought Frank Robinson to Baltimore. Instantly, the Orioles' lineup became the best in the AL.

What was unknown at the time was how would two players accustomed to being the top star co-exist on the same team. Importantly, during the six years that the pair would play together, there was never a hint of tension or jealousy. The team spirit remained strong. Players hung out together after games. Frank later wrote that the black players would get together with white players for dinner or drinks two or three times each week, which had not been the case when he played for the Reds. Brooks would often let Frank know where he was headed, signaling the get-togethers were open to all.

With Frank winning the triple crown and Brooks adding 100 RBI and exceptional glove work, the Orioles finally won their first pennant in 1966. In the World Series, Bauer led the club to a four-game sweep.

By the time the 1966 season ended, the Vietnam War was in full force and several players sought to provide encouragement for the troops. That winter, Brooks joined Joe Torre, Hank Aaron, Stan Musial and Harmon Killebrew to visit American heroes on military bases in Vietnam. This was no mere publicity stunt. The ballplayers made the rounds of battle fronts and military hospitals for 17 days, coming away with tremendous respect for those serving our country.

In the late Sixties, Brooks capitalized on his popularity through paid appearances (making as many as 16 appearances and traveling 5,000 miles one January alone), operating a sporting goods business, and co-owning (with former ballplayer Eddie Robinson) a restaurant called Robinson's Gorsuch House, five blocks from Memorial Stadium, at 511 Gorsuch Avenue near the corner of Greenfield Avenue. His radio show was carried on WCBM.

Brooks and Connie eventually sold their rowhouse to pitcher Dave McNally and bought a comfortable ranch home on a large lot in suburban Lutherville, a better situation for his young children. Yet, as his notoriety grew, his personality remained unchanged, treating everyone he encountered with courtesy, whether an out-of-town reporter, a season-ticket holder, or a child seeking an autograph.

Between 1969 and 1971, anyone who didn't already know how exceptional he was with the glove got to see it on national television three straight Octobers in the World Series. He was at his best in 1970, making sensational plays that helped the Orioles defeat the Reds for the world championship. After the Series, he joked that the journalists wanted to interview his glove.

The mid-Seventies posed new challenges. Though Brooks remained one of the game's elite defenders, his offense diminished. By 1976, young Doug DeCinces was eating into his playing time. Moreover, the team camaraderie was suffering. Key players from the championship years were gone, replaced by newcomers like Reggie Jackson and Ken Holtzman who were not committed to staying long-term in Charm City. Brooks asked the Orioles to trade him to a team where he could play regularly. But he vetoed a summer 1976 deal to the White Sox when owner Bill Veeck would not guarantee a 1977 contract.

Around this time, the media reported that Brooks was suffering financial problems. The sporting goods business he co-owned had initially thrived, selling equipment, embroidering uniforms, stringing tennis rackets, drilling bowling balls – a full-service enterprise. But in 1974, just as the business had taken out a large loan to open a new store in York, Pennsylvania, the economy went into a recession and the store opening got caught up in red tape. Loan payments came due. The new store never opened and the business eventually folded. Brooks personally paid off many of the firm's unpaid loans, so as to put the episode behind him.

Free agency had arrived and the gold rush was on for players to cash in. But it came too late for Brooks. He returned to the Orioles one final season (taking a sizable pay cut) as a player-coach, hitting .149 in 24 games. A pre-game ceremony held in his honor drew more than 50,000 appreciative fans. Brooks retired with a .267 batting average, 268 home runs and 2,848 hits.

Robinson never wanted a managerial or coaching role, but agreed to join the O's telecast team, doing about 60 games per year until 1993, when he and Connie moved to California. Years later, the couple returned to Owings Mills, Maryland and Brooks remained active, leading the Major League Baseball Alumni Association, golfing in charity tournaments, and attending selected autograph shows. "It was just an honor and a treat to walk out on the field with Brooks Robinson every day," Boog Powell commented in 2022, a year before Robinson's passing. "Not only because I loved him as a man, but because of the way that he worked."

RON HANSEN

Ron Hansen played in MLB for 15 years, but one week in the summer of 1968 provided a lifetime of memories. Within a seven-day period, he turned the first unassisted triple play in 41 years, slugged a grand-slam homer, and got traded from the Senators to the White Sox! That's one hell of a week.

Hansen's future in baseball seemed in jeopardy back in 1957 due to a ruptured spinal disc that required delicate surgery. He didn't relish having the operation, but realized he had no choice when he went to a theater to see *The Ten Commandments* and could scarcely lift himself out of his seat. Since he was only 18, he needed his parents' permission to have the surgery.

By 1960, he had recovered enough to deliver a monster rookie season for Baltimore, with 22 home runs and 86 RBI plus a cover story in *Baseball Digest*. Hansen was a key part of the youth movement that catapulted the Orioles from sixth place in 1959 to AL runner-up in 1960. O's manager Paul Richards called Hansen and Brooks Robinson his "sliding doors" because they stopped so many hard-hit balls. Hansen worked tirelessly with coach Jimmy Adair to improve his jump on balls hit to his right.

Ron roomed in Baltimore that year with Robinson and Chuck Estrada, and as the club outperformed all expectations, the three had the time of their lives. When Robinson got married, Hansen was the best man. Looking to the future, Hansen and his wife bought property in rural Baldwin, Maryland, and built a home there. He remained with the Orioles until January 1963 when he went to the White Sox in the Luis Aparicio trade.

The hard-nosed infielder spent five years with the White Sox, delivering solid defense and frequent contributions on offense. His best year there was 1964 when 20 of his hits landed in the grandstands.

Just before the 1968 training camp started, Hansen was part of a six-player exchange that sent him to Washington. Never one to burn a bridge, Hansen thanked the White Sox for treating him so well, and welcomed the trade, since the Senators' ballpark was only a one-hour drive from his home in Baldwin.

Unassisted triple plays had become rare. After six in the 1920s, there were none until Hansen's stunner on July 30, 1968. Ron was at shortstop for the Senators against the Indians, who had two men aboard with none out. Joe Azcue hit a line drive up the middle and both runners took off running. "My momentum was going toward second base when I caught the ball," Hansen related. After snaring the drive for the first out, "I stepped on second base (doubling off Dave

Nelson for the second out) and crossed the bag and by the time (Russ) Snyder could get turned around, I had the momentum going and just ran him down (for the third out)." The triplet-termination occurred so fast that some fans didn't realize its significance. He received only a modicum of applause from the road audience his next time at bat.

Hansen had an endorsement deal with MacGregor sporting goods, and when he got back to his Cleveland hotel room, a company rep phoned and said they planned a big promotion around his achievement. Putting honesty ahead of fortune, Hansen sheepishly confessed that he was using a Spalding glove when he turned the play. That Spalding glove is part of the collection at the Baseball Hall of Fame. (After Hansen's heroics, it was another 24 years before Mickey Morandini of Philadelphia pulled the next unassisted triple play.)

An August 2 trade back to the White Sox was a waiver deal, since the trade deadline had passed, a partial reversal of the February trade, with Tim Cullen going back to Washington and Hansen returning to the White Sox. To cap off his extraordinary week, Hansen walked, doubled, and singled for the White Sox against Washington in his first game back with Chicago.

Hansen played the rest of his career as a spare infielder for the White Sox, Yankees, and Royals. For his career, Hansen hit .234 with 1,007 hits and 156 home runs. He led the AL in assists as a shortstop four times, double plays three years, and putouts twice.

He later worked as a coach for the Brewers and Expos; and as a scout for the Brewers, Expos, Yankees and Phillies. Ron was at the 2008 game at Jacobs Field where Asdrubal Cabrera turned an unassisted triple play and congratulated the youngster. Hansen retired in 2010 and continues to reside in Baldwin, at the same rural location he purchased as an Orioles rookie back in 1960.

BARRY LATMAN

It didn't cost the Indians an arm and a leg to acquire Barry Latman from the White Sox, but it nearly cost the hurler an ear. Decades before Google news alerts, mobile phones and text messages, players sometime learned that they had been traded via the mass media. Latman was getting his hair cut on the eve of the 1960 season when he heard on the radio he had been traded. "I was sitting in a barber chair in Hammond, Indiana, when I heard the announcement on the radio," he told writers. "I sort of jumped up and almost lost an ear when the barber was slow in getting the razor out of the way."

Nicknamed "Shoulders" for obvious reasons, Latman pitched for Fairfax High School in Los Angeles, where he once threw a perfect game with 19 strikeouts. He also played high school football. From 1954 to 1959, Latman exchanged a series of letters with Ty Cobb, which led to Cobb watching Barry pitch in a high school game. Cobb encouraged him to pursue baseball professionally.

Barry was a member of the White Sox's post-season roster in 1959 but did not see action in the World Series. After the season, the Sox traded him to the Indians for pitcher Herb Score. His four-year stay in Cleveland was his longest with any one club. His best season was 1961 in Cleveland, when he started the year 9-0, made the all-star team, and finished at 13-5. He later became a full-time reliever, achieving success with the Angels and Astros. He relied chiefly on a fastball and slider, having learned the latter pitch early on from White Sox coach Ray Berres.

As a representative of Spalding sporting goods, Latman once took a great deal of baseball equipment to Italy for the children of Rome on a goodwill trip. While there, he had a private audience with Pope John Paul at his private retreat, Castel Gandolfo.

Barry was a Californian at heart, comfortable with the area's culture and lifestyle. He didn't dislike Chicago or Cleveland, but he never felt connected to either city. Barry was thrilled when the Indians shipped him to the Angels after the 1963 season, where he could be home year-around. He had a 6-10 record in his first year with the Angels and went 1-1 the following year (while spending part of the year at Triple-A Seattle). His road roommate with the Angels was all-star pitcher Ken McBride.

His final season was 1967 with the Astros, who had several players of Jewish heritage. In addition to Latman, Larry Sherry, Norm Miller and Bo Belinsky were members of that team. After posting a 2.71 ERA in 1966, Latman's ERA ballooned to 4.52 in 1967 and he was waived in August, spelling the end of his pitching career.

The son of a wealthy furniture auctioneer, the pitcher himself invested in a home furnishings business while with the Indians. "My father once told me that when you work for somebody else, you'll never be 100 percent happy. Only when you work for yourself can you control your situation," he said in the April 6, 1963 edition of *The Sporting News*. In 1961, he married the daughter of a well-to-do owner of a California pharmacy chain (Schwab's Drugstore) and they honeymooned in Israel. They raised two children before divorcing in 1980.

He remarried in 1989 and lived alternately in Marina Del Rey, San Diego, and Puerto Vallarta. Together with his second wife, they had five children and eight grandkids. Barry was 82 when he passed away in Richmond, Texas, following a long illness, in 2019. Latman's final statistics included a 35-37 record with a 4.27 ERA over 11 years.

MEL STOTTLEMYRE

Mel Stottlemyre was a slender young man from Mabton, Washington – a valley town of less than 2,500 people originally built around a railway stop, a water tower and a general store. He was an unheralded baseball prospect in high school and community college, commanding no bonus when he signed with New York in 1961. Yet, three years later, he was pitching for the

Yankees in the heat of the pennant race, instrumental in their 1964 success by posting a 9-3 record and winning another game in the World Series.

His not-so-secret weapon was the sinker. He found that placing his fingers on the seams sharpened the sinking motion. Coach Jim Hegan likened Mel's sinker to that of Bob Lemon, a Hall of Fame pitcher, and noted that both pitchers fielded their position well.

Mel won 20 games in 1965, lost 20 contests in 1966, broke even at 15-15 in 1967, and then settled in as one of the league's best pitchers for the next several seasons. Plenty of teams made trade offers – for example the Orioles offered a package built around slugging prospect Mike Epstein – but none prompted the Yankees to pull the trigger.

On July 20, 1965, Mel hit a highly unusual grand-slam, inside-the-park homer at Yankee Stadium against Bill Monbouquette of the Red Sox. Mel connected on a high fastball, drilling it between outfielders Carl Yastrzemski and Jim Gosger. As Mel raced toward home plate, the relay throw got away from catcher Bob Tillman. The Yankees went on to win the game, 6-3.

Rather than carouse with teammates after home games, Mel returned home to his wife Jean. Two sons, one born in 1963 and the other in 1965, kept them both busy. Both sons eventually became major league pitchers.

As Jim Ogle wrote in 1968, "The big city hasn't spoiled Stottlemyre and never will. He won't give it a chance. When the baseball season ends, Mel and his family return to Washington for peace and quiet, hunting and fishing, relaxing and recovering from another summer in New York. The lure of off-season money has never attracted Mel to New York."

Catcher Jake Gibbs told a story about Mel and Mickey Mantle out on a row boat during spring training. Mel was rowing while Mantle was fishing. A couple of other fishermen were in their boat nearby when one of them recognized Mantle, with the other one telling him he was nuts. They rowed closer and as Gibbs told it, one said, "It sure is Mickey and he's got some big, dumb rookie doing the rowing for him."

As David Halberstam noted in *October 1964,* "Stottlemyre thew what professionals call a heavy ball, which meant that it came into the plate hard and heavy. It was hard to catch and hard on the catcher's hands as it broke down. Catching Stottlemyre over a few games almost guaranteed that Jake Gibbs' hand would be swollen and the fingers would be a purplish blue with little circulation in them."

Fifteen starts into the 1974 season, Mel was diagnosed with a torn rotator cuff and missed the rest of the season. Still unable to throw hard in spring 1975, he was released. Catfish Hunter had signed with New York and replaced Mel as the team's ace. The timing was unfortunate for Mel, as the Yankees won three pennants between 1976 and 1978.

He left the game with a 164-139 record and a fine 2.97 ERA, but he didn't stay away long, as he became a longtime pitching coach. He was 77 years old when he died in Seattle in 2019.

Luis Aparicio

This popular shortstop helped change the way baseball was played by reintroducing the stolen base as a lethal weapon. Beginning with his rookie season with the White Sox in 1956, he paced the AL in pilfered bases for nine straight seasons. In a career that spanned until 1973, he was a 13-time all-star and winner of nine gold gloves. An expert bunter, he twice led the league in sacrifice hits. Even at the age of 39, he was a .271 hitter who swiped 13 bases in 14 attempts for the 1973 Red Sox.

Aparicio's father had been one of the best shortstops in Venezuelan baseball history. The White Sox groomed Luis to replace Chico Carrasquel at the position. He became the sixth Venezuelan to play in MLB; Carrasquel had been the third (the first was pitcher Alex Carrasquel, Chico's uncle, who debuted with the 1939 Senators).

Luis starred with two pennant winners. In 1959, the White Sox won the AL crown, dethroning the Yankees. The shortstop stole a career-peak 56 bases and scored 98 runs, sixth-best in the circuit, as the Sox bested the Indians by five games and the third-place Yankees by 25 games. During the 1959 World Series, Aparicio hit a crisp .308, though the White Sox lost to the Dodgers in six contests.

For two more seasons, Luis remained at the top of his game. "He's not only a great base stealer but a great shortstop. I've never seen anyone play short as well as he does," marveled Dick Howser, a rival AL shortstop.

After the 1961 season, Aparicio passed up winter ball and spent the off-season in Chicago, selling tickets and attending meal functions. In 1962, he reported to spring training seven pounds overweight, a problem for a five-foot-nine player who depended on his speed. He got off to a slow start, made more errors, and stole fewer bases. In September, he was bothered by a sore ankle. He finished with a .241 batting average and 31 stolen bases, down from 53 the previous year.

Upon learning his pay would be cut, he proclaimed it would be 20 years before the White Sox would win another pennant. He asked for a trade and the Sox were happy to oblige, sending him and veteran outfielder Al Smith to Baltimore for four players including Hoyt Wilhelm, Ron Hansen, and Pete Ward. Lesson learned about conditioning, Aparicio was in better shape going forward.

Aparicio's second trip to the post-season came in 1966, his fourth year in Baltimore. He hit .276 with six homers, 97 runs scored and 25 stolen bases, and placed seventh in the MVP voting. His club carried the momentum into the fall classic, sweeping the Dodgers. Luis contributed four hits and errorless baseball to the triumph.

After Aparicio hit only .233 for the 1967 Orioles, the club swapped him back to the White Sox to acquire Don Buford.

In a White Sox-Indians game on June 19, 1968, Aparicio was involved in what Cleveland manager Alvin Dark called the strangest half-inning he had ever seen. Wonderful Willie Smith led off the inning for the Indians, wearing Sam McDowell's cleats because he had forgotten to bring his own. Smith hit a grounder to short, stumbled out of the batter's box, hopped a few steps, fell down completely and bounced back to his feet. Distracted by Willie's theatrics, Aparicio threw wildly to first base, and Smith was awarded second base on the overthrow. Dark wisely got Smith out of the game by having Dave Nelson pinch-run. The next batter, Luis Tiant, beat out a spectacular bunt, putting runners on first and third with nobody out. The next hitter, Russ Snyder, hit a chopper to second baseman Wayne Causey, who flipped the ball to Aparicio, but the shortstop was nowhere near the bag. That provided Cleveland's first run, with runners now on first and second. Tony Horton then hit a shot right back to the pitcher's mound that looked like a double-play ball but went right through pitcher Bob Locker's legs for a run-scoring hit. The Indians won the game, 4-1.

Luis spent three more years in Chicago, peaking in 1970 when he batted .313 and made the all-star team. Remarkable for a 36-year-old, only Alex Johnson, Carl Yastrzemski and Tony Oliva had higher batting averages.

That winter, he was traded for a final time, heading to Boston before the 1971 season. He played effectively for the BoSox for three seasons, but the club released him during spring training of 1974, opting to look at younger infielders like Rick Burleson and Mario Guerrero. Although the Yankees offered to sign Aparicio, the proud player instead retired and returned to Venezuela.

Running came naturally to Aparicio. As a child growing up in Maracalbo, his family lived about 20 blocks from the school and Luis would run back and forth to save time. He played plenty of baseball in the streets, but since equipment was scarce, the boys used a tennis ball instead of a baseball and their hands instead of a bat. It was a "baseball meets handball" scenario.

Regarding base larceny, future Hall of Famer Joe Gordon said, "Aparicio rarely makes a mistake. He has a great feel for the exact moment when he has the proper jump on the pitcher." In a *Baseball Digest* interview in 1961, Luis listed Hoyt Wilhelm, Paul Foytack, Whitey Ford and Bud Daley as pitchers who were difficult to steal against. But Wilhelm, he contended, should have been getting called for balks, due to a hitch in his motion.

Back in the 1940s, it was unheard of for an established player to assist a younger player who might someday replace him. But by the 1960s, that was beginning to change. Aparicio, who was young Mark Belanger's roommate on road trips in 1967, provided Mark with fielding tips. "When I would go to the hole for the ball and then make the throw to first base, the ball was dying on me," Belanger said. "Looie noticed this and told me how to grip the ball against the seams so it would have perpendicular rotation and take off instead of die." Sure enough, Belanger replaced Aparicio the next season.

Luis finished with a .262 career average, 2,677 hits, and 506 stolen bases, which as of 2023 placed him 38th on the all-time list. His 78.8 percent stolen-base ratio was particularly outstanding. He was inducted into the Hall of Fame in 1984.

MAURY WILLS

Cool Papa Bell, Negro League star from the Twenties and Thirties, was called "the fastest man who ever put on a pair of baseball shoes" by his contemporary, Judy Johnson. Four decades later, baseball people said the same of Maury Wills of the Dodgers, who followed in the footsteps of Luis Aparicio in making the stolen base a key offensive weapon. Before his arrival, the entire NL had been averaging only 300 stolen bases per year. Wills shattered all norms in 1962, the year he pilfered 104 bags. That was more than the next three most prolific thieves (Willie Davis, Vada Pinson and Julian Javier) combined (94 steals).

The stolen base, a big part of offensive strategy during the sport's early decades, had taken a back seat once the home run became the weapon of choice. The Trolly Dodgers themselves prospered in the Fifties with little need to steal bases. Sure, Pee Wee Reese would swipe his 20 bases, but with sluggers like Roy Campanella, Duke Snider, Carl Furillo, and Gil Hodges, most of the scoring came on extra-base hits.

But in the mid-Sixties, the offensively challenged Dodgers struggled to score. The team's home run output dwindled from 157 to 140 to 110 to 79 to 78. Increasingly, Walter Alston's crew depended on phenomenal pitching to keep games close. In that context, a stolen base, or a hit-and-run, could create the run that made the difference between a win and a loss. And the Dodgers kept winning straight through the 1966 season. Once Wills reminded everyone how effective the steal could be, he not only helped the Dodgers immeasurably, but he set the stage for villains to follow such as Lou Brock and eventually even Rickey Henderson.

Wills did not become an everyday player until age 27 but led the senior circuit in stolen bases each of his six first full seasons. In his remarkable 1962 season, he set the new major-league stolen base record (since broken), eclipsing the mark formerly held by Ty Cobb. Amazingly, he was gunned down only 13 times against 104 thefts; pitchers and catchers knew he would run but were powerless to stop him. Wills generated media coverage everywhere he went, including a feature in the book, *Baseball Stars of 1963*.

The only product of Cardozo High School in Washington, D.C. to make the big leagues, Wills was a five-time all-star. He captured two gold gloves and became a skilled bunter thanks to instruction from Bobby Bragan, his manager at Spokane. Wills said in his autobiography, *On the Run,* that he deployed six different types of bunts, depending on fielders' positioning.

The shortstop wrote that his closest friends on the team were Sandy Koufax and John Roseboro. He credited Roseboro, his first roommate, with helping him adjust to life in the big leagues. Wills also praised coach Pete Reiser for working with him for hours at a time when he struggled as a rookie. Wills never bonded with Duke Snider. He wrote that Snider, then near the end of his career, was taciturn and uncommunicative.

Wills won the MVP award in 1962, as the Dodgers pushed the Giants all the way to a three-game, season-ending playoff series to determine the pennant winner. Wills played in all 165 games, another major-league record. Infielder Nate Oliver, who roomed with Wills at times, said he was "a great player when the game was on the line."

The speedster remained dominant for several years. He was third in the MVP derby in 1964, when he stole 94 bases as the Dodgers captured the world championship. Maury hit .270 or better 10 straight years.

Dodgers vice president Buzzie Bavasi called Wills "a puzzle we could never solve." Part of his frustration goes back to an incident after the 1966 season, when many Dodgers (though not Sandy Koufax, Don Drysdale and Wes Parker) joined a goodwill tour of Japan to visit U.S. soldiers and play 18 exhibition games. Wills made the trip, nursing a knee injury. According to teammate Ron Fairly, Wills told Dodgers owner Walter O'Malley that he wanted to return to California to have the knee examined. O'Malley asked him to stay on the tour, participate in pre-game introductions, and have the knee examined at a U.S. military base in Japan or by a U.S. doctor after the tour. Wills left without permission, which the Dodgers considered a breach of contract. O'Malley fumed when he learned that Wills was in Hawaii performing banjo music in a night club. He expected a higher level of commitment from the team captain.

It wasn't long before the Dodgers traded Wills to the Pirates for third baseman Bob Bailey and shortstop Gene Michael. Peter O'Malley, who was running day-to-day operations, said the deal was a chance for the Dodgers to get younger. Pirates manager Harry Walker said, "He could give us the extra spark we need. And he'll be our general on the field. We don't have anyone who talks to the pitchers, but Wills can do that. He's the type of player who wins pennants."

In Pittsburgh, Wills settled in, became a partner in a night club, and played third base for two solid years, though there were no pennants. He hit better than .300 for only the second time in his career in 1967. Then in 1968, he hit .278 and raised his stolen bases back up to 52.

His final weeks with the Pirates in 1968 were unpleasant. His temper flared after hearing a rumor that the Bucs didn't plan to protect him in the expansion draft and he twice refused to take a late-season physical exam. Handed a letter imposing a $150 fine as he entered the team bus, he turned around and refused to accompany the club on its final road trip to Chicago. "He swore and ranted and raved about the fine," traveling secretary Bob Rice told reporters. "He told me what [general manager Joe] Brown could do with the fine and I simply told him to go tell Brown, not me." Then in a highly unusual move, Wills met with Pittsburgh Mayor Joseph Barr, who successfully advised him to rejoin the team.

Wills was drafted by the expansion Expos, and in a surprising development, he was traded back to the Dodgers on June 11, 1969, with Manny Mota for Ron Fairly and Paul Popovich. Equally remarkable, Wills had a strong enough season in 1971, at age 38, to place sixth in the MVP voting.

Wills retired after the 1972 season with a lifetime batting average of .281 and 2,134 hits. His 586 career stolen bases ranked 20th on the all-time list as of 2024. Bill James' *The New Baseball Historical Abstract* rated Wills as the 19th greatest shortstop of all time.

Well connected in Hollywood social circles, Wills fathered six children and was rumored to have had an affair with actress Doris Day. The story was considered scandalous at a time when interracial relationships were considered rare, and affairs with married women were verboten. Wills later substantiated the story, while Day denied it.

Wills had a successful run as a baseball color commentator but had a disastrous experience as manager of the Mariners for parts of the 1980 and 1981 seasons. Struggling with a drug addiction at that time, he was fired over his unreliability, erratic behavior and a dismal 26-56 cumulative record. He apparently gained sobriety in the late 1980s and was living in a Phoenix-area golf-course community when he passed away at age 89 in 2022.

GARY GENTRY

The Mets' meteoric rise to the 1969 world championship coincided with the arrival of four superb arms: Tom Seaver, Jerry Koosman, Nolan Ryan and Gary Gentry. The team's victory totals rose from 61 to 73 to 100 during that period.

Gentry starred at Arizona State, staying all four years. The Orioles, Astros and Giants all drafted him in separate years, to no avail. He finally signed with the Mets after his senior year.

After just two years in the Mets' farm system, in February 1969, he packed his wife, six-month old baby, and 150-pound St. Bernard into his car and made the long drive from Arizona to Florida for spring training. He made the parent club right out of camp. The dog played a big role in the family's life, standing guard at their New York apartment when Gary was away on road trips. Gentry won 13 games during the regular season and added another win in game three of the World Series, with Ryan providing late-inning relief.

By 1970, Gentry had developed a reputation for being outspoken and short-tempered. He told a sportswriter that baseball players were underpaid compared to their football and basketball counterparts. He complained that he missed turns in the rotation after rainouts whereas Seaver didn't. "I think we all should be treated alike," Gentry opined. He twice made non-verbal gestures on the mound that were interpreted as showing up teammates Cleon Jones and Tommie Agee. After the incident where Agee muffed a play with the bases loaded and Gentry reacted, manager Gil Hodges said he would have a talk with Gentry; he also told reporters he was instituting a system of fines for players making mental mistakes. Gary confessed that he needed to better manage his emotions. He finished the 1970 season with a 9-9 record.

Early in the 1971 season, Gentry's wife and son returned to Phoenix to sublease their apartment. Thinking her son was behind her as she returned to the apartment following an afternoon at the pool, she suddenly realized he was at the bottom of the pool. She performed mouth-to-mouth resuscitation to revive the youngster, who was already fine by the time the paramedics arrived. Upon hearing about the near-tragedy, Hodges advised Gentry to fly to Arizona to be with the family until his next scheduled start.

Gentry had a fine season in 1971, posting a 12-11 record with a career-best 3.23 ERA and 155 strikeouts. A Jack Lang column in *The Sporting News* reported that Gentry had become much better at controlling his anger.

When the Mets traded for Jim Fregosi after the 1971 campaign, they unwittingly insisted on trading Ryan instead of Gentry. Ryan at the time had a 29-38 record, whereas Gentry seemed more accomplished. But in 1972, Ryan emerged as an ace, whereas Gentry's record drifted to 7-10.

The Mets swapped Gentry to the Braves before the 1973 season, landing pitcher George Stone and second baseman Felix Millan. In three years full of arm miseries with the Braves, Gentry won just five more games. Thereafter, he and his family returned to Phoenix, where he built a successful real estate brokerage. His lifetime record was 46-49 with a 3.58 ERA.

SAMMY ELLIS

Four Reds pitchers reached the coveted 20-win plateau in the Sixties: Joey Jay hit the mark in 1961 and 1962; his roommate Bob Purkey joined him in 1962; young Jim Maloney got there in 1963 and 1965; and Sammy Ellis rounded out the list in 1965. Ellis had the shortest career of the four aces but his contributions remain memorable.

He was born in Youngstown and went to school at Mississippi State. He signed with the Reds for a $60,000 bonus but battled the twin demons of wildness and anger. The Reds gave him a look in eight games early in the 1962 season, but he wasn't yet ready to battle big leaguers. By 1964, that had changed.

The 1964 Reds were a hard-hitting squad with three superb sluggers in Frank Robison, Vada Pinson and Deron Johnson, plus solid talent up the middle with Pete Rose at second base and Leo Cardenas at shortstop. The team played the entire season with heavy hearts, for it had been announced in January that manager Fred Hutchinson, just 45 years old, was terminally ill with cancer. Hutch, who had smoked as many as four packs of cigarettes daily, skippered the team as long as he physically could, until August 12, when with his health giving out, a ceremony was held in his honor and he took a leave of absence. At that time, the Reds were in third place and trailed the first-place Phillies by 6.5 games.

Dick Sisler succeeded Hutch and the club went 32-21 down the stretch to become serious contenders. Meanwhile, the Phillies endured their famous late-season meltdown. The race came down to the final weekend when the Reds dropped a pair of season-ending games to the Phillies. By then, the Cardinals – who were in fifth place on August 12 – had raced past everyone else to win the flag. Hutch passed away shortly after the season ended.

But the emergence of Ellis was a happy story. As the Reds made their late run, Sammy delivered one win and three saves over the last two weeks of the season. He finished the year with sterling statistics including a 10-3 record, a team-high 14 saves and a 2.57 ERA. He also fanned 125 hitters in just 122 innings.

Following the season, Ellis made the case that he belonged in the starting rotation. To prove his point, he demanded a contract that would pay him extra if he appeared in more than 45 games. "We don't give out contracts like that," the assistant general manager, Phil Seghi, tersely responded. Seghi was nonetheless quoted in *The Sporting News* as saying he would like to see Ellis in the starting rotation. That led to manager Dick Sisler's equally terse response at the winter meetings of "I'll use Ellis as I see fit."

By the time the season started, Ellis was where he wanted to be, in the rotation. The 1965 Reds won 89 games, good enough only for a fourth-place finish behind Los Angeles, San Francisco and Pittsburgh. Ellis, however, made the all-star team and concluded the year with 22 triumphs. His wife kept a scrapbook with articles about his season, and there was no shortage of highlights.

His favorite memory came on a blazing hot June day when he felt miserable, sapped by a sore throat and a summer cold. He nonetheless persevered through 11 innings, fanned 10 Braves' hitters, and was still around to gain credit for the win. That's how baseball was played in the Sixties.

After the 1965 season, the Reds traded Frank Robinson; Ellis wasn't shy about appraising the transaction. He said the Reds had traded "a superstar for three maybes" and accused owner Bill DeWitt of not wanting to win the pennant. "I'll tell him so to his face," Ellis stated. To which DeWitt responded, "Maybe I should give Sammy a desk in the front office."

It was mostly downhill for Ellis from there. He surrendered more earned runs than any other NL hurler the second straight year in 1966, and this time without Robinson in the lineup to provide run support, his record sagged to 12-19. Ellis was more effective in 1967 but turned in a losing record at 8-11.

Ellis was traded and posted a 9-10 mark for the 1968 Angels. After the season, the left-hander ran into White Sox manager Al Lopez while playing golf in Florida and told Lopez he'd welcome a fresh start with Chicago. The Sox took him up on the suggestion, executing a trade with the Angels. He was ineffective in 10 games with the 1969 White Sox and finished his career in the minor leagues for the Indians, Cardinals, and A's.

Ellis later explained to writer Lew Freedman, "My delivery got out of whack, and before you know it, you can't get anybody out. I wasn't locating my pitches worth a crap." Coupled with shoulder trouble, Ellis exclaimed, "I couldn't even drive a power mower."

Though his pitching career was finished by age 30, he refashioned himself as a successful pitching coach. After retiring a second time, he followed the Reds and the Rays, before passing away in Florida in 2016.

GIL HODGES

One of the great first basemen from the Fifties, Gil Hodges saw his productivity at the plate nosedive with the arrival of the new decade. After batting .276 with 25 homers for the Dodgers in 1959 – and tearing it up for a .391 average in the World Series -- he dropped off to .198 and eight round-trippers in 1960. Gil had dealt with frustrating slumps throughout his career, but this was the first time one lasted almost an entire season. He was 36 years old, and uncertain of his future.

He settled into a part-time role with the Dodgers in 1961 and assumed the same function with the expansion Mets in 1962. That pitiful club lost 120 games, but New York fans appreciated the presence of Hodges, who had been a hero so many times for the Dodgers before they moved west.

The veteran, now 39 years old, opened the 1963 season with the Mets, but played sparingly. A quarter of the way into the season, Hodges was hired to manage the Senators, who were off to a miserable start under manager Mickey Vernon. Until the managerial change, the Senators players were discouraged, the writers were hypercritical, and the fans were already losing interest in their new expansion club.

The hiring of Hodges represented a fresh start, at least at first. The new manager and his wife, Joan, took a luxury apartment at the Shoreham in the affluent Woodley Park neighborhood off of Connecticut Avenue, where his neighbors included senators, representatives, high-profile attorneys, and other noteworthy Washingtonians. The Shoreham was not the closest apartment to the new stadium, but it was the closest one that would afford the couple the services and glamorous lifestyle they wanted. (Most of the players rented far less costly housing in suburban Prince George's County, Maryland, or in Alexandria, Virginia, near National Airport.)

In the book, *Gil Hodges: A Hall of Fame Life* by Mort Zachter, the author wrote, "The Senators had a history dating back to Bucky Harris in 1924 (and Joe Cronin in 1935) of hiring managers with no previous managerial experience. In 1963, Hodges would take batting and infield practice to stay in shape. Since Harris and Cronin were player-managers, the writers interpreted Hodges' workouts as preparation to pencil himself into the lineup." Despite the speculation, Gil never did go active for Washington.

Having never managed in the minor leagues or winter ball, Hodges was practicing in real time. He quickly became known as a disciplinarian. Don Lock, one of his top outfielders, believed that Hodges' later success as a manager with the Mets was due to dialing back the discipline.

Another player who chafed at Hodges' style was Hawk Harrelson. In his book titled, *Hawk,* he wrote, "Joining the Senators was like a prison term. Hodges was the warden." At one point, when Hodges ordered Harrelson to get a haircut, pitcher Bob Humphreys did the honors. When Harrelson was eventually traded back to the A's, he told reporters that all 25 players hated Hodges. Frank Howard responded that Harrelson should speak for himself. Howard acknowledged that Hodges could be difficult to play for, but said, "If my three sons turn out to be half the man as Gil Hodges, I'll be very satisfied."

After a pair of 100-loss seasons in 1963 and 1964, the Senators improved to 70-92 in 1965, a measure of slow progress perhaps, and to 71-88 in 1966. As the 1967 season got under way, Hodges' fifth season in the position, expectations were beginning to escalate. Howard was emerging as a legitimate slugger (36 home runs), as were, to a lesser degree, Ken McMullen and Mike Epstein. On the mound, veteran Camilo Pascual added stability at the front of the rotation. The 1967 Senators closed out the year with 76 wins, another modest improvement. But rumors circulated that Hodges wanted to return to New York.

He had a year remaining on his contract, but when the Mets expressed interest in his services, general manager George Selkirk granted them permission to contact Gil, who accepted the offer. (Selkirk replaced him with Jim Lemon. After an even worse 1968 season, both Selkirk and Lemon were relieved of their positions, and Ted Williams was hired as Senators manager.)

Back in the Big Apple where his career had started, Hodges led the Mets to a 73-89 finish in 1968, and then to the miraculous world championship in 1969. Having survived a cardiac arrest, Hodges seemed more sympathetic and patient with his players. He was the toast of the town, a role he enjoyed even the next two seasons when the Mets were passed in the standings by other clubs.

He was still the team's skipper when he died of a heart attack in West Palm Beach on April 3, 1972. He had just played 18 holes of golf with coaches Joe Pignatano, Eddie Yost, and Rube Walker. The team was not active that day due to a brief players' strike. Hodges was eulogized as a man with a big heart (figuratively), a military veteran who had served at the Battle of Okinawa and a faithful Catholic who attended church every Sunday. He was beloved as a player who approached the game the right way. Gil was inducted into the Hall of Fame as a player in 2022.

Bob Aspromonte

One of the era's most heartwarming stories involved infielder Bob Aspromonte. He was the favorite player of a young fan named Billy with severe vision problems who listened to games on the radio. Aspro visited him each of the three times Billy prepared for surgery and each time, the youngster asked him to hit a home run. Bob was not a power hitter, but he remarkably went deep all three times. For the third of those occasions, Billy was in the grandstands to enjoy the moment in person. That would be a compelling story if it ended there, but that wasn't the half of it.

Three years after Bob retired from baseball, a car battery exploded in his face and left him nearly blind. Now it was Aspro who needed surgery – by the same surgeon who performed Billy's operations. Billy, who had become a successful athlete and even hurled a perfect game as an amateur pitcher, returned the favor, contacting Aspromonte and encouraging him to have faith, just as the star player had done for Billy years earlier.

Aspromonte was a Brooklyn native who appeared in a single game for his hometown Dodgers as an 18-year-old in 1956. Gil Hodges befriended and encouraged Bob right from the start. After the season, Bob was part of the Dodgers' delegation that traveled to Japan for exhibition games. While there, Rachel Robinson, the wife of Jackie, helped Bob pick out a 112-piece China set that the Aspromonte family has cherished ever since.

After spending time in the minor leagues, Bob got into 68 more Dodgers games after the club moved west. His break came in 1962, when he hit .266 for the expansion Houston club. He became an excellent third baseman, twice led the loop in fielding percentage, and set a league record for hot sackers by going 57 straight games without an error.

The franchise played in an old minor league park before moving into the Astrodome. In a 2012 radio interview on KTRH, Aspro recalled, "We had such a relationship with the fans, and it was created on the field as well as off…What was most inspirational was to watch that incredible Astrodome being built. And that's why I give so much credit to Judge Roy Hofheinz…to build that facility and to win the franchise for the city of Houston, which was only about 500,000 people at that time."

He hit .280 with 69 RBI in 1964 and enjoyed another robust season in 1967 when he hit .294 with 58 RBI. He was so popular that on a "Bob Aspromonte Night" in Houston, he was awarded a trip to Italy and 3,000 pounds of pasta (which he donated). Playing for Houston through 1968, Bob roomed on the road mostly with shortstop Bob Lillis and first baseman Rusty Staub.

Aspro next spent two years as a reserve for the Braves, helping the club win the NL East in 1969. Ahead of the 1971 season, Bob planned to play one more season, and accepted an invitation from the Mets to hold down their third base job until a younger player was ready to take it on. The Mets were managed by Hodges, with whom Aspromonte had stayed in close touch over the years, bringing Bob's career full-circle back to New York. Until he retired, he was the last active Brooklyn Dodger. His lifetime average was .252.

Bob's older brother, Ken Aspromonte, played from 1957 to 1963 for the Red Sox, Senators, Indians, Angels, Braves and Cubs. Ken later managed the Indians for three years. Both settled in Houston where they owned a beer distributorship and two Burger King restaurants for many years. They were inducted together into the National Italian Sports Hall of Fame in 2012.

SAL BANDO

Few franchises have experienced higher peaks and lower troughs than the Athletics. After Connie Mack's gang appeared in four World Series in a five-year span ending in 1914, the club finished last in the AL seven straight years. They were back on top from 1929 to 1931 but finished in the cellar all but three years from 1935 to 1946. They went 41 years between pennants, from 1931 to 1972. During that time, they moved from Philadelphia to Kansas City to Oakland.

In the mid-Sixties, the A's were a below-average team with a pipeline of promising prospects. Five farm teams at the A-level or higher had winning records, boasting intriguing prospects like Reggie Jackson, Rick Monday, Joe Rudi, Jim Nash, Blue Moon Odom, Dave Hamilton, Rollie Fingers, and Sal Bando. By 1972, the A's would become world champions with Bando as their third baseman and team captain.

Sal grew up in Warrensville Heights, Ohio, a Cleveland suburb, where he was a high school football and baseball star. Football scholarships rolled in, but it was not until coach Bobby Winkles offered a baseball scholarship at Arizona State that Sal had a chance to continue playing the sport he truly loved. By 1965, Arizona State won the College World Series and Bando was named MVP.

He was soon selected by the A's in the sixth round of the amateur draft and was invited along with prospect Rick Monday to accompany the A's for two weeks. On their first night in New York, Bando who was 21 and Monday who was 19 decided to go out and see some sights. "On our way to Times Square, we met a guy walking around wearing a Viking costume. We turned around and went back to the hotel," Bando later joked.

Playing for Mobile of the Southern League in 1966, he got off to such a bad start at the plate that he was flown to Kansas City for special instruction. The tutoring paid off as he finished strong. He got into 11 games for the A's later that season.

In 1967, the A's moved veteran Ed Charles to the Mets to make room at third base for Bando. "They sold Ed Charles, so they must have confidence in me," Bando said. "I feel the same way about myself." A's manager Alvin Dark gushed, "We feel Bando is going to be another Brooks Robinson." Yet, it was a controversial move. Dark messed with Bando's batting stance and the youngster hit only .192 in 47 games, when not back in the minor leagues. Sal became the everyday third sacker in 1968, enjoyed greater success, and held the position until he left as a free agent before the 1977 season.

He began to hit with power and displayed what writer Joe McGuff called "a truly spectacular arm." He wasn't swift on his feet – some said he was built like a truck – but his reflexes were quick. There was also something else about Bando, an intensity coupled with a determination to win. His teammate Ramon Webster, the first baseman, commended Bando for being vocal throughout each game.

Recognizing Bando's leadership skills, manager Hank Bauer named him team captain in 1969. Sal was only 25 years old at the time. That season was Bando's finest, as he set career highs with 31 home runs and 113 RBI, and made the all-star team for the first of four times.

Bando was one of many Italian-American players who were proud of their ethic heritage. Joe DiMaggio, who was a living legend in the Sixties, was a full-time A's coach in 1968. When the A's visited Cleveland, Sal invited his dad to sit on the bench during batting practice. His pop expressed interest in meeting the reclusive former superstar. Sal told his dad that if he approached DiMaggio, Joe would likely brush him off. But if he just sat on the bench watching practice, Joe might greet him. Sure enough, Joe came out to the dugout and was approached by a couple of sportswriters. Seeking to avoid the scribes, DiMaggio walked over to Sal's dad and the pair had a long, pleasant conversation.

Sal also used to tell the story about calling his mom on the phone long distance with the great news that he had met a wonderful girl – and on top of that, she was Italian! (The young lady was his future wife Sandy Fortunato.) Bando expected his mother to be thrilled. Instead, she asked, "What part of Italy are her relatives from?"

Another Italian-American during that era was Billy Martin, who had retired as a player in 1961 and began managing the Twins in 1969. One of Sal's duties as team captain was to deliver the pre-game lineup cards to the umpire and opposing manager before the game. One weekend, the A's and Twins had engaged in some nasty beanball activity. Martin was also part Italian. The next day when Bando approached the plate, Martin's Twins lineup card, in the Extra Players section, listed Rocky Marciano and a number of other famous Italian fighters. Bando, Martin and the umpire had a good laugh.

With Bando and other young players hitting their stride, the A's finished second in the AL West in 1969 and 1970. They captured the division title in 1971, losing the ALCS to Baltimore. Bando later said the most meaningful of his three world titles was the first one in 1972. The A's beat the Reds in seven games, even though Jackson and reliever Darold Knowles were injured.

Bando later played for the Brewers, signing a long-term deal at age 33. Named team captain, he was productive the first two years, but struggled the rest of the way, retiring during the 1981 campaign. In that regard, he was one of the first examples of the risks of signing aging stars to multi-year contracts.

The Brewers brought Sal back in 1982 as a bench coach, and he helped manager Harvey Kuenn push all the right buttons as Harvey's Wallbangers battled to the pennant. Bando was the club's general manager from 1991 until 1999.

During his playing career, Bando teamed up with John McGlocklin of the Milwaukee Bucks basketball team in a successful business-loan company, which they took public. He was inducted into the Brewers Wall of Honor in 2014 and one of his three sons was head coach for the Marquette High School baseball team. Bando resided in Phoenix for a number of years before relocating back to Wisconsin, where he died of cancer in 2023 at age 78.

JOE MORGAN

Second baseman Joe Morgan did not become an MVP award winner until the Seventies, but he flashed enormous potential as early as his 1965 rookie season. Playing for Houston, he had already adopted his approach to hitting. He would take the first pitch or two, and only swing at pitches that he was confident he could handle. That prevented him from chasing pitches out of the zone, which resulted in plenty of free passes. He led the NL in walks four times.

Once on base, Morgan's God-given speed, coupled with good instincts, allowed him to rattle pitchers and pilfer bases. He swiped 689 bases, which as of 2024 was 11th on the all-time list.

After placing second in the 1965 rookie-of-the-year vote, he made the 1966 all-star team and placed second in the NL in on-base percentage. He spent five more seasons with Houston, though he lost some time to injuries and clashed with manager Harry Walker.

Morgan reached his peak after being traded to the Reds. He won five gold gloves, continued to steal bases, demonstrated surprising home-run power for a smaller player, and won the MVP award in 1975 and 1976. Cincinnati won the World Series both years.

"Joe Morgan became a Hall of Fame player through hard work and maximizing his talent. He was a very disciplined hitter and was a good friend," noted catcher Ron Brand. Johnny Bench called Morgan "the best player I ever saw."

"He was a great example of why size doesn't matter in baseball. It's in the heart," added George Culver, another former teammate. "He was only about five-foot-seven and maybe 170 pounds but what a competitor. He got so much out of that body. Smart as a whip, way ahead of other players in terms of knowing the pitchers on how they were going to be pitching him. He kept a notebook in his locker after every game. He was very self-motivated."

The veteran retired with a .271 average, 268 homers, and 2,517 hits and became a renowned sportscaster. He was 77 when he died from a nerve ailment in in 2020.

John Roseboro

From humble beginnings, John Roseboro became the successor to Roy Campanella and one of the top catchers in Dodgers history. He made four all-star teams and captured two gold gloves.

Roseboro's dad, who had played for the Homestead Grays and Havana Giants, was working as a chauffeur when he noticed an attractive young lady on the front porch of an Ashland, Ohio home. He stopped by, got to know her, and before long the 15-year-old Cecil Geraldine (who went by Geri) was pregnant with a future big-leaguer. John was delivered five months premature. Geri became the first black employee at the city's J.C. Penney's store. John later wrote that Ashland, which is a small college town halfway between Cleveland and Columbus, was the only place he never experienced discrimination.

Growing up, John played high school football and baseball, shot pool, won money from friends playing cards, and enjoyed movies at the town's theater. After graduating from high school, he went to Central State University on a football scholarship, and also played baseball. While there, Dodgers scout Cliff Alexander invited him to a tryout with the club while it was visiting Crosley Field in Cincinnati. The Dodgers offered him a contract with a $5,000 signing bonus, which he happily signed.

He got called up to the Dodgers mid-way through the 1957 season when Gil Hodges went on the disabled list and did a little bit of everything, including playing first base, catching, warming up hurlers, and pinch-running. The starting catcher, Campanella, welcomed the youngster and gave him pointers on catching.

Campanella suffered his tragic car accident that winter, and Roseboro assumed the starting catching duties in 1958. He acquitted himself well, batting .271 with 14 homers, 11 steals, and an all-star selection.

John's batting average sailed lower the next two seasons, and by the end of the 1960 campaign, sportswriters were speculating on who would claim his job. Former major leaguer Dolph Camilli was raving about his son, Doug, a Dodgers' farmhand. But as the 1961 season rolled around,

John was ready for the challenge, as he posted career highs with 18 home runs and 59 RBI. He remained the Dodgers' starting catcher through the 1967 season.

Roseboro handled the pitching staff brilliantly and held his own with the stick. Having developed a following, he even made an appearance on the Mr. Ed television show. He is often remembered for a 1965 incident in which Juan Marichal attacked him with a bat. John suffered a head injury and sued Marichal, later agreeing to a $7,500 settlement. Tension had been running high during the weekend series between the Dodgers and Giants, and John played a role in instigating the incident by firing the ball back to the catcher close to Marichal's ear, and then stepping toward Juan in an intimidating manner. Roseboro later accepted an apology from Marichal as the two made amends.

In his 1979 book, *Glory Days with the Dodgers, and Other Days with Others*, Roseboro described the life of a ballplayer. Black players continued to face discrimination for much of his career, he wrote. Roseboro, who was married, said his social life on the road was quiet compared to many teammates. He wrote that players like Don Newcombe and Maury Wills often personally paid for a separate room on the road so they could entertain women at will, as there was no way a player was going to sit in the hotel lobby until all hours waiting for a roommate to finish his extracurricular activities.

Pitchers appreciated having Roseboro on the field. Phil Regan in 2022 recalled him as "a gamer and an excellent defensive catcher." Infielder Nate Oliver in 2023 recalled, "He was like E.F. Hutton, the silent type. But when he spoke, we all listened."

John was traded to the Twins' and was their starting catcher for two seasons. He hit only .216 in 1968 but bounced back to make the all-star team in 1969. He also led AL catchers in double plays that season, helping Minnesota capture the AL West.

The Twins released John in 1970 and the Senators, managed by Ted Williams, signed him. He learned a lot about hitting in his short exposure to Williams, before being released in August. He retired with a lifetime batting average of .249 with 104 homers. He coached for the Angels from 1972 to 1974.

During his playing days, Roseboro made investments in a Compton apartment complex and upscale nightclub that backfired. By the late 1970s, he was divorced, unemployed, and scraping to find rent money.

A turning point came when Barbara Fouche, an Atlanta-based model and public-relations executive that he had met during his playing days, moved to California. They went into business together, and later married. John also returned to baseball as a minor-league instructor for the Dodgers. He later suffered from strokes, a heart condition, and prostate cancer, and passed away in 2002 at the age of 69, one of the beloved Dodgers players from the Sixties. He is buried in Forest Lawn-Hollywood Hills Cemetery in Los Angeles.

WILLIE DAVIS

Outfielder Willie Davis had such impressive career statistics – including 2,561 hits, a .279 batting average, 182 home runs, and 398 steals – that it seems unjust that he is best remembered for falling short of his potential. Yet, he was such a gifted athlete, and demonstrated so little interest in refining his game, that he could never outlive the bad rap.

The Dodgers, for whom he played from 1960 to 1973, once asked teammate John Roseboro to work with him on his bunting. Davis responded by sarcastically asking Roseboro, a catcher, how many bunts he had beaten out recently. Roseboro concluded that Davis was egotistical and uninterested in improving.

Maury Wills, who at one time held the league record for stolen bases, wrote, "If he (Davis) had wanted to incorporate base-stealing into his game, he could have stolen 200 a year." Pete Franklin, a longtime sportscaster, called Davis the most physically gifted ballplayer he ever saw, though not the most accomplished.

Davis came out of Roosevelt High School in Los Angeles, where he set the city record for the longest broad jump. While playing for Reno in the California League in 1959, he made a name for himself by repeatedly scoring from first base on singles. At Spokane in 1960, he delivered the ridiculous total of 26 triples while batting .346.

By age 21, in 1961, Davis was the Dodgers' starting center fielder, taking over for the aging Duke Snider. It was in 1962 that public expectations began reaching a crescendo. Davis hit .285, walloped 21 homers, stole 32 bases, and led the league in triples. Baseball men and fans alike began to conclude there wasn't much Davis couldn't do if he put his mind to it.

His Dodgers narrowly missed out on a pennant that season, but they captured the flag in three of the next four years. Davis hit only .167, .231, and .063 in those three fall classics, though the Dodgers were victorious in two of them. His weak post-season performances, which included an embarrassing three-error inning during the 1966 Series against the Orioles, reinforced the argument that he was a disappointment. Meanwhile, during the regular seasons, his batting averages alternated – one season up, one season down.

It was not until Davis was in his 30s that he began to command more respect and less ridicule. In 1969, he ran off a 31-game hitting streak, breaking Zach Wheat's team record. He led the loop again in triples in 1970 and was finally tapped as an all-star in 1971 and again in 1973. He also garnered three straight gold gloves from 1971 to 1973.

The Dodgers swapped him to Montreal for reliever Mike Marshall before the 1974 season. Davis played for the Expos, Rangers, Cardinals and Padres over the next three campaigns, and then played in Japan for two years. He concluded his career with the 1979 Angels.

Dodgers executive Buzzie Bavasi articulated the most damning critique, saying, "He could have been a Hall of Famer, but he had million-dollar legs and a 10-cent head." That said, one keeps coming back to his impressive career statistics. The Dodgers kept Davis for 14 seasons. That fact speaks at least as loudly as the cacophony of legitimate criticism.

Davis was a practicing Buddhist. In the mid-1990s, he developed an addiction to illegal drugs. He was arrested at his parents' home in the possession of a samurai sword and knives, threatening to kill them if they did not give him $5,000. Dodgers' executives worked to provide him with the help he needed to confront his demons. Davis passed away at his home on Victory Boulevard in Burbank at the age of 69 in 2010.

JOE MOELLER

When the 1962 Dodgers -- in a fierce pennant race against the Giants -- needed an occasional fifth starter behind Don Drysdale, Sandy Koufax, Johnny Podres, and Stan Williams, they turned to a six-foot-five, 19-year-old phenom from Manhattan Beach, California, named Joe Moeller.

"The Red Sox gave me/my dad $5,000 when I was in Little League at the age of 12 so they could have the last rights to sign me when I graduated from high school," he wrote in 2022. "I was already six feet tall." He continued, "There wasn't a draft yet, so when I graduated, it was a bidding process. The day after I graduated there were four or five cars parked outside our house and my dad had each scout come in and say what they would give as a bonus. After all the offers were presented, we had to call Boston. All they had to do was top it by $1 and we had to sign with them. We had a couple offers around $100,000 and Boston didn't want to go that high, so we were free to negotiate with anyone we wanted."

"We had held a meeting with [Dodgers owner] Walter O'Malley a couple weeks earlier," Moeller continued, "and he knew about our agreement with the Red Sox. One of the reasons that I signed with the Dodgers was because they would give my brother a chance and signed him also. Plus, from a tax perspective my dad was given $15k, my brother $10k and I got $75k."

Early on, Moeller's repertoire was already respected. Ken Harrelson wrote, "Joe Moeller was a big-bonus boy with the Dodgers who really was a right-handed Sam McDowell. His fastball reached the high 90s and you could hear his curveball. The first time I ever faced him, in Reno, he struck me out four times in four at bats."

Being a teenage bonus recipient was not the surest route to popularity in big-league clubhouses. As Joe recalled, "A lot of players resented the fact that I was so young, the large bonus, and only one year in the minors, whereas most guys spent four or five years in the minor leagues. I got more of a bonus than most guys made in five or six years. Maury Wills was incredible to me when I first came up. He would take time to talk to me and include me with things he did. I had the greatest respect for him for what he went through to get to the major leagues and how hard he worked."

Moeller pitched in 19 games that rookie season, going 6-5 with a 5.22 ERA, as the Dodgers won 102 games but still finished second to the Giants, after losing a post-season playoff.

From that beginning came a decade of dedicated effort and persistent arm pain, which cut into his opportunities and effectiveness. Players from the Sixties will tell you that playing through pain was the norm, and Moeller was a prime example. Rarely feeling his best, he took an estimated 60 cortisone shots.

"Without question, my faith helped me get through the injuries and cortisone shots as well as never knowing if I had a job each year. You couldn't tell anyone your arm, elbow or back was bothering you or they would send you down to the minors and bring someone else up," he reflected. "I just had to pitch through it and trust God had a plan for me." Moeller remained with the Dodgers through 1971, when not pitching for their farm teams.

He had plenty of career highlights. "Pitching in the 1966 World Series was my biggest thrill. There are players in the Hall of Fame that have never pitched in a World Series, so I was very blessed to do that. We had one of the best pitching staffs in the history of baseball and I was the fifth starter on a four-man rotation. So, with Koufax, Sutton, Drysdale and Osteen, I thought there was no way I would get a chance to pitch. Drysdale got in trouble early in the first game so working as the long man, I got to pitch."

Other high points included his first start at age 19 in Milwaukee, facing the likes of Hank Aaron, Joe Adcock and Ed Matthews; and collecting his first MLB win. A light-hearted moment occurred in 1965 when Moeller was pitching for Spokane. He was at the plate at Seattle's Sick's Stadium when he hit a home run that passed through a small hole in an advertising sign, winning him a free trip to Hawaii. During his years with Los Angeles, Moeller roomed at times with Jeff Torborg, Don Sutton, Wes Parker and Jim Lefebvre, making lasting friendships.

Another enjoyable experience was playing in Hawaii toward the end of his career. "At the end of the 1971 season, I knew my career was coming to an end with all the injuries and cortisone shots, so I asked Peter O'Malley to sell me to Hawaii in the Pacific Coast League. I made more money pitching for Hawaii ($38,000) than I did playing for the Dodgers after eight years. Plus, they paid for my apartment in Hawaii and my house payment in Manhattan Beach. We had a fun time playing there. Most of the players were guys at the end of their careers." Indeed, his teammates on the 1972 Islanders included aging veterans like George Brunet, John Donaldson, Jim Hicks, Lee Maye, Mike McCormick, Ray Oyler and Dennis Ribant. Rocky Bridges managed the team, which operated independently of any MLB team.

In recent years, Moeller has shared his faith openly. He wrote, "I had accepted Christ into my life at a young age but I wanted to be the architect to draw up my own plans and get God's stamp of approval on what I did. The bright promise of my career was never fully realized. Two failed marriages along with some business failures left their mark. But I see my career and my life from a different perspective now – God's perspective. Success in life is not determined by performance, income or fame. Those things will not get us into heaven." He goes on to provide scripture references that lead to salvation and joy in life.

Joe's lifetime record was 26-36 with a 4.01 ERA in 166 appearances. For more than 15 years, he worked as an advance scout for the Marlins. Being a professional athlete helped him realize the importance of staying in shape, even when traveling, as documented in a March 5, 2014, article in the *Orange County Register.* He said he ran 10K races until the age of 50 and continued to work out with free weights and machines, in addition to a daily walk with his black lab dog near his home in San Clemente.

BRANT ALYEA

Outfielder Brant Alyea drifted away from baseball after his six-year major league career, only to reconnect to the game in an astonishing way.

But first, the background…Alyea was born in New Jersey, attended classes at Rutherford High School, and at six-foot-five, was recruited to play college basketball under coach Butch Van Breda Kolff at Hofstra University.

He signed with the Reds and was snared by the Senators in the 1962 first-year player draft. Alyea slugged 154 minor-league home runs before finding his place with the 1968 Senators. His best season came with the Twins in 1970, when he clipped opposing pitchers for a .291 average and 16 homers. Following injuries, he retired with a lifetime batting average of .247.

Once out of the sport, Alyea avoided the game, turning down free tickets and declining reunion invitations. He worked as a bartender in Washington, D.C. for a while, burned through three marriages, and eventually settled into work in the Tropicana Casino in Atlantic City in the Eighties. Therein lies the remarkable story that rekindled his interest in the national pastime.

The tale begins after the 1965 season, when Alyea played winter ball in Nicaragua. While there, he had a weekend fling with an attractive nurse. He impregnated the woman, and returned a year later signing papers to acknowledge it was his son, who took the name Brant Alyea, Jr. For a time, he sent money to the mother, and visited when he could. But a bloody revolution occurred in Nicaragua, making it impossible for him to return for visits. Then after the 1972 Nicaraguan earthquake, he lost contact with the mother and son altogether. According to a subsequent article by Peter Gammons in *Sports Illustrated,* she wrote to Alyea, but the letters were intercepted by his third wife.

Some 17 years after last seeing his son, Alyea had no knowledge of his whereabouts. One day when he arrived at the casino, his boss had left a newspaper clipping in his mailbox listing minor league ballplayers whose dads had played in the majors. The article indicated that Brant Alyea, Jr., was now playing minor league baseball in Canada. It was a stunning revelation that led to a 1986 father-and-son reunion during spring training in Florida, in which Alyea spent 12 days with his son, taking him to dinner each evening. Watching the young man at the plate, he was amazed at how much his stance and style looked like his own from a generation earlier.

Through his son, Brant's interest in baseball returned, and the pair stayed in close touch. The younger Alyea enjoyed some success in the minor leagues, even driving in 102 RBI one year. But he was unable to make the majors, closed the curtains on his minor-league career in 1990, and settled in North Carolina, where he sells cars. The elder Alyea left the casino after 11 years and later worked for Volvo. He lived in Hunting Valley, Pennsylvania, until passing away in 2024 at the age of 83.

ROBERTO CLEMENTE

Rarely in baseball history has any five-year period seen so many talented outfielders arrive on the scene. Willie Mays and Mickey Mantle debuted in 1951. They were followed by Al Kaline in 1953, Hank Aaron in 1954, Roberto Clemente in 1955, as well as Frank Robinson in 1956. All six hit for average and with power, with good speed and solid defense, and all were first-ballot Hall of Famers. Mays and Mantle had the advantage of playing in the largest media market for much of the Fifties and enjoyed World Series visibility early in their careers. When any of those stars was on the field, it was another beautiful day for baseball.

Clemente played his entire career in a secondary market and got to the World Series only twice, 11 years apart in 1960 and 1971. Though he commanded respect, he received less publicity. Topps baseball cards didn't even publish his real name, shortening "Roberto" to "Bob." Shortstop Maury Wills commented, "Clemente was bitter all his baseball life. He didn't get the attention that Mantle and Mays got. He goes on my team of underrated players."

Clemente was just 20 years old when he entered the Pirates' lineup. While his outrageously strong throwing arm was evident from the start, it took some time for his offense to catch up. For his first five years through 1959, he averaged only five home runs per year and achieved the .300 mark only once.

That all changed in 1960, the year that the Pirates made believers out of every doubter. Clemente batted .314 and drove in 94 RBI, which would be the third-best RBI count of his career. He was true to form, batting .310 in the World Series. He made the all-star team for the first time, and after the season he received the Joseph Horne Company Award for being the most popular Pirate (Horne's was the dominant department store in Pittsburgh for ages, in operation from 1849 to 1994). However, he finished a disappointing seventh in the MVP voting (behind two of his teammates) and it's said he never wore his 1960 World Series ring in disgust.

In 1961, the Pirates had a disappointing follow-up to their championship season, playing below .500, but Clemente won the first of his 12 gold glove awards as well as the first of his four batting titles. Statisticians took note that while he hit .306 in 69 night games, he was unbelievable during day games, batting .415 in 66 contests (baseball in those days had more day games than in modern baseball). He received the 1961 Outstanding Pirate award, presented to him by Lefty Grove, one of the greatest pitchers of all time.

He had a quiet season in 1962 as the Pirates settled for a fourth-place showing. Then came a 1963 campaign in which the team landed in eighth place, despite Clemente hitting .320. The 1964 NL pennant race saw five clubs battle it out, winning between 88 and 93 games. Ultimately, the Cardinals captured the flag and the Pirates landed in a tie for sixth place, wasting a brilliant season from Clemente who batted .339 as the batting champ. Observers praised him for controlling his temper better and improving his ability to hit with two strikes.

He commanded enormous respect. Teammate Dick Stuart referred to him as "the best 169-pound slugger in baseball." Writer Les Biederman called him "the best right fielder in the league." Pitcher Steve Blass later wrote, "He carried himself with grace, pride, and dignity. I was in awe of him. He was so gifted and a thrill to watch play…He was a man of pride who never let his guard down…I considered him a high-ranking officer, while the rest of us were enlisted guys."

Blass continued, "Clemente didn't hit a lot of home runs and his RBI total was not staggering. But Roberto played with such passion and flair that if you didn't see him every day, the numbers wouldn't dazzle you. But we saw him every day, and we couldn't take our eyes off him."

Gradually, Clemente became more outspoken about the challenges that Latino players faced in becoming adjusted to life in the U.S. Highly principled, he was never afraid to take a stand. That was clear in the fundraising work he did to benefit those in his native Puerto Rico, but also in his conduct during the baseball seasons.

For example, one day in 1961, with the team bus waiting to head from the hotel to Candlestick Park for a game against the Giants, Clemente boarded and said the bus would have to wait because pitcher Al McBean had an upset stomach. The players guffawed and protested and the bus finally left for the park, without Clemente or McBean. Clemente later noted that McBean was a rookie and that he wished that someone would have stood up for him like that when he was a rookie. Before the day was out, true to form, Clemente hit a three-run homer and the Pirates won.

Clemente won his third batting crown in 1965. Harry Walker replaced Danny Murtaugh as manager that year and the club improved to 90 wins and third place.

Meanwhile, there was growing talk that Clemente just might be the most complete player in the game. Following the 1966 season, in which he set career highs with 29 home runs and 119 RBI for the third-place corsairs, voters selected him as the league's MVP.

In 1967, following the retirement of Sandy Koufax, the Dodgers were no longer formidable, creating an opening for another team to step forward. Clemente did all he could to propel the Bucs by hitting a league-best .357, but Pittsburgh finished a disappointing sixth, while the Cardinals returned to the top of the standings. Roberto became just the seventh player to win four batting titles, following Ty Cobb, Honus Wagner, Stan Musial, Ted Williams, Rogers Hornsby and Harry Heilmann. After the season, Clemente attended the MLB winter meetings as an alternate player representative and then played winter ball in Puerto Rico.

Larry Shepherd became the Pirates skipper in 1968, but the club again placed sixth. Always candid, Clemente complained of a sore shoulder in August, noting that he would retire in February if it continued to hurt so much. He also required pre-game rubdowns for his arthritic neck. Meanwhile, he hit a solid .291 with 18 home runs and left for a European vacation with his wife after the season.

The 1969 season saw him return to form as he hit .345 and led the NL in triples. "I love playing baseball when I feel right," he told reporters. The Bucs showed improvement but settled for a third-place showing in the NL East, as Shepherd was dismissed during the final week of the season.

When asked about the Pirates moving out of Forbes Field and into Three Rivers Stadium, he said, "Forbes Field has been good to me. I wish I could finish my career playing there. But you can't stop progress. Yes, I'd like to be able to say I played in the new park, too."

Clemente would play three more years, hitting well over .300 each season. In 1971, when the Pirates won the world championship, he hit a robust .341 with 86 RBI during the regular campaign, and his game seven homer in the World Series delivered the title for Pittsburgh. He was named Series MVP.

His final appearance was the last game of the 1972 NLCS, in which the Pirates lost to the Reds. The mood in the Pirates clubhouse after the game was somber until Clemente yelled for them to get their heads up, and approached every member of the team individually, reminding them what a great season they all had.

Clemente's death on a mercy mission plane crash on New Year's Eve of 1972 shocked the entire baseball world but was emblematic of his unselfishness. The entire Pirates team flew to Puerto Rico for the funeral, during which teammate Steve Blass delivered a eulogy. In a highly appropriate gesture, MLB took the unusual step of waiving the normal six-year waiting period to elect him to the Hall of Fame in 1973.

SMOKY BURGESS

At 5-foot-8 and close to 200 pounds, catcher Forrest (Smoky) Burgess never really got into peak physical condition. Then again, it never mattered. The gifted hitter played 18 seasons, made six all-star teams, and batted .295 over the course of his career.

Writer Les Biederman summarized it well: "If you saw Smoky Burgess on the street in civilian clothes, you'd figure he was an instructor at the local high school or perhaps the butcher in the corner supermarket. But once you see Burgess walk to the plate with a bat in his hands and take a cut, you know for certain…that he was made for baseball."

The North Carolina native had so many solid years that it's difficult to pinpoint his peak. He hit everywhere he went and batted .275 or better every year from 1952 to 1963. He never really had a bad year until he was past the age of 40.

Burgess was an undisciplined hitter, but that also didn't matter. The left-handed swinger wasn't looking for walks, nor for certain pitches. If he could get wood on the ball, he was confident he'd get more than his fair share of hits. His lifetime batting average was higher than any of his contemporaries among backstops. And though he never walked more than 50 times in a season, his lifetime on-base percentage was a solid .362.

Burgess spent his first 10 years with the Cubs, Phillies and Reds. The Pirates acquired him, pitcher Harvey Haddix, and third baseman Don Hoak from the Reds before the 1959 season, in a deal that sent slugger Frank Thomas to the Queen City. All three Pirates' acquisitions played a key role in the club's 1960 world championship. By hitting .333 in that year's World Series, Smoky did his part.

A 1961 *Sports Illustrated* article quoted teammate Don Hoak as saying, "Smoky is a great hitter, but he doesn't always bear down. Once in a while I have to tell him not to let this rinky-dink pitcher get him out."

Behind the plate, Burgess was known for chatting up and distracting the hitters. He often told them what pitch was coming – sometimes accurately, sometimes a bluff. Burgess said that Richie Ashburn, in particular, would become agitated by the distractions. Defensively, Burgess led his league in fielding percentage three times. That statistic is a bit misleading, as a shoulder injury sustained in a jeep accident while he was in the military was to blame for subpar throwing.

By the time Burgess joined the White Sox in 1964, he was strictly a pinch-hitting specialist. He hit well in his first two seasons at Comiskey, but poorly in 1967. By then, nobody had to tell him it was time to call it quits.

Burgess set the major league record (since broken) for the most pinch-hits with 145. He slugged 16 pinch-homers, which was second only to Jerry Lynch at the time of his retirement.

After his playing career, Burgess owned an auto dealership, appeared in old-timer events, and served the Braves as a part-time coach and scout. For his career, he had a .295 batting average, 1,318 hits, and 126 home runs. A statue in Forest City memorializes Burgess for the ages.

DON HOAK

Decades after his death, Don Hoak's name resurfaced in the movie *City Slickers* as the answer to Meg Ryan's trivia question, "Who was the third baseman for the 1960 Pirates?" Billy Crystal and the other characters immediately responded, "Don Hoak."

Indeed, Hoak had a memorable season for that Pirates club, which won the NL pennant by seven lengths, and then upset the Yankees in the fall classic. Hoak hit .282, scored 97 runs, and placed second in the MVP balloting. In the World Series, he contributed two doubles and three RBI.

Not much came easy in Hoak's life. He grew up in a scarcely populated community in northern Pennsylvania. Soon after he enlisted with the military in 1945, his father died in a tractor accident, leaving his mother to raise Hoak's three-year old brother. A former boxer, Hoak seemed inclined to get into fights outside the ring, as well. But he also found time to get married, tying the knot at home plate before a game in Fort Worth in 1950.

After seven seasons in the minor leagues, he made it to the majors with Brooklyn in 1954. The following season, he was a part-timer for the Dodgers team that beat the Yankees in the World Series. But Hoak alienated manager Walt Alston by telling him that he wanted to be traded if he didn't play in the Series. Ultimately, Hoak got into three Series games, but following the season he was dealt to the Cubs.

Don's one season at Wrigley Field was an exercise in futility, as he hit only .215 on a last-place club. A November 1956 deal sent him to Cincinnati, where manager Birdie Tebbetts convinced him to change his batting stance. By moving from a deep crouch to a more upright posture, Hoak led the league in doubles and made the 1957 all-star team. He followed up with a decent campaign in 1958.

Following another trade, Don was the Pirates' starting third baseman for four years. He hit a career-best .298 in 1961, and led the league's third-sackers in fielding percentage in 1962. Don played a full season with the Phillies in 1963, and in six games the following year. He retired with a .265 average and 89 homers.

More than anything, Hoak was respected for his toughness. There were countless examples, none more pointed than the time Hoak ripped open a nasty wound while getting out of a swimming pool during a summertime party. Rather than go to an emergency room, he had a surgeon who was at the party clean the wound and insert stitches into the top and bottom of the foot with no anesthesia. Hoak smoked his cigarette, not saying a word. After the procedure, the doc told him he wouldn't be able to play for a while. Hoak told him pointedly he would play two games the next day – and he did so.

Hoak's first marriage ended in divorce, and in 1961 he married Jill Corey, a singer who had been the youngest-ever performer at the Copacabana in New York. Famous for her hit record, "Sometimes I'm Happy," she had previously had a year-long relationship with Frank Sinatra. Hoak was infatuated with the entertainer and convinced her to break up with the Brazilian diplomat that she had been seeing.

Jill gave birth to their only child in 1965 and gave up performing. Hoak by then was busy with his post-playing career, which included two years as a Pirates broadcaster, a stint coaching for the Phillies, and two seasons managing in the Pirates farm system.

October 9, 1969 was a tragic day for the Hoak family. Don had hoped the Pirates would promote him to manager for the 1970 season, and he was dejected to learn that morning that the team had agreed to terms with Danny Murtaugh. Hours later, Hoak looked outside and saw thieves pulling out of the driveway of his Pittsburgh home with his brother-in-law's car. Hoak furiously got into his own car determined to chase them down but suffered a heart attack and died at a local hospital. He was only 41 years old.

BOB SKINNER

After serving in the Army, Bob Skinner was a steady presence in the Pirates' outfield from 1954 until early 1963. He was tapped for a pair of all-star teams and topped out with a .302 average and 20 homers in 1962. Two of his home runs were mammoth blasts that soared over the right field roof of Forbes Field. Not surprisingly, he became one of the most popular of Pirates players.

After a brief stint with the Reds, he moved to the 1964 Cardinals, where he was a valuable bench contributor and delivered two hits in three World Series at bats. Of course, he would have liked to have played more. During the Cardinals' 1966 Father and Son Day promotion, his son Craig confronted manager Red Schoendienst and asked, "Hey, when are you going to start playing my dad?"

Bob retired with a .277 average, 103 homers and 1,198 hits. Throughout his career, he lived in San Diego, where his favorite hobby was working on automobiles. Bob, the father of catcher Joel Skinner, managed the Phillies for parts of the 1968 and 1969 seasons. In total, he spent 66 years in baseball as a player, coach, manager and scout.

NELLIE BRILES

Right-handed pitcher Nelson Briles was a California native who went straight from the Santa Clara University campus to Double-A Tulsa after signing with the Cardinals in 1964. He joined the Cardinals bullpen just a year later.

When ace Bob Gibson went down with a broken leg in 1967, Briles was ready to play a larger role. He posted a 2.43 ERA and led the league in winning percentage based on his 14-5 record. In the 1967 World Series, he threw a complete game victory in game three and hurled a pair of scoreless innings in game six, as St. Louis prevailed over Boston in seven games.

Unlike most pitchers, Briles pitched out of the stretch, as opposed to using a windup. Pitching coach Billy Muffett counseled him to give it a try in order to hide his pitches. Whether by causation or correlation, the change coincided with his sharper effectiveness. Briles followed up with a fine 1968 season with 19 wins, as St. Louis cruised to its second straight pennant. This time, the World Series wasn't kind to him. He lost game two to the Tigers, 8-1 and absorbed a no-decision in the Cardinals 5-3 loss in game five. The Tigers won the series in seven contests.

Appearing in back-to-back World Series provided Briles with notoriety and he found himself in demand as a public speaker at winter banquets and luncheons. The broad exposure also helped his music-performance career. He played guitar and sang in night clubs; he also appeared in shows in Chicago with stars like actress Kaye Ballard.

Briles' next two years in St. Louis proved less satisfying. In 1969, MLB lowered the pitcher's mound and tightened the strike zone to favor hitters. Briles had trouble locating his curve and began relying much more on a slider, but still managed a 15-13 record, as the Cardinals missed the post-season.

Continuing to demonstrate his entrepreneurial flair after the 1969 season, Briles opened an electronics firm specializing in the design of audio and video recording studios. On hand to help publicize its grand opening were fellow ballplayers Dave Guisti, Joe Hoerner, Sonny Siebert, Dal Maxvill and Steve Carlton.

In 1970, Briles battled leg injuries and frustration, winning only six games. Viewing Gibson, Carlton, Jerry Reuss and Mike Torrez as their "big four" for 1971, the Cardinals traded Briles to the Pirates.

Pittsburgh turned out to be Nellie's "baseball home." He went back to a full windup, adding force to his delivery, and enjoyed three winning seasons for the Pirates. In game five of the 1971 World Series, he was a hero, receiving standing ovations. He closed his career with the Royals, Rangers, and Orioles. His lifetime statistics included a 129-112 record, 17 shutouts and a 3.44 ERA.

The personable Briles later worked in public relations, broadcasting, and special projects for the Pirates. He especially enjoyed the latter role, in which he instituted the club's alumni relations program. He was participating in a Pirates golf tournament when he died of a heart attack in Orlando at age 61 in 2005.

MAX ALVIS

Max Alvis was a two-sport star at the University of Texas at Austin, leading his gridiron team to the Cotton Bowl. He chose pro baseball over football when the Indians made him an offer that, after consultation with his father, he couldn't refuse.

He became a two-time all-star third baseman and a team leader. Teammate Ken Suarez called him "the heart and soul of the Indians." Lou Klimchock remembered Alvis as the one most likely to confront a teammate not giving the game 100 percent. Max was the team's player representative to management as well as a superb golfer.

After a fine 1963 rookie campaign, Alvis encountered a crisis during the 1964 season, when he was hospitalized with a life-threatening bout of meningitis. He started feeling poorly on a long flight from the West coast and felt so bad later that night that he woke up his roommate, who contacted the team trainer. The illness is contagious, so the players, coaches and writers on the flight had to take sulfa pills for a week as a precaution.

Though there were concerns that Alvis might never play again, he was back in uniform just five weeks later, and finished the season with 18 home runs and 53 RBI. Perhaps he rushed back too soon, but players in those days tended to do that. Everyone remembered the story of Wally Pipp losing his job to Lou Gehrig, and nobody wanted to take that chance.

Max was rewarded with an all-star team selection in 1965, had a decent season in 1966, and was tapped as an all-star again in 1967, when he hammered 21 home runs and was second in the loop in sacrifice bunts. He became a better fielder as time went on.

Alvis says his favorite manager was Birdie Tebbetts, who gave him the chance to play. He marvels that Cleveland never won a pennant during his eight years there. "We were just never able to combine our fine pitching with enough hitting and fielding," he said.

He played a final year with the Brewers in 1970 and put out feelers about playing again in 1971. Several teams expressed interest, but the offers required Alvis to travel to training camp at his own expense, with no guaranteed contract, so he decided to retire from baseball. He had a .247 career average, 895 hits and 111 home runs (including six against Jim Kaat).

Alvis went into banking in Jasper, Texas, eventually becoming a bank president. He stayed in touch with lifetime baseball friends, including Larry Brown, Fred Whitfield, Gary Bell, Joe Azcue, Vern Fuller and others. He also has enjoyed attending Indians reunions and fantasy camps, golf, hunting and attending his grandchildren's sporting activities.

JIMMIE HALL

Outfielder Jimmie Hall had nearly the same career as Max Alvis, the contemporary third baseman. They were born a month apart in 1938, Hall in North Carolina and Alvis in Texas. Both became regulars in 1963 and were solid performers for five years. Both were named to two all-star teams. Both stopped hitting in 1968, the year of the pitcher, while they were teammates with the Indians. Both were out of baseball after the 1970 season while still only 32 years of age.

The son of a farmer, Hall signed with the Senators in 1956, and got married in 1960. He was originally a second baseman but agreed to move to the outfield. The Senators relocated to Minnesota in 1961, and Hall made the Twins roster in 1963 when Harmon Killebrew sustained an injury. The 25-year-old seized his opportunity, hitting 33 home runs, which broke an AL rookie record held by Ted Williams. In a fearsome Twins lineup with power hitters like Killebrew, Don Mincher, and Bob Allison, he fit right in. On May 3 of that year, he slugged MLB's 75,000[th] home run since 1900, making national headlines. He placed third in the rookie of the year derby.

Hall went deep 20 or more times each of the next three seasons, including 1964, when he lost a week after being hit in the face with a Bo Belinsky fastball. In 1965, he helped the power-laden Twins to the pennant and appeared in two World Series games, though he went just one for seven.

Following the 1966 campaign, he was traded to the Angels in the transaction that sent Dean Chance to Minnesota. Hall remained productive for the 1967 Angels, placing third on the team with 16 home runs. But that would be his last robust season. After a rough start in 1968, the Angels traded him to Cleveland for Vic Davalillo. With the Indians, Hall roomed with a fellow North Carolinian, infielder Billy Harris. He was used in platoon situations against right-handers, and never got on track all summer.

Hall split an unsatisfying 1969 season between the Indians, Yankees, and Cubs, again struggling at the plate; and divided the summer of 1970 with the Cubs and Braves. He retired with a .254 average, 724 hits, and 121 homers (Alvis hit .247 with 895 hits and 111 home runs). After leaving the game, he labored as a woodworker and truck driver. He continues to reside in North Carolina.

RON PERRANOSKI

Ron Perranoski was the envy of every team with a bullpen problem. The lefty was already 25 when he debuted with the Dodgers in 1961, yet he dominated opposing hitters right from the start. His fastball was exceptional, but what set him apart from his contemporaries was his excellent breaking stuff, which made the fastball his secondary pitch.

The results were stunning. Over the first 10 years of his career, his ERA was never worse than 3.18. The tireless flame-thrower led the league in appearances three times, and was the first hurler in Dodgers' history to appear in 70 contests in a season. During a 1963 campaign that was one of the best on record for a relief pitcher at that time, he posted a 16-3 record with a league-best .842 winning percentage, and a 1.63 ERA, good for fourth in the season-end MVP voting. Topps in 1967 called him "the most effective relief pitcher in the major leagues."

It was huge news when the Dodgers traded him to Minnesota after the 1967 season. Perranoski, fellow pitcher Bob Miller, and beloved catcher John Roseboro went to the Twins, in exchange for two fading veterans -- former MVP Zoilo Versalles and pitcher Mudcat Grant. Much as the Dodgers enjoyed the advantage in an earlier trade in which they acquired Perranoski as a minor leaguer from the Cubs, this time it was the Twins who got the upper hand in the swap, thanks to Perranoski's continued excellence.

With the Twins, the southpaw had three more brilliant seasons. The first year, he set up the closer, Red Worthington. Assuming the close-out role in 1969, Perranoski led the league in saves the next two years. When fellow veteran Stan Williams joined the Twins in 1970, not only did Perranoski have a good friend in the pen, but also a premier setup man.

The one flaw in Perranoski's career was the post-season. With both the Dodgers in World Series action, and the Twins in the playoffs, he found bad times to be ineffective. His lifetime post-season ERA was 7.98 in just under 15 very rough innings.

The aging hurler concluded his career with short stints with the Tigers, Dodgers (again), and Angels. He retired in 1973 with a 79-74 mark, 178 saves, and a 2.79 ERA.

Perranoski was born and raised in New Jersey, and pitched college ball at Michigan State, where he was a teammate of hurler Dick Radatz. After retiring, he was the Dodgers' minor league pitching coordinator for eight years, then pitching coach for 14 seasons. Bleacher Report named him the ninth best pitching coach in baseball history.

He has worked in the Giants organization in various capacities since 1995. An inductee of the National Polish-American Sports Hall of Fame, Perranoski was living in Vero Beach, Florida, when he passed away.

YOGI BERRA

It says much about Yogi Berra and Johnny Bench that decades after both retired, fans still debate which of the two was the greatest catcher of all time. Although Bench probably had the edge defensively, Berra held his own and then some offensively. He was a career .285 hitter with 358 home runs who won three MVP awards in the 1950s and placed second in two other seasons.

A tremendous run producer, Berra had nine seasons with 90 or more RBI. Although Yogi was an aggressive hitter who often swung at bad pitches, the most he ever fanned in a season was 38 times, a remarkable feat for a power hitter.

Berra was born in St. Louis in 1925 and got his nickname from a boyhood friend, Bobby Hofman, who also became a major leaguer. Two local franchises (the Cardinals and Browns) lost out on the chance to sign Yogi when they refused to give him the same $500 bonus that the Cards had presented to another local prospect (Berra's friend Joe Garagiola). Yogi instead inked a deal with the Yankees for $500 in October 1942. He enlisted after playing for Norfolk in 1943 and returned to pro baseball in 1945.

After making his big-league debut in September 1946 (homering off Jesse Flores in his second at bat), he became a regular in the Yanks' lineup in the second half of the 1947 campaign. Although he became the first player to deliver a pinch-home run in World Series action, his greatest blessing that year was meeting Carmen Short, a waitress in a St. Louis restaurant co-owned by Stan Musial. The pair hit it off and got married in 1949, with Garagiola as the best man.

Berra made his first all-star team in 1948 and was selected annually thereafter through 1962. Yogi and Carmen had three sons, all of whom were superb athletes. Dale Berra made MLB as an infielder. Tim Berra played for the 1974 Baltimore Colts football team. Larry Berra was a minor-league ballplayer in the Mets' organization.

Behind the plate, the loquacious Berra chatted up opposing hitters to the point of distraction. Some hitters ignored it while others (like Rocky Colavito) told him to knock it off, saying, "Look, you're Italian, I'm Italian, let me do my job." On one occasion, pitcher Jerry Casale of the Red Sox stepped to the plate and Berra asked, "How's the family, Jerry? How's the kids?" Casale recalled, "The first pitch got by me before I realized what he was doing." Casale blasted the second pitch for a home run. As he crossed the plate, he said, "I'm not even married, Yogi."

By the time the 1960s arrived, Berra was seeing as much action in left field and pinch-hitting as behind the plate. The Yankees had a superb catcher in Ellie Howard, moreover Berra's knees were paying the inevitable toll of years of squatting behind the plate. But the ever-popular Berra remained an excellent hitter. In 1960, he had a robust .792 OPS and then collected eight RBI in the Yankees' World Series loss to the Pirates. In 1961, his OPS was nearly identical at .795 and he clubbed his 12th and final World Series home run that fall against the Reds. His hitting dropped off in 1962 but rebounded in 1963.

As the 1964 season commenced, the Yankees were seeking their fifth straight pennant, now with Berra as manager. The club outlasted the White Sox and Orioles in a spirited pennant race but Yogi was ousted as skipper after the Cardinals beat the New Yorkers in a seven-game series. The reason most cited was that Berra had lost control of the team. The cross-town Mets then scored a public-relations coup when they signed him as a coach-catcher for the 1965 season, reuniting him with manager Casey Stengel.

Throughout his life, Berra was known for his sense of humor. One of the reasons that Yogi Berra humor resonated with so many people was the simplicity of the wit. As in Berra being asked whether he wanted his pizza cut into six slices or eight, to which he responded better make it six, he didn't think he could eat eight slices. Or his quote about a restaurant, "Nobody goes there now. It's too crowded." Or his superstitious wisdom to "never answer an anonymous letter." Upon reaching a fork in the road, Berra advised, "take it."

One of pitcher Ralph Terry's favorite stories concerned Berra explaining to Carmen why he was attending so many funerals. "Well, you got to go to theirs, or else they won't go to yours," Berra reasoned.

Writer Dick Schaap told the story about his conversation with Berra in the early Eighties about the rising value of vintage baseball cards. You got any 1951 Mickey Mantle rookie cards, he asked Berra. "Yeah, I think I've got some lying around someplace," Berra replied. You ought to look for them, Schaap offered, since they're valuable. "Nah, I prefer to remember Mickey as he is," Yogi replied.

Berra passed away in 2015 in West Caldwell, New Jersey, remembered as one of the most popular players in major league history.

JOHNNY BENCH

During the 1950s, Yogi Berra and Roy Campanella sharpened the sport's expectations for receivers. Both won three MVP awards, hit with power, were strong defensively, and provided team leadership. As Berra entered retirement, the baseball establishment began to wonder whether the game would see another catcher of that caliber.

Then came Johnny Bench. At the tender age of 20, the Reds receiver was already something special, making the NL's 1968 all-star team as a rookie. As author Bill James wrote, "After a month in the league, nobody tried to run on him." The youngster from a tiny town in Oklahoma also produced at the plate.

In 1969, one could see the formation of the Big Red Machine getting underway. Lee May and Tony Perez hit 38 and 37 homers apiece. The entire Reds outfield batted over .300. And Bench produced 90 RBI, while hitting .293. All the club needed was some additional pitching depth and once the Reds accomplished that goal in 1970, they went on to win the NL West five times in seven years.

Bench approached the game with such confidence that he chewed out even veteran pitchers like Jim Maloney and Gerry Arrigo.

Durable as they come, Bench set a rookie record by catching 154 games in 1968. In the 1969 all-star game at RFK Stadium, he smashed one home run, and was robbed of another when Carl Yastrzemski made his famous over-the-fence catch. In 1970, Bench drove in 148 RBI, one of the best figures ever by a catcher. In one game, he slugged three home runs against Steve Carlton.

There seemingly was little that the Reds' superstar could not accomplish. Bench won a second MVP award in 1972 and finished fourth in the balloting in both 1974 and 1975. He topped the league in sacrifice flies three times. During a two-year period in the middle of his career, he stole 24 bases in 26 tries. He captured the gold glove 10 seasons in a row and made the all-star team 14 years. In post-season action against elite pitching, he delivered a home run an average of once every 17 times at bat.

There was no baserunner in the game, Bench stated as a matter of fact, that he could not throw out. Though he had pitched as a youngster, he and his truck-driving father concluded his future was as a catcher. As William Barry Furlong wrote in *Baseball Stars of 1971,* his father "discerned the abysmal lack of young catching talent in the early 1960s and he figured that Johnny would have a chance to make it big and make it fast as a catcher."

He therefore trained his son not only to shift his weight and transfer the ball efficiently in making a throw to second base, but also to make throws to distances of up to 250 feet with pinpoint accuracy, all to sharpen his ability to make the 120-foot throw to second base with remarkable precision.

In 1983, both Bench in the NL and Carl Yastrzemski in the AL were playing their final seasons. Bench had spent his last several years as a third baseman due to chronic knee trouble. Yaz had played into his forties. Both had made such a mark on the game that MLB expanded the all-star game rosters by one spot on each side, to allow the two future Hall-of-Famers to participate one last time. It was a fitting tribute.

During his baseball career, Bench cultivated a high profile to maximize endorsement opportunities, but he also suffered financial setbacks. Bench has been married four times, and has joked about using performance-enhancing drugs to fuel his love life. He has sold items from his personal collection to generate additional income. In fact, a game-worn Reds uniform from early in his career sold at auction for $55,212 in 2021.

Among numerous other honors, Bench was named starting catcher on baseball's all-century team, and had his number five permanently retired by the Reds. Bench's final numbers included a .267 clip, 2,048 hits, 389 home runs and 1,376 RBI.

JIM MERRITT

As Jim Merritt took the mound in the 1970 all-star game, television analyst Sandy Koufax noted that Merritt was effective because of his control, changing speeds and breaking pitches. Koufax had known Merritt since Jim served as a bat boy and clubhouse assistant for the Dodgers. Jim learned a lot about pitching just observing Koufax and Don Drysdale.

Jim signed his first pro contract with the Dodgers but was snared by the Twins in the first-year player draft. The tall, slender hurler got his break during the 1965 campaign when a couple of Twins pitchers – Dave Boswell and Camilo Pascual – went down with injuries. Pitching both as a starter and reliever, Merritt went 5-4 with a nifty 3.17 ERA. He made a couple of solid relief appearances in the World Series against the Dodgers, and at one point even picked the NL stolen base leader, Maury Wills, off second base.

The Twins slipped to second place in 1966, and Merritt had a 7-14 record, though his ERA was again a respectable 3.38. He tied an AL record by whiffing seven straight hitters in a game that year. The 1967 season brought another second-place finish for the Twins, but this time Merritt went 13-7, and at 2.53 had the best ERA among the club's starters.

Yet, 1968 proved to be a year to forget for both the Twins, who dropped to seventh place under embattled manager Cal Ermer, and for Merritt who mustered only a 12-16 record. Ready to clean house, the club gave up on shortstop Zoilo Versalles, trading him and disgruntled hurler Mudcat Grant to the Dodgers. In a separate deal, they swapped Merritt to the Reds, getting shortstop Leo Cardenas to replace Versalles.

The latter trade set the stage for Merritt's two successful years in Cincinnati. Jim won 17 games in 1969. In winning 20 games for the Reds in 1970, he became the franchise's first lefty to reach that plateau since Eppa Rixey 45 years earlier. He also was featured with a cover story in *The Sporting News* and notched a win in the World Series against Baltimore.

Tendonitis plagued his career which ended with Texas. He finished with a lifetime record of 81-86 and a 3.65 ERA, along with 9 shutouts. After baseball, he and his wife returned to California, where according to a SABR bio, he worked for the Walton Publishing Company. He now lives in Hernet, California.

JIM BROSNAN

To some, he was a fine relief pitcher. To those who read his baseball books, he was an intellectual curiosity. To pitcher Lindy McDaniel, who was assigned to room with him while with the Cardinals, he was a hard-drinking atheist. To broadcaster Joe Garagiola, he was a "kooky beatnik."

Pitcher Jim Brosnan was born in Cincinnati, the city in which he would enjoy his best seasons. As a young man, he played on a 1946 American Legion team (along with Jim Frey and Don Zimmer) that made the national semi-finals. He signed with the Cubs in 1947, lost most of two years to military service, and finally made the show with that franchise in 1954.

The Cubs came to view the six-foot-four, 200-pound Brosnan as a mediocre starting pitcher and traded him midway through the 1958 season to the Cardinals for aging infielder Alvin Dark. The Cardinals, in turn, became dissatisfied and dealt him about a year later to the Reds for another aging ballplayer, pitcher Hal Jeffcoat.

The Reds eventually figured out that Brosnan's best role was that of a reliever, stopping opposition rallies in the middle and late innings. Relying heavily on his slider, he had a brilliant 1960 season, posting a 7-2 record with 12 saves and a 2.36 ERA for a sixth-place Reds club.

After the 1960 season, Commissioner Ford Frick sent Brosnan to Wiesbaden, West Germany, to head up what then was an annual baseball clinic for U.S. armed forces personnel in Europe. Jim Bunning, Harvey Kuenn, as well as several coaches and umpires completed the patriotic delegation, aimed at providing encouragement to the troops. Brosnan was a natural choice for the mission, as a rugged, articulate, high-performing hurler who was also a military veteran.

Brosnan spent the rest of the winter at his 7742 Churchill Street home in Morton Grove, Illinois. Ordinarily, he would have returned to his previous off-season job as a copy-writer for a Michigan Avenue advertising agency, but he was making enough in royalties from his first book, *The Long Season,* to forego trudging into the snowy city every morning. The book sold more than 250,000 copies. Desilu Productions, the entertainment company founded by Desi Arnaz and Lucille Ball, contracted with Brosnan to make a comedy series called, "You Can't Win 'Em All," based on the book, and a pair of screenwriters wrote a pilot. But the project was shelved in early 1961.

Brosnan, meanwhile, had another season to contemplate. The Reds were optimistic about improving in 1961 but few predicted their 26-game surge in the standings to win the pennant. The club's offensive production exploded. The starting rotation was only fair, but that's where Brosnan came into the picture. Appearing 53 times in relief, he won 10 contests and saved 16 others. That solidified his status as a premier fireman. The Reds' dream season finally collided with adversity when they lost the World Series to the Yankees.

The 1962 Reds were again terrific with 98 wins but settled for third place behind the Giants and Dodgers. Brosnan, now 32 years old, was still reasonably effective, posting a 4-4 record with 13 saves and a 3.34 ERA. But his hits-to-innings ratio was much worse, to the chagrin of Reds owner Bill DeWitt, who had another bone to pick.

The standard major league contract specified that a player could not publish anything without team review and permission, a point that DeWitt discussed with Brosnan before the 1962 season. But the hurler's second book, *The Pennant Race,* hit the bookstores without team review. DeWitt told reporters that Brosnan devoted too much energy during the season to promoting the book and not enough to helping the team compete. Following the season, with little leverage but plenty of royalty income coming in, Brosnan agreed to an unspecified pay cut.

Brosnan requested a trade to an AL team, believing hitters' lack of familiarity with him there would work to his advantage. The Reds traded Brosnan early in the 1963 season to the White Sox and Brosnan could not have been happier. He was back on his home turf, meaning more time with family and more time to write for *The Atlantic Monthly* and other publications. White Sox General Manager Ed Short told him that what he did with his off-season time was his business, but that no books or articles were to be published between March and the end of the season, for risk of distracting the team from its mission. Brosnan initially seemed comfortable with that policy.

Bothered by shoulder pain, Jim turned in a mediocre performance in 1963. Following the season, he and his wife joined Chicago advertising executive Arthur Meyerhoff and his spouse for a three-week trip to Europe. Brosnan had previously mused about moving to Europe, but after the trip said he was happy to return to his suburban Chicago home.

In February 1964, Brosnan returned his White Sox contract to the club, now questioning the team's policy of not allowing him to publish articles during baseball season. As a writer, Brosnan argued, he could not dictate to magazines the dates that articles would be published. At this point, the Sox concluded that Brosnan was more trouble than he was worth. After putting him on the trade block and finding no takers, they gave him his unconditional release.

"Let's face it. I wouldn't exactly say Brosnan had a great season," Short remarked. Manager Al Lopez elaborated, saying that Brosnan was released due to the White Sox's abundance of good pitchers, not because of his writing. As fate would have it, the White Sox fielded one of the best bullpens in baseball without Brosnan in 1964, anchored by Hoyt Wilhelm, Eddie Fisher, Frank Kreutzer, and Don Mossi.

Brosnan took out a "situation wanted" advertisement in *The Sporting News*, but no other team proffered the hurler a contract. The Illinois Civil Liberties Union wrote to the White Sox proclaiming that the team had violated Brosnan's right to freedom of speech and press. Team officials said that the ACLU should have determined the facts behind Brosnan's release before writing the letter and releasing it to the news media.

That chapter spelled the end of his pitching career. Brosnan later authored more books and articles, did some broadcasting, and appeared on the television program *To Tell the Truth.* Book critics have credited him with setting the model for a sports diary book that Jim Bouton, Sparky Lyle and others have since emulated. Brosnan died at the age of 84 in Park Ridge in 2014. He had a lifetime record of 55-47 with a 3.54 ERA and 68 saves.

MILT PAPPAS

When the Hall of Fame ballots were issued and newly eligible former pitcher Milt Pappas wasn't listed, he took action that resulted in a change in how names are selected for the ballots. That was pure Pappas – gutsy, confident, cocky, and argumentative.

Over 17 seasons, Pappas posted a 209-164 record with a 3.40 ERA and 43 shutouts. He was the first 200-game victor without a 20-win season. His lifetime statistics were similar to several Hall-of-Fame pitchers, though he was never as dominant.

Hurling for the Orioles, Reds, Braves and Cubs, he was one of those pitchers who consistently located pitches right where he wanted them, often on the corners. He threw fastballs, sliders, and occasionally an off-speed breaking pitch.

He spent the 1957 season as an 18-year-old with Baltimore, appearing in only four games. Teammates largely ignored him and fellow bonus-pitcher Jerry Walker, resenting them taking up a roster spot. In 1958, defying expectations which were for him to be sent to the minors, he made the O's roster and posted a 10-10 record. It was the first of 10 straight seasons with a .500 record or better.

The righty was one of Baltimore's best pitchers through 1965 but developed a reputation, accurate or not, as a "five and fly" guy, looking to turn games over to the bullpen if he had the lead after five innings. Finally, the Orioles traded him after that season in the deal for Frank Robinson. Although Pappas was respectable for the Reds, Baltimore handily got the better part of the deal.

Milt was the player representative in both Baltimore and Cincinnati, but that role also led to controversy. When his teammates voted to play the day in 1968 of Dr. Martin Luther King's burial over Pappas' vocal objections, he threatened to quit the role. It mattered little, as he was traded to Atlanta a few days later. Milt was sold to the Cubs in 1970 and had perhaps his best season in Chicago in 1972, going 17-7 with a no-hitter. He nearly had a perfect game and remained ticked off at the home plate umpire for years to come over what he felt was a blown call. His career ended when he was released in spring training of 1974.

After some coaching assignments, Milt went into sales of industrial supplies. Tragedy struck in 1982 when his wife left for a hair appointment and never returned. It was an unsolved case until her car and body were discovered five years later in a pond near the family home. By then, Pappas had moved on with his life with a new wife. Milt lived to the age of 76, passing away in Illinois in 2016.

STEVE BARBER

Steve Barber was an outspoken, barrel-chested left-hander from Tacoma Park, Maryland, who seemed to have two separate careers. From 1960 to 1966, Barber was an Orioles ace, winning 91 times against 66 losses. During the second half of his tenure, he was a sore-armed traveler, constantly changing teams in search of a comeback.

Barber was blunt in his younger days but mellowed over time. In the final weeks of the 1959 season, the Orioles brought Steve, then a minor leaguer, to Baltimore for a workout. When manager Paul Richards asked, "How come I never heard of you," Barber responded, "Probably because I'm not one of your f***ing bonus babies," as described in John Eisenberg's book, *33rd Street to Camden Yards: An Oral History of the Baltimore Orioles.* Several years later, as Barber and Milt Pappas emerged as aces of the Orioles' staff, they needled one another mercilessly over which pitcher needed the most run support.

During the spring of 1960, Barber decided he needed to dress like a major leaguer. According to *The Sporting News,* he visited a menswear shop and purchased five suits, three sports jackets, eight slacks, eight shirts, eight pair of socks and 14 neckties. "I'm afraid to get the bill," he confessed with a grin.

Barber won 18 games and topped the AL in shutouts in 1961. The following year, he spent time fulfilling his military obligations at Fort Bragg, but still managed to collect nine wins. In 1963, he won 20 games and made the all-star team.

Boog Powell recalled, "Barber was incredible when he was young…Very intimidating. Nobody wanted to stand in there on him." Barber decimated weaker competition like the A's, beating them 12 times in 13 decisions. At times, he was described as the hardest thrower in the league. Boston's Pete Runnells, a former batting champ, told the *Baltimore Sun,* "He knocks the bat right out of your hands."

Arm pain set in around the 1966 all-star break. That was the turning point, as he lost 18 games in 1967. Through 1974, he pitched with the Orioles, Yankees, Pilots, Cubs, Braves, Angels and Giants, and his record was just 30-40 for the second half of his career. As his velocity diminished, pitches that used to get popped up instead got ripped for base hits. His final comeback attempt came in 1975, when he went to spring training with the Indians, courtesy of an invitation from their manager, his former teammate Frank Robinson. Once he was cut by Cleveland, he retired with a 121-106 record, 3.36 ERA and 21 shutouts.

After baseball, Barber worked in sales and as a school bus driver in Las Vegas. He was inducted into the Orioles Hall of Fame in 1988. Barber passed away at age 69 in 2007 from complications of pneumonia.

CURT BLEFARY

The son of an AT&T Bell Labs electronics engineer, Curt Blefary drew scouts' attention with his spectacular play as a third baseman and catcher for his Mahwah, New Jersey high school team. He signed a Yankees contract in 1962, investing most of his $35,000 bonus – at his dad's insistence -- in AT&T stock. When he wasn't playing ball, he was a typical young man of the Sixties, listening to loud music, consuming large amounts of food and alcohol, and exploring what life had to offer.

While playing in the minor leagues first for the Yankees and then for the Orioles, Curt flashed a hot temper, heaving batting helmets and complaining about whatever was on his mind. "This is an intense, impatient and determined young man," wrote sportswriter Doug Brown. Orioles coach Gene Woodling called him "the angriest player I've ever seen."

Blefary made the big leagues in 1965 at age 21 and in just his second game, crushed two home runs and a double against the Red Sox. Pitchers and fans alike took notice. Before that 1965 season was over, the youngster delivered another pair of two-homer games and a career-best .260 batting average. It was enough to win the rookie of the year award. Road roommate Carl Warwick said "Curt feels like he's been up here his whole life."

The Orioles added Frank Robinson to the mix in 1966, and while Robby was winning the triple crown, Blefary enjoyed another productive season with 23 home runs as the Birds won the pennant by nine lengths over the Twins. Only a 1-for-13 World Series performance, and a growing reputation as a sloppy outfielder, cast a shadow on his otherwise strong season, as the Orioles won the world championship.

On June 6, 1967, he blasted three home runs in a game against the Angels. Though the Orioles had a disappointing season, Blefary remained one of their top sluggers. After three seasons, Blefary had 67 career homers, and was still shy of his 25th birthday.

Like many hitters, he suffered during the 1968 "Year of the Pitcher." He still hit 15 home runs but batted only .200. Meanwhile, the Birds were overloaded with outfielders, having Robinson, Paul Blair, Don Buford, Merv Rettenmund, Curt Motton, and Dave May on their depth chart, alongside Blefary.

Following the season, they traded him to the Astros for pitcher Mike Cuellar. Blefary led the Astros in doubles and triples in 1969, but that paled in comparison to Cuellar having a Cy Young award season for Baltimore. A SABR profile on Blefary notes that he roomed with a black player, Houston's Don Wilson, which was unusual for the late Sixties. Jim Bouton, also an Astro for part of the 1969 season, recalled Blefary as a fearless teammate.

Curt spent the next couple of years as a utility man, seeing action at first base and catcher as needed for the Yankees and A's. After bellyaching about a lack of playing time for the 1972

A's, he was traded to San Diego, and played even less. Then seven games into his 1973 season with Richmond, he was released. Though still only 29, he found it impossible to get another offer in North America or in Japan. He had a lifetime batting average of .237, with 699 hits and 112 homers.

Blefary later held a succession of jobs and finally gained a degree of peace in his life after marrying his second wife, opening a bar in Florida, and increasing his baseball old-timer public appearances. He conquered his serious drinking problem in 1994 after attending Sam McDowell's treatment program. Those years of drinking led to chronic pancreatitis, which took his life in 2001. At his request, his ashes were spread at the no-longer-in-use Memorial Stadium in Baltimore, the locale of his fondest baseball memories.

HAWK HARRELSON

Ken Harrelson spent nine years in MLB as an outfielder and first baseman with the A's, Senators, Red Sox and Indians. A legitimate slugger, he led the AL with 109 RBI for Boston in 1968, placing third in MVP votes. A year later, he turned in a 30-homer, 92-RBI season for Cleveland.

One of the joys of Sixties baseball was the popular nicknames. Ken was nicknamed the Hawk -- his nose was broken five times. He grew up in a tough Savannah neighborhood, the son of an alcoholic father who eventually walked out on the family, and he learned to fight for his own interests. "Many a day and night throughout my life, I worked my way out of a tough situation with my 10 knuckles," he later wrote. "These days, my wrists are very painful. Doctors have told me I basically wore them out. It's no wonder, because I spent my life swinging away at something – with a baseball bat, a golf club, or my fists."

Ken loved golf and early in his MLB career spent an afternoon on the course playing 27 holes with teammates Ted Bowsfield, Sammy Esposito, and Gino Cimoli. Called upon to play baseball that evening, one of his fingers was badly blistered. He went up to the plate wearing a golf glove and despite ribbing by his Yankees opponents, he had inadvertently introduced a new product – the batting glove.

The Hawk's temper was on display early on while playing winter league ball in Venezuela in late 1965. He got into physical altercations with two umpires, one of which led to a 15-day suspension and a hefty $200 fine.

Then in 1967, he offered criticism of A's owner Charles O. Finley over Finley's handling of an alleged incident on a flight involving pitcher Lew Krausse. In a fit of anger, Finley released the slugger. He was initially disturbed, but road roommate Mike Hershberger told him this was an incredible opportunity. Becoming a free agent, Ken started receiving offers from other teams, and he cashed in with a lucrative deal with the Red Sox. Overnight, his salary increased exponentially, with a World Series bonus to follow.

Although Boston slipped to fourth place in 1968, Harrelson enjoyed his best season at the plate. With batting champion Carl Yastrzemski hitting ahead of him, the Hawk had plenty of opportunities to generate runs, and finished with 109 RBI while hitting 35 homers and an uncharacteristically high .275.

By the time the 1969 season began, Harrelson had become well-known for his longish hair, sunglasses, alligator shoes, and bright-colored mod clothing. Early in the season, Boston traded him to the Indians for pitching help. Initially upset at leaving Boston where he was immensely popular, the Hawk finally reported after Cleveland businesses lined up some endorsement offers. He took up residence in a high-rise penthouse lakefront apartment on Cleveland's west side and traveled to Municipal Stadium on team owner Vernon Stouffer's helicopter. His first book, co-authored with Al Hirshberg, came out the same year.

Ken reported to Tucson for spring training in 1970 sporting long hair. Skipper Alvin Dark, who was not only Ken's former manager with the A's but also his golfing buddy, threatened to fine him $1,000. Ken got the widely publicized haircut for $15, joking that he saved $985. Popular in Tucson as everywhere else, a street – Hawk Drive in the Escalante Heights development -- was named for him by developer Gene Anderson.

Harrelson broke a bone above his right ankle while sliding into second base during a 1970 Cactus League game, a gruesome injury that caused him to miss most of the season. Gabe Paul tried to cut Hawk's pay, but Dark immediately intervened to say there would be no pay cut. Ken returned in 1971, but got off to a slow start, lost his first base job to rookie Chris Chambliss, and retired in June to pursue a short-lived career as a professional golfer. He later became a popular broadcaster and in 2020 received the Ford Frick award at the Hall of Fame. Ken had a .239 lifetime average with 131 homers.

Dave Morehead

No-hitters were a rare treat during the Sixties, with an average of just 3.4 such gems per season. By contrast, in 2021, MLB saw 13 no-hitters – about one every two weeks.

One of the no-hitters was tossed by Dave Morehead of the Red Sox on September 16, 1965. The Sox were suffering through a miserable season and needed some good news. Dave held the Indians to just one base-runner – a walk. In the ninth inning, Larry Brown hit a line drive to the left side of the infield, but shortstop Ed Bressoud made the leaping catch to keep the no-hitter alive. Following the contest, owner Tom Yawkey went to the locker room to congratulate Morehead, and alert him to watch for a new contract, with a $1,000 pay increase. It was the first no-hitter in the AL since Jack Kralick's jewel with the Twins in 1962.

Only 1,247 fans were on hand at Fenway Park to see Sox history being made. The termination of general manager Pinky Higgins was announced just an hour after the game and stole some thunder from Dave's terrific afternoon. (Higgins himself represents a tragic story. After being fired by the Red Sox, he joined the Houston organization as a scout. In 1968, while driving his car in Louisiana, he struck a road crew, killing one worker and injuring three others. He pleaded guilty to driving while intoxicated and served two months in prison before being paroled. He died of a heart attack the day after his release at age 59.)

Morehead attended the same San Diego high school that produced Ted Williams and Ray Boone. Dave was selected by the Royals in the 1968 expansion draft and won just five more games over two years. He had a 40-64 lifetime record and a 4.15 ERA. Having completed a marketing degree at San Diego State University, he became a manufacturers' rep based in Tustin, California.

Tom Gramly

An injury cut short the career of promising right-hander Tom Gramly and his story exemplifies one of the biggest changes in MLB since the Sixties, as surgical procedures are now available to help rectify many injuries.

Back then, athletes played through pain and serious conditions. Few had multi-year contracts, and there was always the concern that while rehabbing an injury, one could lose his job.

Gramly learned the art of pitching from his father, who was a former minor-leaguer. "I was a control pitcher," he recalled later. "My best pitch was the change-up. My father taught me to go in and out, and up and down. I could throw any pitch at any time."

As a pitcher at Texas Christian University, he was drafted by the Cubs after his freshman year and by the Yankees after his sophomore season, but never signed until he was selected in the fourth round by the Indians after his junior year. He burnished his prospect credentials with 14 wins at Triple-A Portland in 1967.

Tom's experience with the Indians was not positive. "My career was cut short due to an injury that by today's standards was minor. Yet, the Cleveland Indians never sent me to a doctor. They just sent me home. You see, back then the owners had the upper hand, and unproven players were no better than cattle," he noted.

The injury occurred during 1968 spring training in Tucson, when manager Al Dark insisted that players work out using a device called the Exer-Genie. It had been introduced in 1964 and was touted as a breakthrough in combining isometric and isotonic exercise to attain strength and flexibility.

Gramly, coming from a baseball family, didn't need to be told how to keep in shape, but used the machine as instructed, and suffered his injury as a result. Two years later, he was out of baseball, and still had not seen a doctor. He appeared in three games for Cleveland in 1968 and closed out his career with Portland in 1969.

Living outside of Dallas, Gramly admits to having harbored bitterness over that outcome but is grateful for the tremendous support his parents showed him throughout his youth and his baseball career. He worked for State Farm Insurance and Texas Instruments for many years after baseball, before becoming semi-retired.

DON BLASINGAME

Don (the Blazer) Blasingame was the second baseman for the Cardinals (1956-1959), Giants (1960), Reds (1961-1962), and Senators (1963-1965), before making cameo appearances with the A's late in his career. He was a solid defender and a .258 lifetime hitter.

The son of a Mississippi butcher, he replaced Red Schoendienst as the Cards' everyday second sacker in 1956. Over his first four seasons, he batted around .270, garnered an all-star selection, and married a beauty queen who was the daughter of Walker Cooper, a legendary Cardinals catcher. For a time, he was the toast of St. Louis.

After the Cardinals' seventh-place showing in 1959, they traded Don to the Giants for a couple of power hitters, Daryl Spencer and Leon Wagner. His batting average tumbled 54 points in 1960, leading to another trade to the Reds early in the 1961 campaign. He arrived in the Queen City in time to help the Reds to the World Series. Though his hitting again suffered, his classy defense saved a lot of runs. Don bounced back with a .281 average in 1962, though the Reds placed third in that year's incredible pennant race.

Pete Rose supplanted him as the Reds' second-sacker coming out of spring training in 1963, though ace pitcher Jim O'Toole stated that Rose could not turn the double play the way the Blazer did. With Don expendable, the Reds swapped him to Washington for pitcher Jim Coates, and he displaced Chuck Cottier as the second baseman in the nation's capital. Young shortstop Ed Brinkman raved about how helpful Don was in positioning him properly, depending on the hitter.

Don later played, coached and managed in Japan for 11 seasons. His family spent half the year in Japan and half in the States, affording his children the chance to study in a foreign country. The Blazer eventually settled in Fountain Hills, Arizona. He died of heart failure at age 73 in 2005, one day after playing 18 holes of golf. A street and a baseball facility are named for him in Corinth, Mississippi, his original hometown.

PETE ROSE

Brash and witty with a zest for life and a crude vocabulary, this 22-year-old made the Reds roster unexpectedly in 1963, following a season with the Single-A Macon Peaches in the South Atlantic League. A local boy, he became the Reds second baseman (dislodging veteran Don Blasingame) and quickly became a fan favorite in the Queen City.

The Reds in those days were managed by Fred Hutchinson. After four years with the Navy, Hutch became one of Detroit's best pitchers in the late 1940s and then went into coaching. Standing six-foot-two, chain smoking cigarettes and exhibiting a bit of a temper, Hutch was simultaneously a likeable yet intimidating figure. He saw Rose play winter ball after the 1962 season and concluded that the hustling youngster was just what his veteran team needed to shake it out of complacency.

During spring training, Rose demonstrated his trademark brand of hustle, with head-first slides and sprints on the base paths. Hutch told reporters, "There isn't a harder worker in camp, but to Pete it really isn't work, just fun." Hutch said that Rose was timed going from home plate to first base in just 4.1 seconds. "But that's after he'd drawn a walk," the manager joked.

Veteran teammates were baffled that Hutch would award the starting second base job to a player coming out of Single-A ball over a proven veteran coming off a .280 season, on a team just 18 months removed from a World Series appearance.

Moreover, they weren't sure what to make of Rose. Unlike most of the players, who cooperated with the beat reporters unenthusiastically, Rose charmed them and attracted fawning media coverage. At every opportunity, he headed to a track to bet on the dog races or horse races. With white teammates giving him the cold shoulder, he simply gravitated toward the team's African American players (Frank Robinson, Vada Pinson and Tommy Harper) who were more welcoming, which was outside the norms of the era.

Over the next few seasons, he exhibited questionable judgment on a personal level. It was one thing to go to a strip joint, but quite another thing to become part of the act. It was one thing to cheat on a wife (he married late in 1963), but another thing to flaunt it in various cities. The Reds brought in coach Johnny Temple in 1964 to try to temper some of Pete's behaviors but even that experiment ended badly, as Temple was fired after getting into a brawl with another coach.

Although the Reds slipped to fifth place during that 1963 season, Pete hit .273 and won the top-rookie honors, in addition to the hearts of the fan base. After a similar campaign in 1964, he became a .300 hitter in 1965. Pete wasn't the smoothest second baseman so in 1967 he moved to the outfield where he was excellent. He won the first of three batting crowns in 1968 and led the NL in hits seven seasons.

Like most hitters, he had trouble against Sandy Koufax, collecting just 10 hits in 57 at bats. "How the hell you going to hit that curve ball," he asked radio host Colin Cowherd years later. "My first three years in the league, he struck out 1,000." But Rose owned another Hall of Fame pitcher, Warren Spahn, going 17 for 32 against him. Rose said Bob Gibson was "the most aggressive pitcher I ever faced," though he hit .307 against him. Asked about hurler Don Sutton, Rose said, "I wore his ass out."

Rose's least favorite stadium was San Francisco's Candlestick Park where the winds made it difficult to hit. The road team's clubhouse was down the right field line, whereas the road-team dugout was on the third-base side. "So consequently, you don't go to the clubhouse during the game. So, if you've got diarrhea, you are in trouble," Pete recalled.

In 1969, he received the Lou Gehrig Award which was presented for exemplifying the character of Gehrig. At the time, Pete's addiction to gambling and predilection to accumulating debt were not yet public knowledge.

It was not until 1970 that the Reds assembled a championship-quality team. The club became even stronger when Joe Morgan became the second baseman in 1972.

Rose played for five Reds managers, including Hutch, Dick Sisler, Don Heffner, Dave Bristol, and Sparky Anderson. Pete told broadcaster Chris (Mad Dog) Russo that "Dave Bristol created the Big Red Machine, but Sparky [Anderson] developed it…Sparky was the most street-smart guy I ever met in my life." Coming from the street-smart Rose, that was high praise.

While not exceptionally athletic, Rose had strong arms and legs, buffed by working summers loading and unloading railroad box cars. He was always ready to play, and refused to give up an at bat, no matter the game's score. While not often publicized, Rose also used amphetamines (or greenies) to pump himself for games, according to writer Michael Y. Sokolove.

Pitcher Jim Kaat wrote, "Pete Rose…did not have much power, speed, agility or even a strong throwing arm. But he was one of the greatest players of all time. Why? His baseball IQ – the anticipation, the ability to see the whole field, knowing what every player needed to do, not just what he needed to do."

"I always admired the way Pete approached the game," says pitcher George Culver, who was a teammate. "He was all about his own stats but he was also all about winning. It's a shame he got involved in the gambling scandal but if they let the steroids users in the Hall of Fame then Pete should be there also. You can't take away his numbers and his incredible career."

As most readers of this book know, the scandal that Culver references broke into the public when *Sports Illustrated* ran an article documenting Pete's gambling debts to bookmakers with ties to cocaine distribution and suggesting Rose may have violated MLB rules by betting on baseball games. An MLB investigation showed strong circumstantial evidence to that effect.

Pete voluntarily accepted a banishment from baseball in 1989 and pleaded guilty to tax-evasion charges. In 2004, he publicly admitted he bet on baseball and his own team.

In the years since then, Rose has enjoyed playing golf and participating in memorabilia-sales programs, which provide him with a lucrative income. A lifetime .303 hitter, Rose retired in 1986 as the all-time leader in hits (4,256) and games played (3,562).

AL KALINE

Al Kaline began his six-decade affiliation with the Tigers in the most formal of ways – he was wearing his senior prom suit and tie when scout Ed Katalinas arrived and negotiated the contract with Kaline's parents. The pact called for a $15,000 bonus, and a first-year salary of the same amount.

He became one of the steadiest performers of his era. En route to 3,007 hits and 399 homers, he made every all-star team from 1955 to 1967, and was tapped again in 1971 and 1974. Billy Martin called him "Mister Perfection."

In his rookie season of 1953, Kaline was introduced by manager Fred Hutchinson to Ted Williams. Al received hitting tips from the master, including how to square up on low fastballs. The instruction made him a better hitter, and the pair became lifelong friends.

The early days of his career were difficult, he told the *Detroit News* decades later. Baseball rules required bonus babies to stay in the big leagues for a period of time, whether they were ready or not. "It was a dog-eat-dog world back then among players," Kaline recounted. "When I first joined the team, I was looked down on, because I was an 18-year-old kid taking a veteran's job away from him. So, a lot of guys were thinking, 'What the hell is going on here?' It's true, I had a guy grab me on my first day in uniform, saying he didn't want me around."

Kaline answered their skepticism quickly. Whereas many bonus babies rode the bench for two years, and then went to the minor leagues for months or years, Kaline quickly earned playing time. He became the youngest batting champion ever in 1955 at the age of 20, on a fifth-place team.

One-year wonder? No way. In 1956, Kaline hit .314 and drove in a career-best 128 RBI. Continuing to learn the league's pitchers, in 1959, he led the loop in slugging percentage and OPS, while hitting .327, second only to teammate Harvey Kuenn. Beginning in 1957, he captured gold gloves 10 times. His arm was strong and accurate.

Kaline was astute at business, as well. In 1957, He teamed up with hockey great Gordie Howe and others to form an auto parts firm called MAPCO. Kaline took a personal interest in the profitable company.

The 1960 season was frustrating. Detroit fans felt the club had talent, but the team fizzled, traded managers in mid-season, and finished sixth. Kaline stole 19 bases, but his batting average (.278), home runs (15) and RBI (64) were the lowest since becoming a regular.

Bob Scheffing took over as manager in 1961, and the club responded with 101 victories, still only good enough for second place. Al was back on track, with a .324 batting average.

"Kaline became a fixture on the AL all-star team in the early Sixties," wrote Jeff Miller in the book, *Down to the Wire.* "The hitting, the fielding: it all came so easy. But that also became a problem for Kaline…Management feared that Kaline's grace on the field would be interpreted by the fans as indifference. They wanted Kaline to get his uniform dirty, to prove to the fans and the press he was giving everything he had on the field. He often became sullen, which only made matters worse when he got into a batting slump."

Kaline also had a painful foot condition called osteomyelitis. The May 11, 1964 *Sports Illustrated* captured these mixed sentiments with a cover story titled, "Detroit's Al Kaline, Enigma of the Tigers."

Bill Freehan later wrote, "Al's quiet, and I've always wondered why he hasn't gone out of his way to talk it up more, to try to charge up the guys. The main reason, I'm sure, is his basic personality; Al's not a screamer or a shaker away from the park, either. There's merit in having the quiet dignity Al has."

In 1963, Kaline placed second in the MVP balloting, but the Tigers drifted to fifth place, with Chuck Dressen replacing Scheffing as manager. Dressen, standing just five-foot-six, was already in his late-sixties. He was a master strategist who told his clubs, "Just keep it close, boys, and I'll think of something." Dressen suffered a heart attack in early 1965, and missed three months of the season, with Bob Swift managing in his place. The Tigers won 89 games but could not catch the pennant-bound Twins.

In 1966, the Tigers had a 16-10 record when Dressen was hospitalized. In August, he suffered a third cardiac arrest, this one fatal. In the meantime, interim manager Bob Swift, just 51 years old, was diagnosed with lung cancer. Frank Skaff, a coach, managed the rest of the season. Amidst these developments, the Tigers won 88 games, placing third. Kaline again delivered outstanding numbers (.288-29-88).

By 1967, Kaline was surrounded by a group of younger players who would form the core of the Tigers' roster for many years, as well as new manager Mayo Smith. Ed Katalinas had a hand in signing three other stars – Don Wert, Jim Northrup, and Denny McLain. Kaline again led the way, pacing the 1967 team with a 7.5 WAR rating, and placing third in the batting derby. The Tigers battled until the final weekend before being eliminated. Al was again in the top five in MVP voting.

The Tigers put it all together the following year, running away with the 1968 pennant. Despite missing time with a hand injury, Kaline hit .287 with 10 homers. During the World Series, he hit .379 with two home runs.

The Tigers were back in the post-season in 1972. Kaline contributed his fair share, batting .313 with 10 home runs. Detroit pushed Oakland to five games before losing the ALCS.

Kaline played two more seasons, and retired with a .297 batting average, 498 doubles, and 1,582 RBI. He is 44th on the all-time RBI list. He passed away in Bloomfield Hills in 2020 at the age of 85. Pitcher Fritz Peterson likely spoke for many pitchers when he said that Kaline was the best hitter he ever faced. "That's because he never gave up. They could be behind 8-1, and he's still trying to get on base and start a big inning."

RON FAIRLY

Long Beach native Ron Fairly played for the 1958 College World Series champion USC Trojans. Pat Gillick was a college teammate of Fairly at USC and recalled, "He was very talented and you were aware that he had both the mental and physical ability to play at a higher level." Needless to say, Ron also loved playing baseball.

The Dodgers, who had recently moved to the west coast, signed Fairly, giving him the largest bonus in team history. He made his Dodgers debut that same year, launching a 20-year MLB career during which he batted .266 with 215 home runs.

Fairly played on four Dodgers World Series clubs, three of which won the world championship. The last of those pennant winners was in 1966, and his 22 RBI during the month of September helped Los Angeles clinch the title. In 20 games in four fall classics, playing both first base and right field, Ron hit .300.

Fairly never considered playing baseball a real job, but he took his vocation seriously. Wes Parker said Fairly held teammates accountable for being ready to compete and win. Joe Moeller recalled, "He was a good fielder at first base and in the outfield, even though he didn't run well. When he struck out a couple times you didn't want to be around the bat rack as he could trash a dugout."

Ron was a believer in fitness and an evangelist for a baseball-specific exercise program developed by a man named Charlie Brown, who ran the International Sports Institute in Long Beach. "I needed power to hit harder," Fairly said. "Charlie Brown showed me how to get that power." Unlike many players who put on weight as they aged, Fairly stayed around 180 pounds.

Tom LaSorda wrote, "This is a guy who never got the credit he deserved in the majors. He stayed around for 20 years. How many guys could do that? I always thought he was the model of how a player should be. He was a pro." Similarly, pitcher Claude Osteen, who roomed with Fairly on some road trips, remembers him as "a tremendous competitor."

"During my playing days, my teammates and I probably spent more time away from our hotel rooms than the players today," he wrote. "We didn't have computers and video equipment to entertain us. We had one simple rule. Do not criticize a player's ability. Everything else was fair game, as long as it was in jest."

During the low-offense Sixties, Fairly was a consistent 70-RBI man. After getting sent to the Expos in 1969, he helped anchor that new franchise. He made his first all-star appearance at age 34, in 1973, a year in which he hit .298. Fairly was the only man to play for both Canadian teams – the 1969 Expos and the 1977 Blue Jays – in their expansion years. He also played for the Cardinals and A's.

After his playing days, the personable Fairly spent another three decades in the game as an announcer and authored an entertaining book titled, *Fairly at Bat.* He was 81 when he passed away in Palm Desert, California, in 2019.

BOB BUHL

One year into his minor-league pitching career in the White Sox organization in 1947, young Bob Buhl informed baseball commissioner Happy Chandler that he had signed a contract before his high school graduation, a violation of baseball rules. Chandler declared him a free agent, and a host of teams sent scouts to his native Michigan seeking a second chance to land him. Buhl signed with the Braves, getting a new car as his bonus.

In 10 years with the club, he posted a 109-72 record, as well as 16 of his 20 career shutouts. He was among his league's top four hurlers in ERA four different times. His willingness to bust hitters off the plate contributed to his success.

When the Braves won the world championship in 1957 under manager Fred Haney, Buhl had an 18-7 record for a league-topping .720 winning percentage. The only blemish on his season came during the fall classic, when he was knocked out early twice by the Yankees. The Braves nonetheless prevailed in the World Series. They repeated as pennant winners in 1958, but a sore arm limited Buhl to 11 outings. The Yankees prevailed in the World Series rematch.

Buhl bounced back with 15 wins in 1959 and 16 victories in 1960. Enjoying his time with the Braves, he usually roomed on the road with Eddie Mathews, while Warren Spahn roomed with Lew Burdette. The four made a practice of visiting the bars and night clubs at each NL stop. They did not look for trouble, but it often found them, Buhl recalled. In one incident in July of 1959, for example, Buhl and Mathews got into a scuffle shortly before 2:00 a.m. with a couple of patrons at the Zodiac Lounge at the Chase Hotel in St. Louis. Police arrived, finding that the only thing broken was a glass door.

Spahn, Burdette, and Buhl had formed a "big three" on the mound, but in 1961, Buhl lost his efficacy. Birdie Tebbetts was tapped as manager late in the season and yanked Buhl from the rotation. The club soon swapped the 33-year-old to the Cubs but did so prematurely. Over the next four seasons, Buhl registered 51 more victories for Chicago.

Ron Fairly of the Dodgers recalled a story involving Buhl and the Cubs. "On another trip to Chicago, we heard rumors that the Cubs were stealing signs. Bob Buhl pitched for them in the first game of the series. The next day, about the second or third inning, one of our players noticed this guy in the right center bleachers wearing a trench coat. Very suspicious. I can't recall ever seeing a Chicago fan wearing a trench coat. It was Buhl. Then, we noticed he had binoculars and held a scorecard up to his chest on fastballs, but not on curves." The Dodgers sent their traveling secretary out to offer Buhl upgraded seats, which put an end to the outfield sign-stealing saga.

Buhl was kidded by teammates for being a dreadful hitter. No amount of batting practice, nor rooming with Eddie Mathews, made a difference. In 857 at bats, he hit below .100 and never homered. To his credit, he was able to lay down an occasional bunt.

In 1966, Buhl was traded to the Phillies in the deal that brought Ferguson Jenkins to the Windy City. The veteran retired in 1967 at age 38 with a lifetime record of 166-132 with a 3.55 ERA and 1,268 punch-outs. Living first in Michigan and then in Florida for retirement, Buhl attended Braves' reunion events for many years. He died of emphysema and pneumonia in 2000, just two days before his old roommate, Mathews, also passed away.

LEW BURDETTE

When Selva Lewis Burdette hurled three complete-game victories over the Yankees in the 1957 World Series, he became the first pitcher to record that achievement since Christy Mathewson in 1905. Burdette got his third win on just two days of rest before 61,207 spectators at Yankee Stadium, providing the ecstatic Braves with their first world championship since 1914.

Burdette had begun his MLB career with two appearances for those same Yankees in 1950. He said he liked to beat everyone too much for any one opponent to be special.

A light-haired, lean pitcher who won 203 regular-season games, Lew was at his peak from 1956 to 1961. During that run, he won 114 times and lost only 68. In two all-star appearances, he surrendered just one run in seven innings of work. In one of the most memorable games of all time, when hard-luck Harvey Haddix hurled 12 perfect innings before losing in the 13th frame on May 26, 1959, Burdette threw a complete game for the win.

Lew fired a no-hitter of his own on August 18, 1960 against Philadelphia. He faced the minimum number of 27 hitters, getting hit batsman Tony Gonzalez out in a twin killing. Burdette also scored the game's only run. He was a formidable hitter, having smashed 12 home runs, including two against Sandy Koufax.

Opponents accused him of throwing a spitball and joked that his first name should have been Saliva, not Selva. If nothing else, his constant fidgeting on the mound drove hitters to distraction. He also threw from different arm angles, keeping hitters off balance.

Burdette rarely walked a hitter. Only Robin Roberts, Juan Marichal, and Carl Hubbell issued fewer free passes per nine innings, among pitchers since 1920 with 3,000 or more innings.

Originally from Nitro, West Virginia, he played baseball in the streets with friends using a tennis ball. His family lived 15 miles from Charleston, and his dad periodically took him to see minor league games. In high school, he ran track. He met his future bride in a bowling alley. Lew briefly worked in a factory, then spent six months in the military reserves. He later enrolled at the University of Richmond, made all-state collegiate, yet still was still unsure of his future.

With the Yankees organization, he worked his way through the minor leagues, rooming at one point with fellow prospect Whitey Ford. One spring, he contracted pneumonia and a doctor administered penicillin. "I stiffened and turned blue and passed out," Burdette said. "They tell me my hand was like an iron claw." The allergic reaction was temporary, and he was soon feeling fine. Yankees manager Casey Stengel did not even know his name, he remembered. He would call "Hey, you" if he wanted to get Burdette's attention.

By the time Burdette delivered his 1957 World Series heroics for the Braves, he had already been living for several winters in Sarasota. At that time, about 30 current and past major leaguers wintered in the area, according to the *Sarasota Herald-Tribune*. Sarasota at the time was still a small town with a population of less than 30,000. The residents adopted the World Series star Burdette as one of their own.

His 20 wins helped the Braves win their second straight pennant in 1958. This time around, Burdette won game two of the World Series, but lost games five and seven.

Between 1959 and 1961, he won another 58 games. It was not until 1962 that he showed signs of decline. By 1963, with their championships a fading memory, the Braves put Burdette on the trading block. At the deadline on June 15, 1963, Milwaukee sent him to the Cardinals for catcher Gene Oliver and a minor league pitcher. Lew had little impact with the Cardinals, who dealt him to the Cubs about a year later.

One of his Cubs teammates was Lindy McDaniel. On his PitchingfortheMaster blog, McDaniel recalled, "This was late in Lew's career, and he would tell us guys in the bullpen how things were when he and Spahn played together. He told us they would drink at least 10 beers a day, but because they worked so hard running and exercising between starts, it would never affect their pitching. The effects of the beer would just sweat right out of their bodies."

After splitting the 1965 campaign between the Cubs and Phillies, Burdette changed leagues and pitched out of the Angels' pen for two years. With his fastball's success diminishing, he added a knuckleball.

A noted practical joker, his most visible prank was posing for his Topps 1959 baseball card as a southpaw, even though he threw right-handed. Topps proof-readers never caught it, but they pulled an inadvertent stunt of their own, spelling his first name "Lou" instead of "Lew."

Burdette was the Braves' pitching coach in 1972 and 1973 under manager Eddie Mathews. He also tried some entrepreneurial endeavors and worked in public relations for a Milwaukee brewery. He died of lung cancer in Florida in 2007. Baseball commissioner Bud Selig, a fixture in Milwaukee baseball, said, "I think what I remember most is that he was a tremendous competitor. He pitched in pain, he pitched to win." Burdette's lifetime record was 203-144 for a .585 winning percentage with a 3.66 ERA.

EDDIE MATHEWS

Until the arrival of Eddie Mathews in the 1950s and the maturation of Brooks Robinson in the 1960s, Pie Traynor was generally considered the greatest third baseman of all time. Traynor, who spent his whole career with Pittsburgh, played from the 1920s to the mid-1930s. He was a spray hitter and a smooth fielder who placed in the top 10 in MVP voting six years. He hit only 58 home runs over his entire career.

Mathews was a very different sort of third baseman. His calling card was his powerful swing coupled with an excellent eye. Hurlers pitched around him, and he was patient enough to lead the NL in walks four times. He never won a gold glove but was not a liability defensively.

The slugger, who was the only person to play for the Braves when based in Boston, Milwaukee and Atlanta, had four 40-homer seasons and made nine all-star teams. He teamed with Hank Aaron to help the Braves to a world championship in 1957 and pennant in 1958. His own best year may have been 1959, when he clouted 46 home runs, hit better than .300, and placed second in MVP voting. Teammate Johnny Logan said, "He had one of the sweetest swings I've ever seen."

Mathews' final all-star season was 1962 but he remained productive for several more years. His contract was transferred to the Tigers in August 1967 for the season's stretch run. The Bengals brought him back for a final season in 1968, but he went on the disabled list with a bad back on June 8 and underwent surgery at Henry Ford Hospital on July 5 to remove a protruding disc. He rehabbed and recovered in time to collect a hit and a free pass in just four plate appearances during the Tigers' triumphant World Series over the Cardinals. He was only the third future Hall of Famer to retire as a world champion, following Joe DiMaggio and John Mize.

Mathews had a .271 lifetime average with 512 home runs and 2,315 hits. He later managed the Braves for parts of three seasons. In retirement, he returned to his hometown of Santa Barbara, but battled alcoholism and burned through several marriages. He endured and recovered from a serious case of pneumonia, but in 1996 suffered a crushed pelvis when he was trapped between a cruise ship and a dock. His health never fully recovered and he passed away from pneumonia in 2001.

NATE COLBERT

Baseball's expansion from 20 to 24 teams in 1969 was perfectly timed for a number of young players including first baseman Nate Colbert. The St. Louis native signed with his hometown Cardinals and was drafted by Houston, which used him sparingly between 1966 and 1968. Astros manager Harry Walker micromanaged Colbert's swing, which only served to frustrate the player. As MLB expanded, creating 100 more jobs across the sport, the Padres selected him with the 18th pick in the expansion draft.

Managed by Preston Gomez, that first 1969 Padres club was one of the worst in the sport's history with 110 losses. For the first two weeks of the season, Bill Davis got most of the starts at first base, but he was eventually farmed out. During two weeks that Colbert was away for military duty, Roberto Pena started at first base. Otherwise, the job was Colbert's alone, and though he was a strikeout machine, he led his team in home runs (24), RBI (66) and hits (123) while batting .255.

The first home run of his career came early that season. It was a game-winning three-run shot against Houston's Jack Billingham and came just moments after he was brushed back with a knockdown pitch.

Gomez said that Colbert "probably has the quickest bat on the club," adding, "He may be one of those fellows who might never have gotten a chance to play had baseball not expanded."

Going into the 1970 season, Gomez predicted, "Nate's going to be our first baseman for a long time" and that Colbert could hit as many as 35 home runs in a season. Nate didn't disappoint. He slugged 38 home runs for the 1970 Padres, despite striking out 150 times. After launching 27 bombs in 1971, he crushed 38 more homers in 1972.

During the latter season, he produced a record 13 RBI in a double-header. Before he knew what had happened, the Baseball Hall of Fame had taken his bat for its vast collection of memorabilia.

Colbert closed his career in 1976 after time with the Tigers, Expos and A's, retiring with a lifetime batting average of .243, 141 home runs and 833 hits.

After his playing career, Nate became a minor-league coach, ordained minister and talk radio host. The low point came when he was indicted on 12 counts of fraudulent loan applications. He pled guilty and served six months in a minimum-security institution. In his later years, he has battled glaucoma and nerve damage. Now a resident of Las Vegas, Colbert was inducted into the Padres team hall of fame in 1999.

LOU PINIELLA

As the 1968 spring training approached, outfielder Lou Piniella had already proven he could hit Triple-A pitching and was determined to win a roster spot with the Indians. He caught a sore throat en route to Tucson from his native Tampa, but was ready to show the Indians' new manager, Alvin Dark, what he could do.

In an exhibition "B" game against the Cubs on March 30, he delivered a triple, double and single against all-star pitcher Ken Holtzman, but by then it was too late, as the Tribe had just awarded the last two roster slots to other outfielders, Willie Smith and Jose Vidal.

When informed of his demotion, Piniella furiously packed his bags and told farm director Hank Peters he was quitting baseball. Peters got the hot-headed young player to cool down and convinced him that with expansion coming in 1969 and with it 100 more roster spots, that his future was still bright. Piniella changed his mind about retirement and hit .319 at Triple-A Portland.

In the eyes of the Indians top brass, Piniella's fiery personality worked against him. During that 1968 spring training Dark had a fatherly, hand-on-the-shoulder conversation, urging the young outfielder to adopt a more even-keeled approach to his work. Any benefit of the conversation was short lived as a few days later, Piniella struck out, and stormed back to the dugout, nervously paced for a moment, and then angrily stomped his batting helmet to pieces, with Dark watching unamused from the corner of the dugout.

Teammate Tom Gramly recalled an incident in Portland, saying, "Lou hit a grounder to short for the third out of the inning. Now normally, he would come back to the dugout and kick the wall. But on this occasion, he was playing right field, and he was walking to his position very calmly. But then, there's a crashing sound coming from right field. Lou had gone out and kicked the fence and it fell over on him."

While the Indians' leadership had little appreciation for Sweet Lou, others in the organization saw his potential. Infielder Billy Harris roomed with him at Portland – and briefly again with the Royals in 1969 – and couldn't understand why the Tribe wouldn't give him a chance.

Pitcher Stan Williams shared a similar view. "I befriended him in 1966" at Portland, recalled Williams in a 2006 interview. "He was a brash young rookie on the way up. I took him under my wing and we hung out together. I liked the way he played the game. He played with a fire. I taught him how to play gin rummy and won a lot of money from him, though he's a great gin rummy player now."

"Lou was not a tool guy," Williams explained. "He couldn't run. He had an average arm. But Lou was the type of guy who got 150 percent out of his ability. Being fair to the Indians, that part was a little hard to scout because you don't really know what's inside a guy. But if you'd watched Lou much, you'd have known."

Piniella was left unprotected by the Indians in the October 1968 expansion draft. Selected by Seattle then traded to Kansas City, he won the 1969 rookie of the year award with the Royals. He went on to play 18 years in the majors and retire with a solid .291 batting average and 1,705 hits. He was an all-star in 1972 and hit .319 in 72 World Series at bats.

Between 1986 and 2010, Piniella managed the Yankees, Reds, Mariners, Devil Rays and Cubs, compiling a record of 1,835-1,713. He continues to reside in Tampa.

STEVE BLASS

Despite weighing only 165 pounds, Steve Blass became one of the best pitchers on one of the NL's fastest-improving teams in the late Sixties. "He's gone from the bullpen to the number five starter and now he's our stopper," raved Larry Shepherd, who managed Pittsburgh in 1968.

That year, Blass went 18-6, led the circuit with a .750 winning percentage and hurled seven shutouts. Three of those whitewashes came against the hard-hitting Braves. Only four other pitchers bested Blass's 2.12 ERA. Pete Rose observed, "Nobody pitched me like Blass did" in 1968, adding, "He hits the corners with his good pitches and with something on the ball."

Blass was a kid at heart and well-liked in the Pirates' clubhouse. "I still have cardboard boxes of bubblegum cards at home, with pictures of the batters I'm facing," he acknowledged early in his career. He was also great with the fans and autograph seekers. Veteran hurler Bob Friend, his road roommate in the early years, was a valuable mentor.

Steve's first MLB start was one of his career highlights. The Pirates were on the road and he was matched up against Dodgers ace Don Drysdale. Before the game, teammate Bill Mazeroski told him, only half-jokingly, "Pitch a shutout, kid, and we'll play for a tie." Blass took the mound, and with the Dodgers' vulgar third base coach, Leo Durocher, hectoring him with profanities and insults the whole contest through, he pitched a complete-game victory.

Steve hailed from Connecticut, and his family enjoyed listening to Pirates games on clear-channel KDKA-AM after he joined the corsairs. They also made the 100-mile drive to Shea Stadium to watch Pirates-Mets games numerous times. Blass spent his winters back home, working as a truck driver for a company that reconditioned athletic equipment. After his big year, speaking engagements started coming his way, as well.

The Pirates fell short of a division title in both 1969 and 1970, with Blass going 26-22 over the two-year period, but the Bucs hit their stride in 1971 and the righty was a big part of the story.

Blass was a 15-game winner with five shutouts during the 1971 season and won a pair of World Series games against Baltimore, including the pivotal final contest. Following the Series, Blass's hometown held a day in his honor, drawing 4,000 attendees – more than the village's actual population. Schools were dismissed at 12:30 p.m. so students could participate in the festivities, which featured an 18-car motorcade. Republican Senator Lowell Weicker was among those on hand to honor the local hero.

Even in stardom, Blass was humble, commenting, "I don't have the type of fastball to overpower hitters and my curve isn't that good. Now I have direction on my slider and it has made the difference."

He was also thrilled to be making his living by playing a sport. "Nobody loved the baseball life more than I did…I was having the time of my life," he later wrote. "I expected to win. It was fun. I felt, to a certain degree, that I had mastered my craft." While on road trips, he often played poker with teammates.

Blass enjoyed one more brilliant season in 1972, winning 19 games and finishing second in the Cy Young voting. During that year, Steve and his family moved permanently to Pittsburgh, buying a home four houses away from road roommate and drinking buddy Dave Giusti. The Pirates graciously loaned him $25,000 interest-free for the down payment.

Then, after his finest season, came what he called "the worst experience of my baseball life." His control was suddenly gone during the 1973 season, resulting in walks, hit batsmen, wild pitches, base hits and a 9.85 ERA in 23 outings. "There were nights when I would just come home and sit in the backyard, wondering why all this stuff was going on," he recalled. Most mysterious was that his control seemed fine in the bullpen. He compared it to being solid at the driving range and dreadful on the course.

Pirates fans were supportive, sending him about 100 letters of encouragement every week. Steve tried relaxation exercises, hypnotism and Transcendental Meditation. He visited a psychologist who had worked with pitcher Don Sutton. But nothing helped, and he never figured out how or why he went from being an elite star one year to the league's worst pitcher the next.

Impressively, he didn't become a recluse. After failing to regain his control in 1974 and the spring of 1975, he pursued his post-pitching professions, first in class-ring sales with Jostens, operating a baseball camp for 11 years, and public relations for a brewer; and later as the radio voice of the Pirates. His ability to tell amusing baseball stories on the air may have been second to none. Blass, who continues to live in Pittsburgh, had a lifetime record of 103-76 with a 3.63 ERA.

VIC DAVALILLO

An exceptional contact hitter, Vic Davalillo was just the seventh Venezuelan to make the big leagues, playing from 1963 to 1980. At five-foot-seven he was one of the game's shortest players; his brother, named Yo-Yo, a shortstop for the 1953 Senators, stood just five-foot-three. Originally a pitcher, Vic played five years of minor league ball before breaking in with Cleveland.

As a rookie, he flashed signs of stardom, hitting for power and average, blazing around the bases, and covering ample ground in center field. A broken wrist -- sustained on an errant Hank Aguirre pitch -- seemed to rob him of his power, but Vic still finished 1963 with a solid .292 batting average and led the league's outfielders with 10 assists.

In 1964, he became the fourth Indian to win a gold glove. He landed an all-star berth in 1965, when he hit .301 (third best in the league) with a career-high 26 stolen bases.

Gradually, he had more trouble hitting left-handers. Vic also had an affinity for the bottle. Teammate Gus Gil recalled walking into a near-empty hotel bar with him in 1967. Vic ordered and quickly knocked back three rum-and-cokes, strolled back to the bar, and ordered several more, to the surprise of the bartender, who was looking around to see if there were other patrons in the lounge that he had not noticed.

When under the influence, his temper became short. Vic traveled with a portable record player and Gil recalled the night that Davalillo returned to the team's road hotel after drinking and discovered that his roommate, Chico Salmon, was using it. Vic became enraged and started screaming, requiring teammates to intervene to protect Salmon's life and limb. On at least a couple of occasions, Vic showed up at the ballpark under the influence, with teammates making sure he didn't get too close to the manager or coaching staff.

Following a trade to the Angels in June 1968, Vic's bat caught fire again, and he finished sixth in the AL with a .277 batting average. Upset over the end of his first marriage in early 1969, it is believed that he suffered a breakdown and was hospitalized for a couple of weeks. He soon remarried another gal – evidently over the telephone. Off to a poor start in the 1969 season, he was traded to St. Louis for outfielder Jim Hicks.

Later, between 1970 and 1972, he turned in three excellent seasons as a platoon outfielder for the Cardinals and Pirates. The veteran later played for the A's, continued to play ball in Mexico and Venezuela, and returned as a pinch-hitting specialist for the Dodgers. He was a lifetime .279 hitter with 1,122 hits, 36 homers, and 125 stolen bases. After baseball, he returned to his native Venezuela where he lived off his baseball pension and enjoyed giving youth baseball clinics until passing away in 2023.

ROY FACE

Roy Face's pitching career was remarkable for a number of reasons. First, he relied on the forkball more than any other pitcher of his era, an estimated 70 percent of the time. Due to its movement, it was difficult to track, let alone hit. More than once, Face was asked if he knew which way the pitch was going to break. "No, but neither does the hitter," was his standard response.

Second, the Pirates' right-hander was surprisingly durable, enough so to get into 848 games over 16 years. As of 2023, he was still ranked number 39 all-time in pitching appearances. The only time he went on the disabled list, in 1965, it was not for arm trouble, but rather due to knee surgery. He led his league in appearances twice and saves three years.

Third, he is best remembered for his work in 1959 and 1960. In the former year, he posted an 18-1 record and set a still-standing record for winning percentage at .947. Critics noted that a number of his wins came after he allowed the opposing team to tie the score, but his seventh-place finish in the MVP derby reflects the respect he commanded. Then in 1960, when the Pirates won the world championship, Face contributed 10 wins and 24 saves. He notched saves in each of the three games the Bucs won during the 1960 fall classic, as well.

Fourth, Face stood only five-foot-eight, hardly the prototypical specimen for a pitcher. It simply didn't matter. He found a niche with the Pirates, for whom he pitched from 1953 to 1968. He loved Pittsburgh and lived down the street from Churchill Country Club. When he made his 802nd and final appearance for Pittsburgh, he tied Walter Johnson for another record, the most pitching appearances with one team. When the Pirates sold Roy to the Tigers where he could be part of a championship team, his teammates congratulated him one by one, followed by the team's ushers. Before leaving for Detroit, he spent an hour in the Forbes Field grandstands, signing autographs for fans. Then he was on to join his new team.

After concluding his career with the Tigers and Expos, he finished with a 104-95 record, 3.48 ERA and 191 saves. Though originally from New York state, he remained in Pittsburgh, working as a carpentry foreman at Mayview State Hospital. He has lived in the town of North Versailles since 1983.

WILLIE STARGELL

One of the most beloved figures in baseball, Willie Stargell enjoyed a Pirates career from 1962 to 1982. "Willie and I played in Roswell in 1959," recalled catcher Ron Brand. "He was skinny, gangly, and funny. I never would have believed he would become the player he grew into. I hit 11 homers to his nine, and had a higher batting average, and was a better player then. But he got bigger and better every year and wound up in the Hall of Fame."

"Stargell swings what I call a loud bat," manager Danny Murtaugh said in 1964. "When he connects you hear it all over the ballpark." Murtaugh also praised Stargell for reporting to camp 20 pounds trimmer than the previous September. He cemented his role as the Pirates' left fielder that year, but Murtaugh didn't hand him the job. He challenged Willie to compete with Jerry Lynch, Manny Mota and Ted Savage to earn the role. Stargell responded, making the all-star team for the first of seven times.

After that 1964 season, Stargell had surgery to remove a pin from a hip, eliminate bone chips from his left elbow, and repair torn cartilage in his left knee. To strengthen his wrists, he used weights each morning on a tip from Ted Williams.

One of his early-career highlights came on June 24, 1965 at Dodgers Stadium. He slugged three homers in a game and narrowly missed a fourth. The first two shots came against Don Drysdale, the last one against John Purdin. Stargell hit .272 with 27 home runs that season. As his knee periodically needed draining, he would rest for 48 hours after each such procedure. Stargell credited manager Harry Walker with helping him improve as a hitter.

In June of 1966, Stargell pounded nine straight hits, which was one shy of the NL record, last achieved by Woody Williams of the 1943 Reds. Stargell's bid for another hit was stopped by Bob Gibson. When reporters asked him about the streak, the humble slugger said, "I wish you'd talk about the team instead of me." Stargell closed out the season with a .315 clip and 33 home runs for the third-place Buccos.

Stargell's weight was a constant source of friction, never more so than when he reported to camp in 1967 at 230 pounds, which was 20 pounds heavier than the Pittsburgh brass recommended. Their solution was to put him on a crash diet of no potatoes, no desserts, and limited liquids. After three weeks on that regimen, his weight had *increased* to 235 pounds! He finally trimmed down by eating grapefruit for breakfast and lunch, followed by a broiled steak for dinner.

The Pirates dropped to sixth place in 1967, and Stargell's production decline was part of the reason. His .271 batting average and 20 home runs were respectable, but a decline from the previous year. Willie did make history by becoming the first slugger to drive two pitches to the right field roof of Forbes Field in the same season. That winter, general manager Joe Brown said he would be willing to trade anyone – except his wife. But Stargell remained a Pirate.

The Bucs placed a disappointing sixth again in 1968. Willie started strong, hitting .300 through the end of May. One of his season highlights was a May contest against the Cubs in which he delivered five hits, three of which were home runs. But by season's end, his average had declined to .237, with arm, neck and leg injuries hampering his offense.

In 1969, the Pirates boosted their offense from 583 to 725 runs, but settled for third place in the NL East. Stargell was part of that power surge, hitting .307 with 29 home runs – his best season in three years. After being benched against tough lefties for years, new manager Larry Shepherd allowed Stargell to play no matter who was one the mound – to positive results. Cardinals manager Red Schoendienst observed, "The big fellow is dangerous no matter who is throwing the baseball. You make a mistake to him and the ball is gone."

The dawn of the Seventies brought Stargell's most satisfying years. In 1971, he led the NL in home runs and led his club to the division crown. Voters placed him second in MVP voting. During the NLCS and World Series, he went into a frustrating 5-for-38 slump, but the Pirates nonetheless bested the Giants and then the Orioles to become world champions.

Willie's solid 1972 season led to another division title, then an NLCS loss to the Reds. Stargell led the NL in homers, RBI and slugging percentage in 1973. He helped his team to the division crown again in 1974 and 1975.

The career culmination came in 1979 when "Pops" led the "We Are Family" Pirates to the world championship. At age 39, he shared the MVP honors with Keith Hernandez of the Cardinals.

"He had a special warmth and humility," recalled Branch Rickey III. "He never had too little time for a kid wanting to spend time with him. You never had a sense that he was too busy."

Stargell, who played left field and first base, would have benefited from the designated hitter rule in his later years, but that would have required him to move to an AL team and leave Pittsburgh. Neither he nor the Pirates wanted to consider that move. He played through 1982, retiring with a .282 batting average, 475 home runs and 2,232 hits. A diabetic, he died at the age of 61 in Wilmington, North Carolina, in 2001.

DENNIS BENNETT

The next several player profiles are of pitchers who shared one thing in common: Free-spirited personalities. Their stories and levels of success differ but their love of off-the-field adventure are similar.

Southpaw Dennis Bennett attended Shasta College in Redding, California. His brother, Dave Bennett, made a single appearance for the Phillies in 1964 at the age of 18. Dennis was a wild-spirited Californian with imaginative ways to risk bodily injury. He fought wildfires and rode in the rodeo. After becoming a pitcher for the 1961 Chattanooga team, he challenged a teammate to race him down a hill doing summersaults, and messed up his knee in the process, requiring surgery. He evidently carried a gun with him on baseball road trips, and once shot out a hotel room light rather than get up and turn the switch.

Bennett's work with the Phillies from 1962 to 1964 was his best, winning 30 games while losing 28. He was part of the Phillies' collapse in September 1964, and after the season, they swapped him to Boston for first baseman Dick Stuart.

The Red Sox management in 1965 had visions of success from an evolving core of young pitchers including Bennett, but the club endured a 62-100 season, and Dennis was of little help. He had never fully recovered from a broken ankle, pelvis, and shoulder blade sustained in a violent January 1963 auto accident in Puerto Rico. He started the 1965 season hurt and won only six games. "What Bennett lacked was the consistency that would have allowed him to be part of the rotation," wrote Peter Golenbock. "Bennett claims that if healthy he could have produced far greater numbers and I can't disagree."

Bennett and his teammates were in for a shock when Dick Williams became the new manager in 1967. Williams was a disciplinarian, perhaps because some of the players he inherited required considerable discipline. Bennett, in particular, was called out by the new manager, and he was traded part-way through what became their league-championship 1967 season. Dennis concluded the campaign with the Mets.

After a short stay with the Angels in 1968, Bennett finished out his pro career with four seasons mostly with the Hawaii Islanders. The Islanders always seemed to have a collection of aging pitchers. When he won 18 games for Hawaii in 1970 at age 30, he was a spring chicken on a staff that also included Roy Face (age 42), Jim Coates (37), Juan Pizzaro (33), Gary Bell (33), Bob Allen (32), and Phil Ortega (30).

In an interview decades later on the Baseball Historian web site, Bennett said that he threw primarily a fastball and curve, plus a changeup that he learned from a minor-league coach named Ben Tincup. Phillies coach Al Widmar taught him the slider, but he didn't throw it often.

Bennett related that the frightening traffic accident in Puerto Rico was the turning point in his career. He had just completed his rookie season, going 9-9 on a losing Phillies team and was in Puerto Rico to pitch winter ball. The taxi driver had a fatal heart attack, and the cab spun out of control. Bennett was thrown through the windshield. Widmar was in the back seat, along with a player named Joel Gibson and his wife. "If I had it to do over again, I wouldn't have gone to Puerto Rico," he exclaimed.

Following his pitching career, Bennett was briefly a pitching coach in Triple-A ball, and later owned commercial buildings, bars, and retail businesses in Oregon. He and his wife raised nine children. He was age 72 when he passed away in 2012.

TED DAVIDSON

A native of Las Vegas, Ted Davidson was a promising left-handed reliever for the Reds whose career nosedived after he was shot in the chest and abdomen by his estranged wife.

The shooting occurred in March 1967 during spring training in Tampa. The pitcher was in the Park Lane Lounge on Kennedy Boulevard when Mary Ruth Davidson arrived and an argument ensued. The hurler exited the back door, while his wife went out the front door and the shooting occurred in the driveway. She then drove to the Carousel Bar on West Platt Street, where she phoned the police to turn herself in. Charges of "assault to commit murder" were dismissed when Ted twice failed to show up for hearings.

Davidson's wounds required 90 minutes of surgery. Manager Dave Bristol and teammate Tony Perez visited him in a hospital and according to the RedlegNation.com website, Bristol fainted when he saw Davidson's bloodied condition.

Since 1961, Davidson had progressed through the Reds' minor-league system with stops in Palatka, Columbia, Topeka, Macon and San Diego. He was recalled mid-way through the 1965 season with high praise from San Diego general manager Eddie Leishman, who noted that Ted had developed a knuckler to supplement his heat. On his first whirl through the NL, he notched a 4-3 record and 2.23 ERA. The lefty stayed with the Reds through the entire 1966 season but saw too many of his pitches smashed into the cheap seats.

Following his recovery from the 1967 shooting, he appeared in only nine games for the Reds in addition to some outings at Triple-A Buffalo. While hoping for a complete recovery in 1968, he had a bloated 6.23 ERA for the Reds by June, prompting a trade. With the Braves, Davidson had a 6.75 ERA, as well as an 8.47 ERA at Triple-A Richmond. He pitched in the Cubs' and Indians' organizations in 1969.

Little information is available about his life after baseball, other than that he passed away in 2006, just shy of his 67th birthday, in Bullhead City, Arizona, a town alongside the Colorado River, about 90 miles from Vegas.

GEORGE BRUNET

The ultimate blues traveler, George Brunet made 39 stops in a 21-year pro career. He pitched in such obscure loops as the Tar Heel League, the Sooner State League, the Cotton States League, the Big State League, and the Evangeline League. His big-league itinerary featured stints in Kansas City, Milwaukee, Houston, Baltimore, California, Seattle, Washington, Pittsburgh, and St. Louis.

The Californian signed his first contract with Tigers scout Schoolboy Rowe, a former pitching great. Right from the start, he was plagued by control trouble. In a game in 1959 with the A's, he issued five bases-loaded walks (a dubious big-league record). He also had some bad luck. Over one stretch in the minor leagues, his team failed to score in more than 50 innings with him on the mound.

According to Bruce Markusen in *The Hardball Times,* "Though he had a live arm and a repertoire of four pitches, he was often overweight and out of shape. He also had a furious temper, which boiled over when he pitched badly or his fielders flopped behind him. And then there were considerable off-the-field journeys, which found him in bars and unknown hotel rooms. This was a player who once the game ended, headed for the nearest watering hole to begin his latest round of heavy drinking."

Los Angeles Times writer Jim Murray noted in 1965, "Every time there was a song to be sung, a bottle to be opened, a card to be turned over, a town to be closed up or a fight to be started, George was your man."

The classic Brunet story comes from spring training 1959 in West Palm Beach, when he was aspiring to make the A's pitching staff. A half-crocked Brunet finished up a night of drinking by standing in front of the team hotel, directing traffic. One of the cars that approached was occupied by the A's general manager Parke Carroll and manager Harry Craft, who soon enough dispatched him for more minor-league seasoning.

He finally solidified his big-league status with the Angels in 1965 and for the next four and a half seasons, he was one of the club's busiest pitchers. Yet, even in that role, he led the league in losses twice.

Mid-way through the 1969 season, the red-headed lefty was traded to the expansion Pilots, a notoriously poor team that included pitcher Jim Bouton, who was writing *Ball Four.* In the book, Bouton revealed that Brunet didn't wear undershorts, feeling the only time you would need them is when you get into an auto accident.

In 1970, it was on to the Senators and Pirates, where he posted a winning record of 9-7. The Pirates went on to win the world championship in 1971, but Brunet was not there to enjoy it. He was in St. Louis, where he yielded three home runs in just nine innings of work, leading to his unconditional release.

Brunet had no plans and no prospects for employment after baseball. A friend, Chico Carrasquel, invited him to the Mexican League, where he pitched for four more seasons, and then became a manager. Brunet found he liked living in Mexico and was still a resident there when he suffered a fatal heart attack in 1991 at the age of 56.

MARSHALL BRIDGES

Young Marshall Bridges captured the attention of baseball scouts when he pitched for the Negro American League All Stars against the Campanella All Stars during their 1952 tour of the South. The hard-throwing left-hander pocketed a $10,000 bonus when he signed with the Giants.

Subsequently, Bridges' career was characterized by changes of address and extra-curricular episodes. His nickname was "the Rug" – as in "lies like a rug."

Oddly, the Giants auditioned him as a first baseman, which would have been a waste of his great arm. Bridges was acquired by the Braves organization in 1955 and dispatched to the Cardinals farm system in 1958.

Finally breaking into the majors with the Cards at age 28 in 1959, he had a 6-3 record as a rookie. Yet, on August 2, 1960, with the Cardinals 10 games over .500, general manager Bing Devine gave up on him, and the Reds claimed him on waivers. Bridges responded with two great months, posting a 4-0 record down the stretch. In another twist, he proved ineffective in 1961, and the pennant-bound Reds farmed him back to the minors.

The journey continued to the Bronx before the 1962 season, where he played an unexpectedly large role, replacing the aging Luis Arroyo as closer. He won eight games and saved 18 others, with manager Ralph Houk calling him his "life-line reliever."

Marshall's personal luck ran out in October. During the World Series, he pitched in a pair of games that the Yankees lost, in one case serving up the first slam in World Series history to Chuck Hiller of the Giants. The Yankees nonetheless prevailed in the Series.

Bridges' bad luck continued on a Wednesday night the following February. The Yankees held their 1963 training camp in Fort Lauderdale, then a deeply segregated city. One evening before the formal start of spring training, the 31-year-old Bridges went to the "Pride of Fort Lauderdale Elks Lodge" for a drink. The lodge building, constructed in 1932, was a popular gathering spot for the African-American community.

"On the evening of February 13," wrote William Ryczek in *The Yankees in the Early 1960s,* "Bridges was at the Elks Club, making a concerted effort to attract the attention of a 21-year-old woman named Carrie Lee Raysor. Bridges, married with three children, kept asking Ms. Raysor if she would go home with him. She said she wouldn't. When he persisted, she pulled out a small revolver and put a .25 caliber bullet into Bridges' left leg, just below the knee." He was hospitalized for several days and opted against surgery to recover quicker. Some interesting conversations with his wife presumably followed.

The Yankees emphasized that he was not intoxicated at the time and they took no formal disciplinary action. In fact, Houk and his teammates kidded Bridges upon his return. With the bullet still lodged in his leg, he made a full comeback, but played a lesser role for the 1963 Yankees – Hal Reniff took over as closer -- and saw no action in the World Series.

The club sold Bridges to the Senators after the season. He pitched two more seasons for Washington, and later hurled for Hawaii. After baseball, he worked in Mississippi as a handy man at the State Capitol building. Bridges passed away in 1990 due to cancer at age 59, and is buried in Garden Memorial Park in Jackson, Mississippi.

Bo Belinsky

The highlight of Bo Belinsky's pitching career came on May 5, 1962, when the Angels rookie no-hit the Orioles. Team owner Gene Autry and general manager Fred Haney were on hand at Chavez Ravine Park, wearing suits and neckties reflective of the era, to congratulate the 25-year-old lefty. Baltimore's Steve Barber, the losing pitcher in the 2-0 contest, walked over to the Angels' clubhouse to salute the man of the hour. As the league's first no-hitter since 1958, the achievement was big news. Belinsky's record at the time was a perfect 5-0.

Thereafter, any news Belinsky made was nearly always related to his extracurricular activities. "No Angel – no major league player ever – received more publicity for accomplishing less," summarized writer Ross Newhan. Belinsky drew fines and suspensions for breaking curfew and showing up at the park late. He disregarded instructions from the front office, feuded with reporters, hired an agent and took on small acting bits. He dated leading Hollywood ladies, such as shapely blonde actress Mamie Van Doren, Gilligan's Island co-star Tina Louise, dancer Juliet Prowse, and actress-singer Connie Stevens. He later had short marriages to playmate Jo Collins and heiress Janie Weyerhauser.

Belinsky became best friends with teammate Dean Chance, and it's hard to know which pitcher's influence on the other was worse. In one regrettable instance, Belinsky, Chance and two women were hauled into a police precinct around 5:00 a.m. after Belinsky reportedly tried to drag one of the women out of a car, injuring her in the process.

Bo finished his 1962 rookie season with three shutouts, 10 wins, and a decent 3.56 ERA, but the red flag was his league-worst 122 walks in 187 innings. Meaning he was as wild on the mound as he was after hours. Rather than pitch winter ball, Belinsky signed on as an entertainer at the Silver Slipper Club casino in Paradise, Nevada.

His 1963 season was far worse, with a 2-9 record. Chance also endured a disappointing year at 13-18. As beat writer Braven Dyer reported the following spring, "Many feel Belinsky let the team down."

During the 1964 spring training in Palm Beach, Angels manager Bill Rigney surprised everyone by naming Belinsky and Chance as managers for an intra-squad game involving pitchers and coaches only. The final score was 15-15. Laughed hurler Art Fowler, "They warned that the day may come when the inmates take over the asylum. This is it."

That 1964 season proved to be Belinsky's only winning campaign, with a 9-8 record, while Chance emerged as a 20-game winner. Yet, even that season ended with controversy, as Belinsky got into an altercation in August in Washington, D.C. with the 64-year-old writer Braven Dyer in a Shoreham Hotel guest room at 2:15 a.m.

What went down? Dyer's account was that he had waited in the hotel lobby for Belinsky to return from a night on the town to ask him about a report that he was contemplating quitting baseball. After they spoke, the journalist filed his report, and later, Belinsky called his room and threatened him. Dyer said he went to Belinsky's room and the next thing he remembered he was lying on the floor bleeding, with Rigney and the team's trainer standing over him.

Belinsky's version differed. He asserted that Dyer had been drinking, approached Belinsky's room while the pitcher was brushing his teeth, and challenged him with drawn fists. Belinsky claimed he hit Dyer only once with the back of his hand (or perhaps with a water glass) and that any injury must have occurred when Dyer's head hit the doorknob or the floor. According to Belinsky and Chance, Dean was taking a hot bath and did not see the incident.

What was undisputed was that Dyer was taken to an emergency room, required six stitches behind his ear, and that he left the team beat three days later due to blurry vision. The Angels assigned Belinsky to Hawaii, and Bo refused to report without a pay raise, explaining that the demotion would cost him endorsement income and hurt his credit rating. At that point, the Angels suspended him. An editorial in *The Sporting News* said it was a shame that "a personable young man with so many obvious talents would hold them so cheaply and let them fritter away." The paper correctly predicted that his time with the Angels was finished.

Belinsky was traded to Philadelphia for pitcher Rudy May and first baseman Costen Shockley. He was not in the best of shape when he got to Clearwater for the 1965 spring training; in fact, just bending over to grab a batting helmet, he pulled a back muscle. He was 4-9 and 0-2 in two seasons with the Phillies; and just 3-9 in 1967 with the Astros.

In 1968, Belinsky took his act to Hawaii, the White Sox's Triple-A affiliate. Infielder Ernie Fazio roomed with Belinsky, saying later in *This Great Game*, "We had a great time, two single guys in Honolulu. Bo was a great guy to hang out with. He had his choice of any woman he wanted. And that's all I can really say about that."

Belinsky's comeback attempts with the 1969 Pirates and the 1970 Reds both failed. After baseball, his life unraveled, with broken marriages, alcoholism, drug abuse, and troubled relationships with hookers. He finally entered Alcoholics Anonymous in 1976 and, in fits and starts, put his life back together. He was 64 when he died at his home in Las Vegas in 2001. For his career, Belinsky had a 28-51 record with a 4.10 ERA. His minor-league record was 77-77.

DEAN CHANCE

Baseball had limited access to radar guns in the 1960s, meaning that we have incomplete knowledge of how hard each pitcher threw. We do know that Dean Chance was one of the hardest throwers. He was one of the AL's elite hurlers through much of the Sixties, winning 83 games over a six-year span. Dean was a 20-game winner for the 1964 Angels and the 1967 Twins, pacing the league in complete games both seasons.

Writer Maury Allen quoted Mickey Mantle as saying, "Every time I see his name (Chance) on a lineup card, I feel like throwing up." Chance kept his pitches below the waist, which were difficult for Mantle to launch. Decades later, executive Pat Gillick recalled Chance as "a fiery competitor who hated to lose." Teammate Ken McBride, who himself was a three-time all-star pitcher, said, "Chance had Hall of Fame stuff."

Dean grew up on a farm in Wooster, Ohio, a rural college town about an hour south of Cleveland. At West Salem Northwestern High School, there was no football program, so the baseball team played in the fall and the spring. The lanky youngster became a local legend as he threw 17 no-hitters (Rusty Ragg of Louisiana broke Chance's record with 19 no-hitters in the 1980s).

It's assumed that he was already throwing in excess of 90 MPH. Dean's team won the Class A state championship that final spring and he finished with a 52-1 record, which was on top of also leading the school to a state basketball championship. The Orioles signed him to a $30,000 bonus and when the AL expanded, he wound up with the Angels.

For a time, it seemed as if Chance might sabotage his own success. The farm boy married and had a child at a young age, but soon was divorced. In 1962, he posted a 14-10 record for a surprisingly strong third-place Halos team but Chance became mesmerized with Hollywood's social life. When Chance and Bo Belinsky began rooming together, the late nights – hanging out with Frank Sinatra, Dean Martin, and a variety of women -- took a toll. Chance's record dropped to 13-18 in 1963 and the Angels plummeted to ninth place.

Both pitchers tried to tone it down in 1964 and Chance in particular put together a brilliant campaign. Capitalizing on a sinking, heavy fastball and a roundhouse curve, he went 20-9 with a superb 1.65 ERA and 11 shutouts, earning the Cy Young award. Dean sought a mid-season pay hike, which did not go over well in the front office. After a game in which Dean struck out 12 hitters, he took a shot at his teammates, quipping, "I didn't dare let them hit it to anybody." Teammates responded by filling his locker with trash the next day, and everyone enjoyed a good laugh. With the hurler leading the way, the Angels climbed back to fifth place with an 82-80 record.

Chance went 15-10 in 1965 and then 12-17 in 1966. At that point, owner Gene Autry and his front office chose to seek offense, so they traded Chance to Minnesota, getting first baseman Don Mincher, outfielder Jimmie Hall and hurler Pete Cimino in return.

Few were surprised when Chance turned in a brilliant 20-14 all-star season for Minnesota in 1967. His no-hitter against Cleveland was one of a number of highlights. With the Twins battling for the pennant until the bitter end, he lost the season's final game to Boston by a score of 5-3. That allowed the Red Sox to win the pennant, with Minnesota and Detroit tied for second place, just one game out.

Chance went 16-16 in 1968 and led the Twins in wins, innings, strikeouts and shutouts. But in 1969, back trouble put him on the shelf. His Twins made the post-season, but he got shelled in a relief appearance against the Orioles in the ALCS.

When the Twins and Indians executed a six-player trade before the 1970 campaign, Chance welcomed the chance to play closer to home, in front of his parents and old friends. He went 9-8 and before the season was over, the salary-slashing Indians sold him to the Mets.

Dean's final season was 1971 with the Tigers. He had trouble locating his pitches and went 4-6 for Detroit. Never a great fielder, he led the league in errors for a fourth time. He was released after the season and retired with a 128-115 record and an impressive 2.92 ERA along with 33 shutouts.

Chance worked as a boxing promoter, real estate manager, carnival barker and finally as president of the International Boxing Association which he ran from his basement. He remained a close friend of Belinsky and both came to accept Christ as their savior in their later years. Chance, who died in Wooster in 2015 at the age of 74, is a member of the Angels Hall of Fame.

ROGER MARIS

Roger Maris was already a 25-year-old all-star outfielder when he arrived in the Bronx to play for the Yankees. The Indians had sacrificed him in a deal with Kansas City for Vic Power and Woodie Held. Then the A's gave up on him in a seven-player trade. Maris had delivered a solid season for the 1959 A's despite his early-season appendectomy, but after the team placed seventh, the club was determined to make changes.

In Roger's first game as a Yankee in 1960, he delivered four hits including two home runs. That set the tone for the next two seasons in which the Yankees won pennants and Maris received two MVP awards.

Despite his heroics, the 1961 season was personally difficult. As Maris and Mantle chased Babe Ruth's single-season homer record, the pressure particularly affected Maris. He received nasty letters, started losing clumps of hair, and could not open the newspaper sports page without seeing disparaging coverage. Reports circulated that Maris and Mantle were feuding. Nothing could be further from the truth; they were actually sharing a New York apartment with Bob Cerv.

Whereas today a team would set up a post-game press conference, in the Sixties the reporters would crowd around the player's locker, perhaps eight or ten at a time. With 50 or more reporters looking for quotes, Maris would have to answer the same questions, over and over again.

Traditionalists resented Maris having an eight-game longer season, at 162 contests, with which to pursue Ruth's seemingly sacred record. "Maris has no right to break Ruth's record," said Rogers Hornsby, a Ruth contemporary. Commissioner Ford Frick sided with traditionalists, insisting an asterisk be placed next to the name of anyone breaking Ruth's record in more 154 games. The asterisk seemed to cheapen the achievement. Besides the longer season, another factor in Maris's favor was the fact that the AL had expanded from eight to 10 teams, resulting in a 20 percent increase in the number of pitchers. Mantle got hurt and fell out of the chase, while Maris hit the record-breaking 61st homer in the 161st game of the season, against Tracy Stallard.

Although Maris was sometimes dour, aloof and uncommunicative with the press, he was well-liked by his teammates. Pitcher Dick Tomanek recalled, "We roomed together with the Indians and the Athletics. He was a good friend and a great talent." Teammate Bobby Richardson later wrote, "Roger was the most dedicated family man I knew in baseball…He and his wife Pat believed that Kansas City provided a better environment for their kids to grow up in. But being away from his family for a big part of the year was clearly difficult for Roger…Because he was a quiet guy, we had a more reserved friendship than I had with other teammates, but we were close nonetheless."

By the end of the 1962 season, as the Yankees won their third straight pennant, it would have been easy to imagine Maris becoming a Hall of Famer. He recorded his fourth straight all-star season and third consecutive year with 100 RBI. He was also more relaxed. Maris said, "This is so different from last year, you have no idea. I'm in an altogether different frame of mind than a year ago at this time. Last year, the pressure was unbearable. I was beaten and tired after chasing Babe Ruth's record all year. Now, I'm relaxed." The Yankees won the Series over the Giants in seven games.

In 1963, Roger was again productive with 23 homers but missed 72 games due to injuries, and went just 0-for-5 in the World Series. He turned in a solid season in 1964, hitting .281 with 26 circuit clouts, but the next two campaigns were badly marred by injuries.

As he related to writer Peter Golenbock, "In '65, I had a broken hand all year…I slid into home plate, jammed my fingers into the umpire's shoes…This was in May. I dislocated two fingers, and they pulled the fingers back out and put them back in the joint…We left New York the following day and went to Washington. The first time I took a swing in Washington, something popped in my hand and that was it." Although x-rays were taken, Maris did not learn until after the season that the hand was broken. Maris hit only eight home runs in 46 games in 1965. The following season, no longer able to grip the bat in the same way, he went deep only 13 times in 119 games. He batted below .240 both years as the cheers at Yankee Stadium gave way to booing.

In December 1966, after the Yankees traded Maris to the Cardinals for third baseman Charley Smith, Roger contemplated leaving the game. August Busch talked him out of retirement and the Cardinals honored his $75,000 annual salary for the next two seasons, as he played right field on a platoon basis. The Cards won pennants both seasons, giving Maris seven league championship rings in a nine-year period plus World Series bonuses.

Maris retired after the 1968 season, still only 33 years of age. He was a lifetime .260 hitter with 275 home runs and 1,325 hits. In 152 post-season at bats, Maris hit just .217 with six home runs. During his playing days, Maris, his wife, and seven children made their home in Independence, Missouri. After striking up a friendship with Busch, he moved to Gainesville, Florida, where he ran a Budweiser distributorship. He passed away at the M.D. Anderson Cancer Center in Houston in 1985 at the age of 57.

BOBBY RICHARDSON

Second baseman Bobby Richardson was the first World Series MVP to have played on the losing team. The year was 1960, and the Pirates edged the Yankees in seven games, despite New York outscoring Pittsburgh 55-27. Richardson drove home 12 RBI, all but one of them in games that New York won. That performance, coupled with his steady glove work, led to his selection, instead of his opposing second baseman, Bill Mazeroski, who won game seven for Pittsburgh with his walk-off home run. In addition to the honor, Bobby received a new Corvette.

Richardson often saved his best performances for the post-season. In 1961, he contributed nine hits while batting .391. In 1962, he made a miraculous diving stab of a Willie McCovey line drive, with two runners on base, to end the Series, sealing the Yankees' championship. Furthermore, in the 1964 World Series, he set a new series record with 13 hits. His lifetime World Series batting average was .305.

During his stellar career, Bobby was a seven-time all-star who won five straight gold gloves. Though only a .266 career hitter during regular season action, in his standout 1962 campaign, he hit .302 and led the league with 209 hits and 20 sacrifice bunts. He finished second to Mickey Mantle in the MVP balloting and credited coach Wally Moses with helping him improve as a hitter.

He grew up in South Carolina as the son and grandson of tombstone manufacturers. He carved his own bats out of wood and practiced hitting stone chips. He and his family were Cardinals fans, since the KMOX-AM signal carried all the way from St. Louis to his community. At age 14, he was inspired by the movie *Pride of the Yankees*.

The following spring, a Yankees farm team held spring training in his home town. The manager, Mayo Smith, watched the 15-year-old play high school ball, and told him that at graduation time, Smith would ensure he had a chance to sign with the Yankees.

The two stayed in touch, and although Bobby had a wide choice of options, he signed with New York. That led to a trip to Yankee Stadium where for three days he took grounders on the field, watched the club's stars take batting practice and observed games from the stands. When Mantle, already a star, put his arm on Richardson's shoulder and said, "C'mon kid, take some swings," it was the start of a lifelong friendship.

Bobby loved baseball, but considered leaving the game in 1954 amidst a hitting slump, booing and homesickness. Then came a timely letter from a former coach, reciting Matthew 6:33: "Seek ye first the kingdom of God and his righteousness; and all these things will be added unto you." It reminded him to keep everything in the proper perspective.

After that season, good things indeed began to happen. While at church, he met his future wife, Betsy Dotson. Meanwhile, he was promoted to the Triple-A Denver Bears team in 1955. Still only 19, word came that Yankees infielder Gil McDougald had gone onto the disabled list. Hence, Bobby got his first brief taste of MLB, and Mantle was the first one to greet him.

Back at Denver in 1956, the young player tied the knot with Betsy. Jo LaSorda, wife of teammate Tommy LaSorda, helped Betsy adjust to life as a baseball wife. On road trips, Bobby roomed with Tony Kubek, who would be his roomie for most of his career. Bobby's first son was born in 1957. Then in 1958, Bobby's second son was born on the same day in the same hospital as teammate Enos Slaughter's daughter.

Bobby solidified his standing with the team in 1959, when he hit .301. That season, however, the Yankees drifted down to an uncharacteristic third place as the White Sox captured the pennant.

During the 1960 season, the Orioles and White Sox were giving the Yankees a run for their money during the pennant race. Manager Casey Stengel was frustrated at the lack of offense from his infield, and for a time, Bobby was benched, later finishing with a .252 batting average and only 26 RBI, though the Yankees captured the flag. That same year, he and Betsy had built the house they would occupy for more than 50 years.

Following that season, Stengel was fired. As Richardson wrote, "Casey was a good man. But his platooning, his constant lineup shuffling and his love of pinch-hitting had become frustrating to me." Under new manager Ralph Houk, there was never any question who would play second base, as it was always Richardson. The Yankees won the world championship.

Teammates respected Richardson's Christian faith. In his autobiography, Bobby writes that Moose Skowron would spew out profanities after striking out. He would say, "Excuse me, Bobby," as he passed in the dugout, then would resume his profanities.

In 1964 he received the Lou Gehrig Award. Established by the Phi Delta Theta fraternity, the award honors the player who best exemplifies the character of Lou Gehrig on and off the field. Bobby helped the club win the pennant, but manager Yogi Berra was fired after the losing World Series. Richardson felt Yogi had done a good job in light of team members' injuries and disagreed with the notion that Yogi had "lost the team."

In 1965, Bobby began noticing a troubling "me-first" attitude among some of the younger players. He contemplated retirement, but the Yankees, having not groomed a successor, convinced him to play one more year. They paid him $45,000 in 1966 and gave him three $5,000 checks to present to the charities of his choice. In September, he became the 10th Yankee player to have "a day" dedicated to him. With family and friends on hand, evangelist singer George Beverly Shea sang "How Great Thou Art." Among the gifts he received was a gun case (a gift from his teammates) presented by his new road roommate, Steve Hamilton.

The most famous of his teammates was Mickey Mantle. "My whole career was with Mickey," Richardson recalled in an interview in *Risen* magazine. "My 12 years in New York he was there, and we were close in this sense – I didn't go out with him after ballgames, he'd go out with Whitey and they'd be drinking a little bit. I roomed my whole career with Tony Kubek, who knew the Lord, and we'd go out together and eat. We were known as the milkshake twins." But the relationship between Richardson and Mantle was always one of mutual respect.

Mantle retired two years after Richardson. Years later, Mantle gave a televised interview with Bob Costas in which he acknowledged being a heavy drinker and an unfaithful husband. He stated that he had stopped drinking, but still felt a void in his life. Many people had been praying for Mantle to come to know the Lord for years, and they intensified their prayers after that interview.

Not long later, Bobby and his wife received a very early morning phone call from Mantle and his wife. Mantle had undergone a liver transplant operation and was taking heavy drugs to prevent rejection of the new organ. He was miserable and discouraged, and wanted to speak with Richardson about his faith. Through that conversation and subsequent visits, he helped lead Mantle to dedicate his life to the Lord. When Mantle passed away, by his own request, Richardson officiated the services.

Bobby made numerous friends in baseball beyond his Yankees teammates. He counted Brooks Robinson and Albie Pearson as close friends, and sometimes hunted with Billy O'Dell.

As the head baseball coach for the University of South Carolina from 1970 to 1976, Bobby built a winning program and won visibility for the school by holding exhibition contests against the Yankees and the Mets, who were managed by his former teammate Yogi Berra. In 1976, at the request of President Gerald Ford, Richardson ran for Congress as a Republican. Joe DiMaggio, among other baseball figures, traveled to South Carolina at his own expense to campaign for Bobby. After narrowing losing the election, he later returned to coaching at Coastal Carolina University and Liberty University. He has also been a much sought-after speaker at church conferences, and he gave his testimony during five Billy Graham Crusades in the mainland United States, Hawaii, and Japan.

Speaking for many, pitcher Fritz Peterson wrote in 2017, "Richie is an honest, wonderful man, and getting to play with him was one of the greatest honors of my life."

CLETE BOYER

In 1959, the Yankees slipped to an uncharacteristically low third-place, a humbling summer for a proud franchise coming off four straight pennants. The team had several problems, one of which was the hot corner. Hector Lopez was seeing most of the action, and manager Casey Stengel was seeing red at Lopez's defensive deficiencies. Clete Boyer, whom the Yankees had acquired from the A's, saw action at third base as well, but struggled at the plate. Since his fielding and throwing arm were exceptional, the Yankees hoped his bat would improve enough for him to claim the third-base job in 1960.

New York didn't need Boyer to become a big RBI man. They already had Mickey Mantle, Yogi Berra, Elston Howard and Moose Skowron to provide power, and added Roger Maris, as well. What they needed offensively was exactly what Clete delivered in 1960 -- a respectable .242 clip with 14 home runs and seven sacrifice bunts.

Boyer's chief contribution was tightening up the infield defense and that helped the pitchers become more effective. The negativity and back biting from the 1959 season dissipated and the club returned to the top of the standings, eight games ahead of second-place Baltimore.

Although Boyer's hitting dropped off in 1961, the Yankees had six players with 20 or more home runs, so they could afford weak production. Coach Frank Crosetti declared, "I have seen everybody who has played third base for this club since 1932, and this man is the best. What can't he do?" Reds manager Fred Hutchinson, after witnessing Boyer in the 1961 World Series, said, "Now, I have seen. Cletis is something special."

The 1962 season was one of Boyer's finest. He carried a potent bat into the World Series, where he delivered seven hits including a homer in seven games against the Giants.

Anchoring third base in New York through 1966, Boyer led the league's third sackers in assists three times and was in the top three in double plays five straight seasons. Only the presence of Brooks Robinson prevented Boyer from winning AL gold glove awards.

In 1966, after missing the pennant for the second straight year, the Yankees traded Boyer to Atlanta for outfield prospect Bill Robinson and veteran pitcher Chi Chi Olivo. The deal never panned out for New York; Robinson became a productive hitter, but not until he left the Yankees.

Meanwhile, Boyer had a career year in 1967, finishing in the NL's top 10 in home runs (26) and RBI (96), while batting .245. He garnered some MVP votes for the only time ever. Finding himself comfortable in Georgia, he opened a country western bar outside Atlanta called, "The Golden Glove."

After the season, Boyer unwisely ripped Braves teammate Rico Carty in the press for not giving 100 percent effort. When the following season got underway, Boyer found criticism coming back to him, as he endured a season-long slump. He was now making $45,000 per year – a healthy salary at that time – and expectations for his offensive contributions had risen.

Seemingly at risk of losing his position, Boyer rebounded in 1969. He hit .250 with 14 home runs, captured his only gold glove, and helped the Braves win the NL West. He contributed three RBI in Atlanta's three-game loss to the Mets in the NLCS.

Boyer's statistics were similar in 1970, but when the Braves' fortunes turned south, the finger pointing resumed. Boyer publicly criticized his manager (Lum Harris) and general manager (Paul Richards), which is never a wise move. Though still only 34 years old, he was released on June 2, 1971, as the Braves handed his position to young Darrell Evans. To the surprise of many fans, no other MLB team wanted him. He finished the season with the Hawaii Islanders.

Boyer next spent four seasons in Japan, where his roommate for a time was home-run king Sadaharu Oh. In those days, each Japanese team was permitted to have two foreign players. Boyer and Johnny Sipin were the imports on the 1972 through 1975 Taiyo clubs. Boyer flourished in Japan, hitting 71 homers over four seasons. He later coached in Japan and returned periodically for baseball reunions.

Yankees teammate Bobby Richardson wrote, "Even though Clete and I were friends, we lived opposite lifestyles. He was known for his hard living and constant battle with alcohol. I prayed many nights for my good friend. After he retired, Tony (Kubek) and I flew to Atlanta to see what we could do to help. Clete's family was concerned, too. One of his daughters prayed for him year after year." Richardson disclosed that on one of Boyer's visits, he accepted Christ as his savior.

Boyer was the brother of fellow major leaguers Ken and Cloyd Boyer. In 2000, he opened a restaurant in Cooperstown, called Clete Boyer's Hamburger Hall of Fame, where burgers were named for famous baseball stars. He could often be seen working in the restaurant and mixing with customers. A father of six, he passed away from a brain hemorrhage in 2007 in Atlanta. Boyer had a lifetime batting average of .242, with 1,396 hits including 162 home runs.

LUIS ARROYO

The year 1961 was one to remember for this five-foot-eight hurler from Puerto Rico. Although he had made the NL all-star team as a Cardinals rookie in 1958, his career had been inconsistent. The Cardinals, Pirates and Reds had dispatched him, and he had latched on to the Yankees in 1960.

The southpaw pitched in his native Puerto Rico before the 1961 season and led that island's winter league in ERA, which brought him a $300 grand prize. Today, that would be the equivalent of nearly $3,000. At least some of the award money likely went toward cigars, which he enjoyed as much as anyone in baseball.

Then came a frightening incident during the 1961 Yankees spring training camp, in which one player after another sustained injuries. The 34-year-old Arroyo was on the mound in an exhibition game when Jesse Gonder lined a wicked shot toward Arroyo's head. The hurler lifted his right, non-pitching arm to protect his head and sustained a fractured ulna bone, putting him out of action for about three weeks.

When he returned, Arroyo emerged as the league's best reliever. The improved effectiveness of his screwball meant he relied less on his rather ordinary curve. Writer Red Foley quipped, "He has more saves than a Coney Island lifeguard." Come mid-summer, he was tapped for the all-star team. According to writer Marty Appel, on a Whitey Ford Day held on September 9th, Arroyo rode onto the field on a cart with a huge Life Savers package, signifying his role in saving so many of Ford's wins.

When all was said and done, backed by his 15-5 record and 2.19 ERA, Arroyo placed sixth in the MVP voting. He also won game three of the World Series.

Late that summer, Arroyo received a letter that read, "I don't like Puerto Ricans. The next time you go to the mound at Yankee Stadium, I will shoot you through the head." Arroyo and manager Ralph Houk turned the letter over to the authorities for investigation, but Arroyo professed no concern, and nothing came of it.

Following his big season, Arroyo enjoyed a relaxed winter for the first time in 15 years, waiting until January to pitch in a few winter-ball games. Maybe it was the change in prep, but he struggled early in the 1962 season, lost Houk's confidence, and his career unraveled. After a disastrous start to the 1963 season, he spent most of that summer at Triple-A Richmond, hurling for manager Preston Gomez.

Arroyo retired with a 40-32 lifetime record and a 3.93 career ERA. Becoming a coach and scout, he was a popular figure at the annual Yankees old-timer games. Luis was 88 years old when he passed away from cancer in Puerto Rico in 2016.

HORACE CLARKE

St. Croix native Horace Clarke was the Yankees second baseman between Bobby Richardson and Willie Randolph. He took some blame for the Yankees' lean years between two championship eras, but never let it bother him. Looking back, he said, "New York is New York. If you don't win, you're going to hear about it."

St. Croix is the largest of the islands that comprise the U.S. Virgin Islands. Clarke was the fourth Virgin Islands player to make the major leagues, following outfielder Joe Christopher, pitcher Al McBean, and catcher Elmo Plaskett. He initially was not considered a premier prospect, but with each minor league rung he climbed, the more his play attracted the attention of the Yankees' front office.

Though never an all-star, Clarke was a competent fielder who perennially led the junior circuit in assists. A 1967 article by Jim Ogle in *The Sporting News* noted, "One of his biggest assets is the ability to flash far to his right to and turn 'hits' into outs with spectacular plays, which the fans have appreciated." Ogle wrote that "Clarke is the prototype of Charlie Gehringer, famous Detroit infielder, who went about his work so quietly that no one knew he was around."

Clarke told interviewer Kenneth Hogan in 2010, "They said I couldn't make the double play, but Gene Michael and I were tops in double plays a couple of years…My play was consistent over the years. I got on base and scored runs every day. During the time I played, I had the third-best fielding percentage of second basemen." Hogan called Clarke "one of the nicest gentlemen in the game I've ever spoken to."

A lifetime .256 hitter, he usually was among the Yankees' leaders in hits and stolen bases in a career that spanned from 1965 to 1974. Along the way, he collected some great memories. His first two home runs were grand slams. In a single season, he broke up no-hitters by Joe Niekro, Sonny Siebert and Jim Rooker in the ninth inning. His best season was 1969, when he hit .285 and swiped 33 bases.

He is said to be the last Yankee to live near the ballpark. A summer resident of the Concourse Plaza Hotel, he would walk the three blocks to the stadium, he told *The Daily News*. Babe Ruth and Mickey Mantle had lodged in the 1922 structure in its decades-long heyday, but the neighborhood's decline had resulted in mostly low-income renters by the late Sixties, when the facility's property manager was shot to death by an angry resident.

After closing out his career with the Padres, Clarke retired with 1,230 hits and 151 stolen bases. Returning to St. Croix, Clarke enjoyed the water, longtime friendships, and playing music weekly in a Caribbean-style band. Clarke passed away in Laurel, Maryland, in 2020.

STAN MUSIAL

Several excellent books have been written about this Hall of Famer's career, including his own autobiography, co-written with famed writer Bob Broeg. For purposes of this book about baseball in the 1960s, we focus on the latter days of his incredible career.

Musial had been in the majors since 1941, save for the 1945 season that he missed while in the service. He entered the Sixties with nothing more to prove. He already had accumulated more than 3,000 hits, won seven batting crowns, and collected three MVP awards. His Cardinals team had been victors in three of the four Worlds Series in which he had competed. Only Mel Ott had hit more home runs in the NL. Musial was well set financially with restaurant, real estate, and other business interests. Still, even at age 39 and coming off a disappointing 1959 season with a mediocre .255 batting average, he loved the game and had no intention of stepping away.

He spent two weeks with his family in Hawaii and then took a hunting trip to Texas. Only thereafter did he begin workouts under the watchful eye of a fitness coach to prepare for the 1960 season. He voluntarily accepted a pay cut to $75,000 for the upcoming season and worked hard in spring training to maximize his conditioning.

Part-way into the 1960 season, manager Solly Hemus benched Musial in favor of young first baseman Bill White. Broeg, who was always closely allied with Musial, wrote a column suggesting the Cardinals should trade him to the contending Pirates, noting that Musial was born in Donora, Pennsylvania, and had grown up rooting for the Bucs. Three weeks after his benching, *The Sporting News* reported in June that "Rumors have been springing up daily from sources close to Musial picturing him as an unhappy, hurt and puzzled man."

The Cards soon solved the situation by bringing Musial back into the lineup as the left fielder, rather than at first base, where he had played extensively the previous six years. Although the Cardinals settled for a third-place finish in 1960, Musial was productive, improving his OPS from .792 to .841, and his RBI from 44 to 63.

By 1961, Musial was said to be a millionaire on the basis of his baseball and business earnings. His Cardinals had a rough first half to the season, leading to Hemus getting axed and replaced by Johnny Keane. The redbirds finished above .500 but still in only sixth place among eight teams. Musial hit a solid .288 with 15 home runs and it was a foregone conclusion he would return in 1962.

Keane's approach in 1962 was to let Musial play nonstop for a week or 10 days, and then give the veteran a couple of days to rest. It paid off, as Musial enjoyed a better season than anyone expected, with a .330 batting clip and 19 homers. Although the Cardinals settled for a sixth-place finish, there were other highlights. One came in May when Musial was honored by the American Legion as the former Legion ballplayer who best exemplified the spirit of sport. Musial passed Honus Wagner on the all-time NL hit list. He also broke Ty Cobb's all-time mark for most total bases. After the season, he was measured for a bust in St. Petersburg's wax museum.

Musial had a well-deserved reputation for being exceptionally thoughtful. One example came from the all-star break in 1960, when Cliff Evans of NBC's *Today Show* was having breakfast with Musial and Vic Wertz, who were the starting first basemen in the upcoming all-star game. The three were planning a television interview segment, and several fans recognized Musial and approached him requesting an autograph. Each time, he not only obliged, but told the fans, "I'm sure you wouldn't want to miss the chance to get my famous opponent Vic Wertz down there, too, would you," as he handed the pen to Wertz.

Even in the twilight of his career, Musial was popular with his teammates. Catcher Jim Schaffer was a young catcher for St. Louis in 1961 and 1962. He recalled in 2022 that Musial, along with Red Schoendienst, treated him like a son upon his arrival in St. Louis.

With the club performing below expectations, Branch Rickey was brought in as special advisor before the 1963 season. Although 80 years old, he was still one of the most respected minds in baseball. It wasn't long before Rickey and general manager Bing Devine were experiencing disagreements with one of the items being Rickey's belief that Musial should retire and let a younger player step in. Ownership quickly clarified that only Musial himself would decide the appropriate time to leave the sport.

Musial played one final season in 1963 and batted .255, the same average he had during the disappointing 1959 campaign. This time, Musial knew it was time to step away. The Cardinals came in second place and had an exciting future ahead of them, but they would pursue it with Musial in the front office rather than on the roster.

Stan spent three years as a Cards vice president and one year as general manager, but stepped away to devote more time to his business interests. He also served as a physical fitness adviser to President Johnson and appeared occasionally on television shows such as *That Girl*. He received the Presidential Medal of Freedom in 2010.

Remembering his superstar player, Devine later related, "When Musial played with the Cardinals, you never had to worry. Whenever there were problems, he was around. If he didn't help with a hit, he helped as team leader, as the fellow the other players rallied around. His presence in the dugout and the clubhouse alone was enough."

KEN BOYER

The 1964 season was baseball's Year of the Third Baseman. In the AL, Brooks Robinson won the MVP award on the strength of his .317 batting average, league-best 118 RBI, and stellar defense. In the NL, Ken Boyer led the league in RBI, won the MVP award, and helped the Cardinals to the world championship.

In that year's World Series, the Cardinals defeated the Yankees whose own third baseman was Ken's brother, Clete Boyer. When the players' mother was asked who she was rooting for in the fall classic, she quipped, "the guy at third base." Part of a proud baseball family, Ken and Clete rank in the top 10 in homers by a brothers-combo.

A decade earlier, as a young prospect, Ken was rendered unconscious for three days while playing winter ball in Cuba. He recovered and joined the Cardinals in 1955, alongside pitcher Larry Jackson, who became one of his closest friends. Ken enjoyed a solid rookie season. A year later, back when baseball people often talked about the sophomore jinx, he hit over .300 and made the first of seven all-star teams.

After a marginal season in 1957, during which he played in the outfield, he returned to form the next several years, delivering consistent offense. At one point in 1959, he hit in 29 straight contests. He was rewarded with a plump pay increase for the 1960 season and general manager Bing Devine voiced confidence, saying, "I doubt that Boyer has reached his peak. He still has momentum left and the fact that this club will be better will add to his stature." Divine proved correct. Ken slugged his career-best 32 homers in 1960 and placed sixth in the MVP balloting.

He was named team captain in 1961 and responded with a .329 batting average. He continued to amass all-star selections through his 1964 MVP season. The Cardinals won 93 games en route to that year's World Series, during which Boyer slugged a pair of homers. Ken and Clete both homered in game seven.

African American players like Bob Gibson, Bill White, and Curt Flood had become an integral part of the Cardinals in the early Sixties. Boyer, a Missouri native, was initially not sensitive to racial-equality matters, but through conversations with black teammates, and witnessing the discrimination they faced, he came to understand what they went through. Boyer played cards on a regular basis with Gibson and others, as the team became unified on and off the field.

Back pain reduced Ken's productivity in 1965, prompting the Cards to dispatch him to the Mets for pitcher Al Jackson and third baseman Charley Smith. During the 1966 season, Ken shared a New York apartment with coach Whitey Herzog, brother Clete Boyer, and Roger Maris. Despite high expectations with Boyer in the fold, the 1966 Mets finished in ninth place. Boyer contributed 61 RBI, but at age 35, it was unrealistic to expect him to replicate his previous performances. He played part-time through 1969 with the White Sox and Dodgers.

Ken was named manager of the Cardinals early in the 1978 season, replacing Vern Rapp, who was unpopular with his players. The Cards improved to third place under Boyer in 1979, but got off to a horrendous start in 1980, after trading for Bobby Bonds. Team ownership was not patient. Boyer was dismissed between games of a twin-bill on June 8, 1980. His career record as a manager was 166-190.

Boyer stayed with the Cardinals in a scouting capacity and was offered the chance to manage their Triple-A club in Louisville in 1982. He initially accepted, but then stepped away when he was diagnosed with cancer in the esophagus and lungs. After initial treatments in the U.S., he went to Mexico for treatments with laetrile. He died that September at the age of 51.

Boyer's lifetime average was .287 with 282 homers and 2,143 hits. Though remembered today mostly for his hitting, he was also an exceptional glove man, capturing five gold glove awards. In 1999, Bill James rated him the 12th greatest third baseman of all time.

DAVE ADLESH

Long Beach native Dave Adlesh had four different careers, all rewarding in their own way. Career number one was major league baseball. He turned down football scholarships from schools including Notre Dame to ink a $95,000 baseball deal with Houston.

Though a strong defensive catcher, Adlesh struggled to hit, batting just .168 in 106 big-league contests. He was John Bateman's backup for Houston for a couple of years, and one of his highlights was catching a Don Wilson no-hitter. He later caught in the minors for the Cardinals, Braves, and Angels organizations, but never made it back to the show.

Career number two was in the nightclub business. Adlesh fronted much of his signing bonus to join his brother in operating a popular 350-seat night spot called "The Limit" at 4365 Atlantic Avenue in Long Beach, from 1966 to 1971.

The brothers booked acts like Linda Ronstadt, Bo Didley, Ike and Tina Turner, Etta James, Thelma Houston, and Jackie Wilson. Adlesh enjoyed telling an amusing story. The club was looking for a house band, and a group of young musicians applied for the gig saying they wanted to perform their own original music, rather than covers of already-popular songs. Dave's brother, Frank Adlesh, passed on the group. A short time later, the band, Three Dog Night, scored the first of more than 20 hit records.

After the brothers closed the Long Beach club, they opened another rock-and-soul joint called "The Market" in Newport Beach. But musical tastes were shifting toward folk rock, and the struggling new R&B club was short-lived.

Reflecting on his baseball career, Adlesh sometimes noted that appropriately for a night-club owner, his lone homer came against pitcher John Boozer.

In career number three, Dave ran the press boxes at three California horse racing facilities. He wasn't passionate about the job, but it kept him active and paid the bills. His fourth career was his favorite. Always handy with a hammer and a drill, Adlesh partnered with his adult son Darren in a home remodeling business. Adlesh later waged a long and courageous battle with cancer. He passed away in Long Beach in 2016.

Ron Brand

The atmosphere was electric as the Astros suited up for their first exhibition game at the newly constructed Astrodome, baseball's first domed stadium, in 1965. Facing off against Mel Stottlemyre and the defending AL champion Yankees in the third inning, young Ron Brand smoked the second pitch into the outfield between Mickey Mantle and Roger Maris for a triple, and to this day believes he could have scored had the third-base coach not put up the stop sign. That was the first Astro hit at the Astrodome.

"It was a thrill to hear the roar that went up when I tripled for the first Astro hit ever," Brand recalled in 2022. "The stadium had a lot of flaws, but the crowd support was great. We always had a winning record there but lost a lot on the road."

As a youngster, Brand grew up in North Hollywood. He played ball on a field in Burbank near the Lockheed Airport, and later became the shortstop for North Hollywood High School. "It was in the Forties and Fifties, and I didn't realize who lived around me" in terms of film stars, Brand recalled. "The San Fernando Valley was a beautiful place back then with orange groves, young neighborhoods, and just the beginnings of the freeways."

He got to know a local baseball scout, George Genovese, who recommended Brand to Branch Rickey, who ran the Pirates. The Pirates signed Brand in 1957 at the age of 17, and he made his big-league debut for the Bucs in 1963, batting .288 in 46 games. "Of course, it was exciting to be there," he recalled. After another summer in the minors in 1964, Houston selected him in the Rule V draft before the 1965 season.

Brand played for the Astros from 1965 to 1968, sharing the catching duties with John Bateman. He homered in 1965 off two of the hardest throwers in the league, Bob Gibson and Bob Veale.

In 1969, both Brand and Bateman wound up with the expansion Expos. Montreal skipper Gene Mauch used Brand in a utility-man capacity, and Brand believes he is the only player in history who caught 300 games who also made multiple appearances at second base, third base, shortstop, and the outfield. He said he learned more about baseball from Mauch than any other manager. Brand used Rawlings gloves and needed several models for the different positions he played.

The Expos were MLB's first Canadian team. For Expos players, this meant a lot of time spent going through both nations' Customs process at airports. Brand recalled that the Expos' travel was a mix of chartered and commercial flights, and that having to deal with Customs was a time-consuming hassle.

Through the years, Brand roomed on the road with outfielders Mike White and Dave Nicholson while with Houston; and infielder Bob Bailey, catcher John Boccabella, and pitcher Mike Marshall while with the Expos through 1971.

He later managed in the minor leagues and operated a contracting business. In 1994, Gene Michael of the Yankees offered him a scouting position, which he held until 2013. A resident of Prosper, Texas, he continued to instruct young players at a facility called My Batters Box with eight batting cages. His cousin, Glen Brand, won a gold medal in wrestling in the 1948 Olympics in London.

LARRY DIERKER

Sometimes called Mr. Astro, Larry Dierker is revered in Houston for his work as a pitcher, broadcaster and manager. Save for one year with the Cardinals, his entire baseball profession has been associated with the Houston club.

Dierker, a six-foot-four righthander, was born in Hollywood and came out of Taft High School in Woodland Hills, California, where he grew up following the Dodgers. Exhibiting incredible poise, the youngster made his debut for Houston on his 18th birthday in 1964, striking out Willie Mays and Jim Ray Hart in his first inning of work.

Over the next four years, he missed time to military duty, but nonetheless polished his craft and compiled a respectable 35-36 record. His repertoire initially featured mostly only his blistering fastball, but with some tutoring from Jim Owens and Roger Craig, he gradually perfected a curve and developed a change-up. During the winters, he returned to UC Santa Barbara to continue his education.

"Most of the guys on the team smoked cigarettes and consumed large quantities of beer. Back then, the Schlitz Brewing Company was our sponsor and they gave each of us a case of beer every home stand," Dierker wrote. "At first, I gave all of mine to one of our veteran pitchers, Jim Owens. Later, I kept the case myself and we drank together at the Surrey House Motel on South Main Street just across the street from the Dome."

"Larry could go 'pitch for pitch' with all of the good pitchers of his time," noted teammate Ron Brand decades later. "Despite being only 19 years old as a rookie, he had great stuff." Another of his catchers, John Edwards, recalled, "He was an excellent pitcher with exceptional control. He sometimes became too fine in games where he didn't need to be."

In 1968, Dierker became just the 10th pitcher in the 20th Century to uncork 20 wild pitches in a single season. Before anyone gets too critical, two of the other nine pitchers were Hall of Famers Christy Mathewson and Walter Johnson. Moreover, just a year later in 1969, Dierker achieved the number "20" in two other categories – victories and complete games -- while fashioning a career-best 2.33 ERA and making the all-star team.

One of the pitchers on that 1969 team was Jim Bouton, who arrived in a late-season trade. Bouton was taking notes for what became his infamous book, *Ball Four*. Dierker was later asked about Bouton by the *Astros Daily*. He said, "I would say most of the guys liked Bouton. Most of them didn't really feel threatened by him taking notes. I think privately most of them would say they enjoyed reading the book, even though some of them would say he shouldn't have said some of the things he said because it was private business behind clubhouse doors."

Dierker made the all-star team again in 1971 but was on the disabled list at the time of the game. He posted a 12-6 record, with five shutouts that season. He increasingly experienced arm trouble but pitched a no-hitter in 1976 against the Expos. He missed the final month of that 1976 season with a painful shoulder.

By the time the Astros traded Dierker to the Cardinals in November 1976, the big righty owned just about every pitching record in Houston history, except for appearances and saves. The trade did not come as a shock because the Astros were cultivating a crop of young pitchers.

Larry has nothing but good things to say about the Cardinals, though his time with the team was unsettling. He broke his leg in spring training and continued to experience a sore arm. The 30-year-old got into only 11 games before retiring. He finished with a 139-123 record and a 3.31 ERA, as well as 25 shutouts. As of 2024, only two pitchers (Joe Niekro and Roy Oswalt) had more victories for the Astros.

Dierker returned to Houston in 1978, becoming a popular broadcaster, and one of the first to introduce listeners to advanced sabermetrics. He also experienced success as the Astros skipper. He was the NL manager of the year in 1998, and his 1999 club garnered 102 victories. Off the field, his hobbies have included golf and fine cigars. Dierker continues to reside in Texas.

LEE MAYE

Arthur Lee Maye was as well-known as a soul singer as he was as a ballplayer. At age 16, he helped The Platters score their first major hit record, "Only You."

Maye decided to focus mostly on baseball. He joined the Braves in 1959. Playing alongside Hank Aaron, Maye's solid bat kept him in the lineup frequently against right-handed pitching.

But life with Lee could also be interesting. In April 1960, he was ticketed for driving the wrong way on a one-way street and ordered to acquire a Wisconsin driver's license. In September of that year, a court ordered him to pay child support for the child of a woman who was not his wife. In June 1962, Maye encountered breathing problems and was hospitalized with a rapid heartbeat. The next season, Braves manager Bobby Bragan benched him after repeated instances of missing signs. Thanks to his bat, he was back in the lineup before long. In May 1965, with Maye hitting .296 but nursing a leg injury, the Braves traded him to Houston for starting pitcher Ken Johnson.

Not long after his arrival in Houston, Lee accepted an invitation to perform at a night club called Dome Shadows, not far from the new Astrodome. The only problem was that the Astro's headstrong owner, Roy Hofheinz, a former county judge and Houston mayor, was in the middle of a legal crusade against business establishments that were capitalizing on the stadium's name and notoriety. Why it was so important to Hofheinz is unclear; with decades of hindsight, it seems to matter little.

But Hofheinz had a strong will. The team asked Maye to cancel the gig, and he refused to do, which ensured that he would never be one of the owner's favorites. Maye stayed with Houston through the end of the 1966 season, then was traded to the Indians.

Maye was with Cleveland through the midpoint of the 1969 season and always hit well. Loud music and expensive sound systems were not yet a fixture in baseball clubhouses, but Maye often carried a portable radio with him and listened to a variety of types of music. "Lee was outgoing, if you got him going," recalled teammate Sam McDowell. "He would not start conversations on his own very often. But if you started to tease him a little bit, he would interact with you with the best of them. He was a good guy."

Another Indian with warm memories of Maye was Max Alvis, who referenced an occasion after Maye was sold to the Senators. "He approached me before the game one night in Washington and asked if I wanted to meet up for dinner after the game. Lee took me to a soul food restaurant, and I was the only white guy there. The food was great and we had a wonderful time," Alvis recalled.

Maye retired in 1971 with a solid .274 lifetime average. He was unable to find a job in baseball, and instead worked in other fields, including a 12-year stint in baggage handling and ticket sales for Amtrak. He never lost his interest in music and continued to occasionally appear in nightclubs. His recordings never made him much money; about a nickel per record in royalties.

Sadly, he contracted throat cancer shortly after his music career was enjoying a revival, and he passed away in Riverside, California, in 2002 at age 67. Both as a player and a singer, Lee Maye will not be forgotten.

ROCKY COLAVITO

New York native Rocky Colavito attended a high school named for Teddy Roosevelt, who was known for his philosophy to speak softly and carry a big stick. The mantra applied well to

Colavito's baseball career (1955 to 1968), in which the soft-spoken slugger averaged 33 home runs and 102 RBI per 162 games. Pitcher Ralph Terry recalled that it was impossible to throw an inside fastball past Colavito. Terry knew first-hand, as Rocky homered off him 13 times.

From 1956 to 1959, he slugged 129 home runs. He was third in MVP balloting in 1958 when only Mickey Mantle hit more homers. Rocky placed fourth in the MVP tally in 1959, when he led the loop in total bases and tied with Harmon Killebrew for the most home runs. On June 10 of that year, he achieved the rare feat of slugging four home runs in a single game against the Orioles.

Colavito also gained notice for his strong arm. During one nine-game stretch, he threw out six enemy baserunners. Ralph Kiner said that Rocky had "the greatest throwing arm in the history of baseball." Hank Greenberg said he had "the greatest arm I have ever seen." Bob Feller wrote that Rocky had "the greatest arm ever." Colavito credited Bob Kennedy, who was working in the Indians' organization, with helping him to throw with a less exaggerated motion, resulting in more accuracy.

The relationship between Colavito and blue-collar Cleveland was something very special. Bob DiBiasio, the Indians public affairs chief, recalled, "He was the icon of the late Fifties and the Sixties [in Northeast Ohio]. All of us that grew up in that generation, we all walked to the plate in Little League and put the bat behind our head down to the shoulders because Rocky did so. We kneeled on one knee in the on-deck circle because Rocky did so."

According to the book *Rocky Colavito: Cleveland's Iconic Slugger* by Mark Sommer, he signed autographs for hours, not stepping away until the last youngster with pen and paper went away happy. Rocky often ate at Cavoli's – an Italian restaurant on the city's west side that was popular with the players – and at restaurants in the Little Italy neighborhood on the east side of town. Being seen in public, whether at restaurants or the Catholic church, fueled the impression that he was an integral part of the community.

Rocky and his bride Carmen initially resided in a lakefront high-rise apartment in Lakewood, just minutes from Municipal Stadium. After they began a family, they moved into a comfortable home in the suburb of Parma. For a time, teammate Roger Maris lived nearby, and the pair would car-pool to and from Indians home games. He roomed on road trips with pitcher Herb Score, who became a lifetime friend.

Once Frank Lane became the Indians general manager, he openly entertained trade offers for his young slugger. One rumored deal would have sent Rocky to New York for second baseman Bobby Richardson. Another would have shipped the Rock to Kansas City. Finally, just before the start of the 1960 season, Lane swapped his most popular player to the Tigers for Harvey Kuenn, the defending batting champion. Indians manager Joe Gordon told reporters he supported Lane's move. The trade was a punch to the gut of the local fan base. Appalled Clevelanders flooded the switchboards of the Indians and the local newspapers, expressing outrage. But the deal was done.

Kuenn was several years older, not exactly in perfect physical condition, and mostly a singles-and-doubles hitter. The negative impact was swift. The Indians won 13 fewer games in 1960 and saw home attendance crater by more than half a million admissions.

Lane traded dozens of players but seemed to have personal disdain for Colavito, who he called "a dago fruit peddler." The fruit reference pertained to Rocky's work in helping his father-in-law run a fruit-and-vegetable packaging business.

With Detroit, Rocky was never the top star; that role belonged to Al Kaline, a gifted outfielder who had been there longer. Colavito did his best to settle in. He had a decent 1960 season with 35 bombs and then delivered a banner year in 1961 with 45 homers and 140 RBI. After an all-star season in 1962, Rocky was less productive in 1963, prompting the Tigers to trade him to Kansas City, where he gave fans of the beleaguered A's something to cheer about throughout the 1964 season.

The Indians reacquired Colavito ahead of the 1965 season. While the trade was well-received locally, the price tag was steep. The Indians gave up two future stars in pitcher Tommy John and outfielder Tommie Agee, along with catcher John Romano.

He turned in a tremendous 1965 season as he led the AL in RBI and walks, while his .287 batting average was seventh best in the loop. He was the starting right fielder for the all-star game, placed fifth in MVP votes, and became the first AL outfielder to play a full season without committing a single error.

Colavito remained productive in 1966, slugging 30 homers and earning his sixth all-star berth, but his game declined rapidly the following two years, which he divided between the Indians, White Sox, Dodgers and Yankees.

He retired with a .266 career batting average, 374 home runs, and 1,730 hits. Of all players from 1869 to 1969 who are eligible but not inducted into the Hall of Hame, Rocky has the most home runs.

After retiring, he held a number of positions in and out of baseball. His memory is honored by a statue in Cleveland's Little Italy neighborhood.

TITO FRANCONA

When Tito Francona joined the Indians in 1959 at age 25, he was viewed as an average outfielder with questionable health and an uncertain baseball future. He had already played for the Orioles, White Sox, and Tigers, without much success.

That all changed in 1959 when Francona started the season hot as a pinch-hitter and remained on fire most of the campaign. He finished the year with a .363 batting average and placed fifth in the MVP voting. His sterling season earned him a photo on the cover of the Indians 1960 Media Guide.

During that 1959 season, Francona's son Terry was born. Tito had to wait several weeks before getting to see his young boy, who himself would grow up to play and manage in the major leagues. That's another difference from today's game where a ballplayer is permitted to leave the team to be with the mother for the birth of a child.

Tito and his wife considered buying a home in suburban Rocky River but the possibility of being traded weighed on their minds. Instead, the family leased an apartment on the fifth floor of the Commodore Hotel on Euclid Avenue in Cleveland. Tito told MLB.com in a 2013 interview that he would sometimes have to go outside to retrieve a whiffle ball that his young son would hit or throw out the open window. Terry would also peddle his tricycle around the neighborhood. Tito often brought his son to the Indians ballpark with instructions – sometimes followed, sometimes not – to stay out of trouble.

Francona had several more productive seasons with the Indians. In 1960, he hit .292 and led the AL in doubles. He hit .301 in 1961 and was named to the all-star team. He moved from the outfield to first base in 1962 and paced the Tribe in runs scored.

After two more years in Cleveland, the left-handed hitter played as a platoon man and pinch-hitter with the Cardinals, Phillies, Braves, A's, and Brewers. One of his career highlights came on September 12, 1969, not long after he was acquired by Oakland, when he delivered five hits in a 12-5 win over the White Sox.

Francona's lifetime marks included a .272 clip, 125 home runs, and 1,395 hits. After baseball, he was the parks and recreation director for Beaver County, Pennsylvania. His first wife died of breast cancer and he later remarried. Tito stayed close to the game through his son and made several trips to Cleveland after Terry became Indians manager. Tito passed away at the age of 84 in 2018. A Little League baseball complex is named in his honor in New Brighton, Pennsylvania.

SAM MCDOWELL

With a fastball clocked at 103 miles per hour, Sam McDowell was once featured on the cover of *Sports Illustrated* with the question, "Faster than Koufax?" Along with his blistering heater, his arsenal included a sharp-breaking curve, a wicked slider, and a knee-buckling change-up. All of which made him, on many a night, next to un-hittable.

McDowell grew up in the Pittsburgh area. His father had an engineering background and worked as an inspector for the steel mills. "As an engineer, he could explain to me exactly what each pitch should do, and we worked at it until I could throw each one well," he recalled in 2006. His high-school heroics caught the attention of scouts, and he inked a deal with the Indians, pocketing a hefty $60,000 bonus.

From day one, the legend grew. The Indians' brass compared his stuff to that of legendary fireballers Bob Feller and Herb Score. Pitching coach Mel Harder said the prospect's arsenal was incredible, his mechanics were perfect, and he just needed experience. He made his MLB debut in 1961, but did not solidify a spot in the club's rotation until well into the 1964 season. In the meantime, there was plenty of frustration.

"When I came up to the big leagues starting in 1961," he recalled, "I don't think there was a person on Earth who thought I was there for anything other than publicity. And I knew it. And it was that way for the next two years. Because I was a big bonus ballplayer, and the speed that I used to throw. But more importantly, when I was in the minor leagues, there was *nobody* there who could teach me pitching."

"Each time they called me up to the big leagues, everyone was calling my pitches, and doing it like in the Dark Ages. Fastball. Fastball. Fastball. If I got ahead of a batter, then maybe they might call for a curve or a slider or a change-up. I don't care where you're playing, if you keep throwing fastballs to a hitter, he's going to hit one out. And it happened to me. Then they would send me down. They were punishing me because of *their pitch calling*."

"So, each time I was sent back to the minors," he continued, "there was nobody there to call my pitches, so I got into a guessing game and mixed up the pitches as much as I could. That set a bad reputation for me, because they said I was throwing a lot of junk up there. But they don't look at my record and see how well I was pitching."

During spring training 1964, "Gabe Paul called me into his office and says, 'We're going to send you back to Portland to start the season. Maybe that will be a help to you.' I said, 'Do me a favor. Do not bring me up to the major leagues. As long as Birdie Tebbetts is calling my pitches, just leave me in the minor leagues.'"

"He said, 'Well, you're just angry now.' I said, 'No, bull shit. Don't bring me up.' So I go down there and Johnny Lipon, the manager, the very first day says, 'Sam, I know you're down here to learn how to pitch. I was an infielder. I don't know anything about pitching. I apologize, but you're going to have to learn on your own.' I said, 'That's okay, Johnny, at least if I learn on my own, if I get my ass kicked, I will know why.'"

"So, I started out 7-0 with a no-hitter at Portland," McDowell recalled. "I got a call from Gabe Paul, and he said, 'We want you to come to LA to start tomorrow's game.' I said, 'Who is going to call my pitches.' He said, 'Don't start that Sam. We're bringing you up to the major leagues.' I said, 'Never mind. If he's going to call my pitches, I'm not coming.' He said, 'Sam, if you keep that attitude, I'll bury you in the minor leagues.' So, we just hung up and left it unresolved and I really didn't care. I knew I was having success pitching my way."

That exchange made Sudden Sam one of the few Triple-A pitchers ever to turn down a promotion. But he was pitching too well to stay with the Beavers much longer. After hurling another shutout against Hawaii, McDowell's hotel room phone rang again. It was Paul saying, "Okay, you win. Tomorrow, you come to Washington, D.C. to pitch because we have a double-header."

The lefty caught the all-night flight from Honolulu, arriving in the nation's capital at 6:30 a.m. By the time he got to the Shoreham Hotel and ate some breakfast, the players were boarding the team bus for a 9:30 a.m. departure to D.C. Stadium. When the Senators started roughing up starter Mudcat Grant in the fifth inning, McDowell came in, pitched well and got the win in relief.

With managerial interference kept to a minimum, McDowell posted an 11-6 record over the rest of the year. He followed up with a monster season in 1965, winning 17 games and leading the league with a 2.18 ERA with 325 strikeouts.

McDowell went on to win five strikeout titles and became just the second lefty in AL history (after Whitey Ford) to hurl consecutive one-hitters. In 1968, his 1.81 ERA was second best in the league. He became a 20-game winner in 1970, placing third that year in the Cy Young balloting. He threw 23 career shutouts.

His pitching prowess often left teammates and opponents alike grasping for the right adjectives. Reggie Jackson of the A's called him "instant heat." Indians pitcher Stan Williams said, "Sam had four *great* pitches. He was a dominating type."

"What a talent," recalled teammate Max Alvis. "He had more natural talent than anyone else on the Indians' teams." Recalled teammate Duke Sims, "Sam McDowell had the four best pitches I ever saw in baseball."

"But Sam couldn't play today," conjectured Sims in 2006, "because they'd have him out of there by the second or third inning because he'd have thrown 70 or 80 pitches. It was not unusual for Sam to throw 160 to 225 pitches. And he'd be like Nolan Ryan – he'd be better in the eighth and ninth inning that he was in the first or second, with better control."

Though blessed with enormous talent, McDowell, like so many people, was plagued by insecurity and other personal demons that led to an alcohol problem. He later pinpointed the genesis of his problem to a night he joined teammates Gary Bell and Barry Latman for dinner. Though he had seldom drank before then, he imbibed that night until last call, long after his teammates had returned to the hotel. This practice became a routine on nights he wasn't preparing to pitch, whether the team was at home, where he stayed at the downtown Pick Carter Hotel, or on the road.

Stories were all too common. There was the night he exchanged punches with Bob Dolgan, the scribe credited with naming him Sudden Sam. He was arrested for disorderly conduct one night in Tucson in 1967 and fined $500 by the team. Pitcher Tom Gramly said, "I recall rooming with Sam once in Baltimore. He was something."

But there was a little-publicized, more sensitive side to the tall lefty. "Sam and I roomed together on road trips for much of the period of time that I was with the Indians," recalled pitcher Steve Bailey in 2006. "He was a good person and that was not truly understood. He tried to accommodate everyone and had little to say that was negative about his team. Physically, I think he needed to pitch every sixth day, because his recovery was slow from cuts and bruises."

The Indians traded him to the Giants after a disappointing 1971 season and he also pitched for the Yankees and his hometown Pirates before retiring in 1975. He had a lifetime record of 141-134 with a 3.17 ERA. McDowell averaged 8.9 strikeouts per nine innings. At the time Sam retired, only Koufax had a better ratio. In 2006, the Indians welcomed him into the Cleveland Baseball Hall of Fame.

He later became sober, paid off his debts, studied voraciously, and became a highly respected sports psychologist, providing employee assistance program services to dozens of players and others. He also remarried, gave up smoking, and remained in recovery from alcohol. In 2022, he co-wrote a highly insightful book titled, *The Saga of Sudden Sam."* Sam currently resides in The Villages, Florida.

DICK DONOVAN

During a 2022 webcast, Sam McDowell recalled that pitcher Dick Donovan had such precise control that he could place nine out of every 10 pitches exactly where he wanted. The statistics bear this out. From 1955 to 1958, Donovan placed either first or second in the AL in fewest walks per inning. After drifting off the leader board for two years, in 1961 he placed third, and then was back on top the next two seasons. McDowell threw harder and had better stuff but admired his teammate's pinpoint control.

Donovan, a Navy veteran, first made the AL all-star team in 1955 with the White Sox. In 1957, he was second in the AL in winning percentage and during the 1959 World Series, he pitched in three games. Following a trade to the Senators, he led the AL in ERA in 1961, but weak support from his teammates limited him to 10 wins. He was traded to the Indians after the campaign.

Using four pitches, Donovan was all business on the mound. Off the field, he had a wry sense of humor and a propensity to play practical jokes. He was the straight man in Cleveland to Gary Bell, the pitcher with a cut-up sense of humor whose locker was the next one over. Dick brought a degree of maturity, and the Indians assigned him for a time to room with McDowell.

Donovan got off to a fantastic 8-0 start in 1962. Though his effectiveness wavered down the stretch, he managed to win 20 games for the only time in his career. That made him the Indians' first 20-game winner in six years.

The hurler had been on track to win 20 contests once before, with the 1955 White Sox. That year, he had 13 wins before the end of July, before his season went off the tracks. His troubles started on a road trip when he tried to have breakfast at the team hotel's dining room without a sport coat. Angry over being turned away, he stubbornly decided not to return to his room for a jacket, and instead walked a few blocks to a greasy spoon joint. Within hours, Donovan had a rip-roaring upset stomach, which soon gave way to an attack of appendicitis, which required surgery. By the time he regained his health and pitching form, he would win only two more contests that season.

Donovan pitched until 1965, retiring at age 37 with a 122-99 record and a 3.67 ERA. He returned home to Massachusetts, where he worked in insurance and real estate. He was 69 years of age when he died of cancer in 1997.

SONNY SIEBERT

Wilfred (Sonny) Siebert was a dominant pitcher for the Indians in the Sixties, with 61 wins, 48 losses and a 2.76 ERA. Following a 1969 trade to the Red Sox, it took some time for him to learn to pitch in Fenway Park, but he remained a top-shelf pitcher, posting a 57-41 record and a 3.46 ERA with Boston.

His path to pitching stardom was anything but straight. Sonny's first love was basketball, which he played so well at the University of Missouri that he was drafted by the NBA's St. Louis Hawks. He also had a high-profile run in college baseball but as a first-baseman and outfielder, not a pitcher.

"The Indians had a scout in St. Louis," Siebert recalled in an interview, "and he used to follow me around. We were lucky enough to go to the College World Series in 1958, and I had a good series, and hit about .600, and a lot of other scouts got interested in me. I think Cleveland realized this, and they put the full-court press on me, and flew me up to Cleveland to try to sign me."

"I was newly married," he continued, "and they put us up at the old Auditorium Hotel, which was where Rocky Colavito stayed. They took me to the game every night, and I got to take fielding practice in right field with Rocky. And during the day, Rocky would show my wife and I around Cleveland, and that impressed me." Siebert signed with the Indians for a $35,000 bonus.

A cerebral player, Siebert grew bored as a minor-league outfielder, and weary of hitting coaches altering his swing. After his requests to try pitching were rebuffed, he finally packed his luggage to leave baseball, and only then did Hoot Evers, who ran the Indians' farm system, agree to let him pitch at Burlington, North Carolina, the Indians class B affiliate. Once he became a pitcher, he began to experience some success and he made the Indians' roster in 1964, the same year that Sam McDowell and Luis Tiant also had breakout seasons on the North Coast.

"Sonny threw really hard. Nobody knew it. He had spectacular control. And on a given night he might have thrown as hard as Sam," said catcher Duke Sims. "I caught Sonny one night in Baltimore. The first nine outs, seven of them were strikeouts. They had to take him out of the game because he was dizzy with an inner ear infection. Imagine doing that with an ear infection."

Siebert won 16 games in 1965, and duplicated that success in 1966, the year he threw a no-hitter. Even in 1967 when his record slumped to 10-12, he was still third in the league in ERA. In 1968, he led the Indians to a 9-0 win on Opening Day in Chicago, and helped his own cause by dropping three sacrifice bunts. After the game, manager Alvin Dark said, "Siebert's the hardest-working pitcher I've ever seen," explaining why he had to restrict the pitcher's workouts.

Although Sonny enjoyed his time with the Indians, "by then I was looking for a trade," he recalled. "I had pitched winter ball, and knew that a lot of other pitchers with lesser credentials were earning more than I was. I knew I only had a few years left to pitch, and needed to make the most of them."

After Boston, he pitched for the Rangers, Cardinals, Padres and then the 1975 A's where he was reunited with manager Al Dark. Despite joining the A's in mid-season, he was voted a full post-season bonus share of $7,153. Released after the season, he reported to Hawaii for spring training in 1976 nursing a sore back and was released by the Islanders along with fellow veterans Frank Linzy and Sonny Jackson.

His final record was 114-91 for an impressive .551 winning percentage. He later worked as a pitching coach and continued to enjoy golf at his home base in St. Louis. In 2001, the Indians honored him as one of their 100 greatest players of all time.

STEVE BAILEY

Steve Bailey was a promising pitcher from Lorain, Ohio, 30 miles west of Cleveland. When he joined the Indians as a rookie in 1967, he became the first major leaguer from Lorain since pitcher Eli Hodkey of the 1946 Phillies.

Steve made a good first impression. Hank Soar, umpiring a game behind the plate, said Bailey threw harder than Sam McDowell, who pitched the same day. Paul Blair of the Orioles said, "His ball moves a lot. He's got a lot of stuff." Outfielder Leon Wagner, a teammate, saw Bailey as "a potential superstar."

"Steve Bailey was the kind of guy who would run through a brick wall," teammate Sonny Siebert later recalled. "We used to run sprints together. He would never let me win a sprint. He got me into such good shape it was unbelievable."

"Steve was a rookie that year," Siebert said, "and there was a game in Chicago where I pitched 11 innings and came out with the game tied, and Steve came out of the bullpen throwing fastballs and got the win." It was Bailey's first victory, and telegrams flooded in from friends, family, and fans.

Siebert continued, "After the game, [manager] Joe Adcock – he had been a hitter, not a pitcher – told Bailey, 'That's how you're going to pitch every time you come in a game. You're going to throw nothing but fastballs.'" Siebert recalled telling Bailey, "You've got four good pitches. Your fastball is not going to be your best pitch every night. It would be a mistake to throw nothing but fastballs."

But Adcock insisted on that flawed strategy. Bailey complied, getting into 32 games, but hitters began to look for heaters, and Bailey's record dropped to 2-5. By late summer, Cleveland sent him back to Triple-A Portland.

Bailey got into two games for the Indians in 1968, then pitched in the Astros and Cardinals organizations for a couple of years. At one point, he won nine straight games at Triple-A Oklahoma City, but over time, he realized his odds of returning to MLB were growing slimmer, and by 1971, he had completed a physical education degree at Oberlin. He left baseball on his own terms and went on to enjoy a 26-year career as the superintendent of parks and recreation for the City of Lorain.

Looking back, Bailey harbors no bitterness over the trajectory of his pitching career but recognizes the limits to the instruction provided to young players in the Sixties. "They didn't teach much about the internal aspects of the game," Bailey remembered. "They wanted you to throw hard, and provided instruction on how to throw breaking pitches. Nothing about expanding your mind when it comes to pitching. Nothing about Eastern thought. Nothing about anxiety levels. The Indians were not alone in ignoring that aspect of the game." Bailey also remembers Adcock creating one conflict after another in the dugout and clubhouse, leaving it to coach George Strickland to straighten things out.

Retired from his City of Lorain job since 2002, Bailey has enjoyed golf, fishing and bowling.

WILLIE MAYS

Was Willie Mays the greatest player of all time? The case can certainly be made. Standing five-foot-ten, he did not fit the profile for a slugger, but possessed tremendous power. "I don't call myself a wrist hitter," he explained. "I'm a swinger and my power comes from my biceps and my shoulders." Having hit 660 career homers (despite missing nearly two full seasons to Korean War-era military duty), he was third on the all-time homer list for many years. And he was as popular as any other player in the sport.

For 10 straight years, Mays placed in the top six in NL MVP voting. He won the award in 1954, and then 11 years later in 1965. When Mays hit four home runs in Milwaukee on April 30, 1961, he became just the fourth NL slugger to do so in the 20th Century, following Chuck Klein, Gil Hodges and Joe Adcock. The Giants won the game, 14-4.

Nobody loved playing baseball more, leading to his nickname, "the Say Hey Kid." Mays was a charismatic figure who was extremely articulate when interacting with the news media. Extremely intelligent, he always seemed to position himself in the right spot in the field.

Over time, he became increasingly private. He seemed a bit less comfortable in San Francisco (following the Giants' 1958 move) than he had been in New York. Shortstop Ed Bressoud told Ed Attansio in *This Great Game*, "Willie and I never had a conversation that lasted more than a minute. Mays has always been kind of a loner, in my opinion, and I can understand it, actually. The public is always pulling and tugging at him for one thing or another, and…that has to get old after a while. So, he kind of stayed to himself most of the time."

Mays' finances had become a mess after his 1956 marriage to talent promoter Scarlett Marghuerite Wendell, a more worldly figure six years his senior whose first husband was a singer with the Drifters. As announcer Jack Brickhouse put it, "The U.S. Mint couldn't print money fast enough." Rumors of her infidelity and drinking followed. The troubled marriage lasted six years as Willie's sense of idealism and innocence eroded. He aggravated his financial woes through careless spending such as building a 1,200-disc collection of rock, soul and classical records, and given the era's high taxes brackets, Uncle Sam was taking a shocking share of his earnings. He once said in jest that he fainted every time he thought of the income taxes he paid.

Willie had a close relationship with manager Leo Durocher and teammate Monte Irvin in the early-to-mid-Fifties which helped fuel his self-confidence. Bill Rigney succeeded Leo as skipper and did not establish the same rapport with his star. Mays' ties to manager Alvin Dark in the early Sixties were initially cordial but grew distant. He had a very positive relationship with the next manager, Herman Franks, who helped Mays straighten out his troubled finances and redirect his investments.

Throughout the Sixties, the Giants lineup resembled a Strat-o-Matic all-star team. At various times, Mays, Willie McCovey, Orlando Cepeda, Felipe Alou and Jim Ray Hart formed the meat of the order, and they were usually surrounded by other talented players. Ultimately, the club won the pennant just once in the Sixties – in 1962, when Mays led the NL in homers with 49, while hitting over .300. Most of the other years, the squad settled for second place behind either the Dodgers or Cardinals.

In 1964, Willie led the NL with 47 home runs, but hit below .250 the final two months of the season. The Giants placed fourth, five games out of first place, and Dark was given the hook as manager. Pitcher Bill O'Dell later said the Giants missed out on the pennant because some of the players put out "only 60 percent effort." Dark refused to comment on O'Dell's accusation, which Mays denounced. O'Dell's comments were poorly timed, as his ERA that year was an unsightly 5.40.

New manager Herman Franks gave Willie an occasional day off to keep him fresh. The Giants kept Mays' salary stable at $105,000 for 1965, as he remained one of only five players in MLB history with a six-figure salary. Willie applauded the Giants for adding a new layer of topsoil at Candlestick Park, noting that he wore out six pairs of cleats during homestands the previous season.

That same winter, he joined up with Pennsylvania Life Insurance Company to form Willie Mays Agency, a 50-50 partnership aiming to do business in 44 states. But he passed on an invitation to join Franks and some teammates on a wild javelina hunt in Arizona. "While the rest of the boys are on their javelina safari, I'll just stay at the hotel and enjoy the sulfur baths," he joked.

After spending spring training at owner Horace Stoneham's luxurious Francisco Grande Inn along with his teammates, Willie got off to a torrid start to the 1965 season, carrying a .400 batting average with 17 home runs into the third week of May. At the all-star game in July, he made a leaping backhanded catch of a shot by Minnesota's Jimmie Hall, reminding a national audience of his defensive prowess. When Mays came to the plate that day, fans watching the game on television were puzzled why he was wearing a Chicago Cubs batting helmet. It turns out he had forgotten to pack his own and borrowed one from Billy Williams.

By the time the 1965 season ended, Mays led the NL in several categories, including his 52 home runs (a figure that Juan Marichal had predicted before the season) and 360 total bases. The Giants were in contention, but between September 21 and October 1 against the Reds, Braves and Cardinals, the Giants won just three times. They finished two games behind the pennant-winning Dodgers.

The 1966 season was something of a rerun, in that San Francisco missed the pennant by only 1.5 games, again to the Dodgers. Mays, by now 35 years old, slugged 37 home runs, tops on the Giants.

In 1967, the Giants again placed second, albeit 10 games off the pace of the Cardinals. Mays saw his productivity drop off considerably. And in 1968, it was more of the same, with the Giants finishing second, nine lengths behind the Cardinals. Mays was tied for second on the club with 23 home runs.

As the NL expanded to 12 teams in 1969, it also split into two divisions. The Giants finished in their customary second place, three games behind Atlanta. Mays batted .283 but connected for only 13 home runs, as McCovey and Bobby Bonds emerged as the team's top hitters.

An exceptional fielder for most of his career, Mays won 12 gold gloves. His memorable play in the 1954 World Series, where he made an over-the-shoulder grab of Vic Wertz's drive and threw back to the infield to double off a baserunner, is considered one of the greatest plays of all time. By 1971, at the age of 40, Mays led the NL in on-base percentage, but he was no longer an elite defender, committing 17 errors.

Mays finished with the Mets in 1973. For his career, he was a .301 hitter with 660 home runs, 3,293 hits, and 338 stolen bases. After baseball, he did promotional work for Colgate-Palmolive and Bally's Casino. Giants general manager Al Rosen who later hired Mays as a spring training instructor, called him "the greatest player I ever saw." Many who saw Willie play agree with that assessment.

JACK HIATT

Catcher Jack Hiatt, who played for five teams over nine years, once said the best part of being a big-leaguer was the opportunity to play alongside his teammate Willie Mays, the greatest player he ever saw. Mays took a personal interest in Jack when he was first called up to the Giants. Hiatt told Micheal Heinbach in *The News Times* that when Willie noticed Hiatt wearing the same sport coat two days in a row on a road trip against the Mets, Mays took the young man to New York's garment district in a taxi and had the tailor outfit him with several pairs of slacks and sports coats – on Willie's dime.

Back when there were few players with 500 homers, Hiatt witnessed four of the first nine 500th shots. He was behind the plate in June 1968 when battery mate Mike McCormick tried to throw a fastball past Hank Aaron at Fulton County Stadium. Aaron crushed it for number 500. He was also in uniform on the days that Mays, Eddie Mathews and Ernie Banks reached that milestone.

Jack made his big-league debut with the Angels in 1964 and after the season, he was traded to the Giants for outfielder Jose Cardenal. That deal was an important one in Hiatt's career as he played for the Giants from 1965 to 1969, worked winters in their public relations department, and later served 17 years as the franchise's director of player development.

With the Giants, Jack shared the catching duties with Dick Dietz (who was his roommate on road trips) and Bob Barton. He also saw action at first base and pinch hitter. His best season was probably 1967, when he hit .275 in 73 games with a robust .818 OPS. He delivered a grand-slam homer against Roy Face that year. Jack opened the 1968 season as the starting catcher but suffered a separated shoulder in a home plate collision in which he tagged out Ron Swoboda. Then in 1969, he was hospitalized for three weeks with ulcers, before seeing most of the action behind the plate during September's division race.

Jack later played for the Expos, Cubs, Astros and circled back with the Angels. He then was a minor-league manager before accepting the Giants' player-personnel job. Hiatt loved coaching young players and helping them pursue their dream of reaching the big leagues. Jack was sorry to see MLB reduce the number of minor league teams, but nothing will diminish his love of baseball.

Jack and his wife Sherlyn have a first-floor memorabilia room in their Gleneden Beach, Oregon home. It features signed photos, jerseys, autographed bats and balls, and awards. Upstairs, they retain the three world championship rings Jack won as part of the Giants' organization in 2010, 2012 and 2014, as well.

BOB BOLIN

Right-hander Bob Bolin, a 13-year big-leaguer, was quick to credit a couple of baseball men for his success. One was Tim Murchison, the scout who signed him (as well as Gaylord Perry and Jim Ray Hart) for the Giants. Murchison took time to get know Bob and his family personally, which was the biggest factor in his choosing the Giants.

The other mentor was Alvin Dark. Their relationship began in 1961 when Dark was the Giants' manager and Bolin was an up-and-comer. Both were believers in Christ, which helped them bond. Dark gave the South Carolinian a chance and Bolin responded. Just a year later, the young hurler was pitching in front of 70,000-plus fans in a pair of World Series games. Dark eventually moved on, and Bolin pitched for other managers in a career that lasted until 1973. But their friendship endured for decades. Bolin and his wife settled in Easley, South Carolina, Dark's retirement town. They golfed together, worshiped at the same church, and Bolin served on the board of directors of Dark's Christian foundation.

Bolin had an effective sidearm fastball, a durable arm, and a willingness to start or relieve. He had a 14-6 record for the Giants in 1965. In 1968, his record was 10-5 and his 1.99 ERA was second in the NL. Bolin closed out his career with the Brewers and Red Sox. After baseball, he ran an Amway distributorship business and enjoyed hunting and fishing until shortly before his 2023 death. He had an 88-75 record with a 3.40 ERA.

JUAN MARICHAL

The Giants were the first franchise with the vision to make a major commitment to developing players from the Dominican Republic. Catcher Ozzie Virgil, who debuted with the Giants in 1956, was the first of more than 870 major leaguers to hail from the island, though he grew up in the Bronx. The Giants signed and promoted the Alou brothers, as well as Hall of Fame pitcher

Juan Marichal, directly from the Dominican Republic, and these imports contributed to the Giants being a competitive team throughout the Sixties.

Marichal won 243 games, registered a phenomenal 2.89 ERA, and prevailed in 63 percent of his decisions. The right-hander tossed 52 shutouts, including a one-hitter against the Phillies in his MLB debut. Juan was also the winningest pitcher of the Sixties. He was so dominant that Hall of Famer Carl Hubbell said, "He amazes me." Alvin Dark, the manager of the 1962 Giants NL championship club, said, "Put your club a run ahead, and Marichal is the greatest pitcher I ever saw." Juan's trademark high leg kick is a lasting memory for a generation of fans that watched him in person and on television.

When the Giants won the 1962 pennant, Marichal contributed an 18-11 record, and made the all-star team for the first of nine times. He also pitched four scoreless innings in the World Series loss to the Yankees.

Juan was involved in a contest sometimes called "the greatest game ever pitched." It was a Giants-Braves game on July 2, 1963, in which seven future Hall of Famers competed, including starting pitchers Marichal and 42-year-old Warren Spahn. Marichal yielded two hits to Denis Menke but was otherwise untouchable. Spahn was also dominant. The game was a scoreless tie until the 16th inning, when Willie Mays finally blasted a game-winning homer against Spahn. Both starting pitchers – fierce competitors at heart -- went the distance. MLB will never see another game like that one.

From there, Juan exceeded the 20-win plateau six of the next seven years. He won 25 or more games in three seasons (1963, 1966, 1968). In 1967, he became the first non-Dodger pitcher with a $100,000 salary. That proved to be a frustrating season, as he pulled a hamstring muscle in early August. The club shut him down later that month.

In winning 26 contests and hurling 30 complete games in 1968, Marichal almost certainly would have won the Cy Young Award, were it not for Bob Gibson's historic season with a ridiculous 1.12 ERA.

As the 1969 season approached, the Giants team was eyeing the opportunity presented by divisional play. The club was coming off four consecutive second-place finishes and were now the pre-season favorites in the NL West. Between Willie Mays ($125,000), Marichal ($120,000) and Willie McCovey ($85,000), the Giants had three of the game's higher-paid players. Clyde King was the new manager, succeeding Herman Franks, who was in the spring training camp enjoying his new capacity as a retiree.

Juan sustained a groin pull and a sore side muscle early in the 1969 season. On the Fourth of July, the Giants won a pair against Atlanta, but still trailed the Braves by 4.5 games. During the second half, Marichal got back on track, turning in one gem after another. Meanwhile, a superb division race was unfolding. On Sunday, August 31, the Giants were in first place, half a game ahead of the Dodgers and Reds. The Braves were lurking in the background, two games back, and even the Astros were only 4.5 games behind. Juan finished the year with 21 wins, but the Braves surged ahead, and San Francisco finished in its customary second place.

Juan closed out his career in 1975 after short stints with the Dodgers and Red Sox, and was elected to the Hall of Fame on his third ballot in 1983. He resides in Miami.

JOE GIBBON

Joe Gibbon was one of a number of major leaguers from the Sixties who also had great basketball skills. On a 1956-1957 Ole Miss Bulldogs team, the six-foot-four Gibbon was nothing short of resolute, placing second in the nation in scoring at 30.2 points per game, ahead of young stars Elgin Baylor and Wilt Chamberlain. (Only Grady Wallace at South Carolina scored more.) Joe also snared 14 rebounds per contest and was drafted by the NBA's Celtics.

Ol' Miss also had a superb baseball program, and Joe helped pitch and hit his school to the College World Series. Though scouted by the Phillies, Braves and Yankees, he was signed in 1957 by Pirates regional scout Sammy Moses as both a pitcher and outfielder. Just three years later, he pitched for the Pirates against the Yankees in the 1960 World Series.

Joe wound up pitching for 13 years with the Pirates, Giants, Reds and Astros. He won a career-high 13 games in 1961 for the Bucs. He was with Pittsburgh through the 1965 season when he was swapped to the Giants in the Matty Alou trade.

Don Kessinger of the Cubs recalled, "He was a big left-handed pitcher who threw a heavy ball, a sinking fast ball, that produced a lot of ground-ball outs. He was a fine pitcher, and he was also a terrific guy, as friendly as could be." Gibbon compiled a record of 61-65 with a 3.52 ERA.

After his career, Joe raised cattle and coached college baseball. In 2010, he was one of four members of the 1960 champion Pirates healthy enough to participate in a 50th anniversary celebration. When he passed away in 2019 at age 83, the honorary pall bearers included his longtime baseball friends Frank Linzy, Luke Walker, and Ducky Schofield.

AUBREY GATEWOOD

Hurler Aubrey Gatewood was the 101st Arkansan to reach the big leagues, coming right after first baseman Tommy McCraw and just before shortstop Don Kessinger. One of the era's most famous Arkansans was Green Bay Packers star Don Hutson. When Hutson was house hunting in Palm Springs, California in March 1964, he stopped by the Angels training camp and visited Gatewood. The pair posed for a photograph, with Gatewood placing an Angels' cap atop Hutson's head.

Gatewood came to the Angels by way of the Tigers and Mets. In his first start for the Angels, late in the 1963 season, he threw a four-hitter against Boston for a 4-1 win. He described his pitching philosophy to writer Ross Newhan, saying, "Just put a little mustard on the ball and throw it over the plate. With the infield the Angels have, it's an absolute sin to walk anyone. Let 'em hit it, and you have an out."

After starting the following 1964 season in the minors, he was recalled in July and turned in a solid year in manager Bill Rigney's bullpen, registering a 2.24 ERA in 15 outings. Off-season surgery was conducted to remove bone chips from his pitching elbow.

He was hacked off when the Angels shunted him to the minor leagues again at the end of the 1965 training camp. "I am tired of being the scapegoat," he vented. "Each spring I go, and they keep donkeys who have yet to win a game in the big leagues." It appears that he refused to report to the minor-league team, and all talk of goats and donkeys notwithstanding, the Angels soon reinstated him, after which he turned in another solid season, appearing in 46 games.

His 1966 spring training was curtailed by a kidney infection and over the next three years, he labored mostly in the minor leagues, battling arm trouble in the Reds and Orioles organizations. He dabbled with a knuckle ball and last appeared in the big leagues for the Braves in 1970.

Aubrey finished his career back home with the Arkansas Travelers in the Double-A Dixie Association in 1971. (The loop was a short-lived combo of the Texas League and Southern League.) He compiled a lifetime MLB record of 8-9 in 68 games, with a surprisingly good 2.78 career ERA. He passed away in North Little Rock in 2019 at the age of 80. Years later, former teammate Ken McBride recalled him as "a good guy with a very good fastball."

KEN MCBRIDE

Bo Belinsky and Dean Chance got the headlines, but it was right-hander Ken McBride, a sinker ball specialist, who made the AL all-star team each of the Angels' first three years as an AL franchise.

Like his father before him, Ken was a sandlot baseball star, in his case playing at Edgewater Park and Brookside Park on Cleveland's west side. He was playing semi-pro baseball for the Mike's Diner team in 1953 when he signed with Red Sox scout Denny Galehouse, a former pitcher himself. Ken made the big leagues with the White Sox in time to pitch on their 1959 AL championship team. He recalled that club as having true competitors who were determined to do whatever it took to win. Ken roomed on the road that year with outfielder Jim McAnany.

After being selected by the Angels in the expansion draft, Ken went 12-15 with 180 strikeouts in 1961. His 1962 season was off to a sensational start with an 11-3 record when he suffered a cracked rib that put him on the disabled list. Ken rebounded to a 13-12 season in 1963. With the Angels, he roomed on the road primarily with pitcher Barry Latman. He credits coach Marv Grissom with helping him perfect his sinker.

In 1965, plagued by an injured arm, he retired with a lifetime 36-32 record and a 3.46 ERA. Thereafter, he returned to Ohio and worked in private industry. He presently resides in Westlake.

JIM FREGOSI

If any player personified Angels baseball during the new franchise's first decade, it was shortstop Jim Fregosi. He was a hard-nosed competitor, spirited leader, and an intelligent student of the game, who loved to spend time with manager Bill Rigney, discussing the intricacies of baseball.

Born in San Francisco, he attended high school in San Mateo, where he was a state broad jump champion and baseball star. He opted to forego college and signed with the Red Sox for a $20,000 bonus. The Angels snared him in the expansion draft and by the time Jim was 21, he was already the Angels' everyday shortstop.

Like most expansion teams, the Angels struggled during much of the decade, but Fregosi became the face of the franchise, making the AL all-star team six times. He hit .265 for his career with 151 homers and 1,726 hits and rivaled Luis Aparicio as the AL's best shortstop of the decade.

There was a degree of dysfunction on the early Angels' teams. While every club had players who enjoyed the night life, the Angels had more than their share. There were also personality conflicts. Fregosi never got along with the Angels' bonus-baby outfielder, Rick Reichardt, which caused dissension. He also had a difficult relationship, as did most teammates, with 1970 batting champion Alex Johnson. The presence of manager Bill Rigney provided some semblance of stability. Once he was replaced by Lefty Phillips, there was no longer a strong hand to maintain any element of cohesion.

Fregosi's last excellent season came in 1970, as he slugged 22 home runs and drove home 82 RBI, great numbers for a shortstop from that era. The Angels rose in the standings that year under Phillips, raising hopes – albeit falsely – that the team was building a winner.

Then in 1971, Fregosi developed a tumor on a foot. Dick Phillips, the club's general manager, prohibited Fregosi from having surgery until the shortstop finally checked himself into a hospital. His RBI total plunged from 82 to 33, Johnson was suspended several times, and the Angels posted a disappointing 76-86 record.

After the season, the front office made the difficult decision to trade this original Angel to the Mets, despite his popularity. It proved to be one of the greatest trades in franchise history, bringing in Nolan Ryan. The young fire-baller went on to win 138 games over the next eight years, while authoring four no-hitters as an Angel. When the franchise won its first division title in 1979, Ryan was a 16-game winner.

Since the Mets already had a shortstop in Bud Harrelson, the plan was to install Fregosi at third base. Jim had a frustrating 1972 season, and his problems continued into 1973, when he lost the third-base job to Wayne Garrett. That left the Mets paying a high salary to a veteran with no regular position.

In the book, *Tales from the New York Mets Dugout,* Bruce Markusen wrote, "Although only 31 years old at the time, Fregosi would never again attain the all-star status he had shown as a member of the Angels. Some critics attributed Fregosi's unusually early decline as a player to his hard-drinking style, which added to problems with his expanding waistline. New York City, with its 24-hour nightlife, only exacerbated Fregosi's penchant for late hours and barhopping."

Jim eventually became a reserve corner infielder and pinch-hitter for the Rangers and Pirates, retiring as a player in 1978. Just a year later, Fregosi guided the Angels as manager to their first-ever AL West title. The Angels retired his number in 1988. Fregosi piloted the Phillies to the NL pennant in 1993 and later managed the Blue Jays.

During 1999, while managing Toronto, Fregosi and coach Mel Queen (his former Angels teammate) reportedly got into an altercation at a bar with mob figure Joey Merlino. Fregosi emerged from the encounter with a black eye, but Merlino's luck was to take a turn for the worse, as he received a 14-year prison sentence for racketeering.

Fregosi's last position was special advisor to Braves general manager Frank Wren. After Jim died of a stroke in 2014, Wren said, "He lit up a room and had great relationships throughout the game." Wren said it was a constant source of comfort having Fregosi just a phone call away.

BOBBY KNOOP

As Bill Mazeroski was setting the standard for defense at second base in the senior circuit, Bobby Knoop briefly emerged as the AL counterpart. In 1964, the Angels awarded the job to the acrobatic Knoop, who had spent the previous eight years trolling the fields of minor-league ballparks. Knoop went on to lead AL second basemen in range factor and double plays four times over the next five years.

Knoop (rhyming with top) replaced Bill Moran as the second baseman and only hit .216 with seven homers that first season, with the first two coming on consecutive days against Tigers hurlers Dick Egan and Mickey Lolich. Though his batting average was subpar, Angels manager Bill Rigney loved his defense.

He soon began to contribute on offense, too. In 1965, he hit .269 and received some MVP votes. The next season, he produced 17 home runs, 72 RBI, and a league-high 11 triples. While winning three straight gold gloves, the Yorba Linda resident began working for the Angels in the off-seasons in the ticket-sales department, as well as selling insurance.

Fans marveled at the precision with which Knoop and shortstop Jim Fregosi turned the twin killing. The pair were not only keystone partners, but also road roommates and inseparable friends. Knoop set MLB records for most double plays in a game by a second sacker (six) and most putouts in a game (12).

Playing solid defense in the major leagues was actually easier than in the minors, he explained to beat writer Bob Oates. "You pretty much know what an established major leaguer can do, so it is possible to take a defensive position against him. In the minors, you face different hitters every year. You don't have solid information on what they do best," he explained. "Accurate information leads to good fielding."

He quickly became renowned for accurate, off-balanced throws to first base. "I'm lucky in that I can throw from any position," he explained to Oates. "It's just something I was born with."

Knoop was later asked whether second basemen habitually miss touching second base when turning twin-killings. "No sir. I don't think any major league fielder cheats as a matter of habit," Knoop told Oates. He said that as more games are televised, fans would see for themselves how scrupulously infielders adhere to the need to tap the base when turning the double play.

For all of the flash of the Knoop-and-Fregosi pairing at second base, the Angels continued to fall short of serious pennant contention, year in and year out. Part-way into the 1969 season, Knoop was struggling at the plate, and the team was falling short of fan expectations. Meanwhile, Knoop was earning a career-highest $37,500 in player salary. Angels owner Gene Autry had a sentimental streak, but he never let it stop him from making business decisions. The Angels traded Knoop to the White Sox, receiving a younger second baseman who could steal bases, Sandy Alomar, along with reliever Bob Priddy.

Knoop's 1969 season was interrupted when a July 27 baseline collision with Baltimore's Davey Johnson resulted in a broken orbital bone near his eye. After finishing both the 1969 and 1970 seasons with identical .229 batting clips, Knoop wound down his career as a utility man for the Royals. He retired with a .236 average, 856 hits, 56 homers, and 16 stolen bases.

He later spent more than 20 years as a coach, mostly with the Angels. He still works for the Angels in Arizona, observing minor league players, advising the player development team, and hitting fungos. Minor league manager Dave Stapleton said in 2017, "He just brings so much knowledge that young coaches just gravitate to him…Even as long as I've been doing this game, I'm talking to him every day about new stuff." Knoop, however, says its no big deal to still be working and coaching. For one thing, he told *Baseball America,* he doesn't like to be indoors.

For another, his dad lived to age 101. Most of all, he appreciates staying active in the sport he loves.

STEVE BILKO

An enormous guy by baseball standards, Steve Bilko stood six-foot-one and weighed at times as much as 270 pounds. He consumed such large quantities of beer after games, it was written, that he would shut the bathroom door in his hotel room and take a hot shower to steam the alcohol out of his system while consuming can after can.

As the starting first baseman for the 1953 Cardinals, he hit 21 round-trippers with 84 RBI, and tied a record with two doubles in the same inning. But he also led the league in strikeouts and lost his job to Joe Cunningham, a better contact hitter, the following season. The Cardinals sold him to the Cubs, who in turn demoted him to the minors.

In 1955 for Los Angeles in the Pacific Coast League (PCL), the strongman crushed 37 homers. He was just getting started. He added 55 circuit blasts the next year, and 56 the season after that. The personable slugger with an easy smile became well known in the Los Angeles area, which did not yet have a major league team, and supplemented his baseball salary with personal appearances. Bilko said he enjoyed the PCL but hoped to return to the majors.

After bouncing from the Cubs organization to the Redlegs to the Dodgers to the Tigers, the fan favorite wound up back in LA with the Angels for their 1961 expansion season. That gave Bilko one final chance to star at the major-league level and he came through, beating out several competitors for playing time and batting .279 with 20 homers.

The well-traveled veteran spent that winter at his home in Nanticoke, Pennsylvania, and sold the Shamrock Cocktail Bar in St. Louis that he and former player Rip Repulski co-owned, after realizing that it was not particularly profitable. Especially annoying, he told a writer, were incidents like the time a patron had two drinks, put a buck and a half on the bar, and walked out. The bartender put the money in his pocket. When asked why, the bartender said, "The guy left a $1.50 tip, and walked out without paying."

Steve was with the Angels again in 1962 but saw less action and closed the season on the disabled list with a leg infection. His final pro season in 1963 was spent in Rochester, where he shared first base duties with Luke Easter and Joe Altobelli. He retired with a .249 career average and 76 big-league homers.

After baseball, Bilko worked as an inspector for a perfume manufacturer and was just 49 years old when he passed away in Wilkes-Barre in 1978. He was inducted into the PCL Hall of Fame in 2003.

RICK REICHARDT

A baseball and football standout at Stevens Point High School and the University of Wisconsin, Rick Reichardt garnered a jaw-dropping $205,000 bonus in 1964 from Angels owner Gene Autry, who was personally involved in the pursuit of the prized prospect. Autry, a movie producer and owner of the radio station that carried Angels' games, saw investing in Reichardt much the same as hiring a movie star or on-air talent, only with a longer payoff period. To land Reichardt, he outbid clubs including the Yankees and the A's. Autry wanted Reichardt to be an Angel when the club opened its new stadium in 1966.

The bidding war for Reichardt was the last straw for cost-conscious owners, who instituted the first-year player draft the following year. The draft was one major change in the business of baseball that could be traced to Reichardt. Another came indirectly a decade later, when the reserve clause was struck down. The heart of the reserve clause was the argument that amateur players voluntarily selected the team with which they signed, hence they would remain property of that franchise unless traded, sold or released. But the institution of the draft meant that beginning in 1965, amateur players no longer could sign with the highest bidder, hence the underpinning of the reserve clause was gone, and free agency was instituted in the mid-Seventies.

Erudite, intelligent, and articulate, Reichardt came from a wealthy family (his dad was an orthopedic surgeon who treated quarterback Bart Starr) and did not fit the prototype for a ballplayer in the Sixties. Some teammates resented his huge bonus and constant press attention, none more so than shortstop Jim Fregosi, another talented and intelligent player who was the established star in Anaheim. Fregosi contributed to an atmosphere that made Reichardt's tenure with the Angels somewhat uncomfortable.

It wasn't as though Reichardt was unsuccessful. For the six years from 1966 to 1971, he averaged 20 home runs per season. He showed toughness in leading the league in hit by pitches, and finished his career with a respectable .261 batting average. But the consensus in the sport was that the old cowboy who owned the Angels had badly overpaid for this outfielder.

Early in the 1970 season, the Angels finally gave up on Reichardt, packaging him with third baseman Aurelio Rodriguez to Washington for another hot corner specialist, Ken McMullen. Reichardt delivered 19 homers in 1970 for manager Ted Williams, but the Senators swapped him to the ChiSox the following winter for pitcher Gary Janeski, who was coming off a 10-18 season. That showed how markedly Reichardt's value had plunged. His career, plagued by injuries, wound down from there, ending with a single at bat in April, 1974, with the Royals.

Decades later, reflecting on the Angels' decision to rush him quickly to the big leagues, he admitted that he would have been well served by more seasoning in the minor leagues.

After baseball, he settled in Gainesville, Florida, near some of his siblings, and pursued a career in financial planning. He also did some coaching for the Florida Gators. Reichardt was inducted into the College Baseball Hall of Fame in Lubbock, Texas in 2015, alongside Frank Viola and Lance Berkman.

EDDIE FISHER

Eddie Fisher, who pitched in MLB for 15 years, was born in Louisiana, but his family moved to Oklahoma when he was an infant. Oklahoma, at the time, spawned baseball players the way Idaho produced potatoes. Fisher observed in 2006, "Oklahoma just became a hotbed for producing baseball players and was real strong in American Legion baseball. A lot of the players went through that program and really blossomed. It just became a tradition."

Eddie studied at a small rural high school and was awarded a baseball scholarship at the University of Oklahoma. He began experimenting with the knuckler but was forbidden by his coach to throw it in games. Finally, while pitching his way through the Giants' minor league system, he got to the point where he could throw the pitch for strikes, making it a formidable weapon.

His chance to pitch for the 1959 Giants came when Jack Sanford went down with a broken hand. Yet, he struggled in several big-league trials and by the time the Giants had their big year in 1962, Fisher was with the White Sox.

In 1965, he had his best year, garnering a fireman of the year award, winning 15 games while saving 24 others. He pitched in 82 games, registering a tidy 2.40 ERA.

Handling the knuckleball has always been a challenge for catchers. Fisher said that J.C. Martin of the White Sox was probably the most adept of the catchers he worked with at handling the pitch. The ChiSox had both Hoyt Wilhelm and Fisher on their staff and in 1965, as they combined to pitch 309 innings out of the pen. That's a lot of knuckleballs.

Martin, a former first baseman, was a natural at catching the knuckleball because, in Fisher's words, "A first baseman has to go out and catch the ball, and not just let it come to him. And if you let the knuckleball just come to you, it will beat you to death. You've got to reach out and get it."

Midway into the 1966 season, the ChiSox traded Fisher to the Orioles. Eddie remained at the top of his game and led the AL in appearances for the second-straight year. He would have liked to have pitched in the World Series, but the O's had little need for relief pitching in sweeping the Dodgers.

He spent the 1968 season with the Indians. By then, Fisher was throwing the knuckler about 75 percent of the time but mixing in a slider and sneaky fastball that would later be clocked at 88 miles per hour, not bad for a guy who viewed the heater as his third pitch.

He was traded before the 1969 season to the Angels, where he became friendly with team owner Gene Autry. The former cowboy actor gave Fisher a revolver he had used in a movie. Fisher, in turn, gave Autry a gun from his own personal collection. The hurler said Autry was in the clubhouse often, mixing with and encouraging the players. Eddie pitched for the Angels until 1972, then divided one final season with the White Sox and Cardinals. His lifetime marks included an 85-70 record and a 3.41 ERA.

Even during his playing days, Fisher had an enterprising streak. He owned and operated a baseball camp in his hometown of Altus, complete with five playing diamonds (three of which were lighted), pitching machines, sliding pits, and a swimming pool. Youngsters with talent could attend the camp and receive quality instruction from qualified coaches.

After retiring from baseball, Fisher worked as a bank president and as state superintendent of public golf courses, a job that "required" him to play a lot of golf. The jobs provided good income to help Fisher put his children through college. Still residing in Altus, Fisher has also enjoyed attending baseball reunions.

LARRY COLTON

Remarkably, the Pi Kappa Alpha fraternity at UC Berkeley in the mid-Sixties produced three major league pitchers – Rich Nye, Dave Dowling and Larry Colton. Given the anti-war movement and emerging drug culture, it was an insane time to be at Berkeley. But Colton made lifelong friends on campus, five of whom he chronicled in an entertaining 1993 book entitled, *Goat Brothers*.

A 210-pound right-hander (who batted lefty), Colton appeared in just one game in the big leagues – a two-inning relief appearance for the Phillies on May 6, 1968. Soon thereafter, his left shoulder was dislocated in a fight outside a bar. Though not his pitching shoulder, he nonetheless changed his motion and was never the same pitcher. Colton labored in the minor leagues for a couple of more seasons, then devoted his attention to writing.

Colton's first wife was Denise Hedwick, the beautiful daughter of Austrian-American actress Hedy Lamarr and British actor John Loder. The wedding was on Rodeo Drive in Beverly Hills and a photo of Colton and his bride ran in *Life* magazine. The marriage lasted only five years, perhaps not surprising in that Hedy Lamarr herself had already been married six times.

Colton moved to Portland and spent time bike-riding with basketball legend Bill Walton. His first book was about the Walton-led Portland Trail Blazers championship team. *Goat Brothers* was his second book. He spent more than a year on location with Crow Indians in Montana before writing his third book which described that experience. Still another exceptional book focused on baseball and civil rights in Birmingham in the mid-Sixties. Colton continues to live in Portland.

DICK ALLEN

Philadelphia's Shibe Park (Connie Mack Stadium) had a 65-foot-high left-field grandstand, which Dick (Richie) Allen of the Phillies cleared 18 times in seven seasons. Allen's dazzling power prompted opposing slugger Willie Stargell to joke that the reason Philadelphia fans booed Allen was because his home runs were hit so far that they weren't yielding souvenirs for the spectators.

Allen was not the only player in the Sixties on the receiving end of negative feedback from home fans – infielder Ted Lepcio was booed mercilessly by Phillies patrons, Donn Clendenon often heard it from the fans in Pittsburgh, and Frank Robinson got the same treatment in Cincinnati. But few players were more controversial than Allen.

Starting with his spectacular 1964 rookie-of-the-year season, Allen pounded 177 homers in seven years for the Phillies, while topping the .300 mark four times. His offensive heroics – coupled with his ability to be charming when he wanted to – initially won him legions of admirers.

Allen's fielding at the corner infield positions was erratic, but what really fueled Phillies fans' eventual ambivalence was his penchant for voicing every complaint that crossed his mind. He quarreled with managers, teammates and scribes. Sometimes, as with the racism he encountered, those gripes were completely understandable. His confrontation with race-baiting outfielder Frank Thomas led to Thomas becoming an ex-Phillie. A similar fate awaited manager Bob Skinner, who resigned after feuding with Allen.

Other times, Allen seemed to be looking for arguments and confrontations. The classic example was his attempt to avoid taxes on $40,000 in bonus money by giving it to his mother. He took that case all the way to the U.S. Tax Commissioner before being ordered to pay the back taxes.

Smoking cigarettes in the dugout and getting drunk after games was then part of baseball's culture. But drinking before and during games, which Allen started doing, was a problem.

On June 24, 1969, after a night in Jets quarterback Joe Namath's bar in New York, Allen reportedly failed to show up for a twi-night twinbill against the Mets. The Phillies suspended him, noting it was the third time in two years he didn't answer the bell on time to play. He was later reinstated, but on Richie Ashburn's radio show on August 18, Allen said, "I have no intention of returning here. I have taken about as much as I can stand." He also moved his locker out of the main clubhouse, at various times suggesting it was to evade the press or protect his teammates.

The Phils had entertained trade offers from the Mets and Indians after the 1968 season but never consummated a deal. They finally honored Allen's trade request and shipped him to the Cardinals after the 1969 season. The slugger enjoyed playing for Cards manager Red Schoendienst. Although Dick hit 34 home runs for St. Louis in 1970, he rubbed management the wrong way by returning to his horse farm in Pennsylvania after an injury rather than rehabbing with team officials. The Cardinals suffered their first losing season since 1965 and soon after the season traded him to the Dodgers for a pair of young players, Ted Sizemore and Bob Stinson. Allen lasted just a single season at Chavez Ravine, as well, chafing at many of the club's public relations policies such as requiring interaction with fans.

Dick reached his apex in 1972 with the White Sox, turning in an MVP season that saw him lead the loop in home runs, RBI and bases on balls. The White Sox were rebuilding under manager Chuck Tanner and hoped Allen would be the centerpiece of a revival. Allen carried the Sox to a second-place finish in the AL West that year, but the team regressed the next two summers. By the time Allen walked away from the club late in the 1974 season, the Pale Hose, too, were ready to part ways.

Among Allen's other complaints was artificial turf, which was becoming prevalent in the Seventies. "If a horse won't eat it, I don't want to play on it," Allen said. Another target was sportswriters. "I wish they'd shut the gates, and let us play ball with no press and no fans," he said.

Allen's next stop was back where it all began in Philadelphia for the 1975 and 1976 seasons. The aging first baseman was warmly welcomed but had trouble staying healthy, and his production was uneven. His second stay with the Phils ended when he got into a dispute with management over their plan to leave teammate Tony Taylor off the 1976 playoff roster.

Allen made an impression wherever he went. Willie Mays said that Allen "hits the ball harder than any player I've ever seen." Outfielder Don Lock, who played a couple of seasons with him, told writer Graham Womack that Allen would have hit 500 to 520 homers if he had applied himself. Teammate Ron Stone remembers Allen as "very quiet, but an incredible right-handed hitter." Catcher Dave Watkins was a teammate in 1969. "Allen was very quiet and never said much of anything. He let his bat do the talking," he remembered in 2023. "His locker was next to mine and we did strike up a friendship and had conversations about hitting. He liked my explanation of Force = Mass times Acceleration as it applies to striking a baseball."

After a final 1977 season as a DH with the A's, Allen retired with a .292 average, 351 circuit clouts and 1,848 hits. After baseball, Allen largely stayed away from the game for a number of years. He attempted to return to the sport as a hitting coach or scout after the shooting death of his daughter but was unable to land a position. He died at age 77 in his hometown of Wampum, Pennsylvania, in 2020.

HANK ALLEN

While playing for the Senators, Hank Allen developed an interest in horse racing. He spent his free time at a pair of Maryland race tracks, Laurel Park and Pimlico. After his playing days were complete and it became clear that he would not be able to land a baseball front-office job, he remained in Upper Marlboro in Prince George's County and became a trainer and owner of race horses. In 1989, he was the first African American to saddle a horse in the Kentucky Derby.

"It was an unforgettable experience," he told *The Baltimore Sun.* "There's no other day like it. I compare it to the World Series. People are gathered around your barn and they ask you about your rider, your horse. There's a line of people about 10 deep all the way from the barn until you walk onto the racetrack. And that's like an honor that you are walking through."

Allen was born in the small town of Wampum, Pennsylvania, as were his brothers Dick and Ron, who also became major-league players. Hank attended college at Baldwin-Wallace and Youngstown State, signed with the Phillies, and played six years of minor league ball. Versatile enough to man most positions, he saw action in seven MLB seasons with the Senators, Brewers, and White Sox (where he was a teammate of his brother Dick). He remained with Chicago long enough to qualify for his pension.

His best year was 1969 when he got off to a torrid start. By May 4, the Senators had a surprisingly strong 16-11 record, with Allen batting .339 and making national news. Though he cooled off, in 109 games he set career highs in batting average (.277), stolen bases (12), hits (75), and runs scored (42). His success coincided with the arrival of manager Ted Williams and coach Nellie Fox, gentlemen who knew something about hitting.

Allen finished with a .241 lifetime batting average, 212 hits, and six home runs. A longtime scout for the Royals, he recently has been living in Riverview, Florida.

FRANK MALZONE

Third baseman Frank Malzone spent 11 years with the Red Sox, who finished anywhere from third to ninth in the AL during those seasons. By the time Boston won a pennant in 1967, Malzone was still affiliated with the club as an advance scout.

Frank was born in the Bronx, moved to northern New York after getting married, and then began making his home in Massachusetts midway through his playing career. The six-time all-star was with Boston from 1955 to 1965, before one final season with the Angels.

Though few teams scouted Malzone as a prospect, many sought to acquire him later via trade (the Indians, for example, reportedly went so far in 1959 as to offer Rocky Colavito for him). It was not just for Malzone's timely hitting. He was also a spectacular defender who won three gold gloves. He was known for guarding the line, going deep behind the bag to snare hot shots and firing to first base in time to retire the hitter. He was also adept at fielding bunts with his bare hand.

Yankees infielder Gil McDougald commented in 1960, "He has the quickest hands and the way he handles high hoppers, and how he gets into position to field hits into outs, give him an incredible effectiveness." Writer Larry Claflin called him, "a Rock of Gibraltar at third base."

Baseball Writers Association President Dan Daniel said, "He doesn't say much, is all business, and is always in shape." In the later years of his Red Sox run, despite his quiet nature, he was a speaker on the team's winter goodwill caravan through New England. During the off-seasons, Malzone enjoyed bow-and-arrow hunting, and often bowled with teammates Ike Delock, Ted Lepcio and Dick Radatz on Friday nights.

Malzone was an all-star as late as 1964 but saw his hitting drop off the next year. When the Sox released him after the 1965 season, it moved his $35,000 salary off the books.

During the winter meetings, Malzone signed with the Angels. Sportswriters ribbed Angels general manager Fred Haney for running an old-folks home, noting that his mid-winter pickups, Lew Burdette, Frank Malzone and Norm Siebern, were 39, 35, and 32 years of age respectively. The club's roster at the time also included Joe Adcock and Vic Power, who were 38 and 34 years old.

Frank got into 82 games for the Halos but batted only .206. He retired with a .274 average, 133 home runs as well as 1,486 hits. He was part of the Sox organization for more than 40 years, and was inducted into the Red Sox Hall of Fame in 1995. Frank passed away in 2015.

RICO PETROCELLI

Beloved by the Fenway faithful, Rico Petrocelli devoted his whole career to the Red Sox (1963 to 1976). Rico grew up in Brooklyn as a Yankees fan idolizing Mickey Mantle and enjoyed those occasions when his dad took him to games in the Bronx. He pitched and played outfield in high school, but after signing in 1962, the Sox ticketed him to play shortstop.

As the starting shortstop at age 22 in 1965, Rico hit below .240, endured muscle pulls, elbow trouble, and battled personal insecurity. The bad elbow kept him from making sharp throws, and at times sidelined him entirely. Billy Herman, an old-school manager who had been a Hall of Fame second baseman in the 1930s, grew frustrated with his young player missing so much action.

But team captain Carl Yastrzemski was a source of frequent encouragement. "Rico is a sensitive guy," Yaz said in 1966. "He wants to play good for the home fans so much that I believe he presses at Fenway Park. But give the kid a little more time in baseball and you'll see something. What talent."

Yaz and Petrocelli were fast friends, but another source of encouragement was coach Eddie Popowski, who had managed Rico in the minor leagues. He joined the Sox staff under new manager Dick Williams in 1967, after Herman was canned. Rico made the first of two all-star squads that year, and the Sox went all of the way to the World Series. Boston lost the Series to the Cardinals, but Petrocelli bashed two home runs in game six. He then followed up in 1969 with one of the best seasons ever enjoyed to that point by a shortstop. He was just the third player in MLB history to hit 40 home runs with fewer than 100 RBI (Duke Snider and Mickey Mantle were the first two).

For relaxation, he listened to jazz, especially drummer Buddy Rich. He also took drumming lessons, which he believed strengthened his wrists. During the 1967-1968 offseason, he worked in public relations for an oil company. During that time, his family of five resided in Peabody in an apartment complex that was also home to teammates Gary Waslewski, Bucky Brandon and Mike Andrews, as well as hockey star Bobby Orr. Rico and his wife bought a home of their own several months later.

Rico always enjoyed an affinity with other Italian-American players. At different times, the Red Sox employed several such players including himself, Tony and Billy Conigliaro, Tom Satriano, and Mike Fiore. Hurler Jerry Casale said he detected an anti-Italian bias in the Red Sox front office, but Rico never observed it.

Petrocelli remained a top slugger through the 1971 season, which was his first as a third baseman, and he was still a key part of the Sox in 1975. Rico played in all seven World Series games that year and hit .308, but Boston again came up short. He retired after the 1976 season with a .251 average, 210 home runs and 1,352 hits. After baseball, he has worked in sports marketing and hosted radio shows.

JIM GOSGER

In 1965, Red Sox owner Tom Yawkey listed four players who were "untouchable" in the trade market: Carl Yastrzemski, Tony Conigliaro, Dick Radatz, and Jim Gosger. The first three were all-stars. Gosger was a young, athletic center fielder who projected a bright future. Memorable moments came often. He set a Carolina League record with 10 RBI in a game. He homered off Whitey Ford on the last day of the 1965 season. Later, he went deep twice in a 1966 game against Denny McLain. And when he slugged a game-winning homer in the 16th inning of a June 1966 game against the Yankees, it was the seventh "latest" game-winning homer in MLB history.

Billy Herman, his manager in Boston, admired his intensity, defensive range, and accurate arm. Those same qualities made Gosger attractive to the A's, and it turned out he wasn't untouchable after all. The A's acquired him in a June 13, 1966 trade that sent John Wyatt, Jose Tartabull, and Roland Sheldon to Boston. Gosger responded well with the A's and registered career highs of 10 homers and 44 RBI that season.

The emergence of Rick Monday and Reggie Jackson eventually relegated Gosger to defensive specialist and pinch-hitting duty for the A's. He divided the 1969 season between the Pilots, Mets, and Tidewater Tides. Jim gained a new lease on baseball life with the Expos in 1970, and enjoyed the experience so much that he wintered in Montreal, working in the team's public relations department. He later played for the Mets through 1974 and closed the books on his career with a .226 batting average and 30 home runs.

Looking back, Gosger wrote on Facebook, "I always loved the game that I played for 14 years and I know many teammates and friends were treated unfairly but those were the best years of my life." His favorite ballparks were Fenway Park in Boston and Wrigley Field in Chicago. After baseball, Gosger was employed by the Port Huron Utilities Department and worked evenings and weekends as a basketball and football referee. A man who values faith and family, he collects $5 for every autograph request which he sends to the St. Jude Children's Hospital charity. Gosger enjoys music from soft rock artists such as Neil Diamond, Rod Stewart, and the Bee Gees and continues to live in Port Huron, Michigan.

JOE LAHOUD

On June 11, 1969, a Red Sox outfielder blasted three home runs in a single game. One would figure it had to be Yaz, Reggie Smith, Rico Petrocelli, or Tony Conigliaro. In fact, it was Joe LaHoud, a player who had an 11-year career, despite a .223 lifetime batting average.

The game was against the Twins and Joe went yard against Dave Boswell, Dick Woodson, and Bob Miller as the Sox rolled to a 13-5 victory. It was only the second time in the Sixties that a Boston player homered three times in a game, the other being Ken Harrelson in 1968.

LaHoud also played for the Brewers, Angels, Rangers, and Royals. His best season came in 1974 when he batted .271 with 13 home runs for the Angels. His manager there was Dick Willliams, who was previously his Red Sox skipper. Williams and coach Grover Resinger, the Angels' intense bench coach, pressured players to perform at a high level, and berated them when they didn't. As LaHoud ruefully recalled, "They should have had swastikas on their arms."

With Boston, Joe roomed with pitcher Sparky Lyle. The hurler once said in mock annoyance, "He comes from a city of 50,000 people, and about 49,000 of them have called him up" on the phone. The outfielder retired with 65 career home runs and went into business in Connecticut.

JIM LONBORG

Whenever articles are written about the all-time Red Sox heroes, Jim Lonborg is highlighted, based on his magical 1967 season.

Jim grew up following the national pastime and collecting baseball cards in California, where his dad was a professor of agriculture at Cal Poly. Jim was a towering right-hander who starred at San Luis Obispo High School, alongside the team's star shortstop, Mel Queen. Not only was Queen his best friend and a future major leaguer, he married Lonborg's sister. After graduation, Jim studied at Stanford with the intention of becoming a physician but put his studies on hold after signing with Boston for a $20,000 bonus.

In his first two major-league seasons, 1965 and 1966, he turned in records of 9-17 and 10-10. "Bill Monbouquette was one of my mentors," he later recalled of the pitcher five years his senior. "He was a hard worker, especially running, and I tried to match him step for step."

Those Red Sox teams had acquired a reputation of having a country club – or perhaps a night club -- orientation. Jim enjoyed golf, symphony music concerts, and sometimes hung out at rock n roll clubs, but was among the more mild-mannered young men on the team. He roomed on road trips in the early years with utility man George Thomas and catcher Mike Ryan – who would also be a teammate later with the Phillies – and pitcher Bill Rohr.

After the 1966 season, Jim pitched in Venezuela, then spent time skiing at the Heavenly Resport at Lake Tahoe. Skiing was an essential part of his fitness regimen, and where better to ski than at Tahoe, which hosted the 1960 Winter Olympics. Jim went directly from Tahoe to spring training and was in the best condition of his life.

The coming season would be the best of his career. During spring training, pitching coach Sal Maglie trained the youngster to work the inside of the plate, while new manager Dick Williams instilled a sense of discipline on the team. By April 28, when Jim threw a six-hit shutout against the A's with 13 strikeouts, it was clear he was on the verge of something special. By July 4, the Sox were only four games over .500, but Lonborg had a record of 12-3. The club gained ground in the second half, and with one game left, they were tied for first place. With the pennant on the line, Lonborg took the mound one last time on October 1, and beat the Twins at Fenway Park for his 22nd win to clinch the flag.

All hell broke out, with fans rushing the field. "I was trying to get back in the dugout," he related. "Thank God for the Boston police, they were able to control the crowd. It was delirium." He later remembered, "We had to wait in the clubhouse to hear the outcome of the Tigers game. After that news, it was pure joy."

Lonborg not only was the AL strikeout champ but he won the Cy Young Award, as well. During the World Series, Jim hurled a one-hitter in game two and a four-hitter in game five. Williams brought Jim back on just two days rest for game seven, and the Cardinals prevailed, 7-2.

Jim was back on the slopes the following winter but tore two knee ligaments and missed spring training. In changing his delivery, he tore his right rotator cuff. He posted a 6-10 record in 1969 and a 7-11 mark in 1970.

Jim needed dozens of cortisone shots due to the shoulder injury. Asked about the shots decades later, he said, "As long as they were shot into the right place and did the right job, they were not a problem. I had no side effects from taking the meds."

It was not until 1972, while pitching for the Brewers, that he enjoyed another brilliant season with 14 wins and a 2.83 ERA. Jim also had a pair of fine seasons for the Phillies in 1974 and 1976. He retired in 1979 with a 157-137 record, 3.86 ERA, and 1,475 strikeouts.

Elston Howard, who caught him in 1967 and 1968, said, "You really get to know a pitcher when you catch him. Lonborg has a terrific fastball and he throws a curve the way it should be thrown – hard." Lonborg is equally complimentary, saying, "What a fine gentleman. I'm so thankful he was traded to the Red Sox in 1967 as I relied on his experience."

Lonborg married in 1970. The couple bought a historic colonial home that dates back to close to 1700. "We are only the fifth family living in this house. It has great bones and charm." At his wife's suggestion, he went to Tufts Dental School and practiced for 30 years. He also participated regularly in the Jimmy Fund charity where he got to know Ted Williams. In 2017, Jim returned to Fenway to celebrate the champion club's 50th anniversary, alongside Rico Petrocelli, Carl Yastrzemski, Gary Waslewski, Reggie Smith and Hawk Harrelson. A cancer survivor, Jim still enjoys golf and watches Red Sox games on radio or television when he can.

GEORGE THOMAS

During the 1960s, most teams sought to carry a super-utility man who could play four or five positions and also pinch-hit. Since neither league had the designated hitter rule yet, light-hitting pitchers often had to come out for pinch-hitters in the late innings of games. Few players served this super-utility role better than George Thomas.

In addition to defensive versatility and the ability to hit, the best of the super-utility men also had a keen sense of humor. Thomas was a positive influence in the clubhouse and the dugout, often poking fun at how infrequently he was called upon to play. In a career that spanned from 1957 to 1971, he was a member of the Tigers, Angels, Red Sox and Twins. Being a member of the 1967 Red Sox championship club was a highlight of his career and the club's skipper, Dick

Williams, was his favorite manager. George played every position except pitcher – and with his strong arm, he could have pitched if asked.

His best season was 1961 with the expansion Angels, as he hit .274 with 13 homers and 59 RBI. He also put up a pair of impressive batting average for the BoSox in limited action late in his career -- .353 in 1969 and .343 in 1970.

After hanging up his spikes, George coached baseball at the University of Minnesota and then worked in the audiovisual field until retiring in Sarasota, Florida, where he still resides.

MIKE ANDREWS

After years of disappointing finishes, the Red Sox won the 1967 pennant as first-year manager Dick Williams provided the needed mix of inspiration and discipline. Williams was not the only "rookie" driving the team's success. Reggie Smith, playing center field, delivered 15 home runs and solid defense. At second base, rookie Mike Andrews hit .263, scored 79 runs and led the circuit in sacrifice hits. During September, when the pressure of the pennant race was at its apex, Andrews hit .342 and sparked many a Boston rally.

Mike was a native Californian and when the Red Sox made their first visit to Anaheim that season, he had 90 friends and relatives in the stands cheering him on. He also won a following in Boston from knowledgeable fans who appreciated his unselfish brand of baseball. Scribes projected that he could become the best Sox second baseman since Bobby Doerr retired in 1951, if his balky back would hold up. Even as a rookie, Andrews needed whirlpool treatments to relax the back muscles.

After another solid season in 1968 in which only four players had higher on-base percentages (Carl Yastrzemski, Frank Robinson, Mickey Mantle and Rick Monday), Mike became an all-star in 1969, hitting a career best .293 with 15 homers.

He had another solid year offensively in 1970, but he also led the league's second sackers in errors. Meanwhile, the Red Sox missed the post-season for the third straight year. Looking to tighten up their infield defense, Boston traded Andrews and another infielder (Luis Alvarado) to the White Sox for shortstop Luis Aparicio. Boston separately acquired glove man Doug Griffin to supplant Andrews at second base.

Away from Boston, baseball became less fun. Though he hit well for the 1971 White Sox, he played with pain in his wrist, shoulder and back. He led AL second basemen in errors again the next two seasons, mostly on errant throws. That resulted in a switch to first base. When his offensive production dropped off in 1972, it meant less playing time.

The White Sox released him in 1973 and he signed with the A's. His career came to an ignominious end during that year's World Series when he committed two errors in one inning and was berated by team owner Charles Finley into signing a statement saying that he had a chronic shoulder injury rendering him unable to play. Andrews signed the statement and flew home to Massachusetts.

The story didn't end there. The A's players affixed Andrews' number 17 to their uniforms for game three of the Series, after which Commissioner Bowie Kuhn ordered Andrews to be reinstated. Although the circumstances were unusual, he received a World Series champion ring.

Andrews sat out the 1974 season, spending time with family. He played overseas in 1975, where he struggled against Japanese pitching, but the engagement paid well. Thereafter, Andrews led the Jimmy Fund, a Dana-Farver Cancer Institute charity, and participated in various baseball and golf-related fundraisers.

Andrews' final statistics included a .258 batting average, 803 hits and 66 homers. His younger brother, Rob Andrews, played second base for five years with the Astros and Giants. Mike now resides in Jupiter, Florida.

TOMMIE AGEE

Outfielder Tommie Agee is remembered for his splendid 1966 rookie-of-the-year season with the White Sox and for sparking the Mets to the 1969 world championship. Those accomplishments capped his 11-year career with five teams.

The Alabama native signed with Cleveland off the campus of Grambling University for a $60,000 bonus. Late-season call-ups from 1962 to 1964 confirmed both his superb outfield range and his propensity to strike out. The Tribe envisioned moving back the fences in 1965 so that Agee could chase down would-be home runs in centerfield, but abandoned that scheme when he was traded to the ChiSox.

The 1965 campaign was a lost season after he broke a bone in his hand trying to score on a passed ball during spring training. The injury bothered him all summer at Triple-A Indianapolis.

Finally playing big league ball in all of 1966, he led the Sox in batting average, home runs, RBI, runs scored, doubles and triples. Chicago went 83-79, and would have clearly been below .500 without his production. He took satisfaction in his success and enjoyed rooming on the road with teammate Tom McCraw.

Agee skipped winter ball for the first time, and in 1967 endured a slump so severe that he visited Dr. Herbert Nash, who gave him some eye exercises to strengthen the eye. At the time of the exam, Agee was batting .239. It's not clear how hard Agee focused on the exercises, but he finished the year at just .234.

Agee welcomed an off-season trade to the Mets, but the 1968 season brought more misery. During his first exhibition game, he was beaned by a pitch from Bob Gibson, (prompting him to finally start wearing a helmet with an ear flap). In another pre-season game, teammate Ron Swoboda barreled into Agee as he prepared to make a catch. In a third spring contest, a throw from Swoboda took a wicked hop and hit Agee just below the eye, knocking him out of the game. The bad luck carried over into the 1968 regular season, as he hit just .218. At one point, Agee went 0-for-34, tying Don Zimmer's Mets record for futility.

At the suggestion of manager Gil Hodges, he spent a month after the 1968 season in Florida for a refresher course. Coach Whitey Herzog worked with Agee on hitting fundamentals, and both came away convinced a big season was on the way.

The Mets' patience paid off. In 1969, Agee delivered a strong season, hitting .271 with 26 home runs. One highlight was becoming the first player to crush a home run into the fifth (and top) deck of Shea Stadium. He still struck out with an alarming frequency but his all-around excellence propelled the Mets to the division crown, and Agee placed sixth in the MVP balloting.

As the Mets swept the Braves in the NLCS, Agee contributed two home runs and two stolen bases. And though he batted only .167 in the World Series, he delivered a home run and made two spectacular catches in game three – which *Sports Illustrated* called perhaps the greatest single-game performance ever by a center fielder in any World Series. The Mets prevailed over Baltimore in five games.

Agee had one more stellar season in 1970, then began to gain weight, suffer more injuries, and produce less on the field. He remained with the Mets through 1972 and then split one final season between Houston and St. Louis. He retired with a lifetime batting average of .255 with 999 hits, 130 home runs and 167 stolen bases. One of the most popular players in Mets history, Agee later ran the Outfielder's Lounge near Shea Stadium, mingled with fans, and took part in charity events. He died of cardiac arrest in 2001.

Cleon Jones

Outfielder Cleon Jones enjoyed his MLB career and most everything that came with it. After joining the Mets in 1966, he became nationally known in 1969, when he hit .340 and helped propel them to the NL crown.

Adding to the fun was having one of his best friends on the team. Tommie Agee was traded to the Mets ahead of the 1968 season. The pair had been teammates on their high school baseball, football, basketball and track teams in Mobile, and close friends, as well. They were born five days apart in August 1942. With New York, they were roommates on road trips and both traveled with portable record players. Their favorites included Aretha Franklin, Jimmy Smith and Dizzy Gillespie, according to a 1968 article in *The Sporting News.*

By 1969, Cleon was making more money and loving it. "Cleon's tastes run much more expensively," wrote Jack Lang that year. "He's somewhat of a fashion plate with $80 alligator shoes, tailor made silk suits and pastel shirts." After the season, he bought a 14-foot runabout boat with an outboard engine, perfect for fishing.

Jones had blazing speed, covered ample ground in the outfield, and had a decent arm. Although he never had another season quite like 1969, he did bat .319 and tied his career-high 14 home runs in 1971. He was still with the Mets in 1973 when the club won the NL pennant. He hit .300 in the victorious NLCS over the Reds and .286 in the World Series, which the Mets lost to Oakland.

The outfielder concluded his career with the 1976 White Sox. He was a lifetime .281 hitter with 93 home runs, 91 steals and 1,196 hits. Jones, who continues to reside in Mobile, was the 15th person inducted into the Mets Hall of Fame in 1991.

ED CHARLES

The Beatles had a memorable hit record in 1970 with "The Long and Winding Road." The same phrase could be used to describe the ascent of smooth-fielding third baseman Ed Charles. Having grown up in a poverty-stricken section of Daytona Beach as one of nine kids in a broken family, Ed dropped out of school after the eighth grade and moved around Florida working odd jobs. Having drawn inspiration from Jackie Robinson's historic integration of the sport, he never lost his dream to play baseball. He signed with the Braves after a try-out in 1952 and finally made the big leagues in 1962, experiencing countless occurrences of humiliating and infuriating discrimination in the interim.

With the A's, Ed and infielder Wayne Causey were probably the club's best all-around players from 1962 to 1966. Charles hit well, stole bases and played inspirational defense. His best season was his rookie year at age 29, as he set career highs for batting average (.288), homers (17), RBI (74) and stolen bases (20).

He was nicknamed "Easy Ed," and as Skip Lockwood observed, "He was easy to talk to. He had soft hands and seemed able to handle any ball without a question."

In 1967, the A's were looking to shed salary and make room for younger players, so they traded Charles to the Mets. In 1968, he led the Mets in home runs with 15 and was third in RBI with 53. Now in his mid-30s, he also provided a veteran presence on a young team, helping to heal internal rifts and advise young African American players about the discrimination they would still need to overcome.

Ed remained with the Mets as a part-time player on the 1969 team, seeing action in four World Series games. Though the club released him after the season, he was content to go out on top as a world champion.

Charles wrote poetry reflecting his thoughts on humanity's struggle for equal opportunity. He later did some scouting and coaching, and supervised juvenile offenders in security facilities. He returned to Shea Stadium for the last game there in 2008, one of 47 players chosen to reflect the 47 years of Mets baseball there. Ed lived in the New York area and was 84 years old when he died in 2018.

DONN CLENDENON

Not every ballplayer in the Sixties was a strategic negotiator. But Donn Clendenon excelled as both a power-hitting first baseman and a negotiator, and those two paths intersected in 1969, when he landed a lucrative multi-year contract during an era when players had precious little bargaining leverage.

The Clendenon story starts in Georgia, where he played ball for Booker T. Washington High School and was a classmate of future political leader Vernon Jordan. Donn's stepfather was Nish Williams, a successful Atlanta restaurateur and player-manager in Negro League baseball. Donn grew up with stars like Satchel Paige, Roy Campanella, and Don Newcombe coming by the restaurant. Immersed in the sport, it was inevitable he would develop a love for the game. He attended Morehouse College where his "big brother" was Dr. Martin Luther King, Jr.

Donn signed with Pittsburgh and figured prominently in the Pirates' run production for most of the decade. From 1963 to 1968, the big first sacker produced 458 RBI, or an average of 76 per season. In 1963, he made Forbes Field history when he smashed a homer over the right-center field wall between the 436-foot marker and the memorial to Barney Dreyfuss (the former Pirates owner). He was the first right-handed hitter to do so in a regular-season game (Mickey Mantle had done it during the 1960 World Series).

Clendenon leveraged his new home base in Pittsburgh to enter a winter management training program with U.S. Steel and began pursuing a law degree. He put those studies on hold temporarily and moved back to Atlanta when his step-father became ill with colon cancer.

The deaths of his step-father and Dr. King, coupled with his duties as the Pirates' player representative, took a mental toll on him in 1968, as did the booing from his home fans. "I just can't take it anymore. I'm fed up with all the turmoil because I'm not hitting. I press and it causes me to make mistakes," he told a reporter. "I'm fed up with the booing, the criticism and the nervous tension a poor season brings on." A stronger second half helped him finish the year with a .257 average, 17 homers and 87 RBI.

When the 1968 expansion draft arrived, the Pirates' front office was in a quandary, with more good hitters than they could protect. Although Donn had led the team in RBI, he also topped the league in strikeouts with 163. Preferring to protect younger players, the Bucs exposed him to the draft, and he was selected by the Expos, who quickly swapped him to Houston in the trade that sent Rusty Staub north of the border.

While the Astros were excited to add Clendenon to their lineup, the sentiment was not mutual. The slugger knew the Astros manager, Harry Walker, from their days together in Pittsburgh, and considered him a racist. He refused to report, suggesting he would retire from baseball and pursue his business interests instead. Commissioner Bowie Kuhn helped resolve the dispute, with the Expos sending other compensation to Houston, and Donn suiting up for Montreal only after negotiating the multi-year pact.

The best was yet to come. Donn welcomed a June 15, 1969 trade to the Mets. As outfielder Ron Swoboda recalled, "The 1969 Mets were known for the great pitching…, but until Donn Clendenon showed up with his big bat, we had no chance of winning anything." Mets third baseman Wayne Garrett said Donn was the key to the Mets' season. Big Donn blasted 12 home runs in the second half, and three more in the fall classic. So, in less than a year, he had gone from the Pirates to the Expos to the Astros back to the Expos to the Mets, and now was both the World Series MVP and the toast of New York City. Speaking invitations and endorsement opportunities followed.

He remained a productive member of the Mets in 1970, driving in 97 RBI. Injuries set in the next couple of years, and he retired after playing for the Cardinals in 1972. He finished with a .274 average, 1,273 hits, and 159 homers for his career.

After baseball, he completed his law degree and worked in human resources and minority recruitment for several companies. He developed an addiction to cocaine but was smart enough to enter a treatment program. Donn and his family relocated to Sioux Falls, South Dakota, where he worked as an addiction counselor, with access to his law practice in Minneapolis. He passed away from leukemia in 2005 at the age of 70.

JERRY LYNCH

Some ballplayers cannot handle the pressure of pinch-hitting situations, while others respond well. Then there was Jerry Lynch. One of the top pinch-hitters of all-time, Lynch slugged 18 pinch-homers, the MLB record at the time.

In a career that spanned from 1954 to 1966, the outfielder started and finished with the Pirates, sandwiching in a memorable seven-year stint with the Reds. When Cincinnati won the pennant in 1961, Lynch offered major contributions, hitting .315 with 50 RBI in only 181 at bats. He is a member of the Reds Hall of Fame.

In 1964, Lynch became only the eighth player ever to smash a home run in regulation play over the right field roof at Pittsburgh's Forbes Field. The victim of his blast was Dennis Ribant of the Mets.

A left-handed hitter, he played almost exclusively against right-handed hurlers. He had a reputation as a weak outfielder, though his glove work improved over time. His lifetime batting average was .277 with 115 home runs, including three against Hall of Famer Robin Roberts.

In an old-school era, Lynch was even more old school. Pitcher Steve Blass recalls the day from his rookie season that Lynch walked into the clubhouse during pre-game practice and caught Blass loafing. The veteran reamed Blass's ass about being out there with his team for both batting and fielding practice. It was a moment that Blass remembered 40 years later.

After retiring from baseball, Lynch remained in Pittsburgh for many years, joined Dick Groat as business partners in the Champion Lakes Golf Club, and was a guest baseball instructor at Camp Penn Hall. He and his wife, who had four children and 11 grandkids, later moved to the Atlanta area, where he passed away at age 82 in 2012.

CHUCK ESSEGIAN

Chuck Essegian rivaled Jerry Lynch as one of the sport's best pinch-hitters, albeit for a shorter period of time.

The muscular young man of Armenian descent attended Fairfax High School in Los Angeles, and earned money however he could, from digging ditches to selling newspapers outside the RKO movie production lot. He harbored ambitions to become a physician but was too athletic not to gravitate to sports. Within a few years, he was playing college football at Stanford. In fact, he was one of only two athletes to play in both a Rose Bowl and a World Series (Jackie Jensen was the other).

After brief stops with the Phillies and the Cardinals, Chuck joined his hometown Dodgers in 1959. In 41 games during the regular season, he hit just one home run. But in the 1959 World Series, which pitted the Dodgers against the White Sox, he went deep twice, once each against pitchers Bob Shaw and Ray Moore. That made him the first MLB player to slug two pinch-homers in the same World Series. Bernie Carbo would later do so, as well.

Essegian started the 1961 season with the A's and at the trade deadline was swapped to Cleveland, where he quickly became a fan favorite. He was so proficient as a pinch-hitter that fans began cheering the moment he approached the on-deck circle. Timely hits often followed. Chuck hit .289 with 12 home runs in only 173 at bats for the Tribe in 1961. He put up equally strong numbers in 1962, splitting his time between the outfield and pinch-hitting.

Reflecting on his pinch-hitting prowess in 2022, Chuck was modest. "Baseball is not really that different from any other business," he related. "You have to be lucky in the right place at the right time and be lucky enough to produce when you do get the chance."

The Indians, dissatisfied with Essegian's salary request for the 1963 season and looking for pitching help, swapped the slugger to the A's. After a disappointing season with Kansas City, he played one final year in Japan in 1964.

"The Japanese were not as talented as the U.S. players as a group back then, but they understood the game very well," he said. "The salaries were comparable."

At the time, Japanese parks were generally smaller, with the fences around 300 feet down the line and about 360 feet to center field, according to writer Jack McDonald. The wood in Japanese bats at that time was evidently not cured as long as in the U.S., making bats more susceptible to breakage.

Eager to move on to the next stage of life, Chuck earned a law degree, became the prosecuting attorney for the City of Pasadena, and got involved in the real estate business. He remained active in the Dodgers' community affairs programs, as well. He was recently living in Canyon Country, California.

As late as 1978, Louisville Slugger was running print ads recalling some of the greatest achievements in World Series history. Alongside a photo of Babe Ruth noting his .625 batting average in the 1928 fall classic, and a picture of Bill Mazeroski recalling his game-winning homer in the 1960 World Series, the ad depicted Essegian, celebrating his two pinch-homers in the 1959 Series.

JOE NOSSEK

By the early Sixties, college was emerging as a viable route to the major leagues for a growing number of players. One was Joe Nossek, a Cleveland sandlot star who grew up cheering for the Indians.

He was invited to the nation's capital for a tryout and received "some of the best advice I ever received," he recalled in 2022. "After the two-day workout, the Senators – soon to be the Twins – told me to go to college and they would keep an eye on me." At Ohio University, "It was my good fortune to have College Hall of Fame Coach Bob Wren as my mentor. I learned more from him about baseball than anyone else in my career."

The superb-fielding outfielder signed in 1961 and made his Twins debut in 1964. In 1966 with the A's, he hit an inside-the-park home run against Sam McDowell, and enjoyed his best season, hitting 261 in 91 games. That winter, his phone rang at 11:30 p.m. on Christmas eve. To his surprise, it was A's owner Charles O. Finley, calling to award him a generous salary hike.

Joe also played for the Cardinals and later the Evansville Triplets in 1971, a team managed by Del Crandall. "Del was a special person in my life," he reflected. "He gave me my first coaching job in the major leagues. I learned more about pitching and catching from Del than anyone else. He was a good friend." Among other friends, Nossek roomed on the road with Twins teammates Mel Nelson and Dwight Siebler, and with A's teammates Danny Cater, Tony La Russa and Rene Lachemann.

Nossek, who coached for the Brewers, Twins, Indians, Royals, and White Sox, now resides in Amherst, Ohio.

AL SPANGLER

In the 1950s, with World War II gratefully in the nation's rearview mirror, a growing number of aspiring ballplayers chose to play college ball rather than sign out of high school. One of the most prestigious programs was that of Duke University, run by Jack Coombs. Coombs had been a pitcher for Connie Mack's Philadelphia A's and Wilbert Robinson's Brooklyn Robins – and no ordinary pitcher at that. In 1910, he won 31 games for the A's with a microscopic 1.30 ERA. In World Series action, he was a perfect 5-0.

Young Al Spangler was a prep ballplayer at Olney High School in Philadelphia who drew comparisons to Phillies outfielder Richie Ashburn for his exceptional defensive range and speed. As Spangler later recalled, "Coming out of high school, I had accepted a full baseball scholarship to attend Lafayette College in upstate Pennsylvania. During that summer, I attended a baseball camp led by Jack Coombs and Ira Thomas (who was a former big-league catcher). Soon after that event, I received an offer to attend Duke in the fall to play baseball under Coach Coombs and become a civil engineer."

Spangler continued, "Shortly after I started at Duke, Coach Coombs retired and I didn't get to play for him. But in 1953 as a sophomore, we went to the College World Series. Then in June 1954 at the end of my junior year, I signed with the Braves. I did return for two fall semesters and graduated in February 1956 with a degree in mathematics."

The fleet-footed fly-chaser debuted with the Braves in 1959, but the club was loaded with outfielders and there were few opportunities to play. When Al arrived, Braves manager Fred

Haney was not even sure which outfield position Spangler had previously played. When he asked, "Al, where did you play last year," Spangler replied, "Louisville," not realizing he had misinterpreted the question until the manager turned and walked away.

Spangler's role expanded with the expansion Houston Colt 45's in 1962. He performed well, hitting better than .280 each of his first two years in Houston, and leading the NL in range factor in 1963. "Don Nottebart was my roommate. He threw a no-hitter and I caught the final out," Spangler recalled.

Houston lost exactly 96 games each of its first three seasons in the NL, and 97 games in 1965. By then, Al had been traded to the Angels, who demoted him to the minor leagues. His career revived with Leo Durocher and the Cubs from 1967 to 1971. His best season at Wrigley Field was in 1968, when he hit .271 in 88 games. Often used as a pinch-hitter, Spangler told writers that he paid close attention throughout the game, in order to be fully prepared when his number was called. That same power of concentration that helped him earn a college degree made him a better pinch-hitter.

He concluded with a .262 lifetime average and 21 homers. Spangler later was a coach and minor league manager with the Cubs, then a high-school athletic director. He also enjoyed building race cars from scratch. Al resides in Humble, Texas.

JOE SPARMA

Pitcher Joe Sparma came along five years after outfielder Al Spangler (previous entry), but traveled a similar path. A high school baseball and football standout in Massillon, Ohio (the city that produced NFL Hall of Fame Coach Paul Brown), Sparma spurned contract offers and opted for college. Selecting Ohio State, he became their quarterback and led the Buckeyes to a Big Ten football championship.

When he later signed with the Tigers, he pocketed a $20,000 bonus. The blue-chip prospect reached MLB in 1964, just one year after leaving the campus. In his sophomore season in 1965, he delivered tantalizing results with 13 wins while still only 23 years old.

Although Mickey Mantle "owned" dozens of AL pitchers, the right-handed Sparma was not one of them. Mantle faced him 40 times and hit only .150. During a "Mickey Mantle Day" celebration, Sparma walked to plate to shake Mantle's hand, then struck him out.

Joe's big-league career was plagued by peaks and valleys. An incident involving his right hand and a car door led to a disastrous 1966 season. He was so wild that manager Bill Swift reportedly said, "The son of a bitch looks like he never threw a baseball in his life." His record was 2-7.

Unwilling to give up on him, the Tigers sent him to Puerto Rico where he worked on his slider with new pitching coach Johnny Sain. Sparma roomed the following season with catcher Bill Freehan, an arrangement that led to lots of communication over beers about how to retire enemy hitters. Joe came back in 1967 to win 16 contests, third-highest on the Tigers, though his ERA was suspiciously high.

During the Tigers' 1968 championship season, Sparma was inconsistent, although his dazzling complete-game win against the Yankees clinched the pennant. Manager Mayo Smith pitched Sparma less frequently late in the season, as he finished with an unremarkable 10-10 record.

The manager and pitcher feuded in a 1969 season that saw Sparma again struggle with wildness. "You couldn't even play catch with the guy," teammate John Hiller recalled years later. His 1969 season ended with a 6-8 record and a bullpen fistfight against teammate Fred Lasher.

Joe was traded to the Expos after the season, but he never won another MLB game. Before long, Sparma was out of baseball, working in sales for Buckeye Steel in Columbus. In 1986 his heavy weight and cigarette habit contributed to a fatal heart attack at age 44. Sparma's lifetime record was 52-52 with a 3.94 ERA and 10 career shutouts.

TED ABERNATHY

Investors regret the stocks they sell too soon. General managers regret letting go of players like Ted Abernathy, who always seem to have another comeback in their future.

This right-hander was one of baseball's busiest relievers, using a submarine motion so extreme that his knuckles nearly scraped the mound. He adopted the unusual motion after a shoulder injury, finding there was less pain throwing from the side. He copied the delivery from a Senators teammate, Dick Hyde, and discovered that it also made it difficult for hitters to see his release point.

Teams repeatedly gave up on Ted but he never gave up on himself. He was a 28-year-old journeyman with a lifetime record of 8-22 and a seemingly dim future when the Indians bought him from the Braves in 1961. By 1963, he was honored as the Indians' Man of the Year. In those days, winter banquets were held in cities throughout the country. At the Indians' annual Ribs and Roasts Dinner, he was rewarded with a $7,000 salary hike, a color Polaroid camera, and an engraved silver serving set.

After Ted's performance leveled off in 1964, it was the Indians – and their stingy general manager, Gabe Paul – who gave up on him, selling him to the Cubs. It was a short-sighted move. Over the next four seasons, he led the senior circuit in appearances three times. He topped the league with 31 saves in 1965 for the Cubs and again in 1967 with 28 for the Reds.

By 1972, pitching for Kansas City and already 39 years old, he posted a spectacular 1.70 ERA in 45 outings. Despite his superb work for the Royals, the club's general manager, Cedric Tallis, did not offer him a contract for 1973, spelling the end of Ted's career with a 63-69 record, 148 saves and a 3.46 ERA. He returned home to North Carolina, where he worked for Summey Building Company, worshiped at the United Methodist Church, and belonged to the Shriners, before passing away at age 71.

Don Elston

Chicago announcer Jack Brickhouse often told the story of Cubs pitcher Don Elston throwing over to first base 11 times in the 10th inning of a game against the Giants, so as to hold Willie Mays close to the base. On his 12th throw to first, he picked Mays off base, winning the game for the Cubs.

Elston was a "bulldog," according to Brickhouse, a stubborn pitcher with unbridled determination. He spent his nine-year MLB career with the Cubs, except for one outing with Brooklyn. Elston twice led the NL in appearances, and garnered an all-star selection in 1959, when he went 10-9 with 14 saves. That save figure is significant, as it was a Chicago baseball writer watching Elston who created the statistic.

"He had a rubber arm," recalled longtime baseball man Bob Kennedy. "You could bring him in in the worst possible jam and he'd get them out. But don't let him start the next inning. He didn't have the same concentration if he wasn't in a jam."

Elston retired in 1964 with a 49-54 lifetime record and a career ERA of 3.64 and stayed close to the game by co-chairing Chicago Baseball Cancer Charities with former pitcher Billy Pierce. He also worked in sales at Danly Machine Company, a manufacturer of die-making machinery in Cicero, Illinois. Elston had heart trouble for much of his life and died of heart failure in 1995.

Ken Holtzman

If you ask baseball fans which Jewish pitcher won the most games of all time, many would state that it was Sandy Koufax. The correct answer is Ken Holtzman, who began his career as Koufax was bringing his to a close. Ken won 174 games, compared to 165 for Koufax, his boyhood hero. The pair faced off head-to-head just once in 1966. Both pitched well, but Holtzman got the victory.

Growing up near St. Louis, Ken was selected by the Cubs in the fourth round of the 1965 draft. He inked a $65,000 bonus contract, and pitched just 12 games in the minor leagues, before manager Leo Durocher insisted on promoting him.

Ken said that his biggest thrill in baseball was getting called up to the major leagues at age 19. Coach Buck O'Neil picked him up at the airport, drove him to the team hotel, and then accompanied him to the ballpark. Holtzman was given a locker next to Ron Santo, three away from Ernie Banks. As he looked across the clubhouse, surrounded by stars, he realized he was part of the club.

There wasn't much time for stargazing. Durocher wanted him on the mound often, and the youngster posted an 11-16 record as a rookie.

Ken threw a high fastball, which hitters had trouble laying off. His change-up and curve set up the rising heater. In 1967, Holtzman fashioned a perfect 9-0 record with a 2.53 ERA in 12 starts. Once his season was interrupted by military reserve duty, he made only a handful of additional starts as his detail permitted. He won only 11 games against 14 losses in 1968, but was still a young pitcher, with most of his career ahead of him.

On August 19, 1969, the Cubs had a 76-45 record, were starting a 10-game homestand, and seemed destined for a championship. Santo belted a three-run homer in the first inning that day against the Braves, and that was all the Cubs would need. Holtzman threw a no-hitter (oddly enough, without a single strikeout) and the Cubs were beginning to appear invincible.

Ken finished with 17 wins, but the Cubs went 15-25 after his no-hitter, and every fan of a certain age knows the story of their collapse and the ascent of the Mets.

The hurler won 17 games again in 1970, but only nine contests (including his second no-hitter) in 1971. His relationship with Durocher deteriorated to the point where he asked for a trade, having grown weary of an atmosphere in which the manager criticized players in the press, rather than face to face.

Just after Thanksgiving, the Cubs traded him to a burgeoning AL powerhouse, the A's, and Chicago received outfielder Rick Monday in return. Holtzman got to the World Series each of the next three seasons, winning 59 regular season games in that span, as well as two ALCS games, and four World Series contests. With two all-star appearances, he finally received recognition as an elite pitcher.

Gradually, Ken tired of the constant time away from his family in Lincolnshire, Illinois, but pitched five more seasons with the A's, Orioles, Yankees and a return trip to the Cubs. He retired after the 1979 season with a lifetime record of 174-150 and a 3.49 ERA, along with 31 shutouts. After baseball, he worked in insurance and financial services. Holtzman,who resided near St. Louis, passed away in 2024.

Ferguson Jenkins

Fergie Jenkins grew up in rural Chatham, Ontario, amidst the laid-back, friendly small-town lifestyle. His father took him to some ballgames in Detroit in the late Fifties, and he appreciated seeing Larry Doby, the AL's first black player.

Jenkins signed with the Phillies in 1962 and went to the Cubs in a 1966 trade that Philly fans have regretted ever since. Philadelphia received veteran pitchers Larry Jackson and Bob Buhl in the deal. Jackson had two good seasons in Philadelphia, then retired. Buhl won only six more games. Meanwhile, Jenkins began a streak of six straight 20-win seasons in 1967.

Fergie's approach was to pitch down and away, regardless of the hitter. He threw mostly fastballs and had superb control. In his 14-year peak from 1967 to 1980, Jenkins won 251 games, more than any other pitcher during that period. Upon winning 20 games in 1968, he was the Cubs' first hurler with 20 victories in back-to-back years since Lon Warneke in 1935.

Like all of the members of the 1969 Cubs, he regrets his team's late-season fade, which allowed the surging Mets to win the division and eventually the World Series. Jenkins still fondly recalls that many core players joined the team around the same time – himself, Glenn Beckert, Don Kessinger, Adolfo Phillips, Randy Hundley, Bill Hands, Ken Holtzman – and matured together.

Jenkins also recalls the incredible excitement that the club brought to Chicagoans in the spring and summer of '69; and the fun enjoyed by the Bleacher Bums, cheered on by pitcher Dick Selma waving a towel in front of the bullpen. A "Go Cubs Go" record was recorded with vocals from numerous team members including the frequently singing Banks, infielder Nate Oliver who sang tenor, and Wonderful Willie Smith, who added his baritone voice. Others singing on the record included Don Kessinger, Gene Oliver, Ron Santo, Randy Hundley and Billy Williams. The team members were also in constant demand for public appearances.

After the late-season 1969 fade, the Cubs finished above .500 three more years. Fergie won 24 games in 1971. "I made $125,000 in 1971. It was good money then," he told writer Paul Ladewski. "It was one of the first big contracts that the Cubs gave to a pitcher. My family really enjoyed it. I bought a ranch in Ontario, Canada, at the time, and me and my father worked on it. We were pretty happy with that." That season, Jenkins became the first Cubs pitcher to win a Cy Young award.

Jenkins also has fond memories of spring training in Scottsdale, except for the time in 1969 that he and several teammates went horseback riding, and Jenkins got thrown from his horse. The injury caused him to miss Opening Day. "Back then, we'd stay at the local Ramada, and just walk across the street to the field," he recalled in a *Chicago Tribune* interview. "Scottsdale was a small town then, with just a couple of two-lane roads." He also recalled one spring when he was a contract holdout, and spent 15 days in an Arizona hotel, playing long-toss in the back parking lot with his attorney-agent. Jenkins was one of the first Cubs players to employ an agent in negotiations with the Wrigley family.

His career record is similar to that of contemporaries Jim Kaat and Tommy John. Jenkins went 284-226. Kaat was 283-237. John compiled a mark of 288-231. What set him apart was mostly his peak dominance (seven 20-win seasons in eight years), and his pinpoint control. His strikeout-to-walk ratio was 3.2, compared to 2.3 for Kaat and 1.8 for John.

"I could have caught Jenkins with a pair of pliers," joked catcher Randy Hundley in describing how skilled the hurler was in placing his pitches. Jenkins learned to throw the slider in winter ball in Puerto Rico and used it at times. In a feat that is not often recalled, in the 1967 all-star game he fanned Harmon Killebrew, Tony Conigliaro, Mickey Mantle, Jim Fregosi, Rod Carew, and Tony Oliva. If fans didn't yet recognize his name, they did after that game.

"Fergie always was very positive and never complained. He was a great example of going out every start with the goal of completing the game," remembered teammate Rich Nye. On road trips, Jenkins often roomed with Ernie Banks, becoming the closest of friends.

Jenkins was also a good hitter. In his first game with the Cubs, he homered to help his new team win the game. If Jenkins had an Achilles Heel, it was surrendering the home run ball. He was victimized 484 times and led his league in that dubious category seven times, while pitching in smaller home ballparks such Wrigley Field and Fenway Park for much of his career.

When his record declined to 14-16 in 1973, the Cubs, coming off a fifth-place finish, were ready to rebuild. That winter, they unloaded Jenkins along with Beckert, Santo, Hundley, Jim Hickman, Jack Aker, and Bob Locker. Billy Williams was gone a year later. It would be another 10 years before a division title would be celebrated in Wrigleyville. Jenkins had some big years with Boston and Texas, and took a final bow with the Cubs in 1983.

Fergie later was a pitching coach and has participated extensively in public speaking, autograph sessions, and charity events.

BILLY WILLIAMS

One of the most prolific run producers of his era, Billy Williams broke into the Cubs lineup with an 86-RBI season and a Rookie of the Year award in 1961. He remained a mainstay of the bruin lineup through 1974, before closing out his career as a designated hitter for the A's.

At his peak in 1970 and 1972, he was an elite run producer, finishing second in the MVP derby (behind Johnny Bench) both years. He made the all-star team six times. Williams enjoyed 10 seasons with 25 or more home runs, and topped the 200-hit plateau three years. His career statistics included a .290 average, 426 home runs, 2,711 hits, and 90 stolen bases. He was inducted into the Hall of Fame in 1987.

One of the qualities that set Williams apart from his peers, beyond his hitting skills, was his reliability. He kept his body well-conditioned, and set an NL record by playing in 1,117 consecutive games. When he broke Stan Musial's previous NL record of 895 in 1969, he received an array of gifts including a Chrysler Imperial and – from his friend Fergie Jenkins – a Weimaraner dog. The pair later took the dog on pheasant hunts together.

Pitchers realized that he was a constant threat to go deep. Craig Anderson – who pitched for the Cardinals and the Mets – rated Williams among the three toughest hitters he faced, alongside Hank Aaron and Ron Fairly.

He also demonstrated an even temperament. Fellow Hall of Famer Lou Boudreau was the Cubs' announcer for many of those years, and observed, "If he's worried, he never shows it. It helps him mentally at the plate. I don't think he lets outside matters affect him once that game gets underway."

Williams was not flamboyant in the field, and it was possible to overlook him during that era of great outfielders. Willie Mays, Mickey Mantle, Hank Aaron, Frank Robinson, Roberto Clemente, and Al Kaline all arrived before him, and often received more publicity. But his numbers speak for themselves, and former teammates always praised his contributions in glowing terms.

Billy was from Mobile, Alabama. His dad, Frank, was a noteworthy semipro first baseman, and an older brother, Franklin, was a Pirates' farmhand. A Cubs scout named Ivy Griffin visited Mobile to scout Tommy Aaron but signed Williams instead. In 1959, Williams was assigned to Double-A San Antonio where he experienced discrimination so severe that he bolted the club. The Cubs sent scout Buck O'Neill, the former Negro Leagues star to persuade him to return. Billy spent much of the 1960 season at the Houston farm team to work on his fielding, then made his MLB debut later that summer.

Off the field, one of Billy's favorite pastimes was fishing. He owned a boat, and since the Cubs played their home games during the day, he was free to take the boat out onto Lake Michigan and do some quiet fishing on pleasant summer evenings. Jenkins, one of his closest friends, sometimes fished with him. The pair also car-pooled from their South Chicago neighborhood to Wrigley Field for games.

After retiring as a player, Williams and his family initially moved west to the Sacramento area, near his brother. But he became a big-league coach for 19 seasons for the Cubs, A's, and Indians starting in 1980, and when he started the coaching job with the Cubs, he moved back to the Chicago area, where he has remained. He was elected to the Hall of Fame in 1987 and was present to see the Cubs unveil a cast statue of him in 2010.

CHUCK HINTON

Chuck Hinton grew up in the segregated community of Rocky Mount, North Carolina, hitchhiked his way to Baltimore for a baseball tryout, and signed with the Orioles for a $500 bonus. Before long, he eloped with his sweetheart Bunny and was drafted into the military, serving at Fort Bragg.

The military service may have delayed his arrival on the MLB scene but he still played for 11 years as a dead fastball hitter around the knees. His first four seasons were with the expansion Senators and he was one of their top hitters. Chuck and Bunny fell in love with DC area and made it their lifelong home. He partnered with several businessmen to form the Chuck Hinton Insurance Agency, which operated at 14th Street and Rhode Island Avenue NW, and three other locations. He passed his insurance exam and his popularity made the business an immediate success.

A superb athlete who could play multiple positions, Hinton enjoyed his best season in 1962. Although the Senators lost 101 games, Chuck batted .310. Only Pete Runnels, Mickey Mantle, and Floyd Robinson had higher batting clips. He also blasted 17 homers and stole 28 bases, second in the league to Luis Aparicio.

By 1964, the Senators were not moving up in the standings and fingers started getting pointed at Hinton. The tension seemed to start in a game against Baltimore in which Hinton caught a fly ball for the second out of the inning, and thinking it was the third out, jogged in with his eyes on the ground. Two runners tagged up and scored; an infuriated manager Gil Hodges pulled him out of the game immediately. Chuck later missed time after being hit on the wrist by a Gary Bell pitch. Meanwhile, after hitting .362 for the first 43 games, his final numbers included a .274 average and just 11 home runs.

After the season, the Senators traded Hinton to Cleveland for veteran infielder Woodie Held and first baseman Bob Chance. Hinton lamented being made the scapegoat. Shirley Povich of the *Washington Post* wrote, "With the Senators, he [Hinton] showed everything with which to burn up a league, except consistency. Hodges alternately admired him and was pained by him. Not all of the time was his good ballplayer strictly attentive."

In Cleveland, Hinton was a Senator in exile who missed his adopted hometown. He remembered playing for Cleveland in his autobiography, *My Time at Bat: A Story of Perseverance*. "Early and late in the season in old Municipal Stadium, the winds would come up from Lake Erie and shoot through you," he wrote.

Hinton also reflected on being a black player in the Sixties. "In my day, although segregation was in full force, black and white baseball players seemed to get along fine," he wrote. "Color was not a problem in my career. Black players had a special bond with one another. All through the minor leagues, the black players would get together and share places to eat…For those of us who made the big leagues, that didn't change. We were even more protective because we knew we were under a microscope."

"We would hang out with one another," he wrote, "and do our best to make it as good or as easy as we could in our hometown. I often found in talking to white teammates, there was little difference in where we came from or what it took to get where we were."

With quick wrists, Chuck could jump all over a pitcher's mistake. Darold Knowles recalled Hinton smoking one of his curves all the way to the outfield fence. It was enough to convince Knowles, an above-average reliever, to focus on his slider and de-emphasize the curve.

Hinton had three productive seasons in Cleveland from 1965 to 1967. Following a trade to the Angels and an off-year in 1968, Chuck was reacquired by the Indians in 1969. He played three more seasons as a valuable utility player.

After the Indians lost 102 games in 1971, it was their turn to go young, marking the end of the line for the 38-year-old Hinton. He returned to his home on 16th Street NW in Washington and worked as the head baseball coach for Howard University for 28 years, winning seven conference titles.

In 1982, he founded the Major League Players Alumni Association which raises money for charitable causes. Hinton died of Parkinson's Disease in 2013 at the age of 78. His legacy is honored through his membership in the Washington, D.C. Sports Hall of Fame.

JIM FRENCH

Senators catcher Jim French was shaving in the clubhouse bathroom one day when he heard that the President of the United States, Richard Nixon, had entered the locker room to say hello to manager Ted Williams. Excited to see the chief executive, French rushed into the locker room wearing nothing but a shirt and the shaving cream. According to a SABR bio by Paul Hofmann, a photo captured the amusing moment, with Nixon chuckling and Williams looking on. French, who became a banker and attorney, used the photo on the back of his business cards for many years.

"I grew up on a farm in Williamsfield, Ohio in Ashtabula County," he explained in 2019. "The Indians were our team, but I did not have a favorite player. I went to a few games as a youngster, always taken by my father. Jimmy Dudley was the announcer and we would listen to the games on the radio when we had time from the farming. Williamsfield is 60 miles east of Cleveland near the Pennsylvania border and Bill Veeck spoke at one of our sports banquets. I didn't realize how impressive that was at the time, to have him come all of that way for a Podunk school - a great promoter."

French's grandfather was a semi-pro catcher, and his father was a semi-pro shortstop in the years after World War II. Reflecting baseball's popularity in those days, there were sometimes as many as 2,000 spectators at the games, French recalled. His grandfather encouraged him to become a catcher, and teamed up with French's dad to buy the youngster all the gear a young catcher would need. Jim took it from there.

French spent parts of seven seasons with the Senators, from 1965 to 1971. He made enduring friendships with teammates, including Dick Bosman, Frank Howard, Casey Cox, Tim Cullen, Ed Brinkman, and Darold Knowles. His favorite restaurant in DC was Fran O'Brien's, named for its owner, an offensive tackle for the Washington Redskins and close friend of Frank Howard.

His managers included Gil Hodges and Ted Williams. French had a strong relationship with Williams. "As a young man I guess I was in the 'twilight zone' and did not realize what a tremendous life he had led and all of his accomplishments," French remembered. "If I had, I would probably have been star struck. In retrospect he was not a great manager, but he was a great teacher for hitters and for some pitchers. Williams understood the mini-game between the pitcher and hitter better than anyone that ever played. Dick Bosman says Ted made him the pitcher, and later successful pitching coach, that he was. Hodges was a better manager but was very aloof and I was a little afraid of him."

Bosman called French "one of my best catchers. He spent a lot of time in the minors before the big leagues." French, who was considered an excellent catcher defensively, played in 256 games with a lifetime batting average of .196. He earned a bachelor's degree, an MBA, and a law degree. He now resides in Colorado.

DICK BOSMAN

Right-hander Dick Bosman, who led the AL in ERA in 1969, grew up in Kenosha, Wisconsin. The spring weather was often cold, but he and his high-school team simply played through it. He signed with the Pirates, recalling decades later that "their scout, Paul Tretiak, spent a lot of time with me and my mom and dad. They also offered the most money, $7,000."

Dick was drafted in succession by the Giants and then the Senators, for whom he debuted in 1966. His first Senators manager was uncommunicative Gil Hodges. "You know Gil," Bosman once said. "He wouldn't get excited even if the stands were on fire."

Ted Williams replaced Hodges as manager in 1969 and it made a world of difference as he instilled confidence in many of the club's players. By May 4, the squad had a 16-11 record and was in second place in the AL East. Eventually, the club settled for fourth place, but did so with a strong 86-76 record.

Bosman notched a 14-5 record and a 2.19 ERA. Williams declared him the league's best pitcher. "Ted taught me how to set up hitters with the pitches I had. He built up my confidence and my belief in what I could do pitching in the big leagues."

Bosman celebrated his successful 1969 season by marrying Pam Yates, a flight attendant, after the season. "I told him he would report hog fat [to spring training] because of his wife's cooking," joked Williams, "but he made a bet he would match his September weight and I took it. We'll see," the skipper laughed.

Not only did Bosman win the bet, but he won 16 games for the Senators in 1970. His 3.00 ERA was sixth in the league, trailing only Diego Segui, Jim Palmer, Clyde Wright, Fritz Peterson and Sam McDowell.

Like many players from the 1960s, Bosman fondly recalls the camaraderie of daily life in the big leagues. "Hondo (Frank Howard), Joe Coleman, Ken McMullen, Barry Moore and I always lived in Alexandria, at the Hunting Towers and later at the River Towers," he recalled. The location was convenient to National Airport and to Old Town Alexandria. As time permitted, Bosman enjoyed golf with Coleman and Moore. He also did some fishing with teammate Jim Shellenback.

Bosman later pitched for the Indians and the A's. A career highlight came on Friday, July 19, 1974, when he hurled the 13th no-hitter in Indians' history. Among the more than 24,000 on hand to see the gem was broadcaster Joe Gargiola, who watched from the press box. Bosman was the talk of baseball the next day as Garagiola called the NBC Game of the Week.

The 1975 season saw Bosman briefly on the same team as second baseman Duane Kuiper, a third cousin, before being traded to Oakland. Retiring after being released by the A's during spring training 1977, he had an 82-85 record, 10 shutouts, and a 3.67 ERA. Dick worked for a time for an auto dealer near the nation's capital, and later returned to the game as an accomplished pitching coach for the White Sox, Orioles and Rangers. Bosman now resides in Trinity, Florida.

FRANK HOWARD

Standing six-foot-seven and weighing more than 270 pounds, Frank Howard was an imposing figure. Having worked a 100-pound jackhammer as a teen, his arm strength was legendary. Ted Williams said if he had been as strong as Howard, he would have hit 1,000 home runs. From 1968 to 1970, Howard was as feared a slugger as anybody in the game.

"Howard is the strongest, hardest, and biggest bat guy that has ever played this game," Williams said in *Baseball Stars of 1971. "*When he hits it, there isn't any doubt where it's going. It's just a matter of how far it's going to travel."

In 1968, playing for the Senators, Howard led the AL in home runs with 44, as well as total bases and slugging percentage. When Williams became the manager in 1969, Howard's output improved further. After engaging in a season-long battle with Harmon Killebrew and Reggie Jackson for the home run title, Howard finished second with 48 circuit shots. His batting average rose to .296 and he scored a career-high 111 runs. Howard followed up in 1970 by leading the loop in home runs (44), RBI (126), and walks (132).

According to teammate Duke Sims, one night when Howard was with the Tigers, he muscled a tape-measure homer and Sims told him, "You really got all of that one." Howard responded, "Nah, most of it." Later, he homered again, and when Sims made the same comment, Hondo gave the save reply. Sims mischievously asked Howard if *he had ever* gotten all of a pitch. "Nope, never have," replied Howard.

It all began at South High School in Columbus, Ohio, which had never produced a big-leaguer. Frank signed with the Dodgers and in 1960, delivered 23 homers to win the rookie of the year award. Whereas some rookies would have rested on laurels, Howard headed to Puerto Rico to refine his craft in winter ball. Scouting Director Al Campanis visited Howard for three days and came away amazed at his improvement in discerning which pitches to lay off.

Frank had another assignment that winter, which was to learn to play first base. The Dodgers had an abundance of outfielders – Wally Moon, Duke Snider, Tommy Davis, Don Demeter, plus youngsters Willie Davis and Ron Fairly. In the end, the Dodgers continued to play Norm Larker at first base, and kept Howard in the outfield in 1961, where he hit .296 when not injured.

Howard's best season on the west coast was 1962, when he led the team with 31 homers and was second to Tommy Davis in RBI with 119. Frank led the pennant-bound team in homers again in 1963 with 28, plus another in the World Series.

In 1964, the Dodgers drifted to sixth place and Frank's batting average tanked. Convinced they needed another reliable starting pitcher, the Dodgers sent a package of players including Howard to the Senators for pitcher Claude Osteen, infielder John Kennedy, and $100,000. Howard was respectable in his first two seasons in DC, then took his game to a new level from 1967 to 1970, earning the nickname, "the Washington Monument."

After Howard led the AL in homers in 1968, the Indians approached the Senators during the World Series with a five-for-one offer that would have sent pitcher Stan Williams, catcher Duke Sims, shortstop Larry Brown, and flychasers Tommy Harper and Lee Maye to Washington for Howard. The Indians proposed the deal for three reasons: first, to acquire Howard's power bat; second, to boost fan interest; and third, because it anticipated losing Harper soon in the expansion draft. The Senators passed on the deal, retaining their franchise player. Washington also declined California's offer of Clyde Wright, Tom Satriano, Vic Davalillo, Roger Repoz and cash.

Late in the 1972 campaign, with the club now based in Texas, Frank was dealt to Detroit. Hondo delivered seven RBI in just 33 at bats for the division-title bound Tigers and enjoyed being on a winning team again. He spent one last year with Detroit and finished with a .273 batting average, 382 home runs, 1,119 RBI, and 1,774 hits.

Teammates remember Howard with tremendous respect. "What I loved about Hondo was that nobody who ever played the game played ever hustled more consistently, no matter the score, including Charlie Hustle himself...He always gave 100 percent," wrote his one-time roommate, Ken Harrelson. Dick Bosman commented, "Next to my dad, Hondo was the best man I've known. He taught us to be big leaguers by word and deed."

After baseball, Howard became an ambassador for the new Washington Nationals, who had relocated from Montreal. When the new stadium opened in DC, it featured statues of three players: Walter Johnson, Josh Gibson and Frank Howard.

DEL UNSER

Starting in 1968, outfielder Del Unser enjoyed a 15-year career with the Senators, Indians, Phillies, Mets, Expos, and a second tour in the City of Brotherly Love. Though he was initially valued mostly for his skill as a center fielder, he evolved into a solid hitter. For his career, he hit .258 with 87 home runs and 1,344 hits.

Del was born in 1944, just as his dad Al was concluding an MLB career as a catcher. Growing up in the manufacturing town of Decatur, Illinois, the youngster was the bat boy for the Decatur Commodores – the Cardinals' affiliate in the Midwest League – when his father managed the team. Summers were often spent traveling while his dad skippered teams in Augusta, Georgia; Winston-Salem, North Carolina; and Winnipeg, Canada. When home, Del spent hours hitting in a backyard batting cage his father built. "It taught me to hit into the double nets on the left and right, and not into our neighbors' homes," he joked.

The prized prospect opted to stay in college after the Twins selected him in the second round of the 1965 draft and the Pirates did the same in the fourth round of the January 1966 draft. He finally agreed to terms with the Senators after a first-round selection in the summer of 1966.

Unser played with some memorable teammates on the Senators. He remembers Ken McMullen as "the best third baseman at charging a bunt or a slow roller." Paul Casanova was "a happy, fun-loving catcher with a very strong arm." He recalls Mike Epstein as a formidable power hitter who enjoyed his "Supe" nickname, short for "Super Jew." Frank Howard, he notes, "was a great teammate who hit the hardest line drives I've ever seen." Del roomed on the road in those early years mostly with infielder Bernie Allen.

Del shot a lot of pool in college, and played racquetball until he turned 50, but golf has been and remains his favorite pastime. Back in 1973, he won $5,000 alongside Browns running back Leroy Kelly in an American Airlines golf classic in Puerto Rico. He worked as a coach, farm director and scout for many years and now resides in Scottsdale.

JOHN BATEMAN

"Trouble" wasn't John Bateman's middle name but should have been. An NL catcher from 1963 to 1972, Bateman endured his share of hard times, many of his own making. He grew up in a broken family in Oklahoma and ran with a rough crowd during his formative years. Somewhere along the line, in one of his barroom fights, he got beat up badly enough to lose a kidney.

Knowing he had baseball talent, he contacted several teams and Houston invited him to a tryout. He was signed to a contract by scout Red Murff in 1962 and was in the big leagues just a year later. Bateman caught the first no-hitter in the franchise's history, authored by Don Nottebart.

In Jim Wynn's autobiography, the outfielder wrote, "Bateman was a guy with fair defensive skills, some good pop in his bat, and a mind that worked in its own curious and different way." After dropping an easy popup, the catcher explained that he lost the ball in the moonlight.

The one year that John kept his weight down and stayed healthy, he put up remarkable numbers. That was 1966, when at age 25, he was the top hitter on the Astros, batting .279 with 17 homers and 70 RBI. His caustic personality led to a team-high six ejections, as well.

Unfortunately, that season was out of character. The three previous years, he batted .210, .190, and .197. The following season, his average was again below .200. Along the way, Bateman sustained injuries to his fingers, hand, ankle, and back; and engaged in a dispute over taxes with the IRS.

John was left unprotected by the Astros after the 1968 season and was drafted by the Expos. With Montreal, he shared the catching duties, caught a Bill Stoneman no-hitter, and enjoyed a 15-homer season in 1970. But trouble continued. His personality grated on the nerves of irritable manager Gene Mauch and contributed to his 1972 trade to the Phillies. John caught many of Steve Carlton's 27 wins that year, but the Phils nonetheless released him after the season.

Thereafter, Bateman played for the King and His Court softball team, worked in manufacturing plants, and sold insurance. When his remaining kidney began to fail, he underwent dialysis and eventually passed away from heart failure in 1996. His lifetime statistics included a .230 batting average, 81 home runs, and 765 hits.

HANK AGUIRRE

For many years, Detroit had a tradition of prominent athletes pursuing high-profile business careers after their playing days. Earl Wilson, Bill Freehan, Al Kaline, Gordy Howe, Bill Laimbeer and Dave Bing were examples. Tigers pitcher Hank Aguirre was part of that tradition, launching a manufacturing business in the city.

Aguirre pitched for 15 years with the Indians, Tigers, Dodgers and Cubs. Although a reliever for much of his career, he was in the Tigers rotation enough in 1962 to win 16 games and lead the AL in ERA. He followed up with a pair of 14-win seasons. "Hank's the type who can put real enthusiasm into a club," his Tigers teammate Dave Wickersham said in 1964. "He's got that way about him."

In Boston, he is remembered for striking out Ted Williams the first time they matched up, and getting Williams to sign the ball. A few weeks later, while Williams was circling the bases after homering against Aguirre, Ted yelled, "get that ball, and I'll sign it, too."

Aguirre was a California native, the son of Mexican-American entrepreneurs who owned a tortilla factory. The young Aguirre would make early-morning tortilla deliveries, starting at 4:00 a.m., before going to school. The lessons he learned about hard work and entrepreneurship lasted a lifetime.

After several years of baseball coaching, Hank founded his company, Mexican Industries, in 1979 with eight employees. It became a $180 million business, making leather steering-wheel covers, tire covers, and airbags; and Aguirre was named Businessman of the Year by the Hispanic Chamber of Commerce. (Sadly, after his 1994 death and a subsequent vote by workers to unionize, low-wage manufacturers in Mexico undercut the company's prices. It filed for bankruptcy in 2000, and several hundred of its workers in southern Detroit lost their jobs.)

Hank's lifetime record was 75-72 with a 3.25 ERA and nine shutouts. When he died from prostate cancer in 1994, he was remembered as a ballplayer, job creator, and civic leader.

JIM BUNNING

Jim Bunning used a fierce fastball, an excellent slider and curve, as well as more than a little bit of intimidation to power his way to 224 victories, and eventual election to the Hall of Fame. Then for a second career, he entered public service and served for 12 years in the U.S. House of Representatives and 12 more in the U.S. Senate as a Republican from Kentucky.

Bunning's resume included two no-hitters. He tossed the first one on July 20, 1958 against Boston, retiring the Splendid Splinter, Ted Williams, for the 27th out.

His second no-hitter was a perfect game on Father's Day, June 21, 1964, against the Mets. It was the NL's first perfect game since John Montgomery Ward's gem in 1880. "It was just unbelievable stuff he had that day," recalled teammate Tony Taylor. In the ninth inning, Taylor snared Jesse Gonder's hard liner for the first out. Third basemen Richie Allen cleanly fielded a George Altman grounder for the second out. Bunning kayoed pinch-hitter John Stephenson to complete the masterpiece.

As the celebration moved into the clubhouse, a raft of New York and Philadelphia media swarmed in to interview Bunning, while the rest of the players tried to get ready for the second game of a twin-bill (amidst the commotion, pitcher Rick Wise, trying to prepare for the nightcap, had trouble finding a catcher to warm him up). Meanwhile, Bunning was rushed into a taxicab and driven to a television studio to appear on Ed Sullivan's widely watched CBS television show that evening.

He was adept at keeping his pitches low. When asked why, he would respond, "I've never seen a 450-foot ground ball." He didn't miss a start for 11 years. In 1957, he was one of only two AL 20-game winners and finished third in ERA. During the all-star game, he set down nine straight NL hitters. Following the season, he worked a winter job officiating basketball games.

His 1958 season, in addition to the gem against Boston, featured a 14-12 record. In 1959, he won 17 games, and reached the 200-strikeout plateau for the first time, pacing the league. In one memorable contest against Boston, he showcased his hitting skills with a homer, triple, two singles and five RBI.

Bunning topped the league in strikeouts again in 1960 and was second to Chicago's Frank Baumann in ERA. He slipped in 1961 to third in strikeouts, behind Camilo Pascual and Whitey Ford, but had a 17-11 season for the Tigers, who climbed to second place.

He won 19 games in 1962, but the Tigers became concerned when his record slipped to 12-13 in 1963. That latter season, Bunning roomed with Rocky Colavito and they had a running discussion about which of them would get traded first. Detroit ultimately swapped Jim and catcher Gus Triandos to the Phillies for outfielder Don Demeter and pitching prospect Jack Hamilton.

Jim, who made his winter home in Cincinnati, was nowhere near done. In his first year in the City of Brotherly Love, he won 19 games, but as most baseball fans know, the Phillies were surpassed by the Cardinals during late September 1964 for the pennant. Some analysts believed that manager Gene Mauch depended too heavily on Bunning and Chris Short, because he didn't have confidence in his other starting pitchers. The Phillies' collapse down the stretch was one of the decade's memorable storylines.

He won 19 contests again in 1965, this time with a career-best 268 punch-outs. In 1966, he struck out 252 hitters and achieved 19 victories for the third straight season.

By 1967, the 35-year-old Bunning was the highest-paid player in Phillies history with a salary around $80,000 including some deferred payments. Overcoming a mid-summer case of bronchitis, he set a new career high in innings worked with 302, and led the Phillies in wins (17), strikeouts (253), and ERA (2.29). "You're only as old as you feel," he told reporters. "A lot depends on how you take care of yourself." Describing Bunning's pitching style, Mauch said, "Jim operates like a fine heart surgeon. He makes an incision here, then another one there."

Unhappy with their roster (after an 82-80 season) and with Jim's salary demands, the Phillies traded him to Pittsburgh, where he was a disappointment. Coming back too soon from both a groin pull and a twisted ankle, he wound up inflaming a hip and pulling a hamstring. His 1968 record dropped to 4-14. "The only thing that hurts is my ego," he told reporters at one point.

Bunning rebounded partially to a 13-10 season in 1969 for the Pirates and Dodgers, but Los Angeles released him after the season. He returned to the Phils as a free agent for two final seasons and retired with a 224-184 record, a 3.27 ERA, and 40 career shutouts. He led his league in fielding percentage four times. Ever the intimidator, he also led his loop in hit batsmen four years.

Jim was only the second pitcher – after Cy Young -- to collect 100 wins and strike out 1,000 hitters in each loop. When he retired in 1971, he was second on the all-time strikeout list with 2,855, trailing only Walter Johnson. Fellow Hall of Fame pitcher Jim Palmer called him "one of a kind. He always let you know where you stood." Mauch called him "two hundred pounds of pride."

Late in his career, Bunning was among those instrumental in the players' association tapping Marvin Miller as president. The hiring of Miller set in motion many changes that affected the game, ultimately leading to free agency and higher salaries for players in the mid-Seventies.

As a lawmaker, Bunning displayed the same no-nonsense intensity as he did on the baseball diamond, yet he always remembered his friends. When Tony Taylor was coaching and his club made a stop in Baltimore, Bunning invited him to the nation's capital and took him on a VIP tour of the White House. Bunning and his wife Mary also acted as surrogate parents for many twenty-something-year-old congressional staffers who worked in Bunning's office over the years.

Bunning suffered a stroke in October 2016 and passed away eight months later at age 85. He left behind his wife, nine children, 35 grand-children, and 21 great-grand-children.

ART MAHAFFEY

Western Hills High School in Cincinnati once had one hell of a baseball program, producing major leaguers Pete Rose, Eddie Brinkman, Russ Nixon, Dick Drott, Don Zimmer, and Art Mahaffey. *Sports Illustrated* at one point put Mahaffey on its front cover with the headline, "New Hope in Philly." A righty, Art pitched for seven years and made two all-star teams. In his top season in 1962, he won 19 games.

Mahaffey fanned 17 Cubs hitters on April 23, 1961, setting a Phillies record. Ernie Banks and Ron Santo both whiffed three times. "Everything was working," Art recalled. "The fastball was jumping. The curveball was jumping off the table." After the game, he and his wife entered a restaurant, to a round of applause from the patrons. Fifty years later, he marveled, "With some of the pitchers the Phillies have had, it's surprising the record hasn't been broken."

Art is remembered for another game in which his Phillies lost 1-0 to the Reds in September, 1964. In a tied contest with Frank Robinson at the plate and Chico Ruiz on third base, Ruiz broke for home with an attempted steal. "It was the craziest play in baseball," Mahaffey recalled, because "Robinson was a right-handed hitter, and if he swings, he'll crush the runner's skull." Not expecting Ruiz to break for the plate, Mahaffey made a poor throw, and Ruiz was safe with the game's only run. The loss proved to be the start of the Phillies' 10-game losing streak that cost them the pennant.

Mahaffey pitched the final part of his career with a torn shoulder muscle. In those days, teams did not believe in shoulder surgery. That left him in excruciating pain, as his ERA drifted above 6.00 in his final two seasons. He retired with a 59-64 record, 4.17 ERA and nine career shutouts. He ran an insurance agency after leaving baseball. He was recently living in Whitehall, Pennsylvania.

JOHNNY CALLISON

Outfielder Johnny Callison was so popular in Philadelphia that when the *Philadelphia Daily News* ran a cover photo of fans waiting to greet the pennant-contending team at the airport in 1964, it showed a teenage girl holding a "Callison for President" sign.

Philadelphia was a perfect landing spot for Callison, though he didn't initially realize it. A member of the 1959 AL champion White Sox, he and his wife flew to Venezuela after the season for winter ball. Returning from the field one day his wife showed him a newspaper article. Though printed in Spanish, they both understood that he had been traded to the Phillies. Going from one of the best teams to one of the worst, he felt betrayed.

With the Phils, Johnny slowly evolved into a star. He always had a deadeye throwing arm, but for two seasons, his progress at the plate was measured. Then in spring training 1962, he selected a heavier bat, shortened his swing, focused on meeting the ball, and beat out Ted Savage for the right field job. "John has improved very much and there is no doubt he is going to be a star," manager Gene Mauch proclaimed early in the season.

He became a master at playing balls off Connie Mack Stadium's right field fence and firing laser-beam throws to the infield. When runners took the bait, Callison often made them pay, leading right fielders in assists four years (at a time when Roberto Clemente was playing the same position). To this day, Callison is tied for 12th on the all-time list for right-fielder assists. He also topped his league in putouts six times.

With the stick, his best period was from 1962 to 1965, during which he made the all-star team three times, led the circuit in triples twice, and averaged 28 home runs per year. In 1964, he received the all-star game MVP award after hitting a three-run homer. Outfielder Billy Williams later recalled, "He was a helluva player. Strong arms, quick wrists, beautiful swing."

His first year with the Cubs (1970) went well, but he clashed with manager Leo Durocher in 1971. By the time he joined the Yankees in 1972, he was still only 33, but whether it was his achy knees, heavy smoking, or just constant worrying, he was no longer productive. He retired with a .264 batting clip, 226 homers and 1,757 hits.

By his own admission, Callison was "the biggest worrier in baseball." Extreme anxiety diminished his enjoyment of the game, and compared to today, there was less in the way of mental health counseling or pharmaceutical anxiety drugs available for such players. Catcher Dave Watkins recalled, "Johnny became my flying buddy. He hated flying and got very nervous at the slightest bump in the sky. So, we played cribbage the whole flight every time, but he needed a martini just before every flight."

The son of a heavy drinker, Callison grew up in poverty and was ashamed of his family's financial position. He understood that with his talent, baseball could be the route to a better life. So, in 1957, when Babe Herman, a famous Phillies scout, was inside Callison's house talking with John's parents, the eager youngster was outside on the driveway, signing a contract with a representative of the White Sox.

After baseball, Callison tended bar and sold cars near Philadelphia. He contemplated a return to a baseball job, but there was no market for an obsessive worrier. John passed away in 2006 at age 67 in in Abingdon, Pennsylvania, still remembered as one of the finest Phillies in the Sixties.

GERRY ARRIGO

Lefthander Gerry Arrigo relied heavily on the screwball and developed chronic arm soreness. It's hard to escape the conclusion that the two were correlated. Then again, his hobby was bowling, so who knows? Arrigo grew up in Chicago where his next-door neighbor was Carmen

Silvano, a pro bowler who won 17 PBA championships. That relationship explains Arrigo's interest in bowling.

He pitched from 1961 to 1970, posting a 35-40 record and a 4.14 ERA, with the Twins, Reds, Mets and White Sox. Gerry had a reputation as a complainer, though in retrospect, that evaluation seems less than fair. When he was farmed out to minor-league Dallas for the third straight season during spring training 1963, he instead went to Deshler, Ohio, to visit his wife and newborn daughter. In those days, that was considered unreasonable.

He eventually reported to Portland. Then a few weeks later, he refused to board a flight from Dallas to Portland. His explanation: "I wasn't about to get aboard that plane. They were weighing each player as he came up the runway to make sure it wouldn't get over-loaded. It was just a two-engine job and was going to take like 18 hours to make the flight." What were seen as unreasonable demands for family time and safe travel decades ago seem like common expectations today.

"Arrigo is like a hound dog," Phil Howser, the general manager of the Twins' Charlotte farm club, said in a colorful quote in 1964. "The more you whip him, the more he lays down. He came from one of the toughest sections of Chicago. And he just needed someone to talk to him, instead of tongue-lashing him." Whatever that meant, Arrigo acknowledged his room for maturity. "I used to lose control when I thought the umpire booted one. Howser taught me to forget about the umpires and just pitch." Jack McKeon, then managing in the minor leagues, called him "one of the best-looking prospects I've ever seen."

Arrigo pitched the first one-hitter in Twins history on June 26, 1964, as he held the White Sox in check until Mike Hershberger got a hit in the ninth inning. After finishing that season with a record of 7-4, he was traded to the Reds for young Cesar Tovar. Twins manager Sam Mele was not happy with the trade, but Arrigo was pleased, relocating near his wife's hometown.

After a pair of lackluster seasons with the Reds and Mets, he returned to Cincinnati in 1967, where pitching coach Mel Harder helped Gerry improve his slider as an effective second pitch. Arrigo authored another one-hitter against the Mets and concluded that 1967 season with a 6-6 record. His 1968 tour of duty was his best as he posted a 12-10 mark for the Reds with a 3.33 ERA.

In 1969, though still only 28 years old, Arrigo lost his command of the now smaller strike zone. His strikeouts-to-walks ratio plunged from 1.8 in 1968 to 0.6 in 1969. The Reds gave up on him, and he finished up with the 1970 White Sox and the 1971 Richmond Braves.

Closing trivia: Only three Twins ever wore uniform number 42, before it was retired by MLB in honor of Jackie Robinson -- Gerry Arrigo, Jim Manning and Buzz Stephen. The three hurlers combined to win 36 games in the big leagues, with Arrigo collecting 35 of them.

JIM MALONEY

If you put together an all-star team for the 1960s, Jim Maloney might be on your pitching staff. The Reds' ace posted a 134-80 record during the decade, with four 200-strikeout seasons. He was a 23-game winner in 1963, and a 20-game winner in 1965.

Fresno High School was in the enviable position of boasting a team that included Maloney, pitcher Dick Ellsworth and catcher Pat Corrales. Ollie Bidwell was the school's coach and trained the youngsters in the game's fundamentals. Maloney demonstrated potential as a hitter and pitcher and since the initial bonus offers from MLB teams were not to his liking, he played one season of college ball at Fresno City College. When Reds scout Bobby Mattick offered $100,000 in bonus money, Maloney was ready to sign.

He wasn't in the minor leagues long. He already had a great fastball, and Nashville pitching coach Jim Turner helped him refine his curve. Maloney made his MLB debut just a year later, in 1960. The right-hander took some hazing from catcher Ed Bailey for the size of his bonus, but credited veterans Wally Post and Gus Bell with helping him adjust to life as a rookie on a team stocked full of veteran star position players. He said catcher John Edwards was one of his best friends in baseball, going back to their time together in the minor leagues. Edwards, in turn, said, "Jim had a tremendous fastball and a good curve." At his peak, Edwards said, Maloney was a Hall-of-Fame-type pitcher.

The young hurler was not much of a factor when the Reds won the pennant in 1961, posting a 6-7 record as a spot starter and getting hit hard by the Yankees in one relief appearance in the World Series. He progressed in 1962 and was one of the league's top pitchers by 1963.

Recalling the 1964 season, Maloney told the HaughtCorner.com web site that it was difficult to see manager Fred Hutchinson's health decline during the season due to his painful bout with cancer. He said coach Reggie Otero had to help the skipper get into his uniform. Hutch stepped aside in August, turning the role over to Dick Sisler. The Reds were still in pennant contention on the last day of the season but started John Tsitouris instead of Maloney. The Cardinals got to Tsitouris early and won the game, 10-0, to capture the pennant.

Maloney was a decent hitter for a pitcher and was adept at bunting. He recalled that Hutchinson would have the pitchers spend two hours a day in bunting practice during spring training.

With each successful season, Maloney's salary figures grew, and his relationship with the Reds became strained in 1969, when recurring shoulder pain prompted him to ask for extra rest between starts. He finished with a 12-6 record but became embroiled in a contract dispute with Reds president Bob Howsam the following winter that led to him accepting a small pay cut, from $60,000 to $57,500. He reported late for 1970 spring training, only to pop his Achilles tendon on a non-pitching play in his first game of the season, and missed most of the year as the Reds powered their way to the pennant.

By then, the Reds had an impressive collection of pitching with Gary Nolan, Jim Merritt, Wayne Simpson, Jim McGlothlin, Don Gullett and Milt Wilcox, all in their twenties. They were eager to move Maloney's pricey contract, and found a taker with the Angels. But Maloney suffered from hamstring and groin trouble, and was ineffective in seven outings. His career ended in 1972 as a minor leaguer in the Giants' system.

Back home in Fresno, Maloney struggled to adjust to life after baseball. He was slated to take over his father's automotive enterprise -- a business he loathed. Jim began drinking heavily, and eventually divorced. In 1982, the Giants hired him to be pitching coach for their Fresno farm team, under manager Wayne Cato. Part-way into the season, farm director Bob Fontaine called and told him that Cato had been fired. Maloney was elevated to manager, but his drinking continued, with Jim in no condition to mentor his players. Even the fans came to suspect something was amiss when Maloney threw up in the third-base coach's box mid-game.

Things went downhill for several more years until February 5, 1985, when Maloney, by then out of baseball, received a phone call from his former teammate Jim Merritt. Merritt, who had a severe drinking problem in his pitching days, told Maloney he had been sober for six years, and asked if Maloney was open to getting help. When Maloney said yes, Merritt told him to expect a call from John Newton, the medical director for Unocal oil company, who also worked with the Dodgers.

Moments later, the phone rang again. This time it was Newton on the line, along with former pitching legend Don Newcombe. Both Newton and Newcombe were in recovery, and Newton recommended a recovery facility in Arizona where Dodgers outfielder Ken Landreux had just been treated. Newton arranged for the facility to open a bed, and before the day was over, Maloney was on flight to Phoenix. He entered treatment for 42 days and became sober.

Maloney still needed to determine a career path, and experienced God's provision. He was offered a job as the City of Fresno's Director of the Drug and Alcohol Abuse Council, which he held for more than decade, and then another counseling position on the staff of a church. In 1998, he went to a high school reunion and reconnected with his high school sweetheart. He is now retired, happily married and still attends two AA meetings a week. An inductee into the Reds team Hall of Fame, he enjoys returning annually to Cincinnati to welcome new honorees into that honorary club.

GEORGE CULVER

Ballplayers in the Fifties and Sixties often supplemented their income by playing winter ball in Puerto Rico, Panama, Nicaragua, Columbia, the Dominican Republic, Venezuela and Mexico. Some of these leagues started to fold during the Sixties, while others continued to provide winter work-and-development opportunities.

Married players sometimes took their wives along for the experience. Players unaccompanied by wives or girlfriends hung out together, often passing time by playing cards in the hotel. Most would exercise care in where they traveled with safety as a concern.

One player who encountered a strange winter-ball experience was a young pitcher from Bakersfield named George Culver who went on to have a nine-year MLB career. Culver was in Venezuela for winter ball. "You can be walking along, minding your own business, a guy can fall down in front of you and start screaming for the police and next thing you know, you're arrested," Culver told writer Earl Lawson. "I happened to be in the wrong place at the wrong time," he said of the incident that resulted in him spending two days in jail on suspicion of assault and battery.

A judge found him innocent but the "plaintiff," after learning George was a ballplayer, filed a civil suit seeking $15,000 – a huge sum in those days. That led to Culver spending several more days in jail. Eventually, the lawsuit was tossed out, the accuser was found to be in Venezuela on a falsified passport, and about 40 people were arrested for being part of a false-passport ring. Culver understandably had no interest in returning to Venezuela.

George's first MLB team was the Indians, who drafted him from the Yankees. He made the team out of spring training in 1967 and enjoyed a solid rookie year, with a 7-3 record and 3.96 ERA out of the bullpen. Following the season, Cleveland traded him downstate to the Reds for outfielder Tommy Harper.

With the Reds in 1968, Culver won 11 games and pitched 226 innings, tops on the club. Curt Flood called Culver's slider "nasty." Orlando Cepeda said he wished that Culver had remained in the AL, noting that the NL already had enough tough pitchers.

On July 29, 1968, Culver fired a no-hitter against the Phillies. He felt rotten that morning with an upset stomach and an in-grown toenail so painful that he had a Novocain injection minutes before the game. Through seven frames, Culver was on track. Then he walked the first two batters of the eighth inning, which led to a visit from manager Dave Bristol and catcher Pat Corrales. He settled down and completed his gem. Second baseman Tommy Helms, with whom Culver was sharing a Cincinnati apartment, made a nice play to back up his pitcher. In honor of the no-hitter, Culver received a $1,000 pay raise and a steer, which he had butchered and donated to a local orphanage.

Two other 1968 games involving Culver were memorable. One came on July 25, when George and reliever Clay Carroll allowed the Pirates 13 hits but nonetheless held the Bucs scoreless.

The other came in April, with the Reds hosting the Cardinals. Players were trying to decide whether to sit out in memory of slain Sen. Robert Kennedy. With 28,000 fans already in the stands, management wanted the game to go on, making for a tense situation. Culver was on the field warming up and returned to the clubhouse when player rep Milt Pappas urged the team to decline to play and called for a vote.

As the players cast their votes, Culver returned to the field to continue warming up. The vote turned out to be tied, 12-12. Outfielder Alex Johnson, who had not voted, was tracked down. Told he would be the deciding vote, he asked, "I don't know. What does everyone else want to do?" That response elicited some laughs in the midst of the tough situation. Culver returned to the clubhouse a third time when team president Bob Howsam spoke to the players, who ultimately decided to play, to the consternation of Pappas, who was soon traded.

Culver spent a second summer in Cincy in 1969, and then split the 1970 season between the Cardinals and Astros. George had a brilliant 1971 campaign in Houston, as he led the team in appearances and posted a career-best 2.64 ERA. He placed second on the club in appearances in 1972.

George welcomed a 1973 trade to the Dodgers, but before long he was waived and claimed by the Phillies. He divided the 1974 season between Philadelphia and Toledo; and in 1975 he pitched for Nippon of the Japanese Pacific League. He retired with a 48-49 record and a 3.62 ERA.

George roomed on the road with pitcher Steve Hargan with the Indians, infielder Tommy Helms and catcher Pat Corrales with the Reds, and outfielder Norm Miller with the Astros, and at times had his own room. He never observed any managers micro-managing the pitch calling from the dugout. His favorite place to pitch was the Astrodome, which he says was a good pitcher's park. Culver's "Funky George" nickname came from Joe Morgan, who said that Culver threw a funky slider.

The respected baseball man later spent three decades in a variety of coaching capacities. He also is a community leader in Bakersfield who has worked tirelessly with other leaders to support and advance sandlot baseball.

JOHNNY EDWARDS

Catcher Johnny Edwards played for two pennant winners, the 1961 Reds and 1968 Cardinals. Although he delivered four hits in 11 trips during the 1961 World Series, his Reds lost to the Yankees in five games. In the 1968 Series, he struck out in his only appearance, as his Cardinals lost to Detroit in seven games. His experience was a reminder that few MLB players are fortunate enough to win a World Series.

Edwards grew up in Columbus, Ohio, and his favorite player was Jim Hegan, the Indians all-star catcher. He attended Ohio State and by the time he made the major leagues, he too was exceptional at blocking runners at the plate and calling a great game for his pitchers. Edwards twice set NL records for putouts and once went 138 straight games without an error. He had a howitzer throwing arm and was a three-time all-star.

The Reds perfected John's defensive skills by having coach Johnny Temple heave throws into the dirt in front of and to both sides of the dish. Practice did indeed make nearly perfect.

Edwards was involved in a 1963 double-header against the Mets the day that New York fans broke out of control. Attendees hurled apples, oranges, bottles and cans at Reds players from the stands and then rushed the field when play was complete. As the Reds players jogged up the stairs leading to the clubhouse, Edwards later fumed, Mets fans were spitting on them. By the time Reds player representative Bob Purkey submitted a written complaint to the league office, NL President Warren Giles had already laid down the law in a phone call with Mets executive George Weiss, telling him that excuses were unacceptable and adequate police protection was required.

John enjoyed playing home games at Crosley Field. Until Riverfront Stadium opened in 1970, the Reds played at the park named for industrialist and broadcaster Powel Crosley, who bought the team in 1934. The stadium was built in 1912; baseball had been played at that location since 1884. Edwards remembers the big scoreboard in left-center field and appreciated the players' proximity to fans when warming up pitchers.

With the Cardinals, Edwards backed up Tim McCarver. He returned to starting duties with Houston. The two-time gold glover's defensive skills kept him in the game through 1974, even after his hitting results diminished.

"People ask me all the time who was my favorite catcher," noted hurler George Culver. "There were some good ones but John Edwards would rank right up there with the best I ever pitched to. He was a great guy, great teammate, and an outstanding catcher and thrower. He had a great demeanor and I always felt he could have been an outstanding big-league manager if he had wanted it."

For his career, Edwards hit .242 with 81 home runs and 1,106 hits. He lived in Cincinnati and Houston during his baseball days, and later remained in Houston, working for Cameron Ironworks and Baker Hughes. He recently was residing in Magnolia, Texas.

LEO CARDENAS

Leo (Chico) Cardenas achieved the first of his boyhood dreams in 1959 upon joining the Havana Sugar Kings, an elite minor-league team owned and operated by the Reds. He followed the team to New Jersey in 1960 when it relocated due to Cuban political instability. A second dream was realized later that summer when the young shortstop joined the Reds, though like many rookies, he initially struggled at the plate.

In 1961, Reds infielder Eddie Kasko's prolonged slumps helped Cardenas become the starting shortstop late in the season, as Cincinnati won its first pennant since 1940. Leo hit .308 in 74 games. Writer Earl Lawson wrote that the slender infielder was called "the Spider" because "at 150 pounds, he's all arms and legs." Manager Fred Hutchison said, "Cardenas has the edge over Kasko because he has the greater power."

Birdie Tebbetts once called the five-time all-star "the most underrated player in the league." His best season may have been 1965, when he hit .287, led the league in intentional walks, and garnered his only gold glove award. Topps produced a "Manager's Dream" baseball card featuring Cardenas alongside Roberto Clemente and Tony Oliva in 1968.

Following a trade to the Twins, Cardenas anchored the shortstop position for the 1969 division championship club, batting .280. He made his final all-star appearance in 1971, his last season in Minnesota, when he had 18 homers and 75 RBI.

After shorter stints with California, Cleveland and Texas, Cardenas retired with a .257 batting average, 1,725 hits and 118 home runs. One weakness was an inability to shorten his swing with two strikes. He fanned 80 or more times in eight seasons, which was considered a problem in the Sixties, though it would be average or better today.

Not infrequently, Leo's temper got the better of him. An early example came in the second-to-last game of the 1964 season. With his Reds battling the Cardinals and Phillies for the pennant, he was plunked in the back by a delivery from Philadelphia's Chris Short. Rather than simply take the free pass to first base, Cardenas made a move toward the mound with bat in hand, before being restrained by catcher Clay Dalrymple. His action incited the ire of the Phillies bench, and Philadelphia went on to win the game, 4-3. The Reds finished the season one game behind the pennant-winning Cardinals, and teammates regretted his action, which seemed to energize the Phillies.

After baseball, lapses in judgment continued. He reportedly used a baseball bat to break the arm of a man who was having lunch with his wife, and was convicted of felonious assault, resulting in a three-month jail sentence. On another occasion, he got into an auto accident as an uninsured motorist, resulting in additional financial woes. Fans of the Reds and Twins prefer to remember happier days when Cardenas represented those clubs in pennant races and post-season games. Leo was recently residing in Burlington, Kentucky.

LOU BROCK

If it was Luis Aparicio and Maury Wills who reintroduced baseball to the stolen base, then it was Lou Brock who re-institutionalized the weapon. Brock called his prolific base stealing a way of "turning up the thermostats of the game." From 1966 until 1974, Brock paced the NL in steals eight times in nine years. He pilfered 50 or more bags 12 straight seasons.

Along the way, he hit .293, with 3,023 hits and 141 home runs. His 938 career stolen bases are second on the all-time list behind Rickey Henderson, who swiped 1,406 bags.

Brock had already shown flashes of promise for the Cubs by mid-1964 when Chicago traded him to St. Louis to get pitcher Ernie Broglio. The Cubs kept hoping Brock would become a capable center fielder and were disappointed in his glove work and arm. The buzz at the time was that the Cubs had gotten the better of the deal.

Cardinals manager Johnny Keane green-lighted Brock to run whenever the opportunity was presented. Lou became an overnight sensation as the left fielder and leadoff man for the Cardinals, hitting .348 with 33 steals in 103 games. The Cardinals went on to win the 1964 world championship. Brock was one of the stars of the World Series, collecting nine hits and driving in five runs.

Once he became entrenched at the top of the St. Louis batting order, there was no looking back. The Cards won another world championship in 1967, with Brock making the all-star team for the first of six times. He led the league in runs scored and stolen bases in 1967, and produced 21 home runs, 12 triples, and 32 doubles. Then in the World Series, his .414 batting average and seven stolen bases keyed the Cardinals to a seven-game victory over the Red Sox.

A year later, the Cardinals returned with largely the same crew, having also added Johnny Edwards for depth at catcher. The Redbirds again won the pennant handily. Brock hit .298, led the loop in steals and triples, and landed in sixth place in MVP votes. His sterling performances continued into the World Series with a .464 batting average and seven stolen bases, though this time the Tigers bested the Cardinals in seven games.

Brock turned 30 in 1969 but offered no hints of a slowdown. Several of his teammates did, however, and the Cardinals drifted back to fourth place. That was followed by an even more frustrating 1970 season in which the Cardinals dropped to a 76-86 record, again in fourth place. Dick (Richie) Allen spent that season in St. Louis but didn't seem like a good fit, and Steve Carlton endured a 10-19 campaign. Brock hit .304 and stole his usual 50-plus bases, but this time settled for second place as Bobby Tolan of the Reds claimed first place with 57.

Lou never won an MVP award, but came closest in 1974, when he finished second to Steve Garvey of the Dodgers. That was the year Brock shattered the single-season stolen base record, held by Wills, and stole 118 bases in 151 tries, while batting .306. He accomplished these fetes despite a hand injury that caused pain the second half of the season. For fans across the country, especially young people, Brock captured the public imagination with his daring base-stealing success.

During the 1977 season, Brock made national headlines again when he stole his 893rd base, breaking Ty Cobb's all-time record. Brock endured a poor season in 1978 but came back for a fine farewell in 1979, as he batted over .300, stole more than 20 bases, and eclipsed the 3,000-hit mark.

If Brock had a weakness, it was his unsteady glove work as he topped the NL in errors eight years. The Cardinals came to understand that miscues were part of his game, and easy to overlook in light of his enormous hitting and baserunning contributions.

Author David Halberstam said Brock "was driven by a rage to succeed." And succeed he did. The Arkansas native was elected to the Hall of Fame in 1985. In *The New Bill James Historical Baseball Abstract,* the author rated Brock the 15the greatest left fielder of all time, just after Joe Medwick and Jesse Burkett, and just ahead of Goose Goslin and Charlie Keller.

CURT FLOOD

Early in Curt Flood's career with the Cardinals, he kept getting passed over for the center field job as the team tried out Jim Beauchamp, Don Landrum, Charlie James, Carl Warwick, Don Taussig and even Bill White, who was really a first baseman. None could play center field as well as Flood. It was not until Flood's fourth season in 1961, when he hit .322, that the Cards realized his offensive potential.

Flood's initial progress was slowed by Solly Hemus, the manager from 1959 to 1961. Hemus was perceived by some as disliking black players, including Flood and his roommate, Bob Gibson. Johnny Keane replaced Hemus mid-season in 1961.

From 1962 to 1969, Flood hit at least .285 all but one season. He led the league in hits in 1964 and was named to three all-star teams. Once Lou Brock arrived in 1964, Flood slotted in as an excellent number-two hitter. On the defensive side, Curt won seven gold gloves and once went 226 straight errorless games. He did make a costly misplay in game seven of the 1968 World Series, however, which helped the Tigers win the championship.

By 1969, Flood was commanding a $90,000 salary. After the season, the Cardinals and Phillies pulled off a blockbuster trade. Dick (Richie) Allen, the Phillies' top star, was sent to St. Louis along with infielder Cookie Rojas and pitcher Jerry Johnson. The Phillies were initially thrilled with the package coming back, which included Flood, catcher Tim McCarver, relief ace Joe Hoerner, and outfielder Byron Browne.

Flood refused to report, arguing that he should be able to join a team of his own choice. To complete the deal, the Cardinals instead sent two younger players to the Phillies, one of whom was first baseman Willie Montanez. The Phillies were hoping to become instant contenders, and without Flood in the deal, that didn't happen.

The broader implication was that Flood sat out the 1970 season and challenged the sport's reserve clause, which bound a player to a single team. He lost his court case, but by 1976, veteran players gained a path to free agency. It was a courageous move by Flood, who realized he was risking his future by doing so.

Flood returned in 1971 with the Senators at age 33, but his skill set was diminished. He played in just 13 games before quitting the sport and flying to Europe. Flood's lifetime stats included a .293 batting average and 1,861 hits.

In 1997, while suffering from throat cancer, Flood contracted pneumonia and died at age 59 in California. He was survived by his wife and a son from a previous marriage.

CHARLIE JAMES

Growing up in the St. Louis suburbs, Charlie James attended Cardinals games with his dad at Sportsman's Park and dreamed of being a big-leaguer. That dream came true as he played outfield for the Cards from 1960 to 1964, before a final season with the Reds.

One of his highlights was hitting a grand-slam homer off Sandy Koufax in 1962. That was his best season as he hit .276 with 59 RBI. Charlie brought the fans to their feet again during the 1964 home opener, in which he again homered against Koufax. Another thrill was playing in the 1964 World Series, in which the Cardinals defeated the Yankees. Decades later, Charlie still wears the championship ring. Overall, he was a .255 lifetime hitter with 358 hits including 29 homers.

For James, much of the joy of playing MLB was being able to do so in his hometown, as well as the friendships. He roomed on road trips with Julian Javier, Lindy McDaniel and Joe Cunningham. He recalls hunting with teammate Bill White and playing bridge with Bob Gibson. Charlie has nothing but good things to say about Stan Musial, saying, "He was a wonderful teammate, always helpful when asked."

Having completed his master's degree in electrical engineering from Washington University, he became president of Central Electric in Fulton, Missouri. Under his leadership, sales grew from $1 million to more than $22 million.

LARRY JASTER

St. Louis has long been a great baseball town. Seldom have its fans had more fun than 1964 to 1968, when the Cardinals won three pennants in five years.

In team lore, this tall lefty is remembered for throwing five shutouts against the pennant-bound 1966 Dodgers, something MLB likely will never see again. The last time a hurler had done so was Pete Alexander in 1916. Asked about the remarkable achievement in 2023, Jaster reflected, "What amazes me looking back is I only gave up 24 singles in those 45 innings." That year proved to be Larry's best season, with an 11-5 record.

Larry grew up in the 1950s in Midland, Michigan, where baseball as well as fast-pitch softball were exceptionally popular (the local Dow ACs team became national fast-pitch champion). After time in college, he signed with the Cardinals, and reported directly to Winnipeg to start his pro career. Jaster still recalls traveling from one minor league city to the next via bus, with the drivers sometimes getting lost on back roads in the Dakotas.

The Cardinals player-development system was better than many other clubs during those years. Jaster credits spring training coaches Howie Pollet and Joe Becker with helping him become a better pitcher, as well as coaches John Grodzicki in Winnipeg and Jim Konstanty in Tulsa. Larry was called up to St. Louis in 1965 and posted a 3-0 record. With St. Louis, Tim McCarver was his regular catcher. "Tim was smart. He always called a good game and good locations," Jaster recalled.

Larry posted an even better ERA of 3.01 in 1967, while his record was 9-7 and the Cards flew away with the pennant. After beating Boston in the World Series, he remembers, "Most players went out to dinner as a group after the initial celebration. Augie Busch threw a big dinner party."

Jaster pitched with the Cardinals through 1968, spent 1969 with the Expos, and pitched for the Braves off and on from 1970 to 1972. He had a 35-33 record with a 3.65 ERA. His primary road roommates were fellow pitchers Joe Hoerner with St. Louis, Steve Renko with Montreal and Phil Niekro with Atlanta.

Reflecting on those great Cardinals teams of 1967 and 1968, he remembers that the players got along exceptionally well. He said that happy personalities like Orlando Cepeda and Lou Brock set the tone in the clubhouse. Roger Maris was quiet but a good teammate, he recalled. Bob Gibson was the optimal competitor, a good team player with a dry sense of humor.

When able to enjoy some down time, Jaster enjoyed hunting quail and duck. After completing his master's degree from the University of New Mexico, he continued in coaching positions, retiring from the Orioles organization in 2012. He now lives in West Palm Beach, Florida.

BOB GIBSON

For both dominance and consistency, it would be hard to find a better pitcher during any era than Bob Gibson of the Cardinals. He reeled off 13 straight winning seasons from 1961 to 1973, enjoyed five 20-win campaigns and collected nine gold gloves. In postseason action, he was even stronger with a 7-2 record and a 1.89 ERA. With two World Series MVP awards, he shares the record with Sandy Koufax and Reggie Jackson. Gibson could even hit, batting .206 with 24 career home runs. Stan Musial once mused about Bob becoming an outfielder, so that he could hit every day.

Gibson was born in Omaha, Nebraska. As of 2023, the state had produced 119 major leaguers, 11 of whom became all-stars. Gibson, Richie Ashburn and Wade Boggs became Hall of Famers.

Gibson never met his father, who died before Bob was born. An older brother mentored him, while his mother worked doing laundry and domestic work to put food on the table for her seven children. Gibson's first love was basketball and for a time he played for the Harlem Globetrotters, rooming with Meadowlark Lemon. Bob found the experience – playing an afternoon game in one city, then riding a bus and performing another game that evening – less pleasant than he expected. One of his first baseball experiences was playing for former Negro Leagues star Josh Gibson's Y Monarchs team. Bob starred in two sports at Creighton University, where his baseball manager was future NBA coach Bill Fitch.

After signing with the Cardinals, Bob's big-league career got off to an uneven start in 1959 under manager Solly Hemus but blossomed after the Redbirds fired Hemus on July 6, 1961. Whereas Bob had a 2-5 record that season under Hemus, he went 11-7 under new skipper Johnny Keane, who instilled confidence in the youngster, saying he had "the best arm in the league." The team itself improved under Keane, and Hemus never got another MLB manager's job. Gibson ended the season at 13-12, his first winning season.

The fireballer found that he was more successful when he threw his fastball less. By throwing more breaking pitches and palm balls, he could prevent hitters from anticipating the heater. His victory total rose each year from 13 to 15 to 18 to 19 to 20, and finally to 21 wins in 1966.

Gibson lost part of the 1967 season to a leg injury (sustained on a Roberto Clemente line drive) but rebounded to win three games in the World Series over Boston.

In 1968, Gibson took his game to an even higher level, winning 21 times with a microscopic 1.12 ERA. He threw 13 shutouts and during one stretch of 95 innings, surrendered only two earned runs. Behind Gibson, the Cardinals won their third pennant in five years, and he set a World Series record by striking out 17 Tigers in a single game.

Pitcher Al Jackson, who had been both a teammate and opponent of Gibson, observed, "His control is simply great. His slider is his money pitch. It shakes hands with his fastball." John Edwards recalled, "I caught many of his games in 1968 and I pushed him to throw more sliders. His 1.12 ERA will never again be matched."

Slugger Tony Perez joked, "When I faced Gibby, my wife would go to the lady's room. She didn't want to see what was going to happen." Dizzy Dean commented during the 1967 World Series, "I've been saying for five years that Gibson is the best pitcher in baseball, bar none."

Bob's lifestyle on road trips was typically low key. He watched television "until the tube blows out," he joked. His favorite foods included steaks and strawberries, preferably eaten together. A married man with kids, he had no interest in visiting bars.

For a time, Gibson worked the winter banquet circuit, but he quickly tired of the experience. "I challenge anyone who has made many dinners to tell me that the food doesn't vary from good to bad at the banquets," he told *The Sporting News.* "I reached the point in most places that I mostly ate only the meat course and a salad. I lost five pounds traveling about. You know people mean well, but some of the banquet cocktail parties, especially afterward, can get out of hand. At one – and why embarrass nice people by saying where – I endured a racial slur."

Gibby finished with a 251-174 record and 2.91 ERA. After baseball, he managed his personal investments while generally keeping a low public profile. He died in Omaha in 2020 at the age of 84. The street "Bob Gibson Boulevard" in Omaha is named for the first-ballot Hall of Famer.

LARRY JACKSON

Idaho native Larry Jackson wasn't the most spectacular pitcher of his era, but he was one the steadiest, winning 194 games. He was a five-time all-star whose durable arm allowed him to rack up innings. His best pitches were the fastball and the slider. He was with the Cardinals from 1955 to 1962, the Cubs from 1963 to early 1966, and the Phillies until he retired on his own terms after the 1968 season.

Larry led the Cardinals in ERA in 1959. A year later, he won 18 games and topped the league in innings. He won 16 games in 1962, his final year in St. Louis. Coming off four straight winning seasons, he was not a logical candidate to be traded, but the Cardinals coveted Cubs all-star outfielder George Altman and Jackson was part of the price tag.

Jackson spent three full seasons with the Cubs, topping out with 24 victories in 1964, a remarkable total on an eighth-place team. He finished second to Dean Chance in the MLB Cy Young award balloting.

Jerome Holtzman wrote that summer, "In a sense, Jackson is a throwback to the old-style hurler. He rarely misses a turn and his best pitch is still the fastball, even at the age of 33. His fastball isn't the overpowering type, but it's just as effective because it sinks and sails."

While the 1964 season was Jackson's finest, he also had an enjoyable off-season. Sears Roebuck was looking to promote its outdoors-related products and teamed up with WGN-TV in Chicago to sponsor and film a 13-day hunting and fishing trip. Larry was joined by several current and former teammates -- Dick Ellsworth, Bob Buhl, Dick Bertell, Ron Santo and Don Landrum – and his brother came along to shoot the film. Bertell was the chef among the group, putting some of his favorite recipes to work.

After returning from the trip and celebrating the holidays, Jackson met with Cubs' officials who rewarded him with a salary increase. Larry was less effective in 1965, however, as he lost 21 games. He bounced back to top the NL in shutouts in 1966 as a member of the Phillies but settled for a 15-15 record.

After the 1968 season, he advised the Phillies that he would hang up the cleats if he was not traded to a western team. When he was selected by Montreal in the expansion draft, he followed through on his threat.

Larry remained home in Boise, where he became a lobbyist for the Boise Cascade forest-products company. He waged an unsuccessful race for governor as a Republican in 1978 (Harmon Killebrew and Vern Law campaigned for him), then accepted an appointment to the state's Industrial Commission, where he served for 12 years until his death at age 59 from cancer in 1990. He never received a vote for the Hall of Fame, despite finishing in the NL's top 10 in wins seven years. Yet, he was the type of reliable, personable, no-nonsense pitcher that every manager coveted.

DICK HUGHES

Right-hander Dick Hughes was an exceptional one-year wonder. He posted a 16-6 record in 1967, helping the Cardinals win the pennant. His luck ran out in the World Series, as he surrendered five home runs in nine innings of work, though his Redbirds nonetheless won the Series.

Hughes grew up in Louisiana, the son of a World War II Navy veteran. He loved baseball, and admired the ace hurlers on the Indians in the late Forties such as Bob Feller as well as Gene Bearden. By age 10, he already envisioned a pitching career. He went to the University of Arkansas and was signed by Cardinals scout Fred Hahn. Hughes made his MLB debut in 1966 and pitched very well.

Reflecting Hughes' success in 1967, only Tom Seaver received more rookie of the year award votes. Hughes went into the rotation when Al Jackson got off to a rough start, and after Bob Gibson's injury, Dick was briefly the staff ace.

The following season, Hughes pitched through a painful torn rotator cuff, and would have been better off taking time off to rest the injury. He spent the 1969 season pitching with pain in A-ball. He later took over Hahn's scouting territory for several years, before going into full-time animal ranching. Hughes, a resident of Stephens, Arkansas, credits his Christian faith for helping him cope with his career-ending injury.

PETE WARD

Born in Montreal and raised in Oregon, third baseman Pete Ward was the son of an NHL hockey player. He signed with the Orioles but spent most of his nine-year career with the White Sox. Besides having a "life of the party" personality, he also was one of Chicago's most productive hitters for several years.

Ward was "a natural hitter with excellent instincts," recalled Pat Gillick. Pete placed second in the AL rookie of the year balloting in 1963 (losing to teammate Gary Peters, who became a lifelong friend.). Ward's 84 RBI led the White Sox, and his 22 homers tied for the team lead with Dave Nicholson. He batted a career-best .295 as the club won 94 games, finishing second to the Yankees.

Ward was on top of his game again in 1964, with 23 home runs and 94 RBI, both the best on the club. He also added 28 doubles for the White Sox, who pushed their victory total to 98, but still placed second in the league.

For reasons that still draw speculation, he never again matched those levels of production. One explanation is that his hitting may have been adversely affected from a neck injury sustained in a car accident. Ward and teammate Tommy John were in a vehicle that was rear-ended in early 1965 while leaving a Black Hawks hockey game. In 1965, battling neck pain, he hit only .247 with 57 RBI.

During that 1965 season, *Sports Illustrated* scheduled a photo shoot, and laid out a front cover, featuring Ward. At the last minute, the magazine's executives changed gears and went with a cover story about boxer Cassius Clay. The cover of Ward never ran, although Ward retained a copy.

After an injury-plagued 1966 season, he moved to left field in 1967 and led the club with 18 home runs and 62 RBI, while hitting.233. That was the last year of contention for the White Sox, who went into a period of sustained decline. Looking back, Ward always felt the ChiSox should have won the pennant that year, in light of their strong pitching.

Ward was shifted to first base and hit 15 home runs in 1968, but saw his average drift further, to .216. He remained with the White Sox after the expansion draft, but played sparingly in 1969. After the season, he was swapped to the Yankees for pitcher Mickey Scott and a cash payment. New York used him chiefly as a pinch-hitter in 1970.

That drew the curtains on his career at age 32, with a .254 average, and 776 hits, including 98 circuit shots. Though he spent most of his career at run-stingy Comiskey Park, his home-road homer differential was close to even. Oddly, nearly 10 percent of his homers came off just two pitchers, Earl Wilson and Denny McLain.

Ward felt fortunate to have played for two all-time great managers, Al Lopez with the White Sox and Ralph Houk with the Yankees.

In later years, he coached under Joe Altobelli in Rochester in 1971, and managed in the Yankees' farm system. After returning home to Portland to operate a travel agency, he was coaxed back into baseball to coach with the Braves for a year under manager Bobby Cox. As a retiree, Ward closely followed the White Sox, Yankees, Mariners, and Braves before passing away.

JOEL HORLEN

The "workhorse of the White Sox," this right-hander pitched at least 210 innings yearly from 1964 to 1969. Relying on two types of fastball, an overhand curve, and an occasional slider, his best season was 1967 when he made the all-star team, won 19 games and led the circuit with six shutouts and a 2.06 ERA. Only Jim Lonborg received more Cy Young award votes.

Horlen hailed from San Antonio and was an American Legion ball teammate of future major leaguer Gary Bell. Indians scout Bobby Goff offered both prospects a contract. Bell signed, while Horlen chose to go to college.

Joel eventually committed for a $30,000 signing bonus out of Oklahoma State. Ira Hutchinson, his first pro manager, wired the White Sox, "This boy will make it. He's intelligent. He has the arm. And he has the desire." Former Tigers manager Bill Norman watched Horlen pitch at San Diego, and said, "A lot of kids have golden arms, but this boy has it inside, too." Joel, for his part, credited Herb Score with providing tips during training camp on optimal conditioning.

The role of a workhorse was not without its downside. Horlen experienced shoulder pain, began taking cortisone pills, and in 1964 began needing cortisone shots. In that 1964 season, only Dean Chance had a better mark than Joel's 1.88 ERA, though plagued by lackluster run support, Joel's record was only 13-9. Instead of pitching winter ball, he took a job with Jefferson Standard Life Insurance, and dickered with the ChiSox over his salary. He followed up with a pair of .500 seasons in 1965 and 1966, again with sterling ERAs.

During his big season in 1967, *The Sporting News* wrote that Horlen chewed wadded-up tissue paper to relieve stress. Why not gum or tobacco? He said gum caused bloating and tobacco made him nauseated.

Horlen credited isometric exercises with helping him prepare for the 1967 campaign. That September, he threw a no-hitter against the Tigers, helping the Sox stay in pennant contention. Consistent with the era's customs, no teammate spoke to him during the later innings, for fear of jinxing him. Only pitching coach Marv Grissom approached, offering his usual advice to get ahead of every hitter. Horlen struck out four and walked none, with a Ken Boyer error preventing a perfect game.

In the Sixties, a no-hitter had pleasant financial implications for a pitcher. His team would usually boost his salary by at least $1,000. More significantly, it could mean an extra $10,000 to $20,000 in endorsement and appearance money, something a married father like Horlen could appreciate.

After contending all season, the 1967 Pale Hose settled for fourth place. Following the season, owner Arthur Allyn announced that the Sox would begin playing nine home games per year in Milwaukee, the first time such an arrangement was implemented in AL history. In the NL, it had been deployed only in 1957, when the Dodgers played several games in Jersey City.

Already a superb golfer, Horlen took up a new hobby in the late Sixties. He bought a Piper Cherokee seven-seat plane, which he piloted from San Antonio to Florida for spring training. He was quick to add that unlike Denny McLain, he would always travel with the team. Horlen said the plane allowed him to save time in getting to golf and hunting destinations. During the previous winter, he had gone elk hunting with Ron Hansen, Gary Peters, Eddie Fisher and Don Pavletich.

After pitching well again in 1968, Joel's fortunes turned south, mirroring those of the White Sox. Battling knee trouble, his record over the next three summers was just 27-41. Manager Chuck Tanner released him in early 1972, saying Horlen's fastball lacked zip, but the hurler suspected his release was about saving money. He quickly became a valuable relief pitcher for the 1972 A's, winning a World Series ring. He finished with a 116-117 record, a 3.11 ERA and 18 shutouts.

Horlen later divorced, remarried and converted to Judaism. He was a minor-league tutor for the Indians, Mets, Royals, Giants and Padres, before becoming a Giants scout based out of San Antonio. He passed away in 2022.

JIM LANDIS

Outfielder Jim Landis was voted onto the White Sox all-century team in 2000. He began his pro career when he signed with White Sox scout Bobby Mattick. Following a two-year Army stint in Alaska, he reached the big leagues in 1957 and was an instant success defensively. By 1958, he had become a solid hitter, as well, batting .277 with 15 home runs.

The Fresno native played no small role in the Sox winning the 1959 AL pennant. He hit .272, paced the league in sacrifice hits, and swiped 20 bases. The real story was his defense. He stole home runs from Willie Tasby and Gus Triandos with leaping catches and robbed numerous other hitters of would-be base hits. MacGregor Sporting Goods was all too happy to remind people that Landis used a MacGregor glove. During the World Series, Landis batted .292, though his White Sox lost to the Dodgers in six games.

Following the season, owner Bill Veeck wanted to trade Landis for slugger Roy Sievers but manager Al Lopez talked him out of including Landis in the deal, insisting he contributed too much on defense to sacrifice.

Landis went on to win five gold gloves, average about 20 steals per year during his peak, and make two all-star teams. He even had five years in the league's top 10 for getting on base as a hit-batsman. During Jim's eight years in Chicago, the Sox never had a losing season.

In 1964, Jim got into a bitter dispute with White Sox general manager Ed Short. Highly upset, he took his frustrations to manager Al Lopez. The manager, in turn, benched Landis for a number of weeks until writer Jack Kuensler played the role of mediator between manager and player. That marked Jim's third straight year with a batting average below 230. Thereafter, he was a fourth outfielder for the A's in 1965, the Indians in 1966, as well as Houston, Detroit and Boston in 1967.

Landis retired with a .247 batting average and the second-best fielding percentage in history among outfielders. After baseball, he went into private business, and along with his wife raised two sons. Jim lived in the heart of the wine country in Napa, California until his death at age 83 in 2017.

HOYT WILHELM

At age 29, most future Hall of Famers have already enjoyed some, if not most, of their best seasons. Hoyt Wilhelm was just making his big-league debut with the Giants. What a debut it was, as he led the league in ERA and winning percentage in 1952. His record was 15-3 with a 2.43 ERA and 11 saves. His knuckleball danced and darted unpredictably, baffling NL hitters all year long.

Wilhelm followed up in 1953 by making the all-star team. Then in 1954, as the Giants raced to the world championship, Wilhelm was again a central figure, going 12-4 with a spotless 2.11 ERA.

Yet, as soon as he experienced adversity, teams backed away, mistakenly concluding he had lost control of his knuckleball for good. The Giants traded him to St. Louis. Cardinals general manager Frank Lane designated him for assignment. Hoyt landed in Cleveland. The next year,

Lane became general manager for the Indians and cut him again. It takes a special type of executive to twice waive a future Hall of Famer.

This time, Hoyt got the last laugh. The Orioles tried him as a starting pitcher and on September 20, 1958, he threw a 1-0 no-hit victory over the Yankees. It was the first no-hitter for the Orioles, who had moved to Baltimore in 1954 after earlier playing as the St. Louis Browns.

In 1959, Wilhelm started the year with a 9-0 record for Baltimore. The Orioles also used him occasionally in relief, including the outing where he pitched 8 2/3 innings of no-hit relief in an extra-innings game. He became the first pitcher to win an ERA crown in both leagues, as he posted a 15-10 record.

Wilhelm remained with Baltimore until 1963, when at the age of 40, he was traded to Chicago in the blockbuster deal that sent Luis Aparicio to Baltimore. With the White Sox, he anchored one of the top bullpens of all time, alongside Eddie Fisher, Bob Locker, and other firemen. Through the 1965 season, he was working more than 130 innings per year. There were plenty of special moments. On August 30, 1966, he hurled three scoreless innings against Detroit, getting the win in the 12th inning. It was the 803rd appearance of his career, as he moved past Walter Johnson into second place on the all-time appearances list, at the age of 43.

"He may be 43, but he has a young arm," manager Eddie Stanky told writer Edgar Munzel. "There's no end in sight for him. He may be around a long time yet." Munzel said, "This balding old gentleman from North Carolina is baseball's answer to Old Man River."

Indeed, Wilhelm continued to excel throughout the Sixties, including five straight ERAs below 2.00. After the 1968 season, he was drafted by Kansas City and traded to the Angels. He pitched all the way until 1972, finishing up with the Dodgers at age 49. By then, he had passed Cy Young to move into first place on the all-time appearance list. Other records set by Wilhelm included career marks for most relief appearances, most relief innings, most victories in relief, and most games finished. He retired with a mark of 143-122, a 2.52 ERA, 228 saves, and five shutouts.

Brooks Robinson said, "He had the best knuckleball you'd ever want to see. He knew where it was going when he threw it, but when he got two strikes on you, he'd break out one where *even he* didn't know where it was going!"

Charlie Metro, a White Sox coach, wrote in his book, *Safe by a Mile,* that J.C. Martin was the only one who could effectively catch Wilhelm's knuckle ball. Martin told WhiteSoxInteractive.com, "It was exciting because you never knew where the ball was going. Seriously, it could do a 90 degree break, and then double back….You'd have to snatch it when it was right on top of you."

Wilhelm himself explained how he threw the pitch in a 1958 television interview with Bob Woolf, sponsored by Palmolive Shaving Cream. "Well, Bob, it's actually a floater," he said.

"The whole idea of throwing a knuckleball is to throw the ball where it won't spin, and the wind currents meeting the seams of the ball make it do those tricks."

He added, "I throw it right off of the fingertips, and more or less push the ball out…There's days when it doesn't do much, and days when it does too much. But when it's working, that's the pitch I want them to hit off me." Wilhelm threw it with two fingers digging into the ball, while some others threw the pitch with three fingers. Keeping his finger nails the right length was also important, he noted in the interview.

Hoyt was one of 11 children raised on a farm in Huntersville, North Carolina. He began throwing the knuckleball at a young age, after reading a newspaper article about the pitch; by high school, it was already his bread-and-butter pitch. He served three years in the military, and won a purple heart, all before making the major leagues. When he finally did get to the big show, he slugged a home run in his first plate appearance. He never hit another.

For 16 years in a row, the team for which Wilhelm played led the league in passed balls. Catchers experimented with oversize gloves, with mixed success. One of those backstops, JW Porter, said, "You never know what his ball is going to do until the very last instant."

While with the Orioles, Wilhelm loved eating crabs at the local haunts. Boog Powell recalled Hoyt and catcher Dick Brown introducing him to crabs during his first season.

When Wilhelm's career finally ended, he and his wife settled in Sarasota, and he worked as a minor-league pitching coach. Wilhelm passed away in 2000 in Sarasota, due to heart failure, at the age of 80.

LOU KLIMCHOCK

Perseverance was the watchword for Lou Klimchock, an infielder who experienced big-league success as a teen and then waited 10 years to replicate that success. In the interim, he played well over 1,000 minor-league contests, often as one of his league's top players.

Lou came out of Latrobe High School in Pennsylvania and signed with the A's. A year later, in 1958, he put up spectacular numbers for Pocatello in the Pioneer League, earning a call-up to the A's for the final weekend of the season. When he homered against Stover McIlwain of the White Sox, it was the first time in modern baseball that one teen homered against another teen. A year later, Lou hit well during another late-season call-up. From there, he played sparingly for the A's, Senators, Braves, and Mets over the next eight years.

He finally got his chance in 1969, at age 29, when Indians manager Alvin Dark gave him extensive playing time at second base (his favorite position) and third base. Lou hit .287 in 90 games and was grateful for the chance to play. Dark was thankful to get some quality hitting from Klimchock for his last-place team. Lou was courteous and cordial to everyone he met and after the season, the writers covering the Tribe presented him with the annual Good Guy Award at a banquet at the Sheraton Cleveland Hotel.

Lou was relegated to a reserve infielder role again in 1970. He was released that August and concluded his playing career for Denver – a Senators' farm team – in 1971. He credits his Christian faith with helping him to persevere through the highs and lows of a baseball career.

After managing the Indians' Reno farm club in 1973, Klimchock later worked for Coors Brewing in Denver and Coca-Cola in Phoenix, learning superb business skills that he has employed in a leadership role with the Arizona Major League Baseball Alumni Association.

Whitey Ford

This five-foot-ten southpaw commanded respect throughout the game. Hank Bauer called him "the best left-hand pitcher for one big game in the business." Pinky Higgins said, "He'll beat you. He'll never beat himself." Catcher Elston Howard simply called him the Chairman of the Board.

Ford was successful from the moment he arrived in New York until the day he stepped away. As a rookie in 1950, he posted a 9-1 record, before leaving for two years of military duty. In his final season in 1967, Ford made seven starts and notched a stunning 1.64 ERA.

A native New Yorker, he was ideally cast as the ace pitcher in the nation's biggest city and media market. His .690 lifetime winning percentage is one of the five best in the sport's history. Even in World Series action, he was commendable, posting a 10-8 record for a .556 percentage with a 2.71 ERA. Ford spent his entire 16-year career with the Yankees and saw World Series action in 11 of those seasons.

Whitey's demeanor conferred a sense of abundant confidence, but according to Dizzy Dean, who was then broadcasting games, there was more than what met the eye. "Whitey looks like a little Horatio on the bridge when he's on the mound, cool, confident, even cocky. Yet before each game, he's as nervous as a cat protecting a basketful of kittens," Dean stated.

Ford confessed in a *Baseball Digest* article that although he would sleep well the nights before he pitched, that he would tense up after arriving at the ballpark. He would lose as much as 10 to 12 pounds during the game, and then drink milk or fruit juice about once an hour, hardly getting any sleep the nights after he pitched. He said it took about 24 hours after a game for him to relax.

Of course, Ford was also known to enjoy beverages other than milk and fruit juice. He was close to teammates like Mickey Mantle, Moose Skowron, Billy Martin, Hank Bauer and later John Blanchard, who were no strangers at New York's top night clubs. One night out in 1957 proved costly. Ford and several teammates, along with their wives, went to the Copacabana club to celebrate Martin's 29th birthday with their friend, Sammy Davis, Jr., who was performing. When some hecklers in the club yelled racist remarks, a ruckus occurred and one of the hecklers was laid out on the floor with a broken jaw. The Yankees confirmed their players were involved and fined most of them (all except rookie Johnny Kucks) $1,000 apiece. Soon after, Martin was an ex-Yankee, a negative influence removed from the team.

In all of the years that Ford played for Casey Stengel, he never won 20 games. Rather than employ a consistent rotation, Stengel saved Ford for the toughest matchups. Once Stengel was replaced and Whitey got to start once every four days, he enjoyed a 25-win season in 1961 and a 24-victory campaign in 1963.

Early in his career, Ford avoided throwing sliders (due to the pain it caused his arm), but by the early Sixties, pitching coach Johnny Sain had taught Ford to throw the slider with a smoother, longer motion. The pain subsided, and Ford suddenly had another weapon in his arsenal.

As Ford got older, he found that he needed to spend more time on running and conditioning. He credited Ralph Houk with instituting drills that helped him get into game shape. He also developed arm problems that resulted in him needing more rest between starts, prompting him to finally retire in May 1967. He later did some coaching, broadcasting, and investing in race horses. In 2008, he auctioned off many of his baseball mementoes, with proceeds going toward his grandchildren's education and his charitable foundation. His lifetime record was 236-106 with 45 shutouts and a 2.75 ERA. Ford was just shy of his 92nd birthday when he died in Lake Success, New York, in 2020.

John Blanchard

As an 11-year-old boy playing pick-up baseball in Minnesota, John Blanchard repeatedly broke the windows of a nearby apartment building with his powerful hitting stroke. Each time, the boys would take off running. Years later, his power remained evident as he paced the minor-league Joplin Miners and the Binghamton Triplets in home runs. He later became a valuable "tenth man" for the Yankees.

Blanchard signed with New York in 1951 for an estimated $30,000 paid out over several years, the most ever at that time for an amateur player from Minnesota. The young man participated in Casey Stengel's off-season "Preliminary Camp" in Florida, where coach Bill Dickey convinced the organization to move Blanchard from the outfield to catcher.

After two years with the military and a lot of time in the minor leagues, John finally started getting serious playing time in 1960, when both Yogi Berra and Elston Howard were nursing injuries.

In 1961, Blanchard came alive, torching opposing pitchers. He hit .305 with 21 home runs in 93 games and credited manager Ralph Houk for his development as a slugger. "Ralph gave me a new spirit, a new desire to play ball, and made me believe I'm a big-leaguer," Blanchard said. In game five of the World Series against the Reds, he delivered a home run, double and single as the Yankees won 13-5 to seal the championship. Twins owner Calvin Griffith was so impressed with the Minnesotan, he said, "If we could get Blanchard, we'd use him every day in the outfield with Earl Battey doing the catching."

Blanchard's batting average dropped off the next two seasons, but he still delivered 13 bombs in 1962 and 16 more in 1963, dividing his time between first base, outfield and pinch-hitter, with fewer appearances as a catcher. He reprised his super-reserve role again in 1964, adding seven more home runs.

Realizing his baseball days wouldn't last forever, Blanchard became co-owner of a liquor store and a franchisee for a company called Ad-O-Matic. But having developed close friendships with drinking buddies Mickey Mantle and Whitey Ford, he hoped his Yankees career would last forever.

All good things come to an end, and for Blanchard, it was on May 3, 1965, when the club traded him and pitcher Roland Sheldon to the A's for catcher Doc Edwards. It was devastating news for Blanchard who had never been with another organization. Playing for Kansas City and then Milwaukee, his production was miserable. By John's own later admission, he was drinking heavily and his skills were eroding.

After sitting out the 1966 season, he went to spring training with the Braves in 1967 and 1968 but could not get another big-league contract. Blanchard later sold the liquor store and got involved in printing and car sales. He passed away in 2009 in Minnesota at the age of 76, still remembered as a key figure on several great Yankees teams.

MICKEY MANTLE

Many ballplayers in the Sixties attracted respect from their peers but Mickey Mantle commanded awe. Senators catcher Paul Casanova recalled being part of the 1967 AL all-star team, saying, "When Mantle walked into that locker room, it was like God walked in." Indians pitcher Steve Bailey later reflected, "I wasn't much for admiring other players, but when we played the Yankees, I watched Mantle take his swings during batting practice. He was an amazing hitter." Reliever Dooley Womack said Mickey was his hero as a kid and as a Yankees teammate. Pitcher Bruce Brubaker lists fanning Mantle twice in a pre-season game among his career highlights.

In a May 28, 2011 *Boston Courant* article by Don Amore, former pitcher Roland Sheldon said, "Mickey would come into the clubhouse and say he heard a new joke, and we'd all have to gather 'round and listen to him tell it. And it could be the worst joke in the world, but we'd all have to laugh at it. That's what made it funny. I loved being part of that team."

Even pitcher Jim Bouton, whom Mantle would not speak with for many years after the hurler's controversial book was published, felt much the same. As he told writer Peter Golenbock, "I felt in many ways the same way the other guys do about him. They all loved him. I loved him also. He was great around the clubhouse, told great stories, and was just fun to be around…After my first shutout, he laid out white towels from the clubhouse door to my locker. Those are things I will never forget as long as I live."

Mantle's accomplishments – including 536 homers and 1,676 runs scored over 18 seasons – are remarkable for any player, let alone one who played through so many injuries. "He played injured all the time," Bouton recalled. Mantle endured operations on both knees, his right hip and right shoulder. Arthritis eventually set in on one knee. Mantle also suffered through broken fingers, a broken foot, pulled hamstrings, and muscle tears in his groin and thighs. Late in his career, he played with both legs wrapped in elastic bandages from the calf to the thigh to provide support.

"I played with him more than 10 years," commented Elston Howard in 1969 in *Baseball Digest*, "and I cannot remember a time he was not hurting, but he never mentioned it. He was the greatest competitor I've ever known." Dr. Sidney Gaynor, the Yankees' team physician for 28 years, marveled at Mantle's determination to play, saying, "He's the kind of guy you'd like to have in your outfit in war." Or in your lineup.

On September 10, 1960 at Briggs Stadium in Detroit, Mantle crushed a 634-foot home run that cleared the right-field roof and a six-lane road, landing at the base of a lumber yard across the street. The blast was rated by the *Guinness Book of World Records* as the longest homer in history. It was one of his league-high 40 home runs.

Power was one measure of Mantle's greatness. The slugger led or co-led the AL in home runs four times, in runs scored five times, bases on balls five times, and in OPS six years.

Yet, in his prime, his preeminence in outfield defense and speed on the base paths were equally impressive. Mantle won the AL MVP award in 1956, 1957 and 1962 – and he placed second in three other seasons. He also showed respect for his opponents, later saying, "After I hit a home run I had a habit of running with my head down. I figured the pitcher already felt bad enough without me showing him up rounding the bases."

A native of rural Oklahoma, he had rugged good looks to accompany his athletic prowess. His dad, a former semipro player, named his son after catcher Mickey Cochrane. He recognized his son's baseball potential and insisted he become a switch-hitter. Mickey's grandfather threw batting practice. Playing semi-pro ball, Mickey was still only 16 and too young to sign when he caught the attention of Yankees scout Tom Greenwade.

When Mick graduated in 1949, he signed for just a $1,100 bonus and suited up in Independence, Missouri. After the season, he rejoined his dad for winter work in the mines. He also met and began dating his future wife.

In 1950, he hit an incredible .383 for Class-C Joplin in the Western Association and was recalled to New York in mid-September where he observed the team's stars as they completed their season. In spring 1951, the Yankees presented an outfield job to Mantle, still only 19. After slumping, Mickey was demoted to Double-A Kansas City for 40 games. Threatening at one point to leave the sport, he met up with his angry father in a hotel room and his dad packed Mickey's suitcase, telling him he could work in the mines. In tears, Mickey resolved to give it another try. By the time the season was over, Mantle had returned to the Yankees, and hit 13 home runs. By 1952, with Joe DiMaggio retired, Mantle was a .300 hitter, an all-star and the league leader in OPS.

As the 1950s progressed, Mantle experienced an array of conflicting feelings. He was sometimes booed by his home fans. After numerous male relatives including his dad died of cancer at a very young age, he became convinced that the same fate awaited him. Playing in the land of temptations that was New York City, his lifestyle became unhealthy.

It was only during the 1961 season, when Mantle and Roger Maris were chasing Babe Ruth's home run record, that the home fans finally seemed to embrace Mickey as their favorite. He finished the year with 54 home runs and a .317 batting average – 48 points better than Maris, who nonetheless was named MVP.

Mantle missed 39 games in 1962 but still led the AL in OPS while hitting .321. His 1963 season was abbreviated by injuries but by 1964, he was once again one of the league's top hitters, surpassing 100 RBI for the fourth and final time.

By 1965, Mantle was dealing with nonstop pain and struggling to stay in the lineup. When manager Johnny Keane was fired 20 games into the 1966 season, the first person to approach him was Mickey, apologizing that he had not been able to deliver for Keane as he had for previous skippers. Mantle concluded the season with a .288 batting average and 23 home runs in just 108 games.

Mantle played two more seasons, compiling statistics that were, at least for him, subpar. Yet, even in his final campaign in 1968, Mantle was still ninth in the league in OPS. He announced his retirement the following spring.

"Mischievous" is a great word to describe Mantle's personality. Along with the jokes, he enjoyed pulling pranks on rookies and veterans alike. In one case, he left a note in Bobby Richardson's locker to call a certain phone number and ask for Mister Lion. Only after placing the call did Bobby realize he had called the Bronx Zoo.

Richardson continued, "Many people have speculated how Mickey's career might have been negatively affected by his love of the nightlife. I think that if Mickey had taken better care of himself, his statistics might have been a little better, but not much. For one thing, I don't think it would be possible for them to be too much better. They were just too good. Second, tales of

Mickey's partying have become exaggerated over time. His greatest excesses came after his retirement from baseball."

Retirement posed new challenges. Mantle had business interests, enjoyed fishing and golf, and played quarterback in backyard football games with his sons. But now he had a void in his life as the daily interactions with teammates were missing. He became more dependent on alcohol and was briefly banished from baseball after taking a casino job. He separated from his wife for 15 years though they never divorced. In the 1980s, as baseball card shows became the rage, he became active on the show circuit. His appearances were arranged by a young agent, Greer Johnson, who was his business manager and live-in love interest.

Late in life, he became sober, was diagnosed with cancer, broke off contact with Greer Johnson, and publicly acknowledged his regret for many of his actions. He died in Dallas in 1995 at the age of 63. More than 2,000 people attended his funeral service in North Dallas, where Bob Costas delivered a eulogy, and country star Roy Clark performed a song. Bobby Richardson then told the story of Mantle reciting John 3:16 and making a decision for Christ. The first-ballot Hall of Famer had a lifetime average of .298 with 536 home runs and 2,425 hits.

JIM BOUTON

In 1963, the Yankees roared to their fourth straight pennant with 104 victories. Second-year man Jim Bouton won 21 games and threw six shutouts, providing spectacular pitching behind club ace Whitey Ford, who won 24 times. When Bouton followed up with an 18-win season in 1964, coupled with two more triumphs in the World Series, he looked set to become another in a long line of Yankee legends, despite having gained a reputation as a bit of an oddball.

His next four seasons were essentially a bust, as Bouton remained in the Yankees organization but registered just a 9-24 record. He pitched through a painful bicep injury that reduced the elasticity of his arm, endured remarkably poor run support, and began to alienate the club's brass with his candid comments about whatever topics he and the New York sportswriters chose to discuss. Demoted to Triple-A Syracuse in 1967, his record there was just 2-8. When the Yanks finally gave up on Bouton in 1968, nobody was surprised.

Joining the expansion Pilots in 1969, Bouton was used mostly as a reliever. Relying now on a knuckleball, he was moderately effective but susceptible to gopher balls. In 57 outings, his ERA was 3.91. On August 24, he was traded in a waiver-wire deal to the Astros, who still harbored longshot hopes of winning the NL West. He went 0-2 in 16 outings for Houston, as the Astros finished fifth with an 81-81 record.

As readers of this book know, Bouton kept a diary of his observations during the 1969 season, read those observations each night into a tape recorder, and sent the tapes to writer Leonard Shecter, who knew instinctively that the pair had the makings of a blockbuster book. *Ball Four* was one of the most transparent examinations of the game ever written. There were juicy stories about players' sexual escapades, drinking, and amphetamine use, as well scathing appraisals of some of the people in MLB leadership positions. On a deeper level, it was also a seemingly honest account of an aging pitcher trying desperately to hang onto a job in the major leagues. The book created quite the uproar, with criticism from Commissioner Bowie Kuhn on down. But the vitriol aimed at Bouton served to drive more book sales.

The Astros gave Jim an opportunity in 1970, but the right-hander yielded just a 4-6 record and a 5.40 ERA. He didn't make it back to the big leagues until 1979, when he made five starts for Ted Turner's Braves club at the age of 39. In between, he worked as a New York sportscaster, developed a bubble-gum product called Big League Chew, published more books and articles, and pitched in Mexico.

Bouton told writer Peter Golenbock that after manager Johnny Keane was hired in 1965, "It was an unhappy clubhouse. I didn't have any particular trouble with Keane, but Joe Pepitone was really having trouble with him, and so was Clete Boyer, and so were Maris and Mantle. Everybody was always in a bad mood…Maris and Boyer and I had deep resentments of each other. Mostly because Maris was deeply resentful of the press and the fans, and during the same period I had a good relationship with the writers and the fans. The contrast was always there for them to see, and so it accelerated our other differences that we had." Bouton aggravated those resentments by sometimes going to dinner with the beat reporters.

"Keane was absolutely the wrong guy," Bouton told Golenbock. "The players may not have respected Yogi [who managed the team in 1964], but at least they liked him. Keane they didn't respect or like. Johnny was too old for us and much too traditional." Keane lost his job early in the 1966 season after the Yankees lost 16 of their first 20 games. Ralph Houk, who had been the skipper for three seasons before moving into the front office, returned to the manager's office. By 1968, Houk had the team over .500 again.

Bouton and Mantle had been friends but that all changed with the book. His revelations about his teammates created hard feelings that lasted almost 30 years. It was not until 1999 that Bouton was invited to participate in a Yankees old-timers game, a tradition that reunites key franchise contributors every year. His return to Yankee Stadium made for a compelling story of goodwill and acceptance.

About 16 years later, Bouton revealed that he was battling dementia. The devastating diagnosis seemed all-the-more-cruel because Bouton had always been erudite and an independent thinker. He passed away in Massachusetts in 2019 at the age of 80.

Bouton's lifetime record was 62-63 with a 3.57 ERA. Thanks to *Ball Four,* he was one of the most famous .500 pitchers of all time.

TOMMY DAVIS

If you made a list of the 10 best seasons from any position player in the Sixties, Tommy Davis's 1962 season would probably make the list. At age 23, he led the NL in batting average (.346), RBI (153), and hits (230). He was fourth in doubles and total bases, as well as fifth in triples and runs scored. His 153 RBI broke Roy Campanella's team record. Surprisingly, he didn't win the MVP award, placing third behind Maury Wills and Willie Mays.

Davis won another batting crown in 1963 and swatted a pair of triples in game one of the World Series. In game three, he delivered an RBI single to give Los Angeles a 1-0 win. That year marked the Dodgers' first world championship after relocating to the West coast.

His roommate on road trips was Willie Davis (no relation), another talented outfielder. They became lifelong friends through their shared experiences. Like many of his teammates, Tommy grew to dread his contract talks with general manager Buzzie Bavasi, which were more akin to ultimatums than negotiations.

A gruesome ankle injury cost him most of the 1965 season and diminished his foot speed. After a 1966 season in which he missed 62 more games, the Dodgers traded him to the Mets for second baseman Ron Hunt and outfielder Jim Hickman. Hunt, in particular, was coveted by the Dodgers, with infield stalwart Junior Gilliam retiring.

Davis had a productive 1967 season for the Mets, hitting .302 with 16 homers, but the front office seemed determined to trade him. The Indians made an off-season trade pitch, but ultimately the White Sox landed the Brooklyn native.

Davis hit .268 with eight homers in his lone season at Comiskey Park as the 1968 White Sox tanked in the standings, and he was selected by Seattle in the expansion draft. "To be honest," Davis later said, "the Pilots were a better team than the 1968 White Sox." Davis was mentioned a number of times in Jim Bouton's book *Ball Four,* which chronicled the Pilots' 1969 season. Davis said he had no problem with the book because everything in it was truthful. "I thought it was well-written and damn funny," he said.

Tommy later played for the Astros, A's, Cubs, Orioles, Angels and Royals, with the designated hitter rule extending his career. He was a .294 lifetime hitter with 153 home runs and 2,121 hits.

The best day in Davis' baseball life? He said it was the day in 1956 that Jackie Robinson phoned him, urging him to sign with the Dodgers. Tommy had been going to big-league tryouts as a catcher, and teams kept telling him he had too much speed to be stationed behind the plate. He was about to sign with the Yankees when Dodgers executive Al Campanis asked Robinson to phone him. Davis later wrote that Robinson had him convinced as soon as he said, "Hello, this is Jackie Robinson."

"Tommy Davis was headed for the Hall of Fame, be it not for the ankle injury," recalled former teammate Nate Oliver in 2023. "He was also a great person and team player."

Davis penned his own book, *Tales from the Dodger Dugout,* with Paul Gutierrez in 2005. He also worked as a private hitting instructor and as a member of the Dodgers' speakers bureau before passing away in Phoenix in 2022.

DON DRYSDALE

Sandy Koufax and Don Drysdale became universally known as the pitching aces for the Dodgers, who won four pennants in eight years starting in 1959. Koufax was the better pitcher but Drysdale was more intimidating. Standing six-foot-five, his propensity to throw inside kept batters from crowding the plate or getting comfortable. Ron Santo of the Cubs told writer Peter Golenbock, "He threw inside, threw ninety-plus, and he was mean." Willie Mays said, "You can't guess with Drysdale if you want to stay healthy. He pitches you in, and he pitches you out, and you gotta be ready, man."

Case in point, in 1960, Drysdale conked Mays on the arm and Orlando Cepeda in the helmet in the same game. In a 1961 contest, building on tensions between the Dodgers and Reds, Drysdale first threw a pitch behind the head of infielder Don Blasingame, next hurled two inside pitches toward Vada Pinson, and then smacked Frank Robinson in the wrist with a fastball. He was ejected and received a five-game suspension plus a $100 fine from NL president Warren Giles. Reds pitchers Joey Jay and Bob Purkey both said Drysdale's actions were "bush league." Asked whether he thought Drysdale deliberately threw at him, Robinson said, "Let's just say I don't think he's that wild."

Teammate Joe Moeller recalls Drydale as "a nasty competitor. He pitched inside as good as any pitcher I saw. Bob Gibson would also be in that category."

Overall, Drysdale led NL pitchers in hit batsmen in five of his 12 seasons. As recently as 2023, he was on the all-time top 20 list in that category with 154. Gus Weyhing, who pitched in the 1890s, is the all-time leader with 277, and Randy Johnson is the modern leader (post World War II) with 190.

A native of Van Nuys, California, Don was the son of a telephone company executive who was also a part-time baseball scout. Don joined the Dodgers as a teenager in 1956, when they were still based in Brooklyn. True stardom arrived a year later when he won 17 games.

The right-hander's most dominant season was in 1962, when he won 25 games and garnered Cy Young award honors. He registered his 20th win on August 3, making him the fastest NL pitcher to reach that level since Hippo Vaughn of the Cubs in 1918.

After missing out on the World Series for three seasons, the Dodgers were back in the fall classic in 1963. Drysdale, coming off a pedestrian 19-17 record, hurled a three-hit shutout against the Yankees in game three. "The Yankees apparently were looking for low stuff, so I just stayed high," he explained after the whitewash. The Dodgers swept the series four straight.

In those days, the Dodger's hurlers worked on three days of rest. If required, Don would start with only two days off. He was perennially among the league's top two or three workhorses in innings pitched.

Drysdale and Koufax had great personal rapport. Don told writer Bob Hunter, "When I was a lonely rookie from Los Angeles in Ebbets Field, I spent many evenings at Sandy's home with him and his parents. When the team moved to Los Angeles, Sandy visited with me and (wife) Ginger and my folks." They went into the service together at Fort Dix and later teamed up in their salary negotiations, as well.

The Dodgers missed out on the pennant in 1964, with Drysdale going 18-16 and nursing a thumb injury and shoulder tightness. He volunteered as a "Young Democrat" for the election of Lyndon Johnson in that year's presidential race.

Don enjoyed his second and final 20-win season in 1965 with a 23-12 record. In the World Series against Minnesota, he got shelled in game one, but looked good in a Dodgers' win in game four. Los Angeles won the Series in seven games.

Over the next two seasons, Drysdale's record dropped to 13-16 both years. In the 1966 World Series against the Orioles, he lost both of his starts, though he was effective in a hard-luck, 1-0 loss in the fourth and final game. In 1967, with Koufax retired and Maury Wills traded, the Dodgers drifted out of contention.

The last of Don's great achievements came in 1968, when he hurled 58 consecutive scoreless innings, breaking a mark long held by Walter Johnson. The new standard stood until broken 20 years later by another Dodgers' ace, Orel Hershiser. Drysdale closed the book on his pitching career in 1969 with a 209-166 record, 2.95 ERA and 49 shutouts. The eight-time all-star was elected to the Hall of Fame in his 10th year of eligibility.

Pitcher Claude Osteen was a teammate for five years. "He was a great leader of the Dodgers tradition and what wearing the Dodgers uniform meant," Osteen recalled in 2022. "I loved the man. He was a fierce competitor."

During his career, Don and wife Ginger Dubberly, a Hollywood actress, lived year-around in a beautiful Los Angeles home. They divorced in 1982 and he subsequently married basketball star Ann Meyers. Don died of a heart attack in his hotel room in Montreal in 1993. His Dodgers broadcast partner, Vin Scully, described calling the next game as the most difficult in his career.

SANDY KOUFAX

Hall of Famer Willie Stargell said that "Trying to hit Koufax is like trying to drink coffee with a fork." Manager Gene Mauch said that Koufax threw "a radio ball," a pitch you hear but don't see. Ron Santo of the Cubs proclaimed, "He should be in a league by himself." Teammate Claude Osteen called Koufax the best pitcher he ever saw, once the lefty sharpened his control.

Edward Gruver, author of the book *Koufax,* wrote, "For four, maybe five years in the 1960s, Sandy Koufax was not only the best pitcher of his time but also possibly the best pitcher of all time."

Koufax's teammate, Ron Fairly, used to tell a story about an instance where one of the Cubs players had demonstrated how Koufax, in his opinion, was tipping his pitches. Koufax went on to strike out 14 hitters and win the game. "When the game was over (Ron) Santo told his teammate, who claimed he had Koufax figured out, to stand on one of the tables in the middle of the clubhouse and do his demonstration again so all his teammates could once more see how Sandy tipped his pitches."

Another teammate, Joe Moeller, called Koufax "The best pitcher I saw in 56 years in baseball. He absolutely overpowered hitters. Sandy was an absolute perfectionist. He could throw a no-hitter and not be happy with some of the pitches he threw."

Bobby Richardson wrote of facing Koufax in the World Series, recording, "His fastball was just taking off out of his hand, and he was throwing a straight change-up off his fastball. His change-up looked exactly like his fastball coming in, and we would swing so far in front of the pitch that we were helpless to make contact. Plus, his curve would drop off like a dime, and he was throwing it precisely where he wanted to."

Koufax seemingly had two different careers. From 1955 to 1960, he had a record of 36-40. He struck out a lot of hitters, but issued too many walks, with a mediocre ERA. To their credit, the Dodgers resisted the temptation to trade him, realizing that Sandy was still only 25 years old.

Then from 1961 to 1966, he was baseball's best pitcher with a record of 130-47. In 1963, he won not only the Cy Young award, but also the NL MVP award. He led the NL in ERA each of his last five years. Lefty Grove and Clayton Kershaw did it four consecutive seasons, but Koufax is the only one to make it five straight.

There were plenty of hints of future greatness in the years before he became a true ace. In one game in 1958 against the Giants, he tied Bob Feller's modern record with 18 strikeouts. Though Koufax's record in 1960 was just 8-13, he notched a one-hitter against the soon-to-be world champion Pirates and a two-hitter versus the Reds.

During 1961 spring training, catcher Norm Sherry predicted Koufax would win 20 games that season. Sandy himself said, "It took me six years to get it through my thick skull, but I'm not taking such a big windup. I'm throwing easier, and I have more confidence now." Coming close to Sherry's prognostication, he won 18 games and set a new NL record with 269 strikeouts. He was just getting started.

His rise to the top coincided with a change of ballparks. From 1958 to 1961, the Dodgers played their home games in Memorial Coliseum, which Koufax and his pitching mates felt was conducive to "cheap home runs." Indeed, once the club moved into the new Chavez Ravine facility in 1962, Koufax hit his stride. He threw his first no-hitter there against the expansion Mets on June 30, 1962, but his season was soon cut short due to a circulation problem.

His second no-hitter came on May 11, 1963, against the Giants. The press had been reporting rumors that manager Walter Alston's job could be in jeopardy, as the club entered action that day at 15-15. Following that gem, Los Angeles won nine out of 10 and the rumblings quieted.

His third no-hitter came against the Phillies on June 4, 1963 in Philadelphia. His final no-hitter was a perfect game -- at home on September 9, 1965 against the Cubs.

During his career, Koufax's hobbies included reading literature, listening to symphonic music from his 300-record collection, and maintaining his ranch home in Studio City. Writer Melvin Durslag said the home was eclectic, noting, "The living room is contemporary, the bedrooms modern, the kitchen early American and the den Japanese."

Koufax wasn't recalcitrant about having a high profile. He co-owned the Tropicana Motor Hotel in Los Angeles and an FM radio station in Thousand Oaks, California. In the winter of 1962-1963, he joined up with comedian Milton Berle on a six-man Dodgers chorus that performed for a month in Las Vegas and for 11 days in Miami Beach. The other singers were Maury Wills, Don Drysdale, Frank Howard, Willie Davis and Duke Snider.

Koufax was a highly eligible bachelor during his playing days. He married three times thereafter and divorced twice. He did some broadcasting and remained involved in some business ventures. Sandy is currently residing in California. His lifetime record was 165-87 with a 2.76 ERA.

AL FERRARA

Like his Dodgers teammate Sandy Koufax, outfielder Al Ferrara was a native of Brooklyn who attended Lafayette High School. While the pair were not especially close, Al was seated next to Koufax on a flight after the Dodgers lost the 1966 World Series, when the pitcher confided he would soon retire from baseball. Al apparently knew several weeks before anyone else.

The fun-loving Ferrara stayed at a low-cost Los Angeles hotel with teammate Johnny Podres, and together they had great times, whether in the hotel or at the racetrack. He was invited to act in Hollywood alongside actress Zsa Zsa Gabor. He drank 10 cups of coffee every morning and smoked up to five packs of cigarettes a day.

Al has told the story of his first spring at Dodgertown in Vero Beach, where he broke curfew and scaled a fence to get back onto the grounds. A flashlight-wielding Tom LaSorda caught him and told him he would not report him just this once because they were both Italian, but that he better never catch Ferrara breaking curfew again. Several years later, Al made the Dodgers roster. LaSorda called him, asked if he remembered the time he let Al off the hook for breaking curfew, and then asked him to speak at an upcoming civic event. Al felt obliged to say yes. This type of conversation occurred several times with Al fulfilling the request each time. "By the fifth time, I said, 'Geez, Tommy, I wish the f--- you would have turned me in so I wouldn't have to keep making these appearances!'"

The hard-hitting outfielder had three solid seasons. In 1967, he hit .277 with 16 homers for the Dodgers. After missing most of the 1968 season with injuries, he put up similar numbers for the Padres in 1969 and 1970.

Ken Harrelson wrote, "He was competitive, strong as an ox, and loved to have fun." Ferrara got into his share of scrapes but was also an accomplished pianist. Moreover, he was an astute observer of the changes happening in American culture and realized early on that team owners would soon be losing their iron-grip control of the players.

Over time, Al went into the home improvement business and adopted a healthier lifestyle. He sold his business and retired at the age of 65.

NATE OLIVER

In the Sixties as now, every team carried one or two utility infielders. Nate Oliver performed that important role for the Dodgers, Giants and Cubs for seven seasons. He also played in a single game for the Yankees in 1969.

Coming out of Gibbs High School in St. Petersburg (which earlier produced infielder Ed Charles), Nate is the son of a Negro League baseball star. Exceptionally down to earth, articulate, and personable, Oliver was an asset in the clubhouse as well as on the field, where he could pinch run, go in for improved defense, pinch hit, drop a perfect bunt, and play other roles.

Oliver told the "This Great Game" website that the Dodgers' confidence was misconstrued as arrogance. "Every year there was only one goal and that was to get to the World Series," Oliver said. "Everything else was second best." He also credited teammates Junor Gilliam (his frequent roommate on road trips), Maury Wills, John Roseboro, Jim Lefebvre, and others as "tremendous students of the game of baseball."

He called Wills "the greatest base stealer I ever saw." Oliver continued, "He was so valuable to that Dodgers team…What Wills did was create havoc for the other team. He got more fastballs for me and anyone else who batted behind him. He also drew the infielders in because of his speed. And he kept the defense on edge at all times, which basically means they were distracted and out of position. As a result, ground balls that ordinarily would have been infield outs are now going through as base hits, because they're defending Wills and not defending the hitter."

After an enjoyable 1969 season with the Cubs, Nate played two years of minor-league ball and then held minor-league managerial and coaching positions. Nate, who still enjoys talking baseball, is a resident of Oakland.

ED KIRKPATRICK

In the old *Little Rascals* movie shorts, Spanky was the mischievous wise-guy, popular with the other kids, and at the center of every story. Ed Kirkpatrick looked a lot like Spanky McFarland, and was every bit as likable and mischievous. Somewhere along the line, he picked up the nickname, and it followed him for a lifetime.

He was just 17 when he made his MLB debut for the 1962 Angels and he was with that franchise through 1968. But it wasn't until baseball expanded again in 1969 that he found ample playing time as a member of the Royals through 1973. He later played four years for the Pirates before making brief stops in Milwaukee and Texas.

Ed had considerable power. In a May 15, 1969 game in Cleveland, he hit a shot high off the foul pole against Luis Tiant. That led to an argument between both managers and the umpires over whether the ball was fair or foul. One would have thought those ground rules would have been pretty clear. It was ruled a home run, one of 14 he hit that season. His career-best of 18 followed a year later. He showed his muscle again in 1972 against Baltimore, when he went yard three days in a row against Jim Palmer, Dave Leonhard, and Pat Dobson.

He often rotated between catcher, first base, outfield and pinch-hitter. If the team was short on players, he could also play second and third base. Whenever former players are asked about him, they keep coming back to the thought that he was a great guy to have on the team. "Spanky was a good friend, and a good guy," recalled teammate Joe Keough. "Our families were very close."

Ed's later years were difficult. In 1981, he was involved in an auto accident. Within days, he suffered a blood clot, endured brain surgery, and then sustained a heart attack. Confined to a wheelchair, he was blessed to have a wife who looked after him. Partially paralyzed, he lived until 2000, when he died of throat cancer at age 66. Glendora, California, his hometown, established an annual award in his name to honor excellence in youth sports.

TURK FARRELL

In the 1958 all-star game Dick (Turk) Farrell struck out Ted Williams, Jackie Jensen, Frank Malzone and Moose Skowron in order. That showing was understandably one of the high points in his 14-year career.

Farrell was a reliever for six years with the Phillies and Dodgers, before being tapped by Houston in the expansion draft. Becoming a starter, he lost 20 games in 1962, but also placed seventh in the circuit in ERA, and fourth in strikeouts. In registering 52 wins over several seasons, he was for a time the Houston franchise's leading winner. In 1967, he was dealt back to the Phillies, where he worked out of the pen for three more summers.

A tall right-hander with an appetite for night life, Farrell was charged with assaulting a sportswriter in 1955. Once in 1959, he became angry while at a Milwaukee tavern and punched a mirror, causing it to crack.

Ron Fairly, his teammate on the 1961 Dodgers, had vivid memories of Farrell when he wrote his autobiography, *Fairly at Bat,* calling him "a veteran right-hander with a mean streak." Fairly wrote, "One night in Cincinnati, we lost a close game to the Reds, and Farrell, upset about the defeat, had a few drinks after the game. There are happy drinkers and not-so-happy drinkers. Farrell was in the second group. While walking back to the hotel, he broke the antennas on every parked car he passed." Team President Buzzie Bavasi, who was walking behind him, contacted the car owners, paid for the repairs, and deducted the cost from Farrell's paycheck.

Dave Watkins, who caught Farrell in 1969, recalls, "Turk was a 'teenager' his whole life! He was a natural tease and agitator and at one time, a flame thrower."

In his autobiography, Jim Wynn wrote, "Both Farrell and [pitcher Jim] Owens were old-school guys who thought of muscle training as a waste of time, unless it involved the repetitious bending of elbows at whatever bar was handy. They were loud laughing galoots who had no clear idea or caring for where a good practical joke blurred over into an act of outright meanness."

In time, Farrell mellowed a bit. After two failed attempts to revive his baseball career, he took a job with Brown & Root as a safety supervisor on offshore oil rigs in Great Britain. He was killed in an automobile accident there in 1977 at the age of 43. Farrell's lifetime record was 106-111 with a 3.45 ERA.

CHARLEY SMITH

An October 19, 1960 *Sporting News* article about Charley Smith provides insight into how ballplayers planned the most important aspects of their personal lives around their baseball obligations. A South Carolina native, Smith was a Dodgers farmhand playing for the Reno Silver Sox in 1959 when he met a university student named Carole Lee Richards.

The couple became engaged during the 1960 season, which Smith spent in Spokane, before a late season call-up to the Dodgers. He was in the lineup on Friday, September 30, the club's third-to-last game of the season. Charley and his bride tied the knot on October 9, honeymooned at Lake Tahoe, visited his family briefly in Charleston, and then caught a series of flights to Venezuela, where Smith played winter ball.

Smith made the Dodgers' 1961 roster out of spring training, but before the newlyweds could get settled in Los Angeles, he was traded to the Phillies, requiring yet another move. That made for a hectic start for a young couple, but not atypical for a professional ballplayer.

Smith enjoyed several productive seasons with the Phillies, White Sox, Mets, and Cardinals, combining good glove work with periodic home-run power. Still only 28 years old with the 1966 Cardinals, he was already mentoring and looking after the younger players.

As the 1967 season approached, the Yankees needed a third baseman to replace the traded Clete Boyer. In a stunning move, they traded Roger Maris to acquire Smith. Charley had one memorable game as a Yankee, homering twice against Chicago's Tommy John and Hoyt Wilhelm. But after hitting only .224 with a lot of strikeouts, he lost his starting position and backed up third baseman Bobby Cox in 1968. Following a trade to the Giants and a sale to the Cubs, he could say he was one of the few players to suit up with all four of the modern New York and Chicago teams.

Unlike many baseball marriages, Smith's endured. He and Carole returned home to Sparks, Nevada, and had two children and seven grandkids. He participated in some old-timers games, but often declined interview requests, keeping a low profile. He was an avid fisherman and hunter, played in a senior softball league, and was a member of Sparks Christian Fellowship Church. In 1994, he went into Washoe Medical Center for routine knee surgery and wound up dying from a blood clot after the procedure at age 57. The City of Sparks honored Smith after his death by moving all flags to half-staff.

JIM HICKMAN

Jim Hickman played for a pair of memorable teams – the original 1962 Mets and the 1969 Cubs squad that was overtaken by the Miracle Mets in the final weeks of the season. He was also the first Mets player to hit for the cycle (1963), and the first player in franchise history to homer three times in one game (1965).

Hickman grew up on a farm in Henning, Tennessee. When he played for the Cubs, ballpark organist Jack Kearney usually played *Tennessee Waltz* as he approached the plate. Catcher Randy Hundley recalled him as having a rocket of a throwing arm from right field, though he sometimes played first base.

Jim joined the Cubs as a throw-in in a trade for pitcher Phil Regan after broadcaster Vin Scully praised him in a conversation with Cubs general manager John Holland. Manager Leo Durocher began giving Jim more opportunities to play starting in 1969. Increasingly confident, Hickman developed into a slugger, leading to the refrain, "Hickman did it again!"

Fergie Jenkins recalled, "We loved the man from the minute he set foot in our clubhouse in early 1968. He did not always come through in the clutch in his six seasons as a Cub. But when he did, you never forgot his feats. If you talk about dignity and quiet strength, you look no further than the man from Henning with that trusty station wagon in the players' parking lot."

Jim's best season came in 1970, as he hit .315 with 32 homers. He singled home the winning run for the NL in the all-star game, and tied a record with two outfield assists in a single inning. He placed eighth in the MVP balloting. Coming four years after a broken wrist and two years after a demotion to the minor leagues, his big season was a heartwarming story.

Retiring as a member of the Cardinals, his final numbers included a .252 average and 159 home runs. Hickman continued to live in Tennessee but lost his farm to creditors during the agricultural crisis of the 1980s. Jim was 79 when he passed away in 2016 at the age of 79.

DICK GROAT

Dick Groat's athletic career was shaped by several sports legends. Red Auerbach was his cage coach at Duke. Colby Jack Coombs, who had been a 31-game winner with Connie Mack's A's, was his college baseball coach. Lou Boudreau played a major role in Groat's decision not to play two pro sports simultaneously. Branch Rickey signed him to play for the Pirates. He was coached by Pirates legends Paul Waner and George Sisler. Few other players had contact with so many legends before suiting up for a major-league game.

Groat could have made his living playing hoops. At Duke, he was the National Player of the Year for 1951-1952, averaging 26 points per game, and later was the first Duke cage star to have his number retired. (His college roommate was Donald Nixon, brother of the future U.S. President.) Groat was chosen by the Fort Wayne Pistons, the third selection in that year's draft. He played for the 1952 Pirates and for the Pistons before serving at Fort Belvoir in 1953-1954.

Upon completing military duty, Groat, who had local roots at Swissvale High School, became a fixture in the Pittsburgh lineup, without ever spending time in the minor leagues.

The Pirates were a losing team in the Fifties, but the front office was assembling a group of promising players. In 1958, the team surged from seventh to second place, with Groat hitting .300. Then in 1959, Danny Murtaugh's club took a step back, dropping to fourth place. Several team members had gained weight over the previous winter and gone on to perform below expectations, including second baseman Bill Mazeroski and pitcher Bob Friend. Groat was one of several players forced to take a pay cut.

Before the 1960 campaign, the Pirates -- looking to add power -- discussed trading Groat with at least two teams – the Senators and the A's. The Bucs were targeting Harmon Killebrew from Washington and Roger Maris from Kansas City. Killebrew ultimately stayed put, whereas Maris was swapped to the Yankees. Most Pirates fans, appreciative of Groat's leadership skills, were content that he was retained.

In 1960, the Pirates' nucleus of young stars (Groat, Mazeroski, and Roberto Clemente) gelled, supported by veterans like Smoky Burgess, Don Hoak, Bob Skinner, Bill Virdon and Vern Law. Dick was the team captain and was, according to writer Les Biederman, "a bundle of controlled nervous energy."

Branch Rickey III told writer Don Liable in 2020, "He didn't have any power to speak of, couldn't run, and his arm was ordinary. But he was your all-around attention-to-detail man. He had incredible magnetism on the team. Every girl around town recognized him. He was young, handsome and had magical hands on the field. Groat-to-Mazeroski was exciting."

Groat in late May 1960 told a reporter, "I have never been on a team with the confidence this one has…There is no time, even with two out in the ninth when we're behind, that our players don't feel that the next man up will do something to pull us out." By Independence Day, the Bucs had pushed their lead to 3.5 games over second-place Milwaukee. "Everyone is shooting at us," he commented in August, adding that he expected his team to win the pennant.

On September 6, the Pirates were seven games ahead of the second-place Cardinals, and Groat was closing in on a batting crown. That day, his left wrist was broken by a Lew Burdette pitch. Dick Schofield played shortstop most of the rest of the way, hitting .403 over a 21-game span. Groat demonstrated integrity by putting his batting title on the line, coming back cold for the final two games of the season (in what would today be called "meaningless games"). He delivered two hits against Warren Spahn and then another hit on the final day of the season against Burdette, to protect his title. Why did he play? "The most important thing for me is to be in shape for the World Series," he succinctly explained. "I'd prefer to have my timing down pat for the Yankees than worry about the batting title."

The Bucs won the flag with seven games to spare and Groat won the 1960 MVP Award, in recognition of his team leadership, splendid defense, and yes, a league-leading .325 batting average. They went on to win the World Series, as well.

The Pirates sank to sixth place in 1961, then rebounded to win 93 games in 1962, only to finish fourth. Groat played well both seasons but was traded to the Cardinals, but hit .319 with a league-best 43 doubles in 1963, and his Cards were in contention until the last week of the season, before fading.

In 1964, the Redbirds, led by Manager Johnny Keane, captured the pennant. Groat batted .292 and was tapped for the all-star team for the fifth and final time. St. Louis met up with the Yankees in the World Series, and just like in 1960, Groat's club prevailed in seven games. Dick contributed five hits and four walks.

After a decent 1965 season, Groat was traded to the Phillies and concluded his career with the 1967 Giants, retiring with a .286 career clip, 2,138 hits, and 352 doubles.

Groat spent five winters during his playing career working in sales for Jessop Steel. In 1964, he went into the golf course business with teammate Jerry Lynch. The pair also partnered with pitcher Ron Kline on a 24-unit apartment building investment. Dick did radio broadcasts for 40 years and long supported Pirates Alumni Association charities. Living into his 90s, he died in Pittsburgh in 2023.

BILL MAZEROSKI

Bill Mazeroski was one of those rare ballplayers who enjoyed a lengthy career with a single franchise. He broke in with the Pirates while still a teenager in 1956, was a hero of the 1960 World Series, and was still around in 1971 when Pittsburgh next won the world championship. He retired a year later, at the age of 35.

"Maz was just like a river; he ran quiet," said teammate Bob Veale in John Bird's book, *Twin Killing: The Bill Mazeroski Story*. "If anybody deserves being there (in the Hall of Fame) on his own merits, it is my buddy Maz, a great player, and a fine man. He's the kind of man you'd want your son to be like."

After the first six games, the 1960 Series was knotted at three games each. David Schoenfield of ESPN described the setting, writing, "It was two days after the debut of the Andy Griffith Show. It was one day after Nikita Kruschev infamously did or didn't pound his shoe on his desk during the U.N. General Assembly. Later that night, Richard Nixon and John Kennedy would conduct their third presidential debate. But that afternoon at Forbes Field, two determined teams played the game for the ages."

As Schoenfield wrote, "It was a game that saw the lead change hands four times, most dramatically of course, with the only game seven walk-off home run in World Series history. It was a game between the underdog, blue-collar Pirates, from a blue-collar city still bursting with steel mills and the glorious Yankees…It was a game that, oddly, featured not a single strikeout (the only time that has happened in World Series history). It did feature 19 runs and 24 hits and was played in a brisk two hours and 36 minutes. It was full of managerial decisions to second-guess, clutch hits and unlikely heroes, pitchers throwing through pain, and strange, quirky plays." The game was played before 36,683 fans in Pittsburgh and the final score was Pittsburgh 10, New York 9.

Mazeroski, an eight-time gold glover, was mostly known for his exceptional fielding and prowess in turning double plays. His glove work was all the more remarkable considering the perpetually poor condition of the Forbes Field infield. Yet, he also was a productive hitter. His 100th career homer came against Ferguson Jenkins in 1966, making him just the second NL second baseman to reach that level. He set career bests that year with 16 round-trippers and 82 RBI.

In 2001 the second baseman was tapped for the Hall by the Veterans Committee. His offensive numbers were not spectacular: a .260 average, 2,016 hits, 138 homers, and 23 stolen bases for his career. It was his amazing glove work, grace in turning the double play, and heroic World Series home run that formed the case for his election to the Hall.

Maz was a seven-time all-star who was at his best in 31 post-season at bats, batting .323 with two homers and a .944 OPS. He currently lives in Lansdale, a town northwest of Philadelphia.

GENE ALLEY

Once the Pirates traded former MVP Dick Groat after the 1962 season, the $64,000 question was who would replace him at shortstop. Journeyman Dick Schofield manned the position for the next two seasons but was never seen as the long-term answer. All along, the Pirates' front office was watching a young Virginian moving through their farm system. His name was Gene Alley.

Gene played for the Pirates briefly at the end of the 1963 season, worked on his hitting with coach George Sisler during the off-season, and made the Pirates as the reserve infielder in 1964. He began the 1965 season as the second baseman while Bill Mazeroski was recovering from a broken foot. When Maz returned, Alley claimed the shortstop job and Schofield, after catching bench splinters for a time, was traded.

For the Forbes Field loyalists, Alley and Mazeroski were a joy to watch. They turned routine double plays with flare and even made a spectacular play in which Maz made a diving stop, flipped the ball to Alley, who fired it home to catcher Del Crandall in time to tag out baserunner Dick Allen, who was attempting to score a game-winning run.

Alley worked with manager Harry Walker on his hitting and by 1966, he hit .299, and placed 20 sacrifice bunts. He proved adept at Walker's favorite play, the hit-and-run.

Les Biederman wrote, "He (Alley) can do everything Maury Wills and Leo Cardenas can do, and in addition, he has power…He owns an arm just as good as Cardenas' and can pull the trigger just as quickly. He can go into the hole with any shortstop in the league and also behind second."

Biederman's assessment was seconded by other baseball men. Leo Durocher said, "He can do it all." Hall of Fame third baseman Pie Traynor stated, "He's one of the finest shortstops I ever saw. And with Bill Mazeroski at second base, I'd say this is the best double-play combination of my time."

Mazeroski marveled in 1966, "He's never out of position and his arm is accurate and strong." That year, the pair helped the Bucs turn 215 twin-killings, a new league record, and Alley received the first of two gold glove awards. Meanwhile, back home in Richmond, a fan club was established in his honor.

According to coach Alex Grammas, Alley "hated the St. Louis ballpark. As good a player as he was, he just could not make himself field ground balls in St. Louis…That infield at old Busch Stadium," Grammas told writer Larry Moffi, "had him psyched out."

Alley made the all-star team for the first of two times in 1967, but shoulder trouble hindered him the rest of his career. In later years, he shared the shortstop duties with Fred Patek and then Jackie Hernandez, hitting about .240 most seasons.

Having heard Maz express the joys of winning the 1960 World Series, Alley savored being part of the 1971 world champion Pirates, alongside Mazeroski.

The Pirates won the NL East again in 1972, but lost to the Reds in the playoffs, as Alley went 0-for-16. He played sparingly in 1973 and then retired. Like Mazeroski, he spent his entire career with the Pirates. His lifetime average was .254 with 999 hits and 55 dingers.

After baseball, he worked as a sales rep for a packaging supplier, and enjoyed leisure-time golf. In 2006, he returned to Pittsburgh for the 35th year reunion of the 1971 championship team. He recently has been residing in Glen Allen, Virginia.

VERN LAW

Right-hander Vern Law was yet another career-long Pirate, pitching for the Bucs from 1950 to 1967, save for two years of military duty. His lifetime record was 162-147 with a 3.77 ERA.

He was unusual among players in that he didn't drink, smoke, chew or cuss. As a result, he was tagged with the nickname of Deacon.

When the Pirates raced to the 1960 pennant, Law was instrumental to their success. He went 20-9 and won the Cy Young award. In the Bucs' victorious World Series against the Yankees, Law made three starts, recorded two victories, and took a no-decision in game seven, which the Pirates won on Bill Mazeroski's famous home run.

Law was raised by a Mormon family in Idaho. By his freshman year of high school, he already stood six-foot-three, and he starred in baseball, basketball, and football. One summer, he played American Legion ball and got to meet Babe Ruth, an experience that infused his determination to make the big leagues.

Ruth wasn't the only Babe he met. The Pirates sent scout Babe Herman to offer a contract and also had singer Bing Crosby, the team's part-owner, call Law's mother and promise that the organization would take good care of her son. Law signed with the Bucs in 1948 and got married in 1950. He and his wife had five children, one of whom, Vance Law, became a major league infielder.

It was not until 1957, well after his military commitments were fulfilled, that Law finally had a winning season, going 10-8 for a seventh-place team. In one game that season, Law pitched 18 innings of a 19-inning game and was upset that manager Danny Murtaugh wouldn't let him remain in the game. Teammate Bob Friend pitched the top of the following inning and gave up a run. In the bottom of the 19th inning, the Pirates scored twice to win it. Friend, who yielded a run in in his only inning, got credit for the win, instead of Law!

Vern followed up with solid 14-12 and 18-9 records in 1958 and 1959, setting the stage for his robust 1960 campaign.

The tall righty was the Pirates' best pitcher throughout the 1960 pennant run. During the celebrations on the night that the Pirates clinched the pennant, a teammate was horsing around and caused an injury to Law's ankle. Vern continued to pitch but by favoring his ankle, he injured his arm. The injury carried over into the 1961 season, when he registered only three wins.

Law considered retirement after a dismal 1963 season but thought better of it. By the time the Pirates brought on Harry Walker as their new manager in 1965, Law had recaptured his magic one last time. After an 0-5 start, he became the Pirates' best pitcher, and finished the year at 17-9.

By this time, Law had a career's worth of memories. In Larry Moffi's book *This Side of Cooperstown,* Law remembered a game where Ruben Gomez of the Giants threw at Bill Mazeroski's head. Murtaugh ordered Law to retaliate, and when Gomez stepped up to the plate, Law threw a pitch that sent Gomez plunging to the ground. As the umpire issued warnings, Murtaugh came onto the field, and yelled at Gomez, "You throw at one more of our guys, you're going to get one right there!"

As Law recounts the story, "Well, Gomez grabs his crotch. And Murtaugh saw red. He charged after him, and by this time we've got all the players on the field and we've got a free-for-all going. And out of the corner of my eye, I see…Willie Mays, he's got [Orlando] Cepeda pinned to the ground. Cepeda had gone to the bat rack and got the leaded bat and was out there with the leaded bat. Of course, Mays, being a peacemaker, saw that and pinned him…Had Cepeda used that bat, his career probably would have been cut very short."

Law also had great memories of legendary Pirates shortstop Honus Wagner, who was an honorary coach during the early Fifties. "He was just a very kind individual," Law told Moffi. "About the seventh inning, why, he'd go in the clubhouse and have an Iron City beer, maybe more than one…He'd walk home after a ballgame and he would stop at all the bars. And, of course, everybody knew him. He had a lot of free drinks on the way home."

Branch Rickey III shared memories of Law with writer Don Liable in 2020. "He was forceful but sent a powerful message of how baseball players could be. He was unflawed in character and his impact on the Pirates was powerful. He put a polish on practice," Rickey noted.

Law retired after the 1967 season and went on to serve as pitching coach for the Pirates and assistant baseball coach at Brigham Young University. In recent years, when a writer asked him to name his favorite baseball movies, Law listed "42," "The Natural," and "The Babe," among others. He was recently residing in Provo, Utah.

BOBBY DEL GRECO

Robert Del Greco, Jr., is one of the best-known attorneys in Pittsburgh, a "go-to" lawyer who has defended high-profile sports stars and entertainers. He has nearly everything money can buy. Yet, one of his most cherished possessions is a framed photo of himself as a baby, being held by Mickey Mantle at a backyard barbecue party. It was taken when his dad, Bobby Del Greco, was Mantle's teammate on the Yankees in the late Fifties.

Pie Traynor, the Hall of Fame third baseman, was the scout who signed Del Greco to a Pirates' contract. Bobby was a local boy from the Pittsburgh Hill District who quit high school as a sophomore to earn money for his large family. He and a buddy often snuck into Forbes Field to watch games. The youngster also played American Legion ball, where he captured the attention of Traynor.

After signing for a modest bonus and getting some minor-league experience, the 19-year-old found himself in the Pirates' starting lineup on opening day of the 1952 season. He contributed a triple, two singles and a walk against the Reds, with his mother and eight siblings in the audience. On June 9, he connected for his first home run against hurler Jim Wilson. He finished his rookie campaign with a .217 average and 11 outfield assists.

Over the next three seasons, the Pirates rotated a mix of young prospects and aging veterans, trying with little success to find the right outfield formula. Del Greco spent those three seasons in the minor leagues, missing the quality of life of a big leaguer.

He finally got back to Forbes Field in 1956, playing center field and third base. On May 13, 1956, he blasted a pair of home runs against Harvey Haddix of the Cardinals. Obviously impressed, St. Louis traded for Del Greco just three days later, in a swap that sent Bill Virdon to Pittsburgh.

Bobby was dealt to the Cubs early in the 1957 season, and was demoted to their Triple-A affiliate in Montreal. After performing well there, he was acquired in September by the Yankees to back up Mantle. The Yankees' front office was already worried about Mantle's durability. Del Greco contributed three hits in seven at bats for New York.

The start of the 1958 season meant another trip to the bush leagues, this time to Richmond. A local scribe named Jack Fulp wrote, "In order to see better fielding work in the position, one would have to be in San Francisco watching the great Willie Mays." In other words, Del Greco could play center field. But he didn't return to the majors until 1960, when he got into 100 games for the Phillies, hitting .237 with 10 homers. Demonstrating masterful plate discipline, he walked 54 times in only 300 at bats. For the 27-year-old, it was rewarding personally and financially to be back in the show.

He split the 1961 season between the Phillies and A's. In 1962 with the A's, he hit .254 with nine homers, and topped the circuit in hit-by-pitches with 13. That proved to be his best season. Bobby retired in 1967 after several years back in the minor leagues. His lifetime average was .229 with 42 home runs.

In the end, the book on Del Greco was that he was a tenacious competitor and a spirited teammate who loved baseball. He played excellent outfield defense, possessed an accurate arm, and was a great guy in the clubhouse. He played pro baseball for 20 years, and then remained around the game by coaching at baseball camps and throwing batting practice for the Pirates, all while working as a circulation driver for *The Pittsburgh Press*, which was an afternoon daily paper. He enjoyed interacting with fans until shortly before his death in Pittsburgh at age 86 in 2019.

DICK SIMPSON

Journalist Hy Zimmerman wrote in 1965 that outfielder Dick Simpson was "built like a beanstalk, he has the jolt of a giant, the speed of an eye-blink and a piston-powered arm. That he has not learned to use all those attributes for optimum output can be attributed to inexperience and to moodiness." Bob Lemon, who managed Simpson at Triple-A Seattle, said, "This is a young man with all of the tools of baseball. He could be a great one. If he settles down and uses his abilities, he is a sure thing for the big leagues."

Simpson was gratified to reach the majors and saw MLB action in seven seasons, passing among the Angels, Reds, Cardinals, Astros, Yankees and Pilots. In 288 games, he batted just .207 with 15 home runs. He sometimes seemed to try to pull every pitch and often struck out. But teams kept acquiring him because of his great athleticism. His career highlights included leading off a contest with a home run against Mickey Lolich. It would be the only hit Lolich allowed in the game.

Dick went to Venice High School in California, where he was a star in the high jump and broad jump. According to teammate Fritz Peterson, Simpson was one of three Yankees to wear number 9 between Roger Maris and Graig Nettles (Steve Whitaker and Ron Woods were the others). Dick now lives in Culver City, California.

NORM CASH

When Norm Cash closed the books on his career in 1974, the only left-handed sluggers with more AL home runs were Babe Ruth, Ted Williams, and Lou Gehrig. Cash was second to Al Kaline for most homers in a Tigers uniform with 373.

If fans remember Cash chiefly for his power and his role with the 1968 world champion Tigers, teammates remember him as a free-spirited Texan who lived life to the fullest. "He was fun to be around," recalled Kaline, a former roommate on road trips. "Norm had more fun than anybody," opined Jim Northrup.

Cash's lust for life was combined with a long trail of hangovers. Gates Brown recalled Cash relying on showers and Pepto-Bismol to help him recover. Mickey Lolich remembered, "A lot of times we had night games followed by day games, and when Norm came into the locker room, you weren't sure he was going to make it to his locker. But after he took a shower, jumped in the hot tub, took another cold shower, then back into the hot tub, all of a sudden he would perk up, put his uniform on…and say, 'Let's go boys and get 'em.' And we would say, 'If he can wake up, we can too.'"

One very hot afternoon during pre-game workouts, manager Mayo Smith suspected Cash was hung over, and ordered him to execute a series of drills where Cash would field the grounder and toss it to the pitcher covering the bag. Cash didn't complain and executed the drills flawlessly. When it was over, Cash just glanced at his manager and winked.

Hall of Famer Nolan Ryan, a fellow Texan, loves to tell the tale of closing in on his second no-hitter. Cash came to the plate with a table leg instead of a bat. When the umpire told him he couldn't use the table leg, Cash responded, "Why not, I won't hit him anyway."

The Norm Cash story begins in a small town outside Lubbock, on his dad's farm. Cash developed incredibly strong wrists and forearms through farm work. He was an impressive enough high school football player to be drafted by the Chicago Bears, but he chose baseball instead. After completing his military service, Cash was a rookie on the 1959 White Sox pennant club. He was traded during the off-season to the Indians in the Minnie Minoso deal and soon after, was dealt again, this time in a one-sided trade from Cleveland to Detroit for third baseman Steve Demeter.

Beginning with that first season in Detroit in 1960, Cash would hit 15 or more home runs yearly through 1973. A four-time all-star, Cash was at his best in 1961, when his .361 batting average and 193 hits led the league. He produced 41 home runs and 132 RBI during that memorable season, and even swiped a career-high 11 bags. Cash finished fourth in the MVP balloting as the hard-hitting Tigers came in second place.

There would be no more years like that one, but Cash was consistently one of the cornerstones of the Tigers' impressive lineups. In 1966, he swatted his 200th career homer off Yankees' hurler Mel Stottlemyre. The slugger contributed 25 home runs for the 1968 Tigers, and then hit .385 with another homer and five RBI as the Tigers tamed the Redbirds in the fall classic. Perhaps the biggest surprise came in 1971, just as most baseball men thought Cash was on the downswing. Instead, he cranked up the power, and contended for the home run crown all year long. When the season ended, he narrowly missed the title. Bill Melton of Chicago finished on top with 33 home runs, while Cash and Oakland's Reggie Jackson tied for second with 32.

The Tigers were back in the post-season in 1972, as Cash made the all-star team for the fourth and final time. In 1973, he added 19 home runs on an over-the-hill squad that was showing its age. The Tigers finally released Cash in August 1974 as part of a youth movement.

For all of his consistency, Cash never came close to repeating his peak success from the 1961 season. Late in his career, he shared the reason: corked bats. As Daniel Okrent and Steve Wulf wrote in *Baseball Anecdotes,* "Cash, it turned out, broke the rules of baseball to assemble his impressive statistics. He bore a hole about half an inch wide and eight inches deep into the top of the bat, plug the top two inches of the hole with cork, sawdust and glue, then sand the top so no one would notice. Corking a bat makes it lighter, so that a hitter will get the mass of a 36-ounce bat with the whip of a 34-ouncer, resulting in an extra 20 to 50 feet on some line drives." While more recent studies cast doubt on the benefit of corking, Cash was convinced that the practice, along with watered-down expansion pitching, helped him achieve his banner 1961 results.

After living in Eldorado, Texas (a town with fewer than 2,000 people) and then Fort Worth during the formative years of his career, Cash relocated to Detroit in the early Seventies. According to Bruce Markusen on the DetroitAthletic.com website, "He regularly poked fun at his looks and his alleged lack of intelligence. He and Gates Brown used to travel the off-season banquet circuit together, throwing audiences into hysterics with their comic routines and witty by-play."

Cash lived in Bloomfield Hills after retiring, played pro softball for a couple of years, and was a color commentator for the ABC Monday Night Baseball Game in 1976. A stroke in 1979 slowed his gait and his speech, yet he continued to drink heavily. Norm died in 1986 at the age of 51. Along with his second wife and a friend, he had dinner and drinks at a restaurant, and then returned alone on a rainy October night to his 33-foot cabin cruiser boat. He evidently slipped into the cold, 15-foot water when trying to step onto the boat and drowned. Tests found his blood alcohol level was nearly twice the legal limit.

Remembered warmly as a fun-loving ballplayer who enjoyed a fabulous career, Cash was inducted into the Texas Baseball Hall of Fame in 2001. Two baseball fields in Post, Texas were named for him in 2005.

DON DEMETER

Growing up in Oklahoma in the 1950s, Don Demeter sometimes attended Double-A Oklahoma City games. Among the visiting team player autographs he collected was one of infield prospect Don Hoak. Years later, Demeter and Hoak were roommates with the Phillies, and enjoyed a good laugh when Don showed Hoak the autograph.

Demeter was a center fielder for 10 seasons with five teams. In 1959, he was central to the success of the Dodgers as they prevailed over the White Sox in the World Series. His best season was 1962, when he delivered 29 home runs, 107 RBI and a .307 batting average (while playing third base) for the Phillies. After powering 22 more homers for the Phillies in 1963, he was traded to Detroit, and matched that same power output for the 1964 Tigers.

A man of deep Christian faith, Demeter kept baseball in its proper perspective. His faith was shaped by personal experience. His parents divorced and he ultimately lived with foster parents. His foster father was a Sunday School superintendent, and watching how this family lived inspired him to make a decision for Christ. He relied on that faith as he endured the challenges of a career in baseball. Many in the sport considered him a bit of an oddity as he didn't drink, smoke, cuss or display a hot temper.

Don joined Boston in 1966 and was traded in June 1967 to Cleveland, where he played sporadically the rest of the season. Injuries had reduced his outfield range and he no longer was the same hitter. The Tigers reacquired his contract at the end of August but cancelled the transaction when a physical exam detected an arterial circulation problem. Following a winter of family time and prayer, Demeter retired with a lifetime average of .265 with 912 hits and 163 four-baggers.

After his baseball career, Demeter worked in insurance sales and ran his family-owned swimming pool installation company, Spartan Pools. In 2002, he founded Grace Community Baptist Church in Oklahoma City and served as its pastor for 16 years. His congregation included former Yankee pitcher Tom Sturdivant, as well. Don passed away at age 86 in 2021.

PUMPSIE GREEN

During spring training 1959, critical eyes were focused on the Red Sox, the only franchise that had yet to integrate its roster. Pumpsie Green, a 25-year-old African American infielder, was having a sensational spring. The media covered his exploits on the diamond, and also the discrimination Green faced that spring. While the rest of the Sox players stayed in Scottsdale, Green had to stay alone at an integrated hotel in Phoenix.

When the Sox headed north to start the season, Green was assigned to Triple-A Minneapolis. Scrutiny turned to outcry, with writers speculating that manager Pinky Higgins, who had a history of racist remarks, blocked Green on account of his skin color. A group in Boston called for an investigation of the club's hiring practices, noting that even the grounds crew was all-white.

Higgins, who had a drinking problem that seemed to be impairing his job performance, was fired on July 2nd. Less than three weeks later, Green was recalled and joined the parent club on a road trip. Ted Williams, the team's established star, set the example by throwing with Green before every game. Green got his first hit against Jim Perry, demonstrated an ability to drop bunts, and proved reliable in the field. In his first home game, he turned a tough double play, received a standing ovation before his first at bat, whereupon he slugged a triple. After that fast start, he spent the next four years with the Red Sox.

Green was more interested in playing ball than being a civil rights crusader. Born in Oklahoma during the Great Depression, Green moved with his family to California when his father took a job at the military base in Oakland. Pumpsie attended El Cerrito High School along with pitcher Ernie Broglio, two years his junior. Green played catcher and first base, and closely followed the Oakland Oaks minor-league team in his leisure time. He later played college baseball and basketball at Contra Costa College, while his brother Cornell Green went on to enjoy a 12-year football career in the NFL.

By the time Pumpsie joined the Red Sox, he was the franchise's first full-time switch-hitter in 27 years, according to Topps. He batted .233 as a rookie, and gradually improved at the plate over the next couple of seasons.

Two weeks before Christmas 1962, the Sox traded Green to the Mets in the swap that brought Felix Mantilla to Boston. Green reported to the Mets overweight, and soon began experiencing hip pain. He played briefly for the Mets and closed out his career with some time in Triple-A Buffalo. His lifetime batting average was .246 with 13 home runs.

He later coached baseball for the Berkeley Unified School District for 25 years. For leisure, he enjoyed swimming and working out, as well as spending time with family and friends. Green was 85 years old when he passed away in San Leandro in 2019.

BERT CAMPANERIS

The A's team that won three straight world championships from 1972 to 1974 was built player by player, and often prospect by prospect, starting in the mid-Sixties. Shortstop Bert Campaneris was one of the first pieces to fall into place.

When Campy arrived, he knew little English. As teammate Tommie Reynolds recalled in 2024, "When on rehab in 1963, he came to Burlington, Iowa, and all he could order was hamburgers. I could speak Spanish, so I would order food for him!"

It didn't take long to see that the Cuban was a special talent. In his first major-league game in 1964 after being called up from Double-A Birmingham, he delivered two home runs, a single, and a walk against Jim Kaat, and stole a base for good measure. He did so just hours after taking three red-eye flights from Birmingham to Atlanta to Chicago to Minneapolis, where he suited up four hours after landing.

That 1964 A's team lost 105 games. Except for Rocky Colavito's strong season and the Beatles' concert at Kansas City Stadium in September, highlights were few and far between. But Campy's explosive debut opened some eyes.

Entering the 1965 season, manager Mel McGaha envisioned him as a super-utility player. With that in mind, coach Whitey Herzog worked with the youngster in training camp on learning the outfield trade. Campy quickly proved too valuable not to assume a single position.

In a publicity gesture endorsed by owner Charles O. Finley, the A's played Bert in all nine positions on September 8, 1965, and a larger-than-normal crowd of 21,576 saw him make history. Less remembered is that the stunt led to an injury. He was playing catcher – his ninth position – when the Angels attempted a double steal and Campy took a throw from Dick Green, with Ed Kirkpatrick of the Angels barreling down the third base line. Following the inevitable collision, Bert was taken to a hospital for x-rays of his sore shoulder, which proved negative.

Until he built a network of friends, life in the U.S. could be a lonely experience. In the minor leagues, he developed a reputation for throwing helmets and bats. At one point after joining the A's, the unmarried player was hit with a paternity suit. After the news broke, when he approached the plate in a game in Anaheim, the organist played the song, "Yes Sir, That's My Baby."

Writer Joe McGuff explained in *The Sporting News,* "Baseball is Campaneris' whole life and he is playing the game with such spirit and devotion that he is emerging as the most exciting young player in the history of the Kansas City franchise." Further praise came from A's first-base coach Gabby Hartnett, who said, "He's got guts. He's willing to take a chance. You don't often see that in young players." After Alvin Dark became the A's manager in 1966, he said Campy "has a great arm, very good hands, and he is quick. He makes the plays."

He made his first all-star team in 1968, the fourth straight year he led the AL in steals. By then, the A's had relocated to Oakland and were moving up the standings. His 62 steals in both 1968 and 1969 were career highs, although Tommy Harper captured the steals title in 1969.

Bert's best season was probably 1970, when he hit .279 with career highs in home runs (22) and runs scored (97). His finest post-season occurred in 1973. In the ALCS against Baltimore, he hit .333 and stole three bags. In the A's World Series win over the Mets that fall, he delivered nine hits, a home run and three more steals.

The low point was the 1972 playoff game against the Tigers in which he hurled his bat at pitcher Lerrin LaGrow after a brush-back pitch. Witnesses said the bat "spun like a helicopter blade." Mike Hegan of the A's said there was no question in his mind that Tigers manager Billy Martin had ordered LaGrow to throw at Campaneris. The plate umpire restrained and shielded Campy in the brief fracas that followed and both players were ejected. Ike Brown of the Tigers snared the bat and smashed it into pieces. Campy was suspended for the rest of the playoff series and the first seven games of the next season.

After 13 years with the A's, Bert closed out his career with the Rangers, Angels and Yankees. With three championship rings, impressive stolen base achievements, as well as 2,249 career hits, he ranks as one of the top 25 shortstops to ever play the game. He has been involved in coaching and baseball camps after retiring and now lives in Scottsdale.

BUD DALEY

Left-hander Bud Daley represented the A's in the 1959 and 1960 all-star games. One of those classics was held in Kansas City, and Daley relishes the memory of the standing ovation he received from his home crowd. He was a 16-game winner both seasons.

Daley was a product of Woodrow Wilson High School in Long Beach, a school that as of 2023 had sent 20 players to the majors, including Bob Lemon, Bob Bailey, Bobby Grich, Jeff Burroughs, and Aaron Hicks.

A breaking ball specialist, Bud received similar bonus offers from several teams and selected the Indians because of the connection to Lemon, at the time a pitching ace for Cleveland. Daley saw some action with Cleveland, but by his own admission, didn't pitch very well. He was traded to the Orioles, who in turn peddled him to the A's.

After his two fine seasons with Kansas City, 1961 brought disturbing tidings. Insurance magnate Charles O. Finley succeeded the late Arnold Johnson as team owner and hired Frank Lane as general manager. Lane was the frenetic trader who had shipped Daley out of Cleveland. Bud was so certain Lane would trade him again that he and his wife pre-emptively sold their Kansas City house to get a jump-start on an inevitable move.

Sure enough, he was dealt to the Yankees in June. He finished the 1961 season with a dismal 12-17 record but registered a win out of the bullpen in game five of the World Series against the Reds, which was another career highlight.

Daley pitched for the Yankees through 1964 and retired after failing to make the Indians' roster in 1965. His lifetime mark was 60-64 with a 4.03 ERA.

In a 2016 video interview, Daley recalled he was happy when hitters bunted, so they couldn't hit a home run. He credited Johnny Sain as his best pitching coach for emphasizing the psychology of pitching.

Unlike teammates with a taste for the wild life, Daley was a family man who went straight back to the house after home games. On road trips with the A's, he often joined his roommate, pitcher Ray Herbert, spending evenings eating ice cream or watching television in the hotel lobby (some hotels still didn't have TVs in every room). After baseball, Daley and his family moved to Wyoming where he has enjoyed golf, watching pro football, and time with family.

Chuck Dobson

In the five years preceding Oakland's 1972 world championship, Chuck Dobson averaged nearly 14 wins per season. Though never the team's number-one starter, he threw the fastball, slider and curve for strikes. Dobson was a Kansas City native and a hometown hero for the A's before they headed west to Oakland in 1968.

Dobson is also remembered for representing the U.S. in the baseball demonstration at the 1964 Olympics in Tokyo; for hurling a no-hitter for Lewiston in the Northwest League; for being one of the first white players with a black roommate (Reggie Jackson) on road trips; and for being the first player to publicly admit using amphetamines to get amped up for games.

Although Chuck had a fine 15-5 record in 1971, trouble was on the horizon. He missed the final month with an aching elbow and as he confided to Gregory H. Wolf in a profile on the SABR web site, a drinking problem was taking a toll on his body and psyche.

In 1972, as the A's captured the first of three straight world titles, Dobson spent most of the season on the disabled list, save for a few appearances at Double-A Birmingham, where he chummed around with teammate Denny McLain and manager Phil Cavarretta. In 1973, pitching at Triple-A Tucson, his ERA ballooned to 5.23. He was recalled to Oakland in September, made one start, and couldn't make it through the third inning. To be sidelined as his team was winning world championships took a terrible mental toll.

Though the hand-writing was on the wall, Chuck persevered three more years, first in Mexico, then in the Angels' organization, bouncing between the majors and minors, before calling it quits. He had a lifetime record of 74-69 with a 3.78 ERA.

The story eventually gets happier. After losing his first marriage and his janitorial business due to his drinking, Dobson became sober from alcohol in 1985 and worked as an addiction counselor and a house painter for many years. He also enjoyed playing bridge at the Overland Park Bridge Studio, gardening, and world travel.

Among his close friends was high school teammate Tom Tischinski, at whose wedding Dobson served as best man (Tom later caught for the Twins for three years). Dobson was a notoriously heavy sleeper. His A's road roommate for a time, outfielder Jim Gosger, often found it almost impossible to wake up Dobson, especially on the mornings after he pitched. Dobson was 77 when he passed away in Kansas City in late 2021.

BLUE MOON ODOM

In 1964, MLB began developing plans to replace amateur free agency with a first-year player draft. Knowing it could be his last chance to buy up an array of top prospects, A's owner Charles O. Finley awarded $75,000 bonuses to pitchers Blue Moon Odom and Catfish Hunter; and a $100,000-plus bonus to Skip Lockwood, a position player who would soon become a pitcher. Finley also tried to land blue-chip outfield prospects Rick Reichardt and Willie Crawford, who signed elsewhere. In Odom's case, Finley went so far as to help cook a chicken dinner for the young pitcher and his mom, Florence Odom.

Eighteen of the 20 teams scouted Odom and the Giants were the next highest bidder at $40,000. So, selecting the A's was an easy choice. Overnight, Odom went from being a high school pitcher without so much as a checkbook to a wealthy young man who still had to master the art of pitching. He was simultaneously striving to transition into a mature young man while grappling with rampant discrimination such as police stopping him while driving his new sports car. It was a challenging set of circumstances.

After a few minor-league appearances, the A's rushed him to the big leagues late in the 1964 season for publicity, and he turned in one late-season gem, shutting out the Orioles, who were in the thick of the pennant chase. Odom was confident, even a bit cocky, but in need of seasoning.

It was a few more years before he was ready to compete consistently. In 1966, the 21-year-old posted a 5-5 record, and stunned the Yankees with a one-hitter. His control wavered in 1967, leading manager Al Dark to demote him to Vancouver.

It all clicked in 1968 when Odom won 16 games. In one contest against the Orioles, he was within one out of a no-hitter when Dave Johnson delivered a hit. "I'll settle for a one-hitter," he said after the game. "For a no-hitter, someone's got to be looking on you from above." He made the all-star team, as well.

Heading into 1969 spring training, players association president Marvin Miller asked players not to sign contracts until a pension-funding issue was settled. For the A's, only 12 of the 25 pitchers and catchers reported to spring training on time. Among them were Odom, who explained via a note to reporters that: 1) Baseball is his bread and butter; 2) Baseball has been good to him; 3) Mr. Finley has been good to him; 4) He signed in November before Miller said not to; 5) He is reporting as required in his contract; and 6) He needs as much training time as possible to get ready for the season. Also reporting against the wishes of the union boss were pitchers Rollie Fingers, Tony Pierce, Gil Blanco, Bob Meyer, Bob Stickels, Jack Baldschun, Ed Sprague, Paul Lindblad, and Bob Duliba.

Odom followed up with 15 more wins in 1969, despite issuing more than his fair share of walks. Part of the fun during the 1969 season was a war of words between Odom and Cleveland players Hawk Harrelson and Sam McDowell, after Odom boasted of his ability to shut out the Indians. McDowell said, "I resent Odom making cracks about my teammates. You tell Blue Moon I want a piece of his action when we get to Oakland." Odom again was an all-star in 1969.

John's record in 1970 and 1971 hovered around .500, as he endured elbow trouble. He was shot during a street altercation in 1972 but recovered to enjoy his last fine season with a 15-6 record. After a couple more scuffling seasons with the A's, he closed out his career with stops with the Indians, Braves and White Sox, plus two years in Mexico. His lifetime record was 84-85 with a 3.70 ERA.

Later, after some personal turbulence that included an arrest for selling cocaine, another for threatening his second wife with a gun, debt, depression, and a drinking problem, he served time and came out of it clean and sober. In recent years, he has been living in Anaheim.

FELIPE ALOU

The oldest of the three original Alou brothers, Felipe arrived first (1958), played the longest (17 years) and hit the most homers (206). His .286 lifetime batting average trailed that of brother Matty, who was a .307 hitter. Felipe was just the second Dominican Republic native to make the majors, after Ozzie Virgil. By the year 2023, more than 440 Dominican products had played big league ball.

Giants owner Horace Stoneham brilliantly positioned his franchise to develop Latino talent. Relying on a former Negro League shortstop turned scout named Horacio Martinez, the Giants signed the three Alou brothers as well as Dominicans Manny Mota and Juan Marichal. They also landed Orlando Cepeda and Jose Pagan from Puerto Rico.

The Dominican Republic had been run by Rafael Trujillo, a ruthless dictator, from 1930 until his assassination in 1961. "During Trujillo's time," Felipe explained in 1962, "about the only way a young man without other visible means of support could get a passport to the United States was to sign a contract with some big-league organization in America. I was glad to sign for $200."

Baseball diamonds were rare in the Dominican, so the Alou brothers played ball in rural pastures that they shared with grazing cows. Their father, who worked in a cement plant, made baseball bats for his sons on a lathe in his barn. Felipe excelled as a high school sprinter and javelin thrower.

Maury Wills wrote, "The guy could hit, run, throw, and field…Felipe Alou was a total player. He was fast enough to play center and he had a good enough arm to play right." Some clubs also stationed him at first base, as needed. Dutch Reuther, a Giants scout who had been a teammate of Babe Ruth, observed, "He can run and throw with anybody."

Felipe slugged a gargantuan April 1962 home run that broke the glass "Longine's Watch" sign at Cincinnati's Crosley Field. Reds officials said the sign was 382 feet from home plate and 50 feet high, meaning that the blast would have carried at least 450 feet if not impeded.

Alou enjoyed his first all-star season that same year, when he batted .316 with 25 home runs. The Giants won the pennant but lost the World Series in seven games to the Yankees. Felipe hit .269 in the Series.

After the Giants drifted to third place in 1963, general manager Chub Feeney eased the team's logjam of outfielders by trading Felipe to Atlanta for two pitchers and a catcher. He spent four years with the Braves, including his career-best 1966 season when he led the league in hits, runs scored, and total bases, and finished second to his brother Matty in the batting derby. Felipe repeated as the NL leader in hits again in 1968, his third and final all-star season.

In the Seventies, Felipe saw action with the A's, Yankees, Expos and Brewers. He later managed the Expos from 1992 to 2001 and the Giants from 2003 to 2006, when he retired for good at age 71.

Matty Alou – at five-foot nine, 160 pounds – lacked the muscular build of his brothers. Although playing alongside his brothers in San Francisco made for good times on and off the field, he grew frustrated with the windy conditions at Candlestick Park and his growing reputation as a "Punch-and-Judy" hitter.

A trade to Pittsburgh sparked Matty's success, as manager Harry Walker helped him develop into an elite spray hitter. He began using a heavier bat, choked up, and shifted more weight to his front foot. Instead of pulling pitches, the left-handed hitter delivered grounders and line drives to left and center fields, then used his ample speed to his advantage. It was an unorthodox approach that Ted Williams said "violates every hitting principle I ever taught," but Alou won the 1966 batting crown, becoming a national hero back home. In fact, Matty hit .330 or higher four straight seasons (1966-1969), the only NL regular to do so in the decade.

Writer Les Biederman penned, "Matty handles the bat as deftly as a painter handles the brush or an orchestra conductor wields a baton. He may be the best bunter in the league." In 1969, he set a new MLB record (since broken) for most at bats with 698 and led the league in hits, singles, and doubles. Alou also received visibility at the 1969 all-star game in Washington, D.C. Originally slated for a Tuesday night, the game was rained out and played the following afternoon. Matty batted leadoff, delivered two hits, and scored a run, as the NL won the game, 9-3. Matty later played for several other teams and retired with a .307 lifetime average. He passed away in 2011.

Jesus Alou, the youngest brother, had the lowest profile of the three although his career lasted a long time. He compiled a lifetime .280 batting average, despite a terrible habit of swinging at bad pitches. By failing to capitalize on bases on balls, his on-base percentage was never high enough to bat lead-off and he lacked the power to hit in the middle of the order. He did enjoy some decent seasons in the 1970s with Houston and retired with a .280 lifetime average. He later worked as a scout in the Dominican Republic and passed away in 2023 at the age of 80.

Felipe's son, Moises was an all-star outfielder. Other family members to play big-league ball included cousin Jose Sosa and nephew Mel Rojas.

PHIL NIEKRO

Five of the top nine pitchers in innings worked were active in the 1960s. And only three pitchers – old-timers Cy Young, Pud Galvin, and Walter Johnson – hurled more innings than Phil Niekro.

Phil's remarkable career spanned from 1964 to 1987. The knuckleball was not his only pitch, but it was the one that made him a standout pitcher. Because of the minimal strain it put on the arm, it helped him have a very long career. He led the league four times each in home runs and hits surrendered, but he also led his loop in complete games four seasons and was tapped for five all-star teams. His lifetime record was 318-274 with a 3.35 ERA and 45 shutouts.

Niekro first put the NL on notice during the 1967 season, when he topped the loop in both ERA and wild pitches. That was the same year that his younger brother, Joe, broke in with the Cubs. Joe went on to win 221 games. Together, they rank as the top-winning brother combination of all time.

After a decent season in 1968, Niekro was back on top in 1969, winning 23 games and helping his Braves win the NL West. Only Tom Seaver received more Cy Young votes.

Niekro threw his specialty pitch by digging his finger nails into the seams. His dad taught him the pitch, but Phil was initially reluctant to throw it in the minor leagues. Finally, a minor league skipper ordered him to rely on the pitch. Knucklers are famous for being hard to control, but Niekro did it as well as just about anyone. Bobby Murcer said that "trying to hit him is like trying to eat Jell-O with chopsticks."

Phil spent most of his career with the Braves, but also twirled for the Yankees, Indians and Blue Jays, retiring at age 48. A member of the Hall of Fame, Phil was 81 when he passed away in 2020.

SONNY JACKSON

Sonny Jackson was so fast that Topps called him a "mercury-footed youngster" on his 1967 baseball card. The previous season, Jackson swiped 49 bases, a new NL rookie record. He hit .292 for the Astros that season, and led the league in sacrifice bunts, as well. He finished second to Tommy Helms of the Reds in the rookie of the year balloting.

Jackson fought through injuries in 1967 and was swapped to the Braves after the season. Paul Richards, who was running the Braves, called Jackson "a Marty Marion type shortstop." Marion was the exceptional fielding shortstop for the Cardinals teams that captured four pennants in the 1940s. Jackson did not possess an especially strong throwing arm, but neither did Marion, Richards asserted.

Sonny hit below .240 for two seasons, then reached .259 in 1970. He was second on the Braves in stolen bases in 1970 with 11, trailing Felix Millan. That season, Richards called his club's infield, with Orlando Cepeda at first, Millan at second, Clete Boyer at third, and Jackson sharing time with Gil Garrido at shortstop, as the best unit in the league defensively. But after winning the NL East in 1969, the Braves were a sub-.500 club in 1970.

In 1971, Braves manager Lum Harris installed young Marty Perez as the every-day shortstop, and moved Jackson to center field, a position he also enjoyed playing. Harris was fired mid-season, replaced by Ed Mathews as manager.

The Braves' outfield corps became crowded in 1972, as young Dusty Baker emerged as a high-impact center fielder. Even with Hank Aaron moving part-time to first base, the Braves still had Baker, Ralph Garr, Mike Lum, and Rico Carty available for outfield duty. Hence, Jackson was relegated to a utility role the next two seasons.

Sonny hit several inside-the-park homers where he outran the fielders. He was a lifetime .251 hitter. After his playing days, Jackson remained in the game as a longtime coach in the Braves and Giants organizations. A product of Montgomery Blair High School in Silver Spring, Maryland, Jackson recently was living in Palm Beach Gardens, Florida.

GENE OLIVER

For fans who appreciated tape-measure home runs, Gene Oliver was a player to follow. Though he had to battle for playing time, and shuttled between three defensive positions, he was a ready threat to go deep – way deep.

"He was a good-old Quad Cities boy who brought a lot of energy to the game," said former catcher Bob Oldis in an article in the *Quad-City Times*. "He was very competitive, a guy who brought a real tough approach and plenty of pop in that bat. He was a hitter you had to worry about."

Oliver made his debut with the Cardinals in 1959. His best season may have been 1965, when he hit .270 with 21 home runs for Milwaukee. He was one of six sluggers on that Braves team to eclipse the 20-homer mark.

After more than four years with the Braves, he also played for the Phillies, Red Sox, and concluded his career with the 1969 Cubs. As the Cubs were in the early stages of blowing a hefty 13-game lead to the Miracle Mets, Oliver was so confident in his team that he quipped that he'd jump off a Chicago skyscraper if the Cubs didn't prevail. He reconsidered the pledge. Oliver enjoyed the unbelievable bond that the team's fans had with the players at Wrigley Field and remained a Cubs fan for the rest of his life.

In more than 50 at bats against Sandy Koufax, Oliver batted .409. But hitting for average wasn't Oliver's strength. Rather, it was the ability to go deep at a moment's notice. Between 1959 and 1969, Oliver hit 93 home runs with a .246 average and a .742 OPS. Four of the home runs came against Koufax.

After 1969, he remained in baseball for another decade in coaching positions, and then returned home to Rock Island, Illinois, working in various capacities, including social director for Randy Hundley's fantasy camps and writing baseball columns for a newspaper. When he passed away due to lung problems in 2007, he left behind his wife of 51 years and a bevy of friends.

DEL CRANDALL

The son of a citrus plant worker, Del Crandall graduated from Fullerton Union High School in California, which also produced Hall of Famers Walter Johnson and Arky Vaughan. The prodigy catcher was a productive major leaguer by the age of 19. He became an expert handler of pitchers and led NL backstops in fielding percentage four times. Baserunners never learned not to run on him; he led his league in assists six times.

The longtime Brave gradually improved as a hitter, and belted homers in both the 1957 and 1958 World Series. Entering the 1957 season, he vowed to use the entire field instead of pulling pitches, but after his power suffered, by 1958 he was back in his comfort zone as a pull hitter.

Before the 1960 season, Del's back was so painful that he spent two weeks at the Mayo Clinic undergoing tests, which showed nothing seriously wrong. (By contrast, such testing today would almost certainly be done on an outpatient basis.) The back healed and he enjoyed a fine season, hitting especially well after manager Charlie Dressen, on a hunch, moved him to the second position in the batting order, unusual for a catcher. He finished with a career-high 77 RBI and captured the third of four gold gloves.

Crandall missed most of the 1961 season to an inflamed triceps injury but bounced back in 1962 to bat a career-finest .297 while earning another gold glove. Crandall had served as team captain of the Braves. However, when Birdie Tebbetts became the club's manager, he proclaimed, "In my 30 years in baseball I've never been on a team which had a captain and I see no value in one."

By 1963, Crandall's body was breaking down from too many innings crouched behind the plate. Joe Torre had taken over the Braves' starting catcher role, and Bob Uecker was in reserve, making Crandall expendable. Del was sent to the Giants and spent 1964 backing up Tom Haller. He reprised the same role for the Pirates in 1965 and the Indians in 1966, and retired with a .254 lifetime average, 154 home runs and 1,276 hits.

Crandall loved baseball and vowed to stick around. He managed the Brewers from 1972 to 1975 and the Mariners from 1983 to 1984. None of those clubs was exceptionally talented, and all had losing records. He later served as a baseball color commentator and minor-league manager. In 1997, he stepped away from the game to enjoy retirement life with his wife in Brea, California. Until he passed away in 2021 from complications of Parkinson's Disease at age 91, he was the last living player from the Boston Braves.

Joe Pepitone

Since the Yankees captured five straight pennants from 1960 to 1964, no other club in either league has matched that remarkable achievement. To remain on top, general manager George Weiss, followed by successor Ralph Houk, continually tweaked the roster, and when the Yanks surged to a 104-57 mark in 1963, a quartet of young players – Jim Bouton, Al Downing, Tom Tresh and Joe Pepitone – was just as instrumental as the team's famous stars.

The 1963 Yankees seemingly faced formidable challenges. First baseman Moose Skowron had been traded, Mickey Mantle missed nearly 100 games to injury, and Roger Maris was also banged up. The young Pepitone stepped into the void and led the Yankees in RBI and games played. He made the all-star team for the first of three times. That October, though he hit only .154 in the World Series, he set a Series defensive record for first basemen with seven double plays.

In 1964, continuing to hit out of a deep crouch, the charismatic young Yankee solidified his standing in the Bronx by reaching the 100-RBI plateau and hammering a grand-slam during the World Series. His offense slipped a bit in 1965 but his snappy defense won him a gold glove.

In 1966, he rebounded to slug a career-best 31 home runs and took another gold glove, despite injuring the knuckle of his left index finger by punching the dugout wall in a fit of anger late in the season.

Remarkably, he was still only 25 years old, and he was becoming known as one of the flashier players in the game. He wore mod clothes, combed his thinning hair in a bouffant hairstyle, and traveled with a hair dryer to perfect just the desired look. Eventually, he began wearing a toupee to compensate for his thinning hide. During games, he exchanged banter with fans. During off hours, he was equally engaged, enjoying an active social life. He was a gate attraction as well as a potent force in the middle of a batting order.

The 1967 season brought a pair of changes. One was a shift of position, to allow the aging Mantle to play first base, and Pepitone became a capable outfielder. The other change was a drop-off in plate production, which carried into 1968, when he also missed time with injuries. Joe was in good physical condition, but manager Ralph Houk began sitting him out against southpaws in search of more offense.

Jim Ogle wrote in early 1969 in *The Sporting News,* "It is tragic that Joe has not grabbed his great opportunity to become one of the top players in the game. The personable Pepi has lots of talent, great confidence in his ability, and enjoys doing well, yet he just can't settle down to the serious business of playing ball."

With Mantle retired in 1969, Pepitone moved back to first base, captured one final gold glove, and led the Yankees with 27 home runs. But he also suffered from depression during the season and batted only .242.

That winter, the Yankees traded their hometown hero to Houston for Curt Blefary. In truth, some viewed it as a swap of talented players who were wearing themselves down with self-destructive behavior. But Pepitone had some good years left. He split the 1970 season between Houston and the Cubs, belting 26 home runs. Then in 1971, he hit .307 with 16 homers for the Cubs – the only time he breached the .300 mark. On June 13 of that year, he went deep off Gary Nolan of the Reds for his 200th career homer.

Joe split one final summer in 1973 between the Bruins and the Braves and retired with a .258 batting clip and 1,315 hits including 219 home runs.

Pepitone endured more than his share of adversity. At age 17, he was shot by a classmate, the same week that his father died. All three of his marriages ended in divorce. In 1988, he served a jail sentence following an arrest related to cocaine and quaaludes possession, and he was also arrested twice in the 1990s. Pepitone's autobiography, published in 1975, was titled, *Joe, You Coulda Made Us Proud.* He passed away in 2023.

TOM TRESH

This Detroit area native played a big role in the Yankees' fortunes for seven years starting in 1962, when he won the rookie of the year award. He had a superb batting eye, above average power and the versatility to play shortstop or the outfield. Tresh was a two-time all-star who also won one gold glove award.

Tom had royal baseball blood lines; his father, Mike Tresh, was a catcher with the White Sox from 1938 to 1948. Born in 1938, Tom Tresh spent summers as a youngster with his dad in Chicago, hung out at the ballpark, and played with the sons of other ballplayers. So, when it was time for Tom to play in the big leagues, he had an innate understanding of what to expect. Whereas other young players might have been intimidated joining a team with Mickey Mantle, Roger Maris, Yogi Berra, Whitey Ford and other stars, Tresh had a distinct advantage.

That rookie season in 1962 was one to remember. Tresh hit .286 and drove home 93 runs, both of which would be career bests. His Yankees won the pennant with 96 victories. In the World

Series, Tresh delivered a timely home run against Jack Sanford and made some solid defensive plays to help New York best the Giants in seven games.

Tresh's batting averages later declined but he continued to hit with power. After the 1966 season, his father passed away, but Tom took solace that his dad had seen him succeed in the major leagues and in a World Series. Another difficult turning point came in spring training of 1967 when he tore cartilage in his right knee. The Yankees told him to play through the pain, but Tresh was no longer able to make sharp turns on the base paths or approach fly balls head-on. Instead, he had to take an indirect path to avoid blowing out the knee again. His power also diminished from 27 homers in 1966 to 14 blasts in 1967.

Tresh finally was allowed to have knee surgery after the season, but things were never the same. Moving from the outfield back to shortstop in 1968, he batted just .195 with 11 home runs. And in spring training of 1969, he battled phlebitis and strep throat. Mantle had retired, a new generation of Yankees players were moving into key roles, and things just weren't the same.

In June 1969, the Yankees obliged his request for a trade to his hometown Tigers. With Detroit, a slightly rejuvenated Tresh hit 13 home runs over the second half of the season while batting .224. After the season, he underwent the knife for more surgery on the same knee. When spring 1970 rolled around and the Tigers asked him to report to the minor leagues, he walked away for good at age 32.

During his playing days, Tresh had returned each winter to Central Michigan University to pursue his B.A. in physical education. He joked that it took him only four terms to complete the degree – Eisenhower, Kennedy, Johnson and Nixon. But the degree expanded his employment options and his prior affiliation with the Yankees meant a steady flow of invitations to fantasy camps, baseball card shows, and reunions. Tresh enjoyed his retirement and harbored only minimal bitterness toward the Yankees for insisting that he delay the knee surgery. Tresh passed away at age 70 in 2008 in Venice, Florida.

ELSTON HOWARD

There are 19 catchers enshrined in the Hall of Fame. Elston Howard was arguably the "best of the rest," an all-star yearly from 1957 to 1965. The backstop was the AL MVP in 1963 and placed third in the polling in 1964. He was a three-time .300 hitter and won two gold gloves for his work behind the dish. When he retired, he had the best fielding percentage of all time.

Howard compiled a number of firsts for an African American: First to play for the Yankees; first to win an AL MVP award; and first to coach in the AL. He is also credited with developing the donut, which players slide onto their bats when warming up.

A native of St. Louis, Elston began his career in 1948 with the Kansas City Monarchs. In 1950 he played with the Muskegon Reds in the Central League. (In its day, Muskegon was a powerhouse of an industrial and metalcasting center that supported minor league baseball from 1890 to 1951. In recent years, the Muskegon Clippers have revived that tradition.) Howard hit well in Muskegon, then lost two years to military service.

He made the Yankees' roster in 1955. With Yogi Berra as the starting catcher, Ellie saw action in the outfield, at first base, and as a pinch-hitter, in addition to backing up Berra. He batted .290 as a rookie.

As Berra's knees began giving him trouble, eventually it was Howard behind the plate and Berra playing left field. Meanwhile, after becoming comfortable with the Yankees, Ellie and his wife Arlene moved their year-around home to Teaneck, New Jersey.

Howard was also comfortable playing on the game's largest stage. In the decisive seventh game of the 1956 World Series, he delivered a home run and a double, as the Yanks prevailed over Brooklyn. In the 1957 World Series, he slugged a home run against Milwaukee to send a game into extra frames. In the 1958 fall classic again against Milwaukee, he drove in the winning run in game seven, while in the outfield making what Mickey Mantle called "the greatest catch I've ever seen." During the 1960 World Series, Howard provided a pinch-homer in one contest and spanked out two hits in the same inning in another game.

Standing six-foot-two, Howard began his career at less than 190 pounds. Towards the end, he was around 210 pounds, carrying extra weight that didn't help his endurance. His last brilliant season was 1964, when he hit .313 with 84 RBI. He wound down his career with the Yankees and Red Sox, achieving less success at the plate.

Ernie Banks remembered, "Elston could handle everything that came his way. He and I just wanted to play in the major leagues and we had to carry ourselves in the right manner. We had to be impeccable on and off the field." On a personal level, Howard's hobbies included shooting pool, playing pinball, listening to modern jazz, and watching home movies. His story is told in the book *Elston and Me: The Story of the First Black Yankee* by widow Arlene Howard and Ralph Wimbish. He had a lifetime clip of .274 with 1,490 hits including 168 home runs.

STAN BAHNSEN

Four years removed from their last pennant, the 1968 Yankees were desperate for good news and it came in the form of rookie hurler Stan Bahnsen, a hard thrower from Council Bluffs, Iowa. The "Bahnsen Burner" answered the call, posting a 17-11 record. His 161 strikeouts topped the team and his 2.05 ERA was sixth-best in the AL.

Stan had teased his potential on September 22, 1966, when he went the distance in beating the White Sox, 4-1. That contest has the dubious history of the lowest attendance of any contest at Yankees Stadium. With neither team in a pennant race, just 413 patrons attended the game. Broadcaster Red Barber called out the poor attendance and was fired by Yankees team president Michael Burke four days later. Meanwhile, despite his fine outing, Stan spent the entire 1967 campaign in Triple-A ball.

The 1968 Yankees improved their record by 10 wins over the previous year and Bahnsen was recognized with the rookie of the year award --the fifth Yankee to win the trophy in the award's 20-year history. "I'm not the type of pitcher who tries to spot the ball," Bahnsen noted, "I like to rear back and throw it."

The bachelor Bahnsen spent the winter in New York, appearing at banquets, luncheons and youth gatherings. He later acknowledged, "There are too many distractions for a single man living alone in New York for the winter. I guess I made the scene all over town after my rookie year…You might say I didn't get too much rest that winter."

A strep throat just before the 1969 spring training portended a season of bad tidings. Stan struggled to adjust to the lower pitcher's mound, yielded more walks and gopher balls, and saw his record plunge to 9-16. "I don't believe in the sophomore jinx, I've just been lousy," he explained.

The Yankees turned down trade offers, confident the young hurler would rebound, and he settled in as an effective third starter behind Mel Stottlemyre and Fritz Peterson through 1971. As Peterson recalled of Bahnsen, "He was a flame thrower with a very odd delivery. He threw a heavy ball, which is a ball that seemed heavier when you catch it because it has good movement on it."

Bahnsen notched a 55-51 record as a Yankee. He got married, settled down his lifestyle, and went into business with Dave Debuscherre of the Knicks, Spider Lockhart of the Giants, sportscaster Marv Albert and other notables in a sales-promotions business called International Sports Enterprises.

In a steal of a deal, the White Sox acquired Bahnsen, still only 27 years old, for third baseman Rich McKinney before the 1972 campaign. Bahnsen was a good fit in Chicago. He loved being closer to his family and friends in Iowa; and didn't miss the intense New York media scrutiny.

Bahnsen won 21 games in 1972 but pitching for the Sox was not without its challenges. Staff ace Wilbur Wood, the knuckle-ball specialist, preferred starting once every three games. Manager Chuck Tanner acceded to Wood's schedule, which pressured Stan to pitch on shorter rest. His record declined to 18-21 in 1973, and 12-15 in 1974.

Bahnsen pitched through 1982, doing stints with the A's, Expos, Phillies, and Angels. For his career, he was 146-149 with a 3.60 ERA, and 16 shutouts. He later worked as a player-manager in European baseball, a broadcaster, and a cruise promoter with MSC Cruises. He resides in Pompano Beach, Florida.

FRANK FUNK

Pitching for the 1961 Indians, this right-hander had 11 wins, 11 losses, 11 saves and 11 blown saves, a highly unusual stat set. The product of Bethesda-Chevy Chase High School in Maryland had a memorable year in 1960: A no-hitter for Triple-A Toronto over the Havana Sugar Kings; a late-season call-up with Cleveland; and winter ball in Venezuela.

He became the team's most active reliever in 1961, using a fastball, slider and occasionally a curve that he learned from coach Mel Harder. Funk traveled with a Dyna-Wave muscle stimulator to combat elbow pain. "It's an electrical impulse machine that stimulates the motor nerves," he told a writer. "It makes the arm work the way exercise would and promotes the flow of blood and lymph."

After posting a 2-1 record in 47 outings for Cleveland in 1962, he was traded to the Braves, for whom he had another excellent year in 1963. Thereafter, he pitched minor-league ball through 1969. Frank had a lifetime mark of 20-17 with 3.01 ERA. He later was a coach for the Giants, Mariners, Royals and Rockies. Frank lives in Redmond, Oregon.

LUIS TIANT

One of the most popular pitchers of the Sixties, no matter what city he was visiting, was right-hander Luis Tiant. *Baseball Digest* magazine called him "The Man of Many Motions" and catcher Duke Sims considered him "a little magician." Tiant had a good fastball, but what made him unique was how he supplemented the heat with a variety of other pitches, motions and arm angles that made him as entertaining to watch as he was difficult to hit.

A native of Cuba, he pitched three years in Mexico City before suiting up with the Indians' Triple-A club in Portland in 1964. Halfway through the season, Tiant had racked up 15 wins against only one loss, with the hurler wondering after each start why Gabe Paul still had him toiling away in Triple-A ball. Once Cleveland finally called him up, Tiant went 10-4, meaning he had won 25 games for the season.

Now making big-league money, Luis sent most of it home to his wife, and also sent some to his parents in Cuba, hoping it would not be intercepted by Fidel Castro's agents. He also bought a used car, though the radiator malfunctioned as soon as he got to the ballpark.

For the next three years, he was better than average, collecting a lot of strikeouts, but never quite busting into greatness.

That changed in 1968, when he won 21 games, paced the AL in ERA and shutouts, and fanned 264 hitters. On July 3, 1968, Tiant struck out 19 Twins in 10 innings for a 1-0 win. In the process, he set not only the record for most K's in a 10-inning game, but also the most strikeouts over two consecutive starts with 32.

Luis was popular in the clubhouse. He was a practical joker with a loud and infectious laugh, a bulging waist line and an ever-present cigar stinking up the shower room. Teammate Bob Heffner recalled that Tiant had a nickname for every teammate. "The Indians were a fun team to play for," said Eddie Fisher. "Anytime you had Looie Tiant around, it was going to be fun."

Catcher Ken Suarez remembered a game with two outs when Tiant threw a hesitation pitch and Frank Howard hit a screaming line shot toward the hurler's head. "Looie catches it out of self-defense on his follow through and just continues to run. He throws his glove in the dugout and jumps into the dugout which was really deep. By the time I got there, Looie was lying on the floor, with his hand in his shirt, imitating his heart beating, and everyone was laughing. And then he starts yelling to Howard, "I tell you something, Hondo, you big son-of-a-bitch. Next time I pitch you inside, you no hit me, you big son-of-a-bitch!""

Gus Gil recalled an incident in 1967 where manager Joe Adcock was holding an ostensibly serious team meeting. Tiant engaged in some comical conduct out of the manager's line of sight, and several players were biting the blood out of their lips trying not to laugh.

On the field, Tiant always wore long underwear beneath his uniform, regardless of the temperature, to prevent charley horses. On hot summer days and nights, he would perspire profusely. But he never saw snow until one day in December 1968 when he flew to Cleveland to sign his new contract and be honored as the team's Man of the Year. The Indians surprised him by not only raising his salary to $52,000 but also presenting him with a fur-lined overcoat.

In 1969, Tiant struggled to adjust to the lower pitcher's mound and the new strike zone as his record dropped to 9-20. The Indians traded him to the Twins after the season, but injuries limited his availability the next two seasons. He resurfaced with Boston in 1972 and again paced the league in ERA and remained one of the league's better pitchers for most of the Seventies.

While Tiant displayed a genuinely confident and fun-loving persona, his heart was long troubled by the Castro regime's repression and its effect on his family. He had not seen his parents since 1961 and wanted desperately for them to meet his two children. A reunion finally came in 1975, when Castro gave his parents special dispensation to watch their son pitch in the World Series. His father, a former pitching standout himself in Mexico, died just a few months later.

Luis, who continues to reside in New England, closed out his fine career with a 229-172 record, a 3.30 ERA, 2,416 strikeouts and 49 shutouts. Stan Williams, who was a teammate with the Indians and the Twins, spoke for many when he said Tiant personified a true Hall of Famer.

Stan Williams

Stan (Big Daddy) Williams exemplified what a ballplayer will do to preserve his career, even in the face of daunting, painful injuries. His 1967 comeback was one of the inspirational stories of Sixties baseball.

First, some background: Growing up in Colorado, Williams had three brothers, none of whom was interested in sports. He lived across the street from a baseball field, which gave him lots of opportunities to play the game, often against older boys. He attended East Denver High School, which to that point had produced only one big leaguer, a Pirates shortstop from the late Twenties named Cobe Jones.

Williams signed with Brooklyn and by his second minor-league season, in 1955 at Newport News, he dominated his Piedmont League competition, to the tune of 18 wins and a league-record 301 strikeouts. Then in 1957, he won 19 games for St. Paul in the American Association, while still only 20 years young.

The right-hander made his big-league debut in 1958 with a 9-7 record, as Walt Alston used him mostly as a starter. In 1959, he pitched more out of the bullpen and had a 5-5 season. But in the best-of-three playoff season against the Braves – needed because the clubs finished in a tie – Williams emerged as one of the heroes. He hurled three scoreless innings in game two and was the winning pitcher when the Dodgers scored in the 12th inning. He also hurled two scoreless innings in the World Series as Los Angeles toppled the ChiSox.

The hard thrower moved into the Dodgers rotation in 1960, and turned in records of 14-10, 15-12 and 14-12 over the next three years. Williams made his only all-star team in 1960. His 205 strikeouts in 1961 ranked second in the league.

His six-foot-five frame, delivering blistering fastballs that often moved batters off home plate, could be intimidating, to say the least. "I came out of high school not even knowing what a knockdown pitch was," he said in a 2006 interview, "but the Dodgers taught me that well. It was just intimidation. You always threw in front of the hitter and not behind him, because if you threw behind him, you could hurt him. The whole game was played that way in those days."

His Dodgers tenure ended on a sour note in another best-of-three playoff, this time against the Giants in 1962. He let a save opportunity slip away in game two and then walked in the winning run during game three. Following the season, the Dodgers traded him to the Yankees for aging slugger Moose Skowron.

Williams had a 9-8 record for the Yankees in 1963 and acquitted himself well with three fine innings of work in the World Series. But this time it was the Dodgers who laughed last, sweeping the Yankees four games straight.

In 1964, it was clear something was wrong as Williams managed just a 1-5 record in 21 games. The Yankees sold him to the Indians during the 1965 spring training, but arm trouble cost him most of the 1965 and 1966 seasons.

"1967 was the last year I planned on giving it one more go, to see if I could get it back," he said, noting that had his arm not healed, he probably would have gone into business. "I got tired of hurting," he related. "I'm rushing my fastball at 68 and crying. I got so frustrated that I started taking a 10-pound weight and spinning my arm like the propeller of a helicopter, and reaching around and around at different angles. I did that a long time. I figured there wasn't anything I could hurt in there. Along about May or June," he said, "I picked up my shoulder and something popped, and my shoulder hurt like hell, but my arm was okay again."

Evidently, adhesions had formed and he needed to break them loose. "I also spent my time running on my own with a full rubber uniform on and just ran until I never got tired anymore. And whereas I thought I had been in shape all those years, I didn't realize I wasn't until I got into the shape I was at that point, which was remarkable."

Scouts visiting minor league parks regularly checked in with Williams to get his impressions about other pitchers, but his reputation as a chronically sore-armed hurler had become so entrenched that they rarely asked Williams about his own health. Once his arm was again sound mid-way through the 1967 season, it wasn't long before the Indians promoted him from Portland.

In his first start back, Williams not only beat the Orioles, but struck out Luis Aparicio five times and Frank Robinson four times. The next day the newspaper headlines, instead of focusing on his comeback, read, "Robinson Accuses Williams of Throwing Spitball."

Williams posted a 6-4 record after his 1967 call-up. He followed up in 1968 with one of his best seasons with a 13-11 record, 2.51 ERA and nine saves, drawing commendations from manager Alvin Dark. In 1969, Dark called on Williams 61 times to pitch 178 innings and the veteran recorded 12 saves, though his record was only 6-13.

During his stay with the Indians, Williams resided at the downtown Pick Carter Hotel. Whereas some players preferred to stay closer to the airport, Williams enjoyed the perks of city life. He later conceded that the nightly walk from the Stadium to the hotel was not particularly safe in those days.

"Stan was a jokester," related Sam McDowell at a SABR meeting in 2022. "He would play some games on someone, then others would get into it, and that molded us together as a team."

There was one more brilliant season to come for Williams. After the Indians traded him to the Twins, he teamed up with his former Dodgers teammate Ron Perranoski to provide Minnesota with the league's premier one-two bullpen combo in 1970. While the left-handed Perranoski was busy recording 34 saves, Williams turned in a 10-1 record, 15 saves and a 1.99 ERA. The Twins won their division but lost in the ALCS to Baltimore, although Williams pitched well in two outings.

Stan later pitched for the Cardinals and Red Sox, retiring with a 109-94 record and a 3.48 ERA. Most remarkable, he worked 11 innings of post-season baseball without yielding a run.

He later was a pitching coach for five teams (Red Sox, Yankees, Mariners, White Sox and Reds) and an advance scout for the Devil Rays and Nationals. As pitching coach for the 1990 Reds who were managed by his buddy Lou Piniella, he won his second World Series ring. A longtime resident of California, he died in Nevada in 2021 at the age of 84.

JOE AZCUE

In 1963, Cleveland's newly acquired catcher Joe Azcue delivered so many big hits that *Plain Dealer* writer Bob Dolgan coined a nickname that caught on – the Immortal Azcue. As the story goes, Joe was not expected to see action the day he joined the Indians following a trade with the A's. He was taking a nap in the bullpen when starting catcher John Romano got hurt. Azcue came in, began spraying game-winning hits and finished the year with a .284 average and 14 home runs in just 96 games. Incredibly, he even stole home on one occasion.

Beloved by the Cleveland fans, the Cuban native was equally popular in the clubhouse, where he often had a joke to share or a story to spin. "I loved the guy, great personality, funny," recalled teammate George Culver. Despite his jovial spirit, he was also a dedicated family man whose thoughts were with his wife and daughters, especially if one of them was ill back home in Overland Park, Kansas.

When the Indians acquired Azcue, they knew of his reputation for having a sensitive stomach. The syndrome flared up occasionally during his six-plus years with the team. There was a night in 1963 that teammate Early Wynn took Azcue out for a crab dinner – a dish the catcher vowed never to order again. Teammates recalled another occasion when eating too many grapes caused acute digestive troubles.

Azcue's leadership skills and bilingual abilities, coupled with a strong arm, made him a valuable catcher. He helped young pitchers Vicente Romo and Horacio Pina acclimate to life in the big leagues. In 1968, he hit .280 and was tapped for the AL all-star team.

Joe was one of the few players to hit into an unassisted triple play when his line drive against Washington on July 30, 1968 put Senators shortstop Ron Hansen into the record books. After Azcue's next at bat, when he hit into a double play, he sheepishly told manager Alvin Dark to get him out of the game before he did any more damage.

Early in the 1969 season, he was traded to Boston, where he became disillusioned over a lack of playing time and bolted the team, threatening to retire. The Sox quickly swapped him to California. He finished his career with the Angels and Brewers in 1972, then became a player-coach in the Indians farm system in 1973. Thereafter, he worked for an auto dealership for more than 30 years.

Joe was a lifetime .252 hitter with 50 career home runs. When the Indians named their 100 greatest players of all time in 2001, Azcue was in Cleveland as one of the honorees.

LEON WAGNER

"Get your rags at Daddy Wags," proclaimed the sign in the men's clothing store that Leon Wagner and a business partner owned in Los Angeles in the early Sixties. Wagner had started his MLB career with the Giants in 1958, but became a star with the Angels in 1961. Productive at the plate, he placed fourth in the MVP balloting in 1962, after producing 37 home runs and driving in 107 runs.

Wagner was traded to the Indians on December 2, 1963. It turned out to be a banner day for business at his store. He joked that he should get traded more often, because "all the cats" came to the store to see what had happened. Down deep, though, Wagner felt hurt and betrayed that the Angels would trade him at the peak of his career and popularity.

He provided Cleveland with a productive bat, averaging 27 shots per year into the seats through 1966. Wags was also notorious for running inexplicable routes to fly balls, leading to unnecessary extra-base hits. He occasionally would collide with teammates by ignoring their calls for fly balls. He usually only used one hand to catch fly balls, he explained, because the second hand would only get in the way.

He became frustrated in 1967 when the Indians used him on a platoon basis. "I can't figure out why I'm being platooned," he told writers. "Everybody knows we need power in the lineup. But they don't make bats long enough to swing from the bench," he quipped.

During a homestand in May, 1968, several members of the Indians received mysterious chain letters, threatening that they and their teammates would be subjected to a voodoo hex if they did not send out 20 copies of the letter within 96 hours. Most of the players simply threw their letter away Wagner told sportswriters that he was not superstitious, but just to be safe, he burned all four corners of the letter with a match before throwing it in the trash.

Leon enjoyed a strong second half of the 1968 season with the White Sox and last played in MLB with the Giants in 1969. He played two more seasons of minor-league ball. He hung up the cleats with a lifetime batting average of .272 with 211 home runs.

Sadly, Wagner's post-baseball days were troubled. He lost his marriage and his businesses, suffered from drug addiction, and became homeless. He passed away at age 69 in 2004, a sad ending to the life of a player who had brought joy to many fans.

BOB CHANCE

When asked at a Wahoo Club luncheon in Cleveland in 1964 about the size of the bonus he received when he signed with the Giants, Bob Chance drew laughs when he responded, "nuthin."

The six-foot-four, 220-pound Chance not only had a great sense of humor, but during 1964, the rookie first baseman-outfielder hit .279 and drove home 79 RBI in just 120 games for Cleveland. Manager Birdie Tebbets credited Chance's success at the plate to his hard work with coaches Solly Hemus and George Strickland. Chance roomed that season with Leon Wagner, a darn good hitter himself, and that couldn't have hurt.

Another key to Chance's strong season was getting his weight under control. He asked for advice that spring from Tebbetts, who referred him to the Tucson Clinic, which prescribed diet pills.

Chance's power was something to behold. The May 30, 1964 *The Sporting News* reported that fans were mesmerized when, during batting practice before a game in Cleveland, Chance slugged two balls over the right field roof and another deep into the right-center field seats. By the time he returned to the dugout, the number of fans there seeking his autograph swelled.

"That guy's strong. Not only strong, he's aggressive. He wants to kill the pitcher," Wagner told write Phil Pepe.

Chance met his future wife, Carrie Hall, while playing for an Indians' farm team. A wedding was planned for a Saturday afternoon in 1964, with Wagner slated to be the best man. As the wedding approached, the fanfare started to build, to Bob and Carrie's dismay. Their solution was to surprise everyone by getting hitched one day early.

Chance was traded after the 1964 season to the Senators. He spent the next three years in and out of manager Gil Hodges' lineup, with some stints in Triple-A ball. He never recaptured the magic of his 1964 season but the power was always there. Playing for Triple-A Hawaii in 1966, Chance crushed a home run out of the right side of Honolulu Stadium, the first hitter to do so.

He finished his career with the Angels in 1969 and a couple of years in Japan. He later worked for the Charleston recreation department and the West Virginia liquor control department. Bob passed away in 2013 at age 73.

GARY BELL

Gary Bell, a workhorse who pitched in 519 games over 12 years, was a clubhouse comic, always ready to share a laugh or a beer. When young men spend more than 200 days and evenings a year together in cramped locker rooms, hotels, and airplanes, and play a highly competitive sport under an intense public spotlight, it is important to have easy going, good-humor men like Bell around to keep everyone loose.

Bell joked more than once that pitchers like him helped to make Mickey Mantle and Harmon Killebrew into Hall of Famers. Over the years, Bell surrendered eight homers to Mantle, six each to Killebrew and Norm Cash, five to Roger Maris, and four to Yogi Berra. Bell also had a nickname for each of his teammates. It was the same name for each player – Meat.

Even a good-humor man like Bell had his limits. Having roomed on the road all season one year with pitcher Jack Kralick, the pair got on each other's nerves one night at the Shoreham Hotel in the nation's capital. They had a two-punch disturbance, with Kralick losing a tooth and requiring nine stitches. The pair buried the hatchet and Kralick made his next start.

Signed by Texas-based scout Bobby Goff, Bell joined the Indians in 1958 as a 22-year- old and won 12 games. That performance got him a third-place finish in the rookie of the year competition and a pay raise to $9,000 for 1959. Bell's highest win total of 16 came in 1959 as the Indians battled the White Sox until the final weeks of the season before settling for second place. Bell contributed any way he could, saving five games and executing eight sacrifice bunts.

The right-hander was selected for AL all-star squads in 1960 and 1966. In 1965, he stormed out of the bullpen to record a career-best 16 saves. He developed an average slider and curve but relied on an excellent fastball as his out pitch.

In a 2001 interview with writer Bob Dolgan, he recalled how hard it was to get pay raises during his years with the Indians. "We had to get jobs in the off-season. I was a part-time photographer for years, making $125 a week. It was a good job," he recalled.

With the Indians drifting out of contention before the trade deadline in June 1967, they dealt Bell to Boston for promising first baseman Tony Horton and veteran outfielder Don Demeter. "Getting out of Cleveland was like getting out of prison," he told reporters. He suggested that most of the Indians players under manager Joe Adcock were not giving their best effort, a comment he soon walked back and re-worded.

Gary had enough fuel left in the tank to win 12 games for Boston the rest of the way, a huge boost to the Beaneaters' pennant run. Manager Dick Williams deployed him three times during the World Series loss to the Cardinals.

Bell made the AL all-star team for a third and final time in 1968 and had an 11-11 record with a decent 3.12 ERA. Amazingly, he allowed only seven home runs in 199 innings that year, despite pitching at Fenway Park.

Sensing his best days were behind him, the Red Sox exposed the 32-year-old in the expansion draft. He split a frustrating 1969 season between the Pilots and White Sox and was released after the season. As he explained later, he simply lost his effectiveness over the course of one winter. He closed out his career with some time in Triple-A ball with Hawaii.

Bell's lifetime record was 121-117 with a 3.68 ERA. He was in the sporting goods business in Texas after his pitching career and attended numerous baseball reunions. Decades later, his former teammates still remember him as much for his good humor as for his considerable achievements on the field. Bell now resides in Wikenburg, Arizona.

PETE CHARTON

Baseball's old bonus rules required many a young player to spend entire seasons on big-league rosters, before they could be sent to the minor leagues for much-needed development. Pitcher Pete Charton, who spent the 1964 season with Boston, was one such player.

He reflected in 2022 that being a "first-year player" was "boring and frustrating. Pitching nearly all season was unpredictable as to schedule, and I never really got into pitching shape until nearly the end of the season."

Despite the lack of action – he got into only 25 games – Charton enjoyed visiting the other nine AL cities. He took advantage of the opportunity to visit historic and cultural sites in each of them, and particularly liked seeing the Smithsonian and the monuments in the nation's capital. Charton is also grateful to veteran teammate Bill Monbouquette, who he recalled as "an older pitcher who took an interest in me, teaching me how to pitch to opposing hitters. A really great guy!"

Charton, who attended both the University of Tennessee and Baylor, was a right-handed pitcher who batted lefty. His father taught him to bat left-handed because it is 1.5 steps closer to first base, and because fewer hitters bat left-handed, it "provides more openings to play."

Two coaches were instrumental in helping Charton develop his craft. Mace Brown, who had starred with the Pirates in the 1930s, was a Red Sox instructor who helped Pete improve his curve ball. Harry Dorish, another former MLB hurler employed by Boston, helped Charton improve his change-up.

After a shoulder injury ended his pitching career in 1967, Pete studied geology, meteorology and botany at Michigan State. While doing some field work for his degree, he was asked on short notice to deliver the Wednesday night sermon at a Baptist church. He agreed – and in the process met his future wife that same evening!

Charton recalls, "Coming out of a deeply faithful Christian family and a Baptist university, I was not prepared for the priorities off the field in pro baseball. My faith kept me grounded through it all, and when I had career-ending surgery, God's assurance of his leadership saw me through the transition to graduate school at Michigan State, an MA and a PhD, and to a career as a college professor. Having this faith and assurance, I never looked back at baseball and I absolutely loved life working with college students."

After teaching briefly at the University of Illinois, he then was on the faculty at Roane State Community College in Tennessee for more than 30 years. Charton now resides in Irmo, South Carolina.

Tom Cheney

Pitcher Tom Cheney, according to infielder Dick Schofield, was a small-town kid from rural Georgia who was unprepared for life in the big city. He had a nervous personality, lighting one cigarette after another. But Schofield remembered Cheney's curve ball as a very special pitch. It was on display on September 12, 1962, when Cheney, pitching for the Senators, struck out 21 Orioles in a 16-inning complete game. His control that day was better than usual. "He showed me the greatest stuff I've seen from any pitcher," remarked Brooks Robinson. Cheney threw 228 pitches, including screwballs and knuckleballs. The contest illustrates how much the game has changed, as today's starting pitchers rarely throw even 128 pitches. The late-season game attracted just 4,098 spectators at Memorial Stadium.

Cheney began his career with the Cardinals and was with the Pirates in 1960, pitching twice in that fall's World Series. His best year was 1963, when his 8-9 record for the Senators was coupled with a 2.71 ERA but he was shut down that August due to elbow pain. His 1964 season was a bust and he sat out the 1965 season on the advice of Mayo Clinic doctors, who speculated his torn ligaments might heal. His comeback attempt in 1966 was unsuccessful. Cheney finished with a 19-29 record and a 3.77 ERA. It's said that he rarely made public appearances thereafter. He died at Floyd Medical Center in Rome, Georgia from Alzheimer's Disease in 2001.

DICK RADATZ

Nicknamed "the Monster," Dick Radatz stood six-foot-six and fired 94 mile-per-hour fastballs. With Boston, he notched 20 or more saves four seasons in a row. In 1964, he fanned 184 hitters, still the most punchouts by a reliever.

Opponents took notice. Al Kaline said in 1990, "For a couple of years, he was the best reliever I've ever seen." Monte Moore, calling the A's games on radio, often dwelled on how hard Radatz threw.

Dick tinkered with his arm slot in 1965 and struggled with control. He had 22 saves, but his ERA zoomed up to 3.91. His former roommate, Butch Heffner, believes the Red Sox simply burned him out through overuse. The Sox unloaded him in 1966. He had short stints with the Indians, Cubs, Tigers and Expos, but never got back on track, retiring in 1969.

In a 2014 interview on the Passed Ball show on MTR Media, Heffner recalled Radatz as a generous and fun teammate who often ordered room service meals, especially large quantities of cheeseburgers. But Dick was all business on the mound, Heffner said.

Radatz later worked at Eastern Container, played in old-timers games and enjoyed golf tournaments. In his later life, he gained weight and suffered from health problems. He tragically passed away in 2005 at age 67 from injuries sustained when he fell down the stairs in his home. He had a 52-43 record, 3.13 ERA and 120 saves.

GEORGE SCOTT

George Scott grew up in poverty in the segregated community of Greenville, Mississippi, after his father died working in the cotton fields when George was just a year old. While George loved to play baseball and was inspired by Willie Mays, he also was motivated to excel at the game in order to reach the big leagues and earn enough money that his mother would never have to work again, according to Ron Anderson, who wrote the biography, *Long Taters*. He had a home built for his mother just two years into his MLB career.

Scott was a gifted athlete who contributed at the plate and defensively. His power prompted teammate Joe Foy to nickname him "Boomer" and Scott himself called the circuit shots "taters." The first baseman received eight gold gloves, while also making three all-star teams. He was also strikeout-prone, outspoken and quick to anger, qualities that also marked his 14-year MLB career.

Former big-leaguer Milt Bolling signed Scott to his first contract for the Red Sox in 1962. By 1966, George was the AL rookie of the year.

A notorious bad-ball swinger, Scott struck out at an alarming rate early in his career, and was periodically benched by managers Billy Herman and Dick Williams, but his overall production those first two seasons was nonetheless impressive.

After the 1967 World Series, which the Red Sox lost in seven games, Williams commented, "I would have hated to put him (Scott) on the scales during the World Series, because I know his weight was way up again. But George knows when he lets his weight go up, he will pay for it."

Then the 1968 "year of the pitcher" affected Scott more than most. After hitting better than .300 with the 1967 Sox, he batted just .171 in 124 games the following year. Never getting into a groove, he was one of a number of players who clashed with Williams in 1968. Although Williams had publicly proclaimed Scott was a better defensive first baseman than even Gil Hodges, Scott told sportswriters, "I would rather pick cotton than play for him again."

After the season, Scott played winter ball in Santurce, Puerto Rico, where his manager was Frank Robinson. Robby helped Scott both mentally and at the plate, preparing Scott for a fresh start in 1969. In Boston, with hot sacker Joy Foy drafted by the Royals, Williams moved Scott over to third base at the start of the 1969 season. Scott's hitting recovered and the third-place Red Sox parted ways with Williams before the end of the season.

After two more summers at Fenway, the Sox traded Scott to Milwaukee. His best season was 1975 with the Brewers, when he paced the circuit in home runs, total bases, and RBI. The slugger rejoined Boston in 1977 and slugged 33 home runs. He played through 1979, splitting his last season between Boston, Kansas City and the Yankees. Scott left MLB with a .268 average, 271 home runs and 1,992 total hits, but continued to play ball in Mexico for a number of years.

As time passed, he transitioned into low-level coaching roles in independent leagues and in Mexico, but was resentful that the Red Sox organization never brought him back into the organization. In 2006, he was inducted into the Red Sox Hall of Fame, but expressed disgust that nobody came to his banquet table to congratulate him.

In his later years, his weight increased to more than 400 pounds as he suffered from diabetes. Scott passed away in Greenville in 2013. According to Anderson, "George was a man of great character. He felt misunderstood. He didn't think the game had given him a chance that he deserved." At the time of his passing, only Keith Hernandez and Don Mattingly had won more gold gloves at first base.

PHIL REGAN

Ever since MLB outlawed the spitball in 1920, grandfathering in only 17 pitchers, there have been rumors of hurlers throwing the wet stuff. Variously called a "mud ball," "emery ball," or "shine ball," these doctored pitches move in ways that "clean pitches" seldom do. They were banned after Indians shortstop Ray Chapman was killed by a thrown pitch during the 1920 season.

Phil Regan had a 13-year run as a starting pitcher with the Tigers and a reliver with the Dodgers, Cubs and White Sox. His best season was in 1966, when he anchored the Los Angeles bullpen with a 14-1 record, 1.62 ERA and league-best 21 saves. He was also effective in two World Series games against the Orioles. The righty threw a hard slider for much of his career, supplemented by a sinker and a curve.

He was also known to throw the wet stuff. In one game, White Sox manager Al Lopez became convinced Regan had a foreign substance in the bill of his cap. Lopez had the umpire ask Regan to remove his cap, but the official found nothing. A decade later, when asked about the incident, Regan quipped, "It wasn't in the bill of my cap."

At the time, however, Regan did not relish the accusation about cheating. In 1968, he was quoted in *The Sporting News* as saying, "I've got four children and the oldest one, a girl, she's 11, and old enough to know what's going on. She reads about it in the paper and she sees it on TV…Last night, I came home and could see that it really affected her. She asked her mother if daddy was cheating." The pitcher also devoted a great deal of time to meeting with youth groups, church organizations and civic clubs, and was concerned about damaging his public image.

Phil enjoyed success against Roger Maris, who managed only two hits in 26 at bats. Regan pitched him low and away; the slugger never did get a good read on Regan, who was nicknamed the Vulture.

He then went into coaching and as recently as 2019, at age 82, was serving as pitching coach for the Mets. Regan even spent one year as a big-league skipper with the Orioles in 1995.

Asked in 2022 what he hoped people will remember about his career, he noted that he pitched professionally for 17 years without ever going onto the disabled list. Regan, who made his home in Grand Rapids during his playing career, now lives in Port Saint Lucie, Florida.

RICH NYE

The Midwest Bird & Exotic Animal Hospital in Elmwood Park, Illinois, is the first and most prominent exotic species veterinary clinic of its type. Its co-founder is Rich Nye, a former MLB pitcher. Nye, a southpaw, played ball at UC Berkeley and is remembered for his fast start with the Cubs. At age 21, he jumped from A-ball to the Cubs during the 1966 season, fashioning a 2.12 ERA in three outings.

"It was awesome," he recalled in 2022. "The players were all friendly to me and very supportive. Leo (Durocher) didn't say much except in the newspapers. The veteran pitchers were 'calming' mentors with many good tips."

Nye responded in 1967 with a 13-10 record, as the Cubs finished 13 games over .500, their first winning season in four years. Playing home games during the afternoons left the evenings free. "Many evenings were spent dancing on Rush Street," he reminisced. "If there was daylight, like on a day off or after games, I played golf."

Nye roomed on the road with pitcher Joe Niekro, who became a good friend. "We were very supportive of each other, and he was always a positive force in my life," he said. Rich originally signed a contract to use Wilson gloves, getting a set of golf clubs as part of the deal, but later switched to Rawlings, preferring that company's leather.

Nye was asked what it was like having more education than many baseball people. "I believe most of the coaches harbored a little resentment for the college 'whizzes' who spent little time in the minors. Especially Leo, one of the old guard who seemed to always fall back to the way things were when he played."

Rich turned in a 7-12 record in 1968 and then in the following year, he was called upon so rarely that he never really got on track. He turned in a decent 1970 season with the Cardinals and Expos, despite persistent arm pain. In early 1972, after confirming with the commissioner's office that he had just enough service time to qualify for a baseball pension, he said goodbye to his first career.

Like most teams, the Cubs in the Sixties had a roving minor-league pitching coach. Nye recalled that former Cardinals pitcher Fred Martin, who held that role for the Cubs, "gave me the positive reinforcement to throw any of my pitches at any count. He liked my control and said to 'just throw strikes. You have a great team behind you who can make all the plays.'"

Having continued his studies while pitching, Rich graduated from UC Berkley, earned a master's degree in engineering, and then pursued a degree in veterinary medicine. After baseball, Nye initially spent mornings working with his brother-in-law at the Chicago Mercantile Exchange as a commodities broker, while building a veterinary practice in the afternoons. Finding that working with animals was his true passion, he founded the exotic animal hospital, which treats everything from birds and dogs to turtles and snakes. His co-founder was a lady who later became his wife. Nowadays, Nye is affiliated with a different clinic and resides in Batavia, Illinois.

BILL HANDS

Ferguson Jenkins told writer Paul Sullivan of *The Chicago Tribune*, "At the end of the '66 season, when we'd just lost 103 ballgames, Leo (Durocher) took Bill Hands, Joe Niekro, Rich Nye, Kenny Holtzman, and myself, and told us, 'You five guys will battle for four spots in the '67 rotation." The pitchers welcomed the clarity of Durocher's message. Jenkins became a 20-game winner the very next season, and by 1968, Hands was also a cornerstone of the Cubs rotation.

In the four years from 1968 to 1971, Hands averaged 266 innings per year. Nowadays, such numbers are rare. In 2021, for example, no NL pitcher hurled even 220 innings.

In 1969, Hands went 20-14, with a 2.49 ERA and set career highs in innings worked (300) and strikeouts (181). On August 9 in Los Angeles (on the same night that Sharon Tate, the pregnant wife of film director Roman Polansky, was murdered by followers of Charles Manson in nearby Hollywood), Hands shut out the Dodgers. As invincible as the Cubs looked that night, few could have predicted that they would be surpassed by the Mets just a few weeks later. Hands went 6-6 down the stretch; the humbled Cubs went 18-28 over the same period.

Bill continued to pitch well in the following seasons but had less to show for it in the won-loss column, and slowly, the window of opportunity that Durocher contemplated at the end of the 1966 season began to close, as the Cubs' win totals went from 92 to 84 to 83 to 85 through 1972. Durocher was replaced as manager by Whitey Lockman midway through the 1972 season. By then, the Cubs began to retool their roster.

Hands, who threw a sinking fastball along with an excellent slider, joined the Twins in 1973 and the Rangers in 1974. He closed out his career in 1975 with a lifetime mark of 111-110 and an impressive 3.35 ERA.

Teammate Rich Nye remembered Hands as a very hard worker who loved playing cards, be it bridge, poker or hearts, in his spare time. Hands also enjoyed gardening, fishing, and time with family.

After baseball, Hands owned a gas station in Orient, New York, adorned with baseball photographs. Friends likened it to a setting from Floyd's Barber Shop on the Andy Griffith Show, where people would congregate to pass the time and trade stories. Bill continued to follow baseball and was pleased when the Cubs finally won a World Series in 2016. He passed away after a brief illness in 2017 at age 76.

DON KESSINGER

It was 1964, the last year before MLB adopted the amateur draft, and Don Kessinger, an all-American in baseball and basketball at Old Miss, had many choices of where to sign. Having played in the 1964 College World Series, his stock was high. He selected the Cubs, calculating correctly he could get to the majors quickly. It was a prudent call. In 1965, Don began getting Cubs playing time after fellow shortstop Roberto Pena had fielding problems. By 1966, Don was a .270 hitter and by 1968, he was an all-star.

"I would go out there before everyone else," he told an interviewer, "and have a coach hit ball after ball to me, and I'd throw ball after ball to first base. I finally felt like I could throw to first base with my eyes closed." At one point he went 54 straight games without an error, breaking Chico Carrasquel's record for shortstops. He also led his league in assists and double plays four years.

Baseball purists came to love his game, and not just his fielding. He dropped bunts and advanced runners. In 1969, the year that the Mets overcame the Cubs to win the division and then the world championship, Kessinger hit .273 and scored 109 runs. Manager Leo Durocher almost never rested his key players. Don was a case in point, playing in 158 games. He believes that during the stretch run, when the Mets made their move, the Cubs' regulars were a bit worn down, with the club going 8-18. He thinks they may have been better equipped to compete with a bit more rest.

Don became a six-time all-star and two-time gold glover. He was still the regular shortstop in 1975, by which time the Cubs were rebuilding. They traded him to the Cardinals. The shortstop had 10-and-5 rights and could have blocked a trade, but happily accepted the change. Late in his career, he was traded to the White Sox. Don felt awkward at first, since White Sox fans often held the Cubs in disdain. To his delight, he received a standing ovation upon entering his first game. In 1979 he was asked by owner Bill Veeck to serve as a player-manager, but walked away from both roles that summer. He retired with a .252 batting average, 1,931 hits, and 100 stolen bases.

When Jake Gibbs retired as the head coach for Old Miss, Kessinger accepted the job, which he called "a dream come true." He never hesitated to share his faith. "My opportunity to influence people for the Lord is the greatest thing for me," he stated. He continues to live in Oxford.

GLENN BECKERT

Reflecting the nationwide popularity of baseball, the Hearst media company sponsored the Hearst Baseball Classic for 20 years after World War II. It was a one-day exhibition game of the nation's top high-school phenoms, held in the hallowed Polo Grounds in New York. The grandstands were always packed with family and friends of the players, and with baseball scouts, eager to identify the stars of tomorrow. Pittsburgh native Glenn Beckert gained notoriety by starring in that game. He further burnished his prospect credentials a couple of years later at Allegheny College, where he earned a political science degree.

Strictly a shortstop and third baseman in the minor leagues, Beckert began in the Red Sox chain before being drafted by the Cubs. He was pressed into action at second base in 1965 after the tragic death of Cubs' second-sacker Ken Hubbs in a plane crash. Beckert compiled a 14-game hitting streak at one point in his rookie year, even as he learned his new position.

After the season, he was invited to a winter banquet where he sat on the dais with newly hired manager Leo Durocher. "It's very seldom a .240 hitter gets to the speakers' table," Beckert quipped. "But Mr. Durocher's here, so I'm not alone."

Beckert held down the position for nine years, became adept at hitting to all fields, and rarely fanned. He registered six straight years with batting averages of .280 or better including 1966, when only Felipe Alou, Pete Rose and Roberto Clemente had more hits. During the year of the pitcher, 1968, he batted .294 and led the league with 98 runs scored. Glenn had the longest hitting streak in the majors that season at 27 games, and won the gold glove award, as well.

A year later, when the Cubs enjoyed a rollicking season before losing their grip on first place in the late going, he hit a nearly identical .291 His banner season came in 1971, when he compiled a .342 batting average, before sustaining a season-ending thumb injury in early September. Only Joe Torre and Ralph Garr finished higher.

A slick fielder, Beckert was initially teamed with Roberto Pena in the Cubs' keystone, but Don Kessinger captured the shortstop job for good in 1966. Beckert and Kessinger practiced an hour and a half per day during spring training, rehearsing double plays and force plays at second base. The pair remained lifetime friends, and even stayed in touch during the Cubs' successful 2016 march to the world championship. Glenn also was tight with Billy Williams, as well as his sometime-roommate Ron Santo, and hurler Ferguson Jenkins. Glenn served as best man at Jenkins' wedding.

Beckert loved being in the big leagues. He told an interviewer in 1965, "If everybody in the minors could realize what the big leagues are like, they'd work a lot harder." Cubs official Lou Klein called him "a strong kid and a scrappy, aggressive player."

Williams fondly recalls, "He couldn't sit still for five minutes, and he used to walk up and down the aisles of the plane all the time. He always had to be talking to somebody. And he'd always hit you up for cigarettes and matches. You wouldn't get your pack back or matches."

Teammate Ken Rudolph remembers, "He played hard and was razzle and dazzle, but always got the job done. He was a pesky hitter, rarely struck out, and played the game as it was supposed to be played."

Beckert is fourth all-time in Cubs' history for the most games played at second base, behind Ryne Sandberg, Billy Herman, and Johnny Evers. He played his final two seasons with the Padres and when he retired after the 1975 campaign, he had a .283 lifetime average with 1,473 hits. Beckert passed away from natural causes in Florida in 2020.

RON SANTO

Any ranking of the greatest third basemen of all time will include Ron Santo. Beginning in 1963, he was an all-star in nine of the next 11 seasons. He had everything a third baseman needed – a rocket of an arm, range in both directions, quick reflexes, and a powerful batting stroke.

Unlike his contemporary Ken Boyer, Santo never won an MVP award. The highest he ever got in the voting was fourth. But in 1964, the year Boyer was named MVP, Santo hit .313, led the NL in walks and on-base percentage, and snared the gold glove honors. Whereas Boyer's OPS that year was .854, Santo's was an astounding .962. Had Santo played on a better team, he may have been elected MVP.

A product of Franklin High School in Seattle – the same school that produced manager Fred Hutchinson – Santo grew up in a broken home after his parents divorced. He saw his mother work hard to put food on the table, and Ron resolved to make something of himself and do his mother proud. He discovered his athletic skills as his Pony League team went all the way to the national finals in Washington, D.C. After graduation, he played in the Hearst all-star game. He initially was a catcher but much preferred third base. To earn money while still in school, he worked at Seattle Stadium as a bat boy, usher and clubhouse attendant.

Santo was diagnosed at age 18 with juvenile diabetes, but did not let that setback dampen his spirit, and he waited more than a decade to disclose the condition to the public. His step-father advised him to sign with the team that offered the best opportunity, not the most money. Ron followed that advice, spurning interest from the Yankees, Indians and Reds, to sign with the Cubs. He received a bonus of about $18,500 according to Ferguson Jenkins.

Early in his career, Santo would get anxious in clutch-hitting situations and asked Cubs batting instructor Rogers Hornsby for advice. Hornsby, a former .400 hitter, told Santo that in clutch situations, it is the pitcher who should be nervous. Santo credited Rajah's counsel for helping him to relax. As a hitter, Santo early on stopped trying to guess what the pitcher would throw or where he would throw it. Too often, he found, he was guessing wrong and not ready for the actual delivery.

He also prided himself in playing every day. To try to keep his blood sugar balanced, he would often have a candy bar and/or a cola drink mid-game. The diabetes, he was quoted as saying in Rick Swaine's book, *Beating the Breaks: Major Leaguers who Overcame Disabilities,* "was one reason I played so hard. I kept thinking my career would end one day. I never really wanted out of the lineup." In 1966, he was struck with a Jack Fisher fastball just under the eye, breaking the cheek bone. He was back in the lineup – and homering – a week later.

Along with Ernie Banks, Glenn Beckert and Don Kessinger, Santo formed what has been called the best infield in Cubs' history. Yes, even better than the Tinker-Evers-Chance infield of the dead-ball era.

Ahead of the 1973 season, he vetoed a trade to the Angels before accepting a swap to the White Sox. Ron was miserable with the Sox, had a tense relationship with teammate Dick Allen, and retired after the season. He finished with a .277 career average and 342 homers.

Santo sometimes could have chosen better ways to communicate his feelings, as when he berated Cubs outfielder Don Young or tried to choke manager Leo Durocher. Teammate Rich Nye recalled, "Lots of ego as a player, he had conflicts. He became a good friend after he started announcing." Teammate Billy Williams, who played more than 2,000 games with Santo, said, "What I learned from Ronnie is he loved the game, he loved the people in the game, and he loved the fans of the game."

An entrepreneur, Santo co-owned the Old Heritage Life Insurance Company and worked at the agency during the winters alongside Beckert. Former Cub Ellis Burton worked there, as well. Santo also owned a business called "The Pro's Pizza" and co-owned a chain of filling stations, another income source.

Ron raised tremendous amounts of money for diabetes research and enjoyed a long run as the Cubs color commentator. He died in Scottsdale at the age of 70 in 2010 and was elected to the Hall of Fame the following year.

RUSTY STAUB

When Rusty Staub was growing up in New Orleans, his parents hoped he would go into medicine, and they were disappointed by his decision to pursue a career in baseball. The red-headed youngster answered their concerns and then some with a 23-year MLB career.

A lifetime .279 hitter with 2,716 hits and 292 homers, Staub was a six-time all-star. He was the first player in history to collect 500 or more hits with four different clubs.

Houston executives relished the thought of a confident New Orleans boy becoming one of their first stars. In his initial year of pro ball in 1962, he won the Carolina League player of the year award, convincing Houston to bring him to the big leagues at age 19 in 1963. Awed by his potential, the brass finally concluded he needed some Triple-A seasoning and sent him to Oklahoma City for part of the 1964 campaign.

By 1966, he was the top run producer on the Astros. Then in 1967, he enjoyed the first of many robust seasons, batting .333 with a team-high 44 doubles. He credited maintaining concentration and hitting the ball hard for his success.

Staub put down some roots in Houston, buying a V-shaped, ranch-style house with a backyard pool. Driving his powerful Cadillac El Dorado, he could make it from the house to the Astrodome in three minutes flat, so long as no police cars were along the route. His daily routine included getting eight hours of sleep, rising for a meal, taking a 90-minute nap before night games, and then going out after the game on dates or hanging out with friends.

Yet, after he hit .291 with only six homers in 1968, there was front-office consternation that he had not developed into a power hitter, especially after he moved from the outfield to first base, a position where home run production is expected. Houston's new general manager, Spec Richardson, was less beholden to the original crop of Houston players.

Spec's discussions with Jim Fanning, his counterpart in Montreal, led to a high-profile 1969 trade that sent Staub north of the border. "This man isn't only a .300 hitter, he's a potential champion," Fanning beamed. Maury Wills, whom the Expos had already acquired, said, "It's a great trade. Staub's a great player and a young player. He's a great man to build a new ballclub around." Staub became known in Montreal as Le Grand Orange and hit .302 with 29 home runs that first season, taking advantage of the smaller dimensions of Jarry Park.

Rusty was with Montreal through 1971; the Mets from 1972 to 1975; and the Tigers from 1976 until mid-way through the 1979 season. He closed out his career with stops in Montreal, Texas, and five years as a pinch-hitter with the Mets. In 1983, he tied an NL record with eight straight pinch hits. He became just the second player – after Ty Cobb – to homer before age 20 and after age 40.

He eventually transitioned into announcing Mets games and operating two restaurants in New York, as well as continuing to run his charitable foundation. His health began to decline in 2015, when he went into cardiac arrest on a flight from Scotland that was headed to the States, but reversed course to Ireland so he could receive treatment. He passed away three years later in West Palm Beach.

Julio Gotay

Julio Gotay was a relatively obscure infielder, but he had a rare specialty: The hidden-ball trick. After executing the trick on Julian Javier on June 5, 1968, he told *The Sporting News* he had pulled it off twice before in the major leagues and about 10 times in professional baseball. Few plays in baseball engender more embarrassment for the opposition, or as much satisfaction for the player responsible for the trickery. For Gotay, it was a source of personal pride.

Gotay was a Puerto Rico native who played for the Cardinals, Pirates, Angels, and Astros over a 10-year period. He backed into the starting shortstop role in St. Louis in 1962, after Bob Lillis and Daryl Spencer were found wanting. He hit okay, but the Cards weren't thrilled with his fielding and packaged him in a deal with Pittsburgh to land veteran Dick Groat, who helped St. Louis win the 1964 world championship. Julio was mostly a reserve infielder through 1969, and retired with a lifetime batting average of .260.

After baseball, he moved back to Puerto Rico and pursued a second career as a school principal. He died of prostate cancer in 2008 at age 69.

DON WILSON

Don Wilson was both a top pitcher and a tragic figure. He had enormous talent, compiled some memorable achievements, and died a sorrowful death.

He grew up in Compton, played Little League ball with Roy White and Reggie Smith, and studied at Compton Community College. After three seasons of minor-league action, he entered the Houston rotation in 1966, producing a 10-9 record and a no-hitter versus the Braves. A year later, during a 13-16 season, he joined Bob Feller and Sandy Koufax as the only pitchers to record an 18-strikeout game. His manager that season, Grady Hatton, raved about Don's high-riding fastball and tight, effective curve.

Wilson threw another no-hitter against the Reds in 1969. He said the achievement was particularly satisfying because Reds' manager Dave Bristol had been yelling from the dugout, calling him gutless. That same season, Wilson and Curt Blefary became road roommates, at a time when interracial rooming was uncommon in the sport. Wilson finished the year with 16 wins, but knew he had to improve on his 4.00 ERA and league-lead in wild pitches. By the time that 1969 season ended, he had a 40-37 record, and had yet to celebrate his 25th birthday.

Saddled with an explosive temper, Wilson on two occasions tried to physically assault manager Harry Walker, only to be held back by teammates. Jim Wynn later wrote, "It wasn't easy being a close friend to Don Wilson. He didn't make it easy for anyone to like him. In fact, he did his damnedest sometimes to make liking him a complete challenge. He had a violent temper; he drank way too much, as did a lot of us back in those days, and he could foul-mouth you faster than just about anyone else I've ever known." Wynn described one incident in particular where Wilson's actions could have cost Wynn his life. 'With a little stability in his life," Wynn concluded, "Wilson could have gone on to become one of the great pitchers in baseball history."

Remaining in the Houston rotation through 1974, Wilson remained an effective pitcher. He was both a drinker and a smoker, and in December 1974 had been diagnosed with a minor kidney ailment, but was not known to be having any illegal drug-abuse or marital problems. In fact, he was working that winter for the Astros' speakers bureau. Yet, on an afternoon in early January 1975, he was found dead of carbon monoxide poisoning on the passenger side of a car in his garage. His blood alcohol level was .16. Police believed he had arrived home around 1:00 a.m. and might have passed out in the car.

The gas had seeped into the house, killing his young son, and causing brain damage to his daughter. His wife was unaffected by the gas, but had an injury to her jaw. As police questioned her, she retained an attorney. Investigators ruled the deaths of the pitcher and his son as accidental. Speculation was rampant that Wilson had committed suicide, but teammates Doug Rader and Dave Roberts stated emphatically that Wilson was emotionally stable and would not have taken his own life.

A couple of players interviewed for this book noted that Wilson was exceptionally talented, but not always as focused on pitching as he should have been. Recalled one of them, "He was one of the weird pitchers. When he was motivated, he was tough to beat."

In 1975, without anyone suitable to replace Wilson in the starting rotation, the Astros' record plunged to 64-97. The right-hander would have been just 30 years old, and likely had many solid seasons ahead of him. Wilson had a 104-92 record and a 3.15 ERA, along with 20 shutouts and 1,283 strikeouts at the time of his passing.

MIKE CUELLAR

In winning 125 games over six seasons (1969 to 1974), this Cuban lefty was the premier screwball hurler of his era. He learned the pitch from pitcher Ruben Gomez and threw it at three different speeds with near-pinpoint control. Factor in his plus fastball, a curve and slider, and it's easy to understand why he so often baffled hitters.

Cuellar was already 29 years old when he first tasted big-league success with Houston in 1966, a "10-year project," as coach Jim Busby put it. He posted a 12-10 record, placed second in the circuit in ERA behind Sandy Koufax, and became the first Houston pitcher to toss six straight complete games.

He roomed on the road that year with infielder Felix Mantilla. When the club arrived at spring training in 1967, Mantilla was no longer with Houston, and Cuellar was told he could room with anyone he wanted. Reflecting his new-won star power, he said he preferred to room alone, and the front office granted his wish.

Cuellar had a great sense of humor – Houston manager Grady Hatton called him "a comedian." He enjoyed solitude and on long flights, he sometimes drew cartoons to relax.

He added 16 wins in 1967 and was 8-11 with a good ERA in 1968. The Astros were concerned about their lack of run production, and unwittingly traded Cuellar to the Orioles for Curt Blefary ahead of the 1969 season. The O's made the trade on the recommendation of Earl Weaver, who had seen Cuellar dominate some of the game's better hitters in winter ball. It was a landslide of a swap, as Cuellar won 23 games and shared the 1969 Cy Young award honors in his first year in Baltimore. The co-winner was Detroit's Denny McLain, in the only instance of a tied vote for the Cy Young award.

Weaver appreciated that Cuellar could start on short rest when needed. Three straight seasons he hurled 290 or more innings. "He could screwball you to death or curve you to death," former teammate Jim Palmer recalled.

Cuellar remained a dominant hurler through 1974, when he won 22 games. He managed a respectable 1975 season with 14 wins, but by 1976 was pitching on fumes. His career ended with two appearances for the 1977 Angels.

Cuellar, who died of stomach cancer in Orlando in 2010, had a lifetime record of 185-130 with 36 shutouts and a 3.14 career ERA. In 1982, Cuellar and Luis Aparicio became the sixth and seventh former players selected for the Orioles Hall of Fame.

Jim Wynn

Jim Wynn grew up in a two-bedroom rowhouse in Cincinnati, so close to Crosley Field that he could say hello as Reds players headed to the ballpark. Jimmy was so well regarded as a baseball prospect that on one afternoon, Frank Robinson and Vada Pinson of the Reds stopped by the house, inviting him to come down for a tour of the clubhouse. What was already a memorable day got even better when Robinson gave Jim a baseball glove.

After playing ball at Central State as a shortstop, Wynn signed with the Reds for a modest $500 bonus and began his minor league career playing third base. After one year, he was drafted by Houston. Imagine the optimism of Houston fans in 1963, with a new stadium on the way and a minor league system stocked with promising talent. Wynn was 21 when he broke in with Houston that summer. Late that season, Houston garnered publicity by starting an all-rookie lineup one day against the Mets, with Wynn, Sonny Jackson, Ernie Fazio, Jerry Grote, Brock Davis, Rusty Staub, Aaron Pointer (whose sisters became a top-ranked musical act), Jay Dahl, and a young second baseman who would become Wynn's closest friend in baseball, Joe Morgan.

Jim was in the big leagues to stay in 1965, the year the team moved into the Astrodome and rechristened their name as the Astros. Wynn hit 22 homers, stunning competitors who never expected such prodigious power from a compact, five-foot-ten body. Jim later told writer Richard Justice, "I lifted weights without people knowing about it. I kept my upper body, my hands, my wrists strong. That's where my power came from." It wasn't long before he was nicknamed "The Toy Cannon."

He missed almost two months of the 1966 season with an injury sustained when he crashed into a wall, trying to make a catch in Philadelphia. But in 1967, he and Hank Aaron waged a season-long battle for the NL home run crown. Aaron wound up on top, but Wynn finished second with

37 circuit clouts. Three of those blasts came in a June game against the Giants, making him the first Astro to achieve that fete. His homer totals were remarkable considering he played half his schedule at the Astrodome, a facility he said was "built for pitching and defense."

Nearly half-way into the 1968 campaign, Houston replaced manager Grady Hatton with Harry Walker, who had been the hitting coach. Walker tried to get Wynn to hit the way Walker had hit as a player, emphasizing batting average over power. Wynn's 1968 season was respectable, but in 1969 he delivered 33 homers and set a club record by drawing 148 free passes, tops in the league. Being pitched around was a sign of respect, but also frustrating for the young slugger.

As he settled in with the Astros, he moved his year-around home from Cincinnati to Houston, developed an interest in jazz music, and worked as a broadcaster during the winter. After rooming on the road initially with outfielder John Weekly, he then roomed with Morgan for seven years. Wynn was more of a night owl, while Morgan tended to retire early.

After the 1970 season, the Dodgers offered outfielder Willie Davis and reliever Jim Brewer for Wynn, but Houston turned it down. Jim enjoyed success until 1971, when he mustered only a .203 average and seven homers, a miserable year in which his first marriage had ended. For the first time, Houston fans were booing him. Things came to a head on July 16 when Wynn swung on a 3-and-0 count with the bases jammed and popped out.

Wynn met with Walker after the game and as writer John Wilson described it, "Wynn stalked out of the manager's office, angry and cursing. Walker followed him into the main clubhouse and the shouting began in front of the whole team. Wynn picked up some objects, a food plate and watermelon rind, and hurled them at a trash can standing between him and the manager." Wynn also threatened to "beat the shit" out of the writer if he ran the story in the newspaper, but Wilson did so. Wynn was reportedly fined $100 for the transgressions.

Writers figured Wynn would be gone after the season, but he was still with the Astros in 1972 and enjoyed a solid comeback, collecting 24 homers and 90 RBI. After he struggled in 1973, Houston traded him to Los Angeles for Claude Osteen, a recent 20-game winner.

Arriving in Los Angeles, Wynn found an entirely new atmosphere. Led by manager Walt Alston and third base coach Tom LaSorda, the Dodgers brass was respected by the players, who in turn were excited about the team's future. Jim found himself meeting Hollywood celebrities, and making guest appearances on the Tonight Show with Johnny Carson and the Sonny & Cher Show. Jim homered in his first three games as a 1974 Dodger and the club won the NL pennant. He later closed out his career with the Braves, Yankees and Brewers.

Summarizing Wynn's abilities, teammate Ron Brand said, "Jim was a tremendous talent – power, speed, arm, and range for not a very big guy." He was a three-time all-star with a .250 career average, 1,665 hits, and 291 home runs. Wynn died in Houston in 2020. While Cooperstown may never call his number, he is remembered as a pivotal figure in Houston baseball.

TOMMY HARPER

Until 2023, nobody in MLB history had stolen more than 70 bases and hit more than 30 home runs in a single season. In fact, only two players had done so in different years. One was Eric Davis. The first to do so was Tommy Harper.

Harper was a four-sport star at California's Encinal High School (where he was a teammate of Willie Stargell). Playing later at San Francisco State, he caught the eye of Reds scout Bobby Mattick. Just over two years later, he was wearing a Reds uniform.

Spending parts of five seasons with the Reds, Harper turned in one exceptional campaign, in 1965, when he led the NL in runs scored and swiped 35 bases. But injuries and inconsistency prompted the Reds to trade him to Cleveland. He spent one year with the Tribe in 1968, complained about a lack of playing time and hit just .217.

With the Pilots in 1969, manager Joe Schultz gave the speedster the green light. As Schultz put it, "Go when you like. You are my Lou Brock. So go out there and steal yourself some bases. Make yourself some money." That was music to Harper's ears as he stole 73 bases, tops in the AL. Schultz batted him leadoff and encouraged him to be patient at the plate (95 walks). And he deployed Tommy in both the infield and the outfield to utilize his versatility.

The Pilots moved eastward to Milwaukee, becoming the Brewers in 1970. Harper racked up 31 homers along with 38 steals, making him a 30-30 man. He led the AL in stolen bases again in 1973 with 54 as a member of the Red Sox.

Tommy also played for the Angels, A's and Orioles. Over 15 seasons, he batted .257 with 146 home runs, 408 stolen bases and 1,609 hits. His post-playing career included a number of coaching positions. In recent years he has lived in Sheboygan, Wisconsin.

JIM O'TOOLE

Portable tape recorders were not terribly common in the early Sixties, but Reds pitcher Jim O'Toole traveled with one to record his observations about opposing hitters and his own performance. He also used a black marker to write the letters T-H-I-N-K on his Wilson baseball glove. Unconventional as those practices were, they helped O'Toole become a winner.

In 1958, the youngster won 20 contests for the Nashville Volunteers. Months later, in *The Sporting News,* writer Earl Lawson said, "Jimmy O'Toole is a handsome, 22-year-old Irish lad out of Chicago whose broad shoulders and strong left arm are destined to carry him to greatness."

Lawson wrote that if O'Toole couldn't make the grade in baseball, there would be roles for him in Hollywood because of his good looks.

It never came to that. O'Toole had a dandy 1961 campaign in which he went 19-9 with a 3.10 ERA (second-best in the league). Late in the season, after the Reds clinched the NL title, the club assigned him, pitcher Joe Jay, and catcher Darrell Johnson to scout the Yankees. O'Toole had a front-row seat the day that Roger Maris broke Babe Ruth's single-season home run record. Jim went on to pitch well in games one and four of the World Series but his Reds were swept by the Yankees.

The lefty enjoyed three more winning seasons, with records of 16-13, 17-14, and 17-7, with an all-star selection in 1962. He had legions of fans, none more loyal than his dad, who was a Chicago police officer, and his wife, whom he married in 1960 and credited with helping him settle down and focus on pitching. John Edwards, his catcher with the Reds, said his cut fastball was uniquely effective. He was also respected as a team leader.

O'Toole struggled in the 1965 and 1966 seasons, which led to a trade to the White Sox. With Chicago, he hurled one more gem, a 10-inning two hitter on May 13, 1967. He went on the disabled list that July, concluding his season. Hoping for a comeback, O'Toole split the 1968 season with two minor-league clubs. In 1969, he went to spring training with the Pilots. When they assigned him to their Triple-A affiliate, he chose to retire instead.

For his career, O'Toole had a record of 98-84 with a 3.57 ERA. His younger brother, Denny O'Toole, pitched for the White Sox from 1969 to 1973. Jim O'Toole and his wife stayed in Cincinnati, where they raised 11 children. He held positions in insurance and trash-collection sales, and maintained a close affiliation with the Reds organization, which inducted him into its team hall of fame.

Joe Jay

Joe Jay was the first Little League player to reach MLB and also a large-bonus recipient in 1953. The joy of becoming a pro ballplayer gave way to facing resentment from veteran players. Joe later said, "I fitted in nowhere." He gradually won some teammates over in 1958, when he contributed to the Braves' pennant run with seven wins and a spotless 2.14 ERA.

Over the next couple of seasons, Jay was an unexceptional pitcher, the Braves were a former championship team in decline, and the tense clubhouse vibe reflected that status. A week before Christmas 1960, the Braves traded him and fellow pitcher Juan Pizarro to the Reds for shortstop Roy McMillan. Joey was happy to move on.

Starting fresh with the 1961 Reds, he won 21 games, hurled a league-high four shutouts, represented the Reds on the all-star team, and placed fifth in the MVP voting. A highlight was a one-hit win over the Phillies, and it had to be equally satisfying that he won all four decisions against his former mates on the Braves. He pitched and won game two of the World Series, despite issuing six free passes. He started game five but failed to make it out of the first inning and the Yankees clinched the championship.

The Reds had a powerful lineup, with the likes of Frank Robinson, Vada Pinson, Wally Post, Gordy Coleman and Gene Freese. Joe won 21 games again in 1962 as the Reds settled for a third-place finish. "Jay had above-average stuff and if he was in control, he was hard to beat," remembered his Reds catcher, John Edwards.

Over time, Joe became more focused on his business interests, including a chicken farm in Florida and J&B Drilling in West Virginia. He got into a dispute with Reds manager Fred Hutchinson over leaving the club briefly to tend to personal business. At the 1966 trade deadline, the Reds traded him to the Braves, who released him after the season. Jay left baseball at age 31 with a 99-91 record and a 3.71 ERA. In his post-baseball years, he owned oil fields, taxi and limousine services, and other enterprises. He now calls Largo, Florida his home.

VADA PINSON

Vada Pinson's career illustrates how difficult it can be for a hitter to remain at an elite level over an extended time frame. Pinson played for the Reds from 1958 to 1968 and then for four other clubs from 1969 to 1975.

Early on, Pinson was an extraordinarily tough out. He led the league in hits, doubles, and triples twice each and runs scored once. His spectacular 1961 performance, when he batted .343 with 16 home runs and 23 stolen bases, helped spark the Reds to the pennant. He played with poise and displayed blazing foot speed.

When Vada's offensive production tailed off at the age of 29 in 1968, some baseball officials wrote it off to being a result of "the year of the pitcher." Reds manager Dave Bristol chalked it up to him being overly aggressive and swinging at bad pitches.

Taking no chances, the Reds traded him to the Cardinals, who retained him for only one season. With the exception of an outstanding season for Cleveland in 1970, Pinson was essentially a replacement-level performer until he retired. He had a .286 lifetime batting average and 2,757 hits of which 256 were home runs. He also stole 305 bases, made two all-star teams, and won one gold glove.

Pinson, who hailed from Oakland, was widely viewed as an asset not only on the field but also in the clubhouse, where he was popular with teammates. He had a mischievous sense of humor. When Indians general manager Alvin Dark criticized him for driving in "only 82 runs" in 1970, Pinson responded, "If you put more men on base, I'll drive them in."

Vada's temper may have gotten the best of him during a regrettable incident while with the Reds in 1963. The backdrop was that two writers, Lou Smith in *The Cincinnati Enquirer* and Earl Lawson in *The Cincinnati Post and Times-Star,* wrote articles alleging that Pinson had foregone opportunities for base hits – and perhaps for the batting title – by stubbornly refusing to bunt.

Lawson said that Pinson confronted him about the article, pushed him, roughed him up, and tore his shirt. Pinson apparently aggravated the situation by appearing on a news show the same day and saying he regretted not punching the writer. Lawson filed charges, Pinson was arrested, and the Reds' business manager, John Murdough, had to go to the detention center to get Pinson released on $300 bail.

Lawson filed an assault and battery civil case against the outfielder. The case went to court in late 1963 and resulted in a hung jury. Lawson eventually dropped the charges ahead of the rescheduled court date. Pinson finished that season seventh in the batting derby with a .313 average and mended fences with Lawson.

Another perspective of Pinson came from pitcher George Culver, his Reds teammate in 1968. "He was the cleanest guy I ever played with. We would be on a late-night flight from the East Coast to the West Coast and Vada, always a great dresser, would get off the plane looking like he just got out of the shower, coat and tie, heading for a formal party somewhere. Not a wrinkle or anything out of place. The rest of us looked like we'd been in a street brawl."

"Maybe the nicest guy I ever played with," Culver continued. "Never drank that I know of, always ready to play baseball and happy to be on the field. I saw him playing for Visalia in the California League when I was in high school here in Bakersfield, and you could tell then he was going to be a star."

Pinson roomed on road trips with outfielder Dick Simpson, a fellow Californian, in 1966 and 1967. Vada enjoyed visiting jazz clubs with Jim Hicks when the pair were teammates in 1969. "I took the trumpet with me on the road. Used to practice in my room at the hotel or in the stairwells, some corner of the ballpark. Always dreamed of being onstage playing my horn," he told writer Greg Hoard.

After two years in Cleveland, Pinson played two years each with the Angels and the Royals. From 1977 to 1994, Pinson held coaching positions within the Mariners, White Sox, Tigers and Marlins organizations. He passed away from a stroke in 1995 at the age of 57.

JIM RAY HART

Jim Ray Hart went from picking tobacco and corn at his family's rented farm in North Carolina to becoming a star third baseman and outfielder for the Giants. But his initial welcome to the big leagues in July 1963 could hardly have been ruder as he sustained a broken left shoulder blade from a Bob Gibson pitch. Soon after it healed in September, he was beaned by Curt Simmons, resulting in a season-ending concussion. Hart got into only seven games.

Such injuries might have deterred men with less mettle, but Hart went on to have a big rookie season in 1964, hitting .286 with 31 jacks. He racked up those numbers despite being hit in the ribs by pitches from Don Drysdale and Claude Osteen on May 3 and 4, requiring a brief trip to a hospital. "I haven't seen any Giant since Mays' rookie year who impressed me more," boasted manager Herman Franks.

Hart averaged more than 90 RBI over his first four years and led the Giants in hits three straight seasons. Defense was never his forte. In 1965, Jim, who used MacGregor gloves, made a league-high 32 errors. Part of the problem was his sidearm throws were sinking as they approached the first baseman. He also claimed that tall grass at Candlestick Park made it hard to get to ground balls. The club ordered the grounds crew to reduce the length of the grass by 50 percent, a move that won Hart's approval.

Injuries began taking a toll in 1969, with Hart playing part-time the next several seasons. He was sent down to Triple-A Phoenix in 1971 and 1972 for a time, while battling shoulder trouble.

With the advent of the designated hitter rule in 1973, it seemed likely that Jim would wind up in the AL. The inevitable occurred on April 17, 1973, when the Giants sold him to the Yankees. In the Bronx, Hart hit 13 home runs, drove in 51 RBI, and batted a respectable .254. It was during his stint with the Yankees that Horace Clarke said Hart "has arms like a bull, legs like a bull, strength like a bull."

Hart had many fine attributes but taking care of himself wasn't one of them. He gained too much weight and drank too much alcohol. Nagging injuries took a long time to heal. When he started the 1974 season poorly, he was released, marking the end of his MLB career. His final numbers included a .278 batting average and 170 home runs. Hart gradually became obese and refused to attend Giants reunions or autograph shows. He died in 2016 at the age of 74 in Acampo, California, following a lengthy illness. Though divorced, he was survived by four children and 12 grandkids.

CHRIS SHORT

From 1962 to 1968, Phillies southpaw Chris Short was one of baseball's best pitchers. During that run, Short had a record of 103-75, made two all-star teams, and had seasons with 20, 19, 18 and 17 victories. In 1964, only Sandy Koufax and Don Drysdale had a better ERA. When Short won 20 times in 1966, he was just the second Phillies lefty to ever reach that plateau. In 1967, only Phil Niekro and teammate Jim Bunning had finer ERAs. Though there were no pennants in Philadelphia during his stretch of excellence, he contributed plenty of highlights, including 24 shutouts.

As a youngster, Short pitched three seasons at Lewes High School near the resort town of Rehoboth Beach, and his senior year at a military academy in New Jersey. When he hit a batter in the head with a pitch his sophomore year and left him unconscious, Short learned he had to be careful not to hurt enemy hitters.

Living so close to the water, it's not surprising that Short developed a love of fishing. In March 1966, Chris and his teammate Clay Dalrymple won the second annual All-Star Fishing Tournament at Cypress Gardens, Florida (nosing out Harmon Killebrew and Don Mincher of the Twins) with a total weigh-in of four pounds and 14 ounces. The happy pair each won a Johnson outboard engine as first prize.

Often remembered for his role in the Phillies' collapse at the end of the 1964 season, Chris finished the year with a sterling 17-9 record, but failed to register a win in his last three starts. Manager Gene Mauch was criticized for starting Bunning and Short twice on two days rest, as the Phillies endured a stunning 10-game losing streak. The Cardinals and Reds moved ahead of Philadelphia in the standings, with the Cards clinching the pennant on the last day of the campaign.

Before the 1966 season, Bunning took a page from the book of Sandy Koufax and Don Drysdale, and encouraged Short to join him in a joint contract holdout. Short wound up signing the Phillies' initial offer, leading a frustrated Bunning to label him "the worst negotiator."

As Short gained a following, collectors wondered why he was not appearing on Topps cards. The explanation goes back to an exclusive contract that he signed with Fleer. (Maury Wills, Jack Reed, and Marshall Bridges signed similar pacts.) Fleer issued a short-run set in 1963, and then no more cards for a generation. It was not until 1967 that the legal morass was cleared, and Chris appeared on his first Topps card, by then in his seventh season.

He lost most of the 1969 season to a back injury that required surgery and rehab. When he returned in 1970, his dominance was gone. He went just 20-36 thereafter. The Phillies remained loyal as long as they could, retaining him through the 1972 season. He spent one final season as a spot starter with the Brewers.

After hanging up the cleats, he ran an insurance agency and coached at the Suburban Baseball Camp in Pennsylvania. One day at his office in 1988, Short suffered a ruptured aneurism. With staggering medical bills accumulating, former teammate Art Mahaffey organized what became an annual golf tournament for several years to raise funds for Short's medical care. Chris never came out of a coma and passed away three years later at the age of 53, survived by three sons. Short ranks fourth on the Phillies' all-time list of victories, trailing only Steve Carlton, Robin Roberts and Grover Cleveland Alexander.

DAVE WATKINS

What was it like to play for a losing team in the Sixties? Dave Watkins shared the catching duties with Mike Ryan on the 1969 Phillies, who had a 63-99 record. "I did not have much problem about keeping positive because I was at the top of my profession," he recently recalled. Bob Skinner was replaced as manager by George Myatt two-thirds of the way into the season. "George was a calm, old-fashioned, grinding-it-out, hard-nosed, run-manufacturing character. He promoted teamwork and handled Richie Allen fairly."

The bullpen coach on that team was Andy Seminick, who had caught for the Phillies decades earlier. He had been Dave's manager at Double-A Chattanooga and Macon, and was the most influential coach throughout Dave's career.

Watkins recalls teammate Cookie Rojas as "a natural leader. A smart baseball thinker, he had his head in the game every minute. He made the best of the skills he had." Dave is also complimentary of infielder Tony Taylor. "He was another 'head-in-the-game' ballplayer." On road trips, Dave roomed with pitchers Al Raffo or Woody Fryman.

Originally from Kentucky, Watkins was inspired to catch by his grandfather who was a semi-pro ballplayer. After Tigers scout Max Macon – a former MLB pitcher -- sat on the family's front porch several times and promised that the club would help fund Dave's college education, he signed with Detroit, only to be drafted by the Phillies a year later. By the time Dave made the majors, he was ready to move on. "I had to make a choice between trying to advance in baseball or pursue a medical career. My stats were not great and even though I felt I had the skills and potential, I felt medicine was the better choice," he explained. Now retired from practice, Watkins continues to reside in Kentucky.

RON STONE

Ron Stone, a fleet-footed outfielder, debuted with the 1966 A's and had his longest run with the Phillies from 1969 to 1972. Yet, his favorite two coaches were Earl Weaver and Cal Ripken, Sr., under whom he played while an Orioles farmhand. He had signed with the birds for a $25,000 bonus.

Stone grew up in northern California in a family with a storied, multi-generational history of military service. Ron served in the Army Reserves and came out of his six-month military stint in remarkable physical shape which carried over to his baseball performance.

His best season was 1970 when he hit .262 in 123 games. Notably, he played most of the 1971 season with three broken ribs, sustained in a collision at second base with Pittsburgh's Bill

Mazeroski. One of his 1972 highlights was delivering the ninth-inning pinch-hit that helped Steve Carlton get his first win as a Phillie.

Ron roomed extensively on road trips with pitcher Chris Short and considered pitcher Woody Fryman a good friend. During the off-seasons, he played basketball with several teammates to stay in shape and sold tickets for the Phillies. In 1972, he was one of 60 athletes to join President Nixon at a White House event aimed at encouraging young people to stay clear of illegal drugs. After baseball, he founded Cascade Dealer Services, a firearms distributor. He now resides in Portland, Oregon.

RICHIE ASHBURN

Center fielder Richie Ashburn played for the Phillies from 1948 to 1959 and represented his team as an all-star four years. He was constantly among the leaders in batting average, walks and on-base percentage. A defensive wizard, he topped NL center fielders in putouts nine times. Ted Williams once said Ashburn had "twin engines."

With the arrival of the Sixties, Ashburn was joining a new team, the Cubs. He was 33 but had more to offer. Although Charlie Grim's 1960 Cubs squad could do no better than seventh place, Ashburn hit .291 and led his league in both walks and on-base percentage.

A year later, the Cubs implemented an experimental management system in which coaches would rotate between assignments managing the parent club and visiting minor-league affiliates. Ashburn, as the team's player representative, acknowledged that the system "could be confusing" but praised the organization as a good one for which to work. And in late May, when the Cubs were off to a slow start, Ashburn and teammate Don Zimmer convened an off-the-record team meeting to allow players to sound off in confidence. Ashburn played part-time as the Cubs again finished seventh.

In 1962, the expansion Mets strategized that the best way to compete with the Yankees in the New York media market was to stock up on well-known personalities. Casey Stengel was brought in as manager. The roster was full of recognizable, veteran names like Gil Hodges, Gene Woodling, Frank Thomas and Don Zimmer.

Ashburn was added to the mix and hit .306 in 135 games. The hapless squad lost a record 120 games but won a broad fan base. Rich was named the team's MVP and the prize was a 24-foot boat, which he docked in Ocean City, New Jersey. Not unlike the Mets, the boat soon sank to the bottom of the waterway.

Ashburn joined the Phillies' broadcast crew in 1963 and spent 35 memorable years in the booth. He was still working as a color analyst at the age of 70 when he passed away in 1997. The Hall of Famer was a lifetime .308 hitter with 29 home runs, 2,574 hits and 234 stolen bases. Few names are better remembered in Philadelphia baseball.

ROBIN ROBERTS

From 1950 to 1955, Robin Roberts may have been the sport's most dominant hurler. The Phillies' right-hander won 138 games, led the league in starts all six years, innings pitched five times, wins four times, and WAR for pitchers five times. Demonstrating immaculate control, he also had the best ratio of walks-to-innings hurled four years. Except for the 1950 NL championship team, he accomplished these fetes on mostly middle-of-the-pack squads.

By 1956, the high workloads had taken their toll. His ERA surged and he led the loop in losses two straight years. Manager Mayo Smith urged him to diversify his pitch repertoire, but the hard-headed Roberts seldom heeded counsel. He continued to pitch for the Phillies, well after Smith was dismissed mid-way through the 1958 season. In 1960, his record was 12-16 and he led the NL in home runs surrendered for the fifth time. Things finally bottomed out in 1961 when Roberts, battling knee trouble, went 1-10 with a 5.85 ERA. He had gradually gone from being the league's best pitcher to the worst.

His contract was purchased by the Yankees after the 1961 season, mostly as an insurance policy in case any of their young pitchers got drafted or sustained injuries. When that didn't happen, the Yankees released him, without him throwing as much as a single regular-season pitch.

The revival came with the Orioles. In a rotation where the other starters were ages 24 or under (Milt Pappas, Steve Barber, Chuck Estrada and Jack Fisher), the 35-year-old Roberts offered a helpful veteran presence. And it wasn't long before Roberts got a chance to show the Yankees what he could still do. On June 11 in the Bronx, Yankees' starter Bud Daley beaned Boog Powell, requiring the rookie slugger to be removed from the field on a stretcher and hospitalized. When it was the Yankees' turn to bat, Roberts' first pitch sailed several feet over Roger Maris' head. Within seconds, players from both teams swarmed the field and police intervention was needed to end the fracas. Roberts got the last laugh, emerging as the game's winning pitcher.

The Meadowbrook, Pennsylvania, resident provided the Birds with three straight winning campaigns from 1962 to 1964. These were, in some ways, among Roberts' most satisfying seasons, as he knew he was contributing long after his peak, and by being in Baltimore, he could return to Philadelphia to see his family.

He finally began to weave curves and change-ups into his mix. Ed Liberatore, a Reds scout who covered AL teams, was quoted in *The Sporting News* in 1962 as saying, "It's hard to believe the way he has been pitching after so many people were saying he was 'washed up.' He can throw as hard as he used to except that he mixes in the other stuff and only pops that good fastball when he has to." Roberts finished the 1962 season with a 2.78 ERA, second best in the AL to Hank Aguirre.

Roberts notched a 14-13 record for Baltimore in 1963 and a 13-7 mark in 1964. In spring training 1965, he told reporters, he shed 16 pounds. (Teammate Luis Aparicio responded that if he lost 16 pounds, he'd be a horse jockey.) The Orioles released Roberts on July 31, 1965, yet after a strong finish with Houston, Roberts ended the year at 10-9 for his fourth straight winning season. He split his final season in 1966 between the Astros and the Cubs.

The Hall of Famer's lifetime record was 286-245 with a 3.41 ERA and 45 shutouts. He struck out 2,357 hitters, and made seven straight all-star teams. Some baseball fans compare his stats to those of Jim Kaat and Tommy John, but they overlook the sheer dominance he displayed for six years in the early Fifties. Roberts was 82 years old when he passed away in Florida in 2010.

JACKIE BRANDT

Baltimore returned to major-league status in 1954 when the St. Louis Browns became the Orioles and took occupancy at Memorial Stadium on 33rd Street in Charm City. But it wasn't until 1960 that the Orioles acquired a capable center fielder. In fact, the Birds traded a pair of solid pitchers in Billy Loes and Billy O'Dell to acquire that center fielder, Jackie Brandt, along with a couple of fringe players.

Brandt was already an established big-leaguer when he arrived at spacious Memorial Stadium. In a 1956 rookie season split between the Cardinals and Giants, he led the league in fielding and hit for a .298 average. The initial word around the sport was that Brandt had a pure swing, could cover plenty of ground in the pastures, but that his sense of humor was off-beat and that he gave off an air of indifference.

He lost the 1957 season to military duty and saw only brief action in 1958. When he returned to the Giants' regular lineup in 1959, he hit .270 and won a gold glove. The Giants were willing to surrender him only because of their need for pitching and their own plethora of flychasers.

The right-handed Brandt had a fair first season for Baltimore in 1960 but his best performance came in 1961 when he made the AL all-star squad. Writing in *The Sporting News,* Doug Brown said Brandt "conceals his intelligence behind a curtain of indifference" and "has the swing of a natural hitter." Brandt spent the first six weeks of the season hitting around .400 and by the season's end, he had delivered the tying or go-ahead run in the late innings 13 times. He finished with a .297 clip, 16 wallops into the seats and 72 RBI.

After insisting on a more lucrative contract for 1962, Jackie won a vote of confidence during spring training from his new Orioles manager, Billy Hitchcock. The skipper designated Brandt as the "captain" of the outfield, responsible for positioning fielders. He added, "Brandt has some real good baseball intelligence. I understand you fellows (reporters) think he's flakey. He has everything it takes to be a top star." Brandt, in turn, vowed to get even better on defense.

He set career highs in homers (19) and RBI (75) for Hitchcock in 1962, though his batting average tumbled by 42 points. He spent three more seasons in Baltimore, hitting about .245 each season. He never achieved the "top star" status that Hitchcock envisioned but was nonetheless productive.

With the 1966 season approaching, the O's traded him to Philadelphia. Brandt batted .250 for the 1966 Phillies, but slumped to .213 in 1967, finishing the year with the Astros, who released him after the season.

On road trips, Brandt enjoyed the camaraderie of roommates Boog Powell with the O's and Dick Groat with the Phillies. For his career, Brandt hit .262 with 112 home runs and 1,020 hits. After baseball, he worked for UPS. Originally from Omaha, Nebraska, he now lives in Wildwood, Florida.

DAVE MCNALLY

Four straight 20-win seasons from 1968 to 1971 made Dave McNally one of the top lefties of his day. During that golden era for the Orioles, McNally had a stunning record of 87-31. The Montana native threw a three-hit shutout against Kansas City in his big-league debut in 1962 at the age of 19. Later, with his team in route to a sweep of the 1966 World Series, Dave hurled a four-hit shutout against the Dodgers. According to Pat Gillick, "Even at 21, he had the moxie of a major-league veteran and the correct 'feel' for pitching."

He was tapped for three all-star games and was the first pitcher ever to win 12 games in a row three different times. His success extended to post-season action, where he was 7-4 with a 2.49 ERA.

After initially living near Memorial Stadium, McNally and his wife moved to Lutherville, Maryland, and he worked at Orioles owner Jerry Hoffberger's brewery during the off-season. To stay in shape, McNally joined up with teammates Brooks Robinson, Bobby Floyd, Dick Hall, Jim Palmer, Eddie Watt and Pete Richert on a basketball squad that squared off against high school faculty teams.

Author Doug Wilson, in his Brooks Robinson biography, wrote, "McNally, who had originally signed with the Orioles for over $70,000, their second largest bonus ever, would become a close friend of Brooks's. Quiet, rarely displaying emotion on the field, McNally did not possess the overall speed or stuff that some of the other pitchers had but he developed into a very smart picher."

McNally was the first Orioles pitcher to earn $100,000 in a season. Executive Frank Cashen remembered him as an extremely dogged negotiator every off-season. The Orioles therefore were not especially surprised when McNally challenged baseball's reserve clause. They were simply happy to have traded him before the 1975 season when his trade value was high, landing outfielder Ken Singleton and pitcher Mike Torrez in return.

After baseball, Dave returned to Montana, where he ran an auto dealership with his brother. He was later named by *Sports Illustrated* as that state's athlete of the century. True to his personality, he waged a long battle with lung and prostate cancer before passing away at age 60.

PAUL BLAIR

The 1966 World Series pitted the defending champion Dodgers against the AL pennant-winning Orioles. To the surprise of many, the Orioles won the first two games. The clubs were locked in a 0-0 tie in the fifth inning of game three, when young Paul Blair delivered a solo homer against Claude Osteen. His blast accounted for the only scoring, giving Baltimore a three-games-to-none edge.

Osteen said after the game, "It was a fastball outside, right where I wanted it. He just jumped all over it." Blair had homered only six times during the season, during which he shared centerfield duties with Russ Snyder.

One game later, Jim Lefebvre of the Dodgers hit a shot that looked likely to be an extra-base hit. The 22-year-old Blair made a superb running catch, preserving another 1-0 win and the world championship for the Orioles.

That Series captured Blair's skill set – a two-way player who won games with his offense and defense. Nicknamed "Motormouth," the confident young player was the life of every room he entered. During the off-season, he sold sporting goods at Montgomery Wards during the day and made public relations appearances for the Orioles at night. He was a natural for both roles.

Blair had grown up in Los Angeles with hopes of playing for the Dodgers, but when they showed little interest, he signed with the Mets. Left unprotected after one season, the Orioles drafted him and never regretted it.

Blair played a short center field, which reduced the risk of hits falling in front of him, and relied on his speed and agility to race back and snare most anything hit over his head. Watching the two-time all-star make spectacular plays was one of the joys of following Orioles baseball at Memorial Stadium during that glorious era in Baltimore. He won eight gold gloves over 17 years.

Offensively, Paul was fifth in the AL in hitting with a .293 clip in 1967 and first in triples. After an off-year in 1968, his best season came in 1969, when he hit .285, launched 26 home runs and pilfered 20 bases. He paced the AL in sacrifice bunts, as well.

On May 31, 1970, Blair was hit by a Ken Tatum pitch that broke his nose, cheek bone and orbital bone below his eye. Pitchers thereafter sensed he was gun-shy about inside pitches. Blair disputed the notion, arguing that he hit .474 just four months later in the 1970 World Series. While his offense fluctuated over the years to come, his defense never wavered.

In all, Blair won four World Series rings. His lifetime average was .250 with 134 home runs and 171 stolen bases. Former teammate Don Buford reflected, "He played with assuredness. When you talk about the greatest defensive center fielders, he is right in the mix." Frank Robinson said, "He was to the outfield what Brooks Robinson was to the infield. He was our glue out there." Robinson added, "He was a great guy to have on the ballclub. He kept you loose. He was always talking. He loved the game."

Blair later made his home in suburban Baltimore and was married to his second wife, Gloria, for 42 years. Active in sports right up to the day he passed away at age 69, he had golfed in the morning, and was participating in a celebrity bowling match in the evening when he lost consciousness. Blair was a 1984 inductee to the Orioles Hall of Fame.

JIM PALMER

Jim Palmer's illustrious career began on May 16, 1965, when the 19-year-old not only beat the Yankees, but slugged a two-run homer to help seal the victory. Sixteen months later, he became the youngest pitcher to win a World Series game, delivering a master class in pitching by shutting out the Dodgers in game two of the 1966 fall classic.

Palmer was one of the game's most promising pitchers until he tore his rotator cuff, costing him much of the 1967 season. Recovering without surgery, he saw minimal minor-league action in 1968 and went undrafted by the two AL expansion clubs.

In early 1969, he pitched winter ball in Puerto Rico, trying a pain-killing drug called Indocin that he remembered pitchers Wally Bunker and Mike McCormick had taken. He pitched largely pain-free, returned to the States, and worked out at a YMCA. When the season opened, he reclaimed a spot in the rotation. Despite missing 41 days due to back trouble, he went 16-4, good for a league-best winning percentage. And on August 13, he fired a no-hitter against the A's (though teammate Frank Robinson, judge of the team's kangaroo court, amusingly fined him after the game for a base-running gaffe).

Palmer went into the post-season as the Birds' number-three starter behind Dave McNally and Mike Cuellar. "Once you've had an arm problem," he told reporters during the 1969 World

Series, "you always think of it and you never know when your career can be in jeopardy." He picked up a win over Minnesota in the ALCS but lost his only start to the Mets in the Series.

From 1970 to 1978, Jim won 20 games eight times. He pitched through 1984, winning 268 games with a sterling 2.82 ERA. Remarkable for someone with a history of shoulder trouble, he led the AL in innings pitched four times, and won the Cy Young Award three times. A Hall of Famer, author of three books and former color commentator, Palmer makes his residence in Corona Del Mar, California.

LUIS ALCARAZ

In any era, the vast majority of minor league players never reach the big leagues, and for many years, it looked as if that would be the fate of infielder Luis Alcaraz. A native of Puerto Rico, he signed with the Braves in 1959, and commenced his career with the McCook Braves in the final year of the old Nebraska State League. Five players from that team eventually made the show, including Phil Niekro.

Alcaraz refused to give up on baseball, and every off-season he worked on his hitting with Orlando Cepeda, a boyhood friend and Puerto Rico neighbor. Finally, in 1967, now a part of the Dodgers organization, Alcaraz won the Texas League batting crown at Double-A Albuquerque as well as the George M. Trautman trophy. The honor was named for Trautman, who was president of the National Professional Baseball Leagues for 16 years.

Intrigued by this 26-year-old dark horse prospect, Dodgers Manager Walt Alston played Alcaraz during the final weeks of the 1967 season, and he hit .233 in 60 at bats. The Dodgers were not in contention for the first time in five years, which opened up the opportunity to play some youngsters. Alcaraz had finally reached the majors and his next goal was to stay there.

In 1968, the Dodgers marked out a role for Alcaraz as a reserve infielder, but his bat failed. He hit only .151 with two home runs in 41 contests. After the season, his contract was sold to the expansion Royals.

Alcaraz saw action for Kansas City in both 1969 and 1970. He was one of three Puerto Rican players on the inaugural Royals club, alongside Jackie Hernandez and Ellie Rodriguez. This was an unusual concentration of Puerto Rican players, as Alcaraz was only the 30th player from the island to break into the major leagues.

In 1971, the Royals traded him to the White Sox for veteran second baseman Bobby Knoop. Alcaraz played in the minor leagues thereafter in the White Sox, Braves, and Pirates systems and later played in Mexico through 1980.

HARMON KILLEBREW

While promoting his book on a radio program in the early 1970s, slugger Harmon Killebrew was asked about his batting average by a youthful caller. Killebrew confessed he had never hit much for average. In fact, in 1962, he set the major league record for the lowest average ever by an RBI champion, hitting only .243.

But he needed to make no apologies, as he was a spectacular run producer. Striking fear into the hearts of pitchers who often chose to pitch around him, he had a disciplined batting eye, and led the AL in walks four times. His 1,559 career bases on balls are still among the all-time leaders.

Home run power was his forte. A six-time home run champion, he slugged 573 homers. When he retired in 1975, he was fifth on the all-time list, trailing only Hank Aaron, Babe Ruth, Willie Mays and Frank Robinson.

In 1964, Killebrew reached the 40-homer mark for the fourth straight time. He was only the fifth player to do that, following Ruth, Ralph Kiner, Duke Snider, and Ernie Banks.

He also made time to spend in the community. On the morning of May 20, 1964 in New York, he visited an eight-year-old boy named John Guiney who was hospitalized with burns after his robe caught fire while lighting church candles. "Who knows, maybe I'll hit you a couple," he told the youngster. That afternoon, with John watching on television, Harmon indeed slugged a pair of home runs.

Tape-measure homers were almost the norm, as Killebrew authored some of the longest blasts on record at Minnesota's Metropolitan Stadium, Baltimore's Memorial Stadium, and Detroit's Tiger Stadium.

Defensively, he was chiefly a corner infielder, but he also saw action in the outfield, second base, and late in his career as a DH. He never balked at changing positions.

Harmon said the toughest pitcher for him was the one who probably threw the slowest, reliever Stu Miller. Stu was exceptional at changing speeds, keeping hitters off-balance with a deceptive pitching motion.

The son of a pro football player, Killebrew grew up in Idaho where he worked as a farmhand. He starred in four sports in high school and became famous throughout the state. He originally planned to attend the University of Oregon with a football and baseball scholarship. Idaho Senator Herman Welker, it is said, told Washington Senators owner Clark Griffith to check out Killebrew. Scout Ossie Bleuge did so and signed the youngster with an appropriate bonus.

Six different times, he led the AL in homers. The Killer missed the last half of the 1968 season following an injury in the all-star game. When he returned in 1969, he was nearly impossible to stop. He led the league in homers (49), RBI (140), walks (145), and on-base percentage (.427). In that first year of divisional play, the Twins roared to a 97-65 record. During the ALCS, the Orioles prevailed in three straight games, pitching around Harmon extensively. The following year, the same two clubs connected for a championship series rematch. This time, Killebrew crushed a pair of home runs, but the Orioles again swept the series.

An 11-time all-star, he spent his entire career with the Senators-Twins organizations, save for his 1975 season with the Royals. He was elected to the Hall of Fame in 1984. "Harmon was a Hall of Famer on and off the field," said former teammate Joe Nossek. "He always had kind words and good advice for the rookies and he was one of my all-time favorite people." While inducting Harmon into the Hall of Fame, commissioner Bowie Kuhn emphasized his character.

When the 1975 season ended, Harmon flew to Minnesota and asked owner Calvin Griffith to name him Twins manager, as skipper Frank Quilici had just been let go. The owner said he wanted someone who had managed in the minor leagues. Later, the Rangers offered him a chance to manage, but he declined, preferring to remain a color commentator, and to remain focused on his insurance and auto-dealership businesses.

Over the years, he raised millions of dollars for charities. He retired for good in Scottsdale and passed away in 2011 of esophageal cancer. Upon his death, the Twins issued a statement, noting, "No individual has ever meant more to the Minnesota Twins organization and millions of fans across Twins territory than Harmon Killebrew."

ZOILO VERSALLES

This popular shortstop played an instrumental role in the Twins winning the pennant in 1965. He led the AL in doubles, triples, total bases and runs scored and won the gold glove (though he made 39 errors). The Twins lost to the Dodgers in the World Series, but following the season, he was named the league's MVP.

Versalles was the first player not born in the U.S. to win the honor. Some baseball historians have said that others were more deserving – suggesting Tony Oliva, Brooks Robinson or Rocky Colavito. But none of those stars would have been a clear choice either. Following the season, Zoilo's salary nearly doubled to $40,000.

Contrary to popular perception, Zoilo was no one-year wonder. The Cuban-born star was in the Twins' daily lineup from 1961 to 1967, led the AL in triples three straight years and was tapped for two all-star teams. In the all-star game in Cleveland in 1963, he reached base in all three plate appearances.

His offensive production plunged during a 1966 season plagued first by the flu and later by lower back trouble. By 1967, his batting average declined all the way to .200. Coupled with lackluster fielding, his days with the Twins were numbered.

Zoilo loved the Twin Cities and felt even more at home once his older brother Lazaro joined him and his wife in Minnesota. Though often described as moody, Zoilo was very devoted to the Twins. He was working at a team promotional appearance after the 1967 season when he received the news that he had been traded to the Dodgers. It's not an exaggeration to say that the trade left him broken-hearted.

Thereafter, he mostly bounced around as property of the Dodgers, Padres, Indians, Senators and Braves through 1971. He played three more seasons in Japan and Mexico.

Zoilo remained in Minnesota thereafter, but suffered from heart attacks, financial troubles and home foreclosures. He separated from his wife as well as his children and lived off his baseball pension. He was found dead, likely of heart trouble, in 1995 at the age of 55. Eleven years later, the Twins inducted him into the team's hall of fame.

EARL BATTEY

Rifle-armed catcher Earl Battey won three gold glove awards with the Twins. He was the starting catcher on the 1965 Twins pennant club, providing leadership on the field and humor in the clubhouse. In a career that lasted until 1967, he hit 104 home runs and compiled a solid .270 lifetime batting average.

Growing up in California, both of Battey's parents played competitive baseball. In a June 1961 *Baseball Digest* cover story, he said he was offered contracts by every team except the Yankees, Indians, and A's. He signed with the White Sox and was on their 1959 pennant squad but was soon traded to the Senators in a deal for slugger Roy Sievers.

Battey immediately captured a starting job in 1960 and was in the top 10 in MVP voting. When the Senators moved to the Twin Cities in 1961, he had another solid year, batting a career-high .302.

Battey made the all-star team for the first of four times in 1962, but put up even better numbers in 1963, with 25 home runs and a .285 batting average. Around this time, there was a rumor that Battey would be traded to Cleveland for Joe Azcue, a younger catcher who produced some lofty numbers early in his career. But the rumors proved unfounded, and Battey remained with the Twins for the balance of his career.

In the 1965 World Series, Battey caught all seven games, and hit just .120 with two RBI. But without his .297 batting average and solid pitch-calling during the regular season, the Twins likely would not have reached the fall classic at all.

Earl led the league in assists several times. Corner infielders needed to be alert, since he never hesitated to attempt to gun down baserunners straying from the bag. Battey also spoke Spanish, which enhanced his ability to communicate with Latino hurlers.

Battey was personable, approachable and popular with teammates and their families. Teammate Jim Kaat remembered, "When we flew in from a road trip, my son would be there, and he would gravitate toward Earl."

Starting in 1963, Battey worked part-time for General Mills, promoting physical fitness. According to a company blog written by Jim Thielman on July 14, 2014, "He was eloquent, and had his own radio show when he played for the Washington Senators before the franchise moved to Minnesota in 1961. He joined Consolidated Edison after he retired from baseball in 1967 and helped the power company's baseball community relations program in New York." He later earned a degree and worked as a baseball coach.

During the civil rights era, Battey stood firm for what he believed. In 1962, the Twins were the only team still segregating their white and black players during spring training in Florida. Battey brought the issue to the attention of the Minnesota State Commission on Discrimination, which intervened. That same 1962 season, the all-star game was held in the new stadium in Washington, D.C. Newspapers around the country ran a photo of Battey shaking hands with President Kennedy at the start of the game.

Battey retains a prominent spot in Twins' history. In a 2017 article on a website called Twins Trivia, he was rated the third-best catcher in team history, after Joe Mauer and Butch Wynegar. Lefthander Jim Merritt, who had an 11-year MLB career and went on to become a 20-game winner, recently said, "Earl helped me a lot. He and Johnny Bench were the greatest catchers I worked with."

A native of the Watts area of Los Angeles, Battey devoted countless hours to working with at-risk kids. He passed away at age 68 due to cancer in 2003 in Gainesville, Florida, leaving behind a large family. His brother-in-law, Ed Sanders, was an Olympian boxer.

MUDCAT GRANT

By the time Jim Grant made his major league debut in 1958, his reputation as a prospect preceded him. The youngster had spent four years in the Indians farm system, winning 70 games and losing only 28 times. His best pitch, the fastball, was dubbed the "comet ball." He was considered one of the best young arms in the sport.

Grant grew up in a segregated town in Florida, west of Orlando, and followed the news about Jackie Robinson and Larry Doby integrating baseball as he delivered newspapers throughout his neighborhood. Through this experience, Grant developed pride in the African American players who came before him.

At age 18, Grant signed an Indians contract offered by scout Fred Merkle, who was infamous for the "Merkle's boner" baserunning mistake in 1908. Grant was still only 22 years old when he toed the rubber for his first major league start in 1958. Fewer than 3,000 fans were on hand at Municipal Stadium on a Thursday afternoon in April for his debut, but Grant made it memorable, going the distance for a 3-2 win over the A's. He posted a 10-11 record that rookie season.

His roommate that season was none other than Doby. It was at first awkward to room with his boyhood hero, but they became close friends. Through Doby, Grant got to meet many of the era's great entertainers at night spots in Cleveland, New York and Washington. These included the likes of Duke Ellington, Count Basie, Sarah Vaughan and Moms Mabley. Years later, Grant himself would become a night club entertainer.

Baseball fans were not Grant's only followers. One morning when the Indians were in Detroit, President John Kennedy invited him to breakfast, where they discussed segregation and civil rights. It turns out that the President, too, was a fan.

Grant had experienced segregation and discrimination first-hand, and had deeply held convictions about racial inequality, which he did not hesitate to voice. Late in the 1960 season, as the National Anthem was concluding before a game, following the words "The land of the free and the home of the brave," it's said that Grant sang, "as long as you're white." The bullpen coach, Ted Wilks, took offense and harsh words were exchanged, including an offensive racial epitaph by Wilks.

According to reports at the time, Wilks apologized to Grant (and to teammate Don Newcombe, who was also there), but Grant refused Wilks' apology, left the stadium without permission, and was not used for the rest of the season. But he was back with Cleveland in 1961 and won 15 games.

In 1964, the Indians, eager to shed salary expenses, traded Grant mid-season to the Twins. A year later, Grant won 21 contests for Minnesota, helping the Twins to the AL pennant, despite tendonitis in his knees. He won game six of the World Series, forcing a seventh game that the Dodgers ultimately won.

After his big season, Grant publicly requested a $50,000 salary for 1966. Tight-fisted Twins owner Cal Griffith publicly replied, "If he asks for $50,000, let him stay in the entertainment field, because he's not going to get it. I read that he's booked through August with his nightclub act. Let's see how long he stays booked if he doesn't play baseball." Grant ultimately signed for something closer to $35,500 which then was still a healthy salary.

Grant pitched .500 ball in 1966, and following a poor season in 1967, he was sent to the Dodgers. It was a good move for Grant, who had a fine year out the bullpen (despite feuding with coach Lefty Phillips) and eventually made the LA area his permanent home. He also experienced success in 1970 for Oakland and Pittsburgh, posting an 8-3 record, 24 saves, and a 1.86 ERA.

After failing to make the Indians' roster out of spring training in 1972, Grant moved on to a post-baseball career that included sportscasting and night club performances as Mudcat and the Kittens. He also sang with the Count Basie and Duke Ellington orchestras. After former teammate Harmon Killebrew died in 2011, Grant sang "What a Wonderful World" in his memory at Target Field.

In his later years, he attended autograph shows, and wrote a book, *The Black Aces,* about African American pitchers who achieved 20 or more wins in a season. In 2008, on the 50th anniversary of his MLB debut, he threw out the first pitch at Progressive Field and was presented Cleveland's "key to the city." He received an honorary doctorate of letters degree from Whittier College in 2016. Grant was 85 years of age when he passed away in Los Angeles in 2021.

Mudcat was back in the news in 2023. Shohei Ohtani had just started a game on the mound, homered and stole a base. The last player to have done that was Mudcat, way back in 1964.

JIM KAAT

Jim Kaat pitched in two different World Series, 17 years apart. In 1965, Jim beat Sandy Koufax in game two, but lost to Sandy in games five and seven, as the Twins were blanked in both losses. Then in 1982, the 43-year-old lefty came on in relief in four contests as his Cardinals topped the Brewers in seven games.

Jim grew up in rural Zeeland, Michigan, down the street from the Mead Johnson chemical plant. He inherited his dad's love of baseball and when the Braves relocated to Milwaukee, he became a Braves fan. Jim pitched for Zeeland High School and then for Hope College, where he caught the eye of Senators super scout Dick Weincek (who signed 72 major leaguers including four Hall of Famers). The White Sox tendered a $25,000 offer but Kaat's dad, knowing that the larger offer would have required his son to catch splinters on the Sox bench for two years due to the bonus rule, convinced him to take the lesser offer, so he could continue refining his craft in the minor leagues.

After signing in 1957, Jim spent the 1958 season in Class C ball in Missoula, Montana, rooming with outfielder Sandy Valdespino. He told *The Minneapolis Star Tribune* in 2023, "I was six-foot-five and white as snow and Sandy was five-foot-six and a black guy in Montana 65 years ago. We made quite the pair strolling down the streets of Missoula. We were joined at the hip that summer. They had prizes for the home players at the ballpark. Sandy was our leadoff hitter, and if you scored the first run of the game, you'd get a Stockman's pizza. And if a pitcher struck out 10, you'd get two sundaes at the Dairy Queen. Both free pizza and a trip to the Dairy Queen the same night. That was our goal all summer."

In 1959, Kaat bought his first car – a green 1954 Plymouth coupe – and made his MLB debut. He stayed with the team as it relocated to Minnesota (becoming the Twins) in 1961.

Surprisingly for a guy with 283 career victories, Kaat made only three all-star teams. One was in 1962, when at age 23 he enjoyed an 18-14 season. He was still battling wildness and led the league in hit batsmen and wild pitches.

The Twins won the AL pennant in 1965. The Yankees had captured the flag the previous five years, but Kaat's road roommate, pitcher Johnny Klippstein, had been a member of the 1959 Dodgers championship club, and he told everyone on the team that the Twins had the talent to prevail. Jim had a solid year in 1965, but Mudcat Grant was the team's real ace with 21 wins. Kaat's weight had ballooned from 210 to 240 pounds, and the kicker came when a photographer joked that he would need to use a wide-angle lens. That got Jim's attention…and prompted him to lose weight. That winter, he played handball four times a week and cut back his typical dinner to just one steak, two baked potatoes and a large salad.

His best year followed in 1966, with 25 wins, 304 innings and 19 complete games, all league highs, as the Twins placed second in the AL. After the season, Twins manager Sam Mele said he could no longer work with pitching coach Johnny Sain, prompting Sain and bullpen coach Hal Naragon to join the Tigers. Kaat denounced the team for allowing Sain to leave. Over the next five years, Kaat was steady but less spectacular, going 71-62.

Jim's 1967 season ended on a frustrating note. He had 16 wins heading into the Twins' second-to-last game, with Minnesota leading Boston by one game in the battle for the pennant. Jim hurt his left elbow in the third inning and headed for the trainer's room. The Red Sox won that game and the next one, clinching the pennant.

After the Twins endured an unusually mediocre 1968 season under disciplinarian manager Cal Ermer, the club hired the fiery Billy Martin to manage in 1969. The team fired on all eight cylinders, winning 97 games. Kaat appreciated that Martin did not force the pitchers to do a lot of pre-game running, and that he gave the starting pitchers a long leash. However, he didn't appreciate Martin's second-guessing or periodic dishonesty. Although the Twins won the division that year, Martin was involved in some off-the-field incidents (see entry on Bob Allison) and was sent packing after the season.

Kaat won 14 games in 1970 and 13 in 1971 but became aggravated with the Twins' practice of cutting his salary each season. Jim got off to a blazing start in 1972 but missed half the season to a wrist injury, finishing with a 10-2 record. He spent the rest of the season at home, away from the team.

In spring training 1973, Kaat held out for $60,000 (well above the $46,000 the team offered) and eventually, the Twins gave in. Kaat won the battle but the relationship with the team was permanently damaged. They exposed Kaat on the waiver wire later that summer, and he was snared by Chicago, where pitching coach Johnny Sain helped him re-establish himself as a star for the White Sox. The next two years, he reached the 20-win plateau, now using a quick-pitch, slide-step approach that kept hitters off balance. He was an all-star again in 1975.

Jim later pitched for the Phillies, Yankees and Cardinals, retiring at age 44. His lifetime record was 283-237 with a 3.45 ERA and 31 shutouts. He struck out 2,461 batters and won 16 gold glove awards. According to Kaat, from 1961 to 1975, he was first in MLB in wins, second in complete games and third in strikeouts.

"Jim's work ethic had a good influence on all of the young players," Twins teammate Joe Nossek later recalled.

Kaat worked a couple of winters for the St. Petersburg recreation department, and in the mid-Sixties began broadcasting high school basketball games and co-hosting radio shows in Minneapolis. After serving as the Reds' pitching coach for two years under Pete Rose, he became an acclaimed baseball color commentator. A resident of Blue Diamond, Nevada, he was a 2022 inductee to the Hall of Fame.

RED WORTHINGTON

Those who remember Al Worthington as the Twins' relief ace in the mid-Sixties may not realize the challenges he faced getting to that point. One of three brothers from Birmingham who played professional baseball, Al became the only one to reach MLB in 1954 with the Giants. In his first two starts, he blanked the Phillies and the Dodgers. Though he did not pitch in the World Series, he considered it a thrill to witness Willie Mays' famous catch of Vic Wertz's long drive.

That initial success was followed by a series of struggles to remain in the major leagues. By the time the Giants announced their upcoming move from New York to San Francisco, Al's lifetime record was just 19-35 when not assigned back to the minor leagues. He did not register a winning season with the parent club until 1958 when he went 11-7. Giants manager Bill Rigney used him as a long reliever and spot starter.

One night in 1958 changed his life forever. Al and his wife attended a Billy Graham crusade at the Cow Palace in San Francisco and became born-again Christians. That decision shaped his world view thereafter and gave him the faith to endure whatever challenges were to come his way.

Over time, there were new hurdles. He had a respectable season for the Giants in 1959, notable for his courage in confronting Rigney about reports that the team had a man with binoculars in the stands, stealing opponents' signs. Al understood that sign stealing was part of the game, but believed that using binoculars was cheating and at odds with Christian values. To Rigney's credit, the skipper agreed to put a stop to the practice.

During the 1960 season, Al got off to a terrible start with the Reds and was sent over to the White Sox. Al again received reports of sign-stealing using binoculars. This time, manager Al Lopez and general manager Hank Greenberg essentially communicated that what the team did to gain a competitive advantage was none of Worthington's business. Exercising great faith and courage with a wife and children to support, Al returned home to Alabama, took a part-time job, and resumed his studies.

He didn't make it back to the big leagues until 1963 with the Reds, who discovered that Worthington was a better pitcher when used exclusively in relief. Early in the 1964 season, the *Saturday Evening Post* ran an article titled, "A Bible in the Bullpen," in which author John Devaney wrote that Worthington would never be a star. How wrong he was.

Following an early-season 1964 trade to the Twins, Red had a knock-out season, registering a 1.37 ERA in 41 outings. In 1965, his 10 wins and 21 saves helped the Twins to the pennant. He credited his pitching coach for his success, telling *The Sporting News,* "No man alive knows more about that little baseball and how to throw it than Johnny Sain." Al pitched four scoreless innings in the fall classic, in which Minnesota was bested by the Dodgers.

As late as 1968, at the age of 39, Worthington led the AL in saves and registered his fifth-straight season with an ERA below 3.00. Though he retired after the season, he agreed to return to the Twins in May 1969 for one final tour of duty. After retiring for good, he sold insurance, served as Minnesota's pitching coach, and then coached baseball at Lynchburg Baptist University, where he became athletic director. But if you ask Worthington, his most important vocation has been to continue to spread the gospel of Jesus Christ by speaking to youth groups and in mailings back to those requesting autographs by Mail. Now in his 90s, he continues to reside in Birmingham.

ROD CAREW

Rod Carew was born in a railroad car in Panama and as a young boy listened to ballgames on the Armed Forces Radio broadcast, dreaming of being a major league player. His father, a painter for the Panama Canal, was so mean-spirited that his mother sent Rod to live with family members in Manhattan. "The first time I flew into New York, I was a nervous, excited 15-year-old kid," he would later say.

The youngster was playing ball in New York when a bird-dog scout for the Twins, Herb Stein, arranged for a tryout during the club's next visit to Yankee Stadium. All it took was one visit for Twins manager Sam Mele to advise the club to sign the youngster to a contract.

Three years later, in 1967, Carew made his big-league debut. He got a hit against Dave McNally in his first at-bat, and eventually won the rookie of the year award, hitting a solid .292. His game was still raw; for example, he was successful on only five of 14 stolen base attempts. His defense left much to be desired. But he made the all-star team, as he would for an incredible 18 years in a row.

"He can do it all," Twins owner Calvin Griffith exclaimed that spring. "He can run, throw and hit. He has some growing up to do, but it looks like he has made some great strides." The Twins that season had one of the highest payrolls in baseball, but they also had the best bargain with Carew on a rookie salary.

Rod was swinging for the fences as a rookie, but Griffith advised him to just get on base. The Twins had plenty of power hitters, the owner counseled, and what they needed most was a great table setter.

In 1968, Carew showed substantial improvement on the base paths and credited first base coach George Case (a former Senators speedster himself). "Last year I was involved in a lot of mix-ups on the bases," Carew reflected. "That was because I was running with my head down and wasn't picking up the signs from Billy Martin at third. I think I'm getting a better jump. George has been keeping me farther from the base, instead of staying close."

By 1969, Carew won his first batting title, while setting the table for a Twins team that won the AL West. He seldom slumped until the post-season, when the Orioles' staff mostly shut him down during the ALCS sweep.

One of baseball's most exciting plays is the steal of home and that season, Carew stole home seven times, tying Pete Reiser's big-league record. Usually, manager Billy Martin would signal him to run. On at least one occasion, with California's Tom Murphy on the mound, Carew took off from third base on his own. The batter, Harmon Killebrew, didn't realize Carew was approaching until the last moment, and fortunately, he did not swing. "Rod could have been a double down the left field line if Harmon had swung," Martin mused.

Carew was off to a fantastic start again in 1970, when he collided with a base-runner, Mike Hegan of the Brewers, near second base. He missed most of the season, finishing with a .366 batting average in limited action.

From 1972 to 1978, Carew was the league's leading hitter every season save for 1976, when he finished a close third behind George Brett and Hal McRae of the Royals. Though he never hit .400, Carew flirted with that mark all through the 1977 season, sparking speculation that he might get there. In fact, his quest was the talk of baseball that season. He ultimately finished at .388, the highest mark the sport had seen since Ted Williams hit for the same average in 1957.

Carew was traded only once -- to the Angels in 1979. Baseball's economics had changed due to free agency, and the Twins were operating as if the change had not occurred. Money was the primary reason Rod was traded, coupled with the star's desire to play for a contending team. The Angels captured the AL West crown in Carew's first and fourth seasons in Anaheim.

While playing for the Angels, Carew had a tense relationship with manager Jim Fregosi. Rod observed Fregosi making snide remarks about his contributions to the team and chalked it up to a play that had occurred years earlier, when Fregosi was the Angels' shortstop. On that play, Carew slid into second base, spikes high, and both Fregosi and second baseman Bobby Knoop took offense. In Carew's Hall of Fame induction speech, he recognized former managers and team owners Billy Martin, Calvin Griffith, Gene Mauch, and Gene Autry, but did not reference Fregosi.

Carew played until 1985, and was still a .280 hitter, albeit with no power. The Angels opted not to bring him back, and no other team made an offer. Carew, one of the game's all-time legends, was out of work, and angry about his status.

Over time, his bitterness faded, and the lifetime .328 hitter was mostly smiles when he was inducted into the Hall of Fame. "That's one of the great things about this country," he said of the United States. "You can achieve what you set out to do."

TED BOWSFIELD

Pitcher Ted Bowsfield remembers the 1950s and 1960s as "the best of times for baseball." He was a major leaguer from 1958 to 1964 and later enjoyed a career in sports facilities management. He loved both careers.

As a ballplayer, Ted was unusual in several ways. He threw lefty and batted righty, which he said came about naturally. He was a native of Pentincton, British Columbia, where hockey and basketball were the more popular sports. He also met Fidel Castro, who had pistols mounted on both hips, when Ted was a member of the Minneapolis Millers in Havana to play the Sugar Kings in the American Association playoffs. The Sugar Kings won game seven of the series, and it was the last NABPL-sanctioned baseball game in Cuba for decades to come.

Ted posted a 4-2 record for the Red Sox as a rookie in 1958, rooming on the road with a fellow freshman, Bill Monbouquette. Ted called Red Sox owner Tom Yawkey "a very nice man and a great owner." His best years came with the Angels in 1961 and 1962, when he recorded marks of 11-8 and 9-8, while rooming with all-star pitcher Ken McBride. His favorite manager was

Bill Rigney with the Angels. Ted also pitched for the Indians and A's and retired in 1965 with a 37-39 record and a 4.35 ERA along with four shutouts.

A resident of California, golf has continued to be his favorite pastime. He remembers Albie Pearson and Del Rice being the best golfers among the many baseball men with whom he walked the course.

ALBIE PEARSON

Standing five-foot-five, outfielder Albie Pearson overcame tremendous odds to excel at a game where literally everyone was taller and heavier. He hit .270 in a nine-year career with the Senators, Orioles and Angels. Key achievements included winning the rookie of the year award in 1958 with Washington, leading the AL in runs scored in 1962 as a member of the Angels, and representing that club in the all-star team in 1963, when he hit. 304. "He wasn't big, but he played huge and was a good teammate," commented pitcher Ted Bowsfield.

Albie's performance nosedived in 1964, with his batting average dropping about 80 points. How to explain the drop-off? Angels general manager Fred Haney said after the season, "He hurt his elbow soon after spring training started last season and he began to worry. Then, like he says, he began to try too hard when things didn't go his way." Haney added, "Albie's a born competitor and has a lot of pride," noting he expected a strong comeback.

Things started poorly in 1965 as he injured his hand punching a heckler in Palm Springs (a rare act of losing his temper), soon followed by an inner ear infection. But in time, Haney proved right, as Pearson's batting average rebounded to .278. Pearson spent the off-season selling Angels' season tickets on commission, making the calls from his country club home in Riverside, about 20 miles from the club's new park in Anaheim. He also lifted hand weights that winter to strengthen his wrists and hands.

Pearson took some time out during the 1966 spring training to play, once again, in the Baseball Players Golf Tournament in Miami. After winning the tourney in 1958 and in 1965, he placed an impressive fourth this time, trailing only Ken Harrelson, Ralph Terry and Davey Johnson.

Going into the 1966 season, Pearson was 30 years old, and knew the Angels would be taking a long look at young outfielders Jose Cardenal, Ed Kirkpatrick, and Rick Reichardt. But nothing could have prepared him for what happened next. During a spring intrasquad game, he injured his back while sliding and required hospitalization for traction treatments.

In July, he got into a pair of games before the Angels offered him two options. One was to retain his salary (estimated at $33,000) but play at the Triple-A level. The other was to accept an unconditional release, with an invitation to the 1967 spring training as a non-roster invitee. Pearson opted for the release.

He intended to try out for the 1967 Angels, but aborted his comeback when he realized he had "lost two or three steps." He also abandoned hope of becoming a golf pro, noting that his drives were no longer as powerful. The loss of income forced Pearson, his wife and four daughters to sell their lovely Riverside home and move into more modest accommodations. He publicly thanked Angels fans, manager Bill Rigney, his family and especially God "for showing simple belief, you can be a winner forever."

Albie's disciplined personal life stood in contrast to many of his teammates. Infielder Paul Schaal once said, "I think Albie Pearson was the only player on the team who wasn't a serious drinker and carouser."

Pearson signed on with the Yankees as a California-based scout and in 1968 became general manager of the Hesperia Golf and Country Club. But he ultimately answered to a higher calling. According to an article in *The Orange County Register,* Pearson became an ordained minister, set up churches and orphanages in the U.S., Ecuador and Zambia, and opened Father's Heart Ranch, a refuge for abused and neglected children with 35 employees. He died in 2023 at the age of 88.

DON LEE

What was more difficult in the Sixties – to reach the major leagues or to stay there?

Righthander Don Lee, whose MLB career spanned from 1957 to 1966, was asked that question in 2022. Lee pitched for the Tigers, Senators, Twins, Angels, Astros and Cubs.

"For me, it was harder to stay there," he noted. "I made the Tigers out of spring training in 1957 after just two months in A-ball in Augusta." That was a light-speed advancement to the majors, but Lee was soon demoted, and saw minor league-action in five of the next 10 seasons.

Though Don grew up in Arizona, he was no stranger to big-league parks. His dad was Thornton Lee, a venerable, longtime pitcher from the 1930s and 1940s, mostly with the ChiSox. "I was at the ballpark all the time after age six or seven," he recalled. "I had a real White Sox uniform so I could get on the field during batting practice."

Thornton Lee had been a college man and insisted that his son also have at least two years of college education before signing a pro contract. Demonstrating tremendous potential, Don received contract offers from 15 teams – every club except the Reds. Don agreed to terms with the Tigers, whose scout, former infielder Marv Owen, had been a teammate of his father.

Both a starter and reliver, Don's best season was 1962 with the Angels, when he posted an 8-8 record. He stayed with the Angels through1965 and recalls catcher Bob Rodgers as "a very sound player who called a good game." Lee says in his experience, the catcher and pitcher always called the pitches, never anyone on the bench. Don's lifetime record was 40-44 with a 3.61 ERA. He continues to reside in Tucson.

CHARLIE DEES

Charlie Dees was a tall and slender first baseman born in Birmingham and raised in Chicago. He demonstrated the ability to hit .300 in the minor league ranks and showed some power, setting a modern Texas League record with four straight homers for the Double-A El Paso Sun Kings against Amarillo in 1962. Appreciative fans rained $79 in small bills and pocket change onto the field in appreciation. His team, which also included future big leaguers Jesus Alou and Cap Peterson, captured the pennant, and Dees won the batting crown. Charlie was also voted his team's most popular player, winning a transistor radio from a local appliance shop.

Sold by the Giants to the Angels after the season, the surprise came when the 27-year-old rookie proved he could hit .300 at the MLB level, as well. In 60 games, he batted .307 with a solid .777 OPS. His Achilles Heel was his questionable defensive play at first base.

Over the next two years, he moved to the outfield and spent extensive time in the minors, while struggling in very small sample sizes with the Angels in 1964 and 1965. Then in May 1966, he sustained a broken elbow from a pitch thrown by Pete Craig, putting him in a cast for three weeks. After hitting only .240 for El Paso that summer, his career drew to a close. He was a .265 lifetime hitter.

JIM HICKS

Outfielder Jim Hicks grew up in East Chicago, Illinois, where his pastimes were fixing old cars, listening to progressive jazz, and playing baseball. He called Pete Rucinski, his UI Champagne-Urbana baseball coach, "the greatest man I've ever known," because "He took me off the streets and made me an athlete. I guess you could say I was on the road to becoming a hoodlum at that time."

Hicks labored in the White Sox farm system from 1959 to 1967, with only brief tastes of MLB life. It took a toll on his psyche. "You can't play one day and then sit out two weeks and expect to be any good," he told writer John Ferguson. Some winters he played in Nicaragua and others he devoted to completing his college degree. He refined his game in the minors, crediting coach Les Moss as particularly helpful.

The highlight of Jim's career was a 10-week period at the start of the 1969 season when he was a pinch-hitter for St. Louis. He loved the proximity to the city's jazz clubs and in one memorable photo, he and teammate Vada Pinson posed with their brass instruments. Before the trade deadline, the Cards swapped him to the Angels for Vic Davalillo. Saddened to leave St. Louis, Hicks hit just .130 in 56 games.

He was 30 years old and his MLB career was soon done, but the adventure was not over. For three years, he starred with the Hawaii Islanders. Then he played two years in Japan, making the best money of his career.

Hicks only hit five MLB homers, but all came against all-star pitchers: Gaylord Perry, Jim Kaat, John Hiller, Hank Aguirre and Dave McNally. Hicks later worked for 30 years at an airport, and after retiring from that job, he lived in the Houston suburbs until his death in 2020 at age 80, survived by his wife and six children.

NELLIE FOX

The word "unique" is overused, but there truly was no other player in his era like Nellie Fox. And none since then.

The second baseman was nearly impossible to strike out. Though he played in 19 seasons and led the AL in plate appearances five times, he never struck out even 20 times in a season. Fox once went 98 games (that's games, not at bats) without a strikeout. He stood just five-foot-eight, which made for a small strike zone, and nearly always put the ball in play.

He hustled on every play, was a team leader, exemplified the role of a holler guy, all while playing with an ever-present wad of chewing tobacco. "I don't think anyone liked to play [baseball] more than I did," he told a writer.

For the years that such statistics were kept, Fox was the third-hardest player to strike out of all time, fanning just once every 42.7 at bats. The only two ahead of him were Joe Sewell and Lloyd Waner, who played when punchouts were less common.

Fox led his league in hits four years and compiled a .288 lifetime average. He also got on base by sacrificing his body, getting hit by 142 pitches, which ranked ninth on the all-time list at the time of his retirement in 1966.

He played in 798 consecutive games between 1955 and 1960, which is still one of the 15 longest streaks of all-time. Defensively, only four men played more games at second base – Eddie Collins, Joe Morgan, Roberto Alomar and Lou Whitaker. His fielding wizardry led to three gold glove awards and he paced the league in fielding percentage six times.

He spent nearly his whole career with the White Sox from 1950 to 1963. He was with the A's briefly at the beginning of his tenure (having been signed by Connie Mack), and with Houston for two final seasons. With Houston, he served as a mentor to younger teammates. "Nellie was a great asset for the young Colt 45 players to have him teach and work with us," reflected Bob Aspromonte. "He was one of the best in the game."

Fox deserved much of the credit for Luis Aparicio's early-career base-stealing success. George Case, a former stolen base champion himself, was coaching for the Senators in 1962 when he said, "Fox takes a lot of pitches and that gives Looie more of an opportunity to steal. Fox is also very good on the hit-and-run and protecting the runner who is trying to steal. No one ever helped me the way Fox helps Aparicio."

Fox was a 12-time all-star who approached the mid-summer classic with nearly the same determination as every other game. His 14 hits in all-star competition are tied with Ted Williams for third place, trailing only Willie Mays and Stan Musial. His batting average in all-star games was .368.

When the White Sox won the pennant in 1959, Fox was the highest-paid player on the team at $45,000. Commenting on Fox's value before the season, co-owner Charlie Comiskey said, "Just as important, maybe even more important, are his leadership, his fiery spirit that keeps the whole club on its toes, and his gritty durability." Fox hit .306 and won the MVP award that year.

Nellie supplemented his baseball income by serving as a member of the Wilson Sporting Goods advisory board and making public appearances. He also owned a bowling alley in Merion, Pennsylvania, though he spent much of his winter off-seasons hunting.

He transitioned into a coaching role, first with Houston, and later with the Senators and Rangers. He was just 47 years old when he died from complications of skin cancer in 1975. Fox was elected to the Hall of Fame by the Veterans Committee in 1997.

RAY HERBERT

The best pitching coach of the Sixties may well have been Ray Berres. A former catcher, he was the White Sox pitching tutor for almost 20 years. Numerous hurlers were grateful for his counsel.

Ray Herbert was a journeyman right-hander until he emerged as a 20-game winner for the 1962 White Sox. At one point, he twirled 38 straight scoreless innings, a streak that ended when John Orsino hit a ball beneath a protective iron railing on the top of the fence. Manager Al Lopez and Sox outfielder Dave Nicholson argued it should be a ground-rule double, but the official declared it a home run.

Herbert spent considerable time with Berres, learning to better command his curve ball. Manager Al Lopez explained, "There are two differences in his pitching this year. One is better control and the other is an improved curve ball." Nor was it just a one-year pop. In 1963, he had a 13-10 record and hurled seven shutouts, best in the AL.

Already in his mid-thirties, he pitched three more seasons thereafter, one with Chicago and two with the Phillies. His lifetime record was 104-107 but with Berres and the White Sox it was 48-32.

On a personal level, Ray was born and raised in Detroit where his dad, a former semi-pro player, stoked his family's love for baseball in general and the Tigers to be specific. Ray signed with the Tigers for a $4,000 bonus. He was in the big leagues with the Tigers just a year later, but between two years of military duty, and infrequent use when on the roster, he was not an instant success, and was sold to the A's in 1955. He joined Chicago in 1961.

Instead of buying overpriced bar drinks, Ray saved money for the family. In the off-seasons, he worked at a Montgomery Ward store and enjoyed hunting trips with friends. After his pitching career ended, he remained in the sporting-goods business, threw batting practice for the Tigers from 1967 to 1992, and headed their alumni affairs program.

TOMMY JOHN

This southpaw won 288 games over 26 years for six different franchises. He began with the Indians in 1963 at age 20 and closed out his career with the Yankees in 1989. He made four all-star squads and was a three-time 20-game winner. He threw a sinker and a curve, and never really developed a strong third pitch. These days, he is best known for the arm surgery that bears his name.

Growing up in Terre Haute, Indiana, Tommy was a fan of the Cubs, but he also followed the Phillies, who had a farm club in his community (the Terre Haute Phillies, who operated from 1946 to 1954). His favorite player was pitcher Robin Roberts. It was ironic that his first major-league victory came in the second game of a twin-bill on May 3, 1964, defeating Roberts and the Orioles by a score of 3-0. The game was completed in just one hour and 34 minutes.

After playing basketball and baseball at Indiana State, John signed with the Indians for a $40,000 bonus. The Indians had offered $35,000 and in a meeting at Cleveland Stadium, John's dad demanded another $5,000. "Gabe Paul jumped up and said 'yes' so fast, we both knew my dad had undersold me," John recalled.

He pitched in cities like Dubuque and Charleston, where the entire coaching staff consisted of just one person – the manager. No three-person coaching staffs like minor-league clubs have today. The Indians had a roving pitcher instructor, Hal Newhowser, who mostly told John just to keep doing what he was doing.

When he got to Cleveland, the pitching coach was Early Wynn. "He sucked," John told Northeast Streaming Sports in 2021. "He was a terrible pitching coach. He offered nothing." John's record for Cleveland in 1964 was just 2-9. "So, I get traded to the White Sox and the guys that helped me were Al Lopez and their pitching coach, a (former) catcher by the name of Ray Berres." With Chicago, he became an accomplished hurler, leading the White Sox in victories in 1965, 1966 and 1970.

John enjoyed playing not only for Lopez, but also for White Sox manager Eddie Stanky who had a lot of passion and fire. He later was under pitching coach Johnny Sain, who wanted everyone to throw the slider or the "short curve" as Sain called it. John said Sain was a micromanager, able to describe every possible pitch, but unable to detect flaws in a pitcher's mechanics.

John was traded to the Dodgers in the deal that brought Dick (Richie) Allen to the White Sox. In Los Angeles, John took his game to an even higher level with help from pitching coach Red Adams. John is quick to note that the biggest reason for his success with the Dodgers was that he was surrounded by better ballplayers. He led the NL in winning percentage in 1973 based on his 16-7 record.

In 1974, he had a 13-3 record when he threw one pitch that led to pain like he had never felt before. He went to see Dr. Frank Jobe who suspected that John had torn an elbow ligament but with no MRIs in those days, there was no way to confirm the diagnosis. Several weeks later, Dr. Jobe told him about the ground-breaking concept of ligament-replacement surgery, which had never been performed on a pitcher's arm. Realizing it was the only hope – even if a remote hope – to get back to the big leagues, John agreed to the operation. The surgery took close to three hours. He watched his teammates in the World Series wearing a cast.

John told broadcaster Tony Kubek after the surgery, "I tried to pitch. I think I waited about eight or nine weeks, then rested some, and tried to come back and throw. It just got to the point where all I could throw was maybe three-quarters speed…and I couldn't throw a good curve ball." Against heavy odds, John made a full comeback in 1976. Beginning in 1977, he won 20 or more games in three of the next four seasons.

Since retiring, his hobbies have included golfing with his wife and fishing. In late 2020, he contracted Covid-19 and recently he has dealt with complications of Guillian-Barre Syndrome which has kept him off the golf courses. John is not bitter about being excluded from the Hall of Fame but his career statistics are comparable to some Hall of Famers. As of 2024, John ranked eighth all-time among pitchers for most games started and 26th for most victories. John resides in Indio, California.

GREG GOOSSEN

Several major leaguers from the Sixties appeared in Hollywood films and television, but none could match the experience of Greg Goosen, whose physical appearance was so similar to Gene Hackman that he served as his stand-in in more than a dozen films. Greg was so ruggedly handsome that teammate Jim Bouton said he had the look of a bouncer at an English pub.

Goosen was born not far from the Hollywood hills, the son of a police detective, and signed with the Dodgers through scout Ben Wade for a bonus of nearly six figures. Less than a year later, he was snagged by the Mets in the waiver draft for $8,000. He spent parts of three seasons with the Mets as a catcher, first baseman and pinch-hitter, showing power but struggling to hit even .200. His defensive skills behind the plate were also in question. Just before spring training got underway in 1969, the Mets traded him to the Pilots for a player to be named later (outfielder Jim Gosger).

Greg enjoyed his best year with the Pilots, hitting .309 with 10 homers in 1969 in just 52 games. All of the homers came at his undersized home ballpark, Sicks Stadium. He could never replicate that success and in total, played for more than 30 different major, minor, and Mexican league teams. "Everybody either wanted me or wanted to get rid of me," he joked. He also said, perhaps only partly in jest, that he played best with a slight hangover. His lifetime stats included a .241 average and 13 homers in 460 at bats.

The obvious question is how Gene Hackman met Goosen in the first place. After baseball, Greg and his brothers operated a boxing club. Hackman dropped by one day while doing research for the movie, *Split Decisions.* The pair became friends, and Hackman began stipulating Goosen's stand-in role in his movie contracts. Goosen lived until 2011, when he passed away from a stroke at the age of 65.

DON LEPPERT

Don Leppert was a scrappy, tobacco-loving catcher who played with the Pirates and Senators, after serving in the Air Force Military Police.

Exemplifying how the game was played in the Sixties, Don was the protagonist in an on-field tiff during a Richmond-Columbus game in 1961. He tried to score from third base on a wild pitch. With Richmond pitcher Gary Blaylock covering the plate, Don came sliding in with spikes elevated. Blaylock took a swing at Leppert and both benches emptied. Richmond skipper Cal Ermer, who later claimed he was trying to be a peace-maker, wound up at the bottom of the pile-up, with minor lacerations.

Though Don didn't reach the big leagues until age 29, he homered off Curt Simmons in his first MLB at bat. An all-star with the Senators in 1963, his season highlight was a three-homer game against Boston. He had a lifetime batting average of .229 with 15 homers.

Don's leadership skills were recognized as early as the winter of 1962-1963 when he was playing winter ball for Ponce. The club ditched its manager, Bill Adair, mid-season, and Leppert was a player-manager the rest of the way. Don later coached for the Pirates, Blue Jays and Astros between 1968 and 1985.

An avid outdoorsman, he eventually retired to Naples, before moving to Ohio in 2019. After he died in 2023, Hall of Fame pitcher Jim Kaat called him, "a true baseball guy."

WILLIE HORTON

The 1970 book *The Willie Horton Story* by Hal Butler tells of an athletic youngster who grew up on the streets of Detroit, became a member of the Tigers baseball team, and helped them win the 1968 World Series one year after riots tore the city apart. Horton devoted spare time as a player to encouraging young people in the neighborhoods to avoid violence and pursue life on the straight and narrow. Though written more than 50 years ago, the book still resonates today. Willie devoted much of his energy to that important cause even in the years after his illustrious baseball career.

As a local product, Horton captured the attention of Tigers' fans as he played ball locally and then progressed through the minor leagues. His arrival with the Tigers was as eagerly awaited as the next hot release from Motown Records. As one analyst later put it on the night of Horton's 2012 appearance at the Robert H. Jackson Center, "When Horton joined the Tigers, it was as if the connection had finally been made."

Playing left field for Detroit for more than a decade, Willie was often the team's most productive hitter. He was a four-time all-star with three 100-RBI seasons. When the Tigers won the world championship in 1968, he was second in the league in homers (36) and fourth in RBI (85). Battling through injuries later in his career, he still managed to hit .300 or better in 1970 and 1973. Angels manager Bill Rigney once said, "This guy petrifies my pitchers."

In May 1969, Horton went AWOL for four days. Initially, it was thought that he jumped the club out of frustration over a hitting slump and being booed by the fans. During his time away, he met with Tigers executives, urging them to acquire more black players. Although Horton was fined for his transgression, the Tigers heeded his counsel.

Bill Freehan said Horton was one of the strongest people in baseball, though sometimes moody. Horton's temper was explosive. Not infrequently, he became embroiled in arguments with umpires that got the entire stadium buzzing with fervor. Opposing pitchers sometimes stoked his fury. Duke Sims, who was both an opponent and teammate of Horton at various times, recalled that Freehan and Gates Brown could slow Horton down, but nobody could stop him.

Willie became the Tigers' full-time designated hitter after Al Kaline retired. In 1975, he responded with one of his best seasons, batting .275 with 25 home runs and 92 RBI. His salary eclipsed the $100,000 plateau for the first time the next season.

The nomadic conclusion of his career began the first week of the 1977 season, when the Tigers, in full rebuilding mode, traded him to the Rangers for pitcher Steve Foucault. He was traded to Cleveland in February 1978, released by the Indians that July, signed by Oakland the same month, then traded to Toronto a month later.

With modest public expectations, Horton signed with Seattle as a free agent for the 1979 campaign. He enjoyed one more robust year, batting .279 with a career-best 106 RBI and leading the league in games played. With a 13-year gap between 100-RBI seasons, he established a major league record (since eclipsed by Harold Baines). Then a subpar 1980 season put the lid on his career. His final career numbers included a .273 batting average, 325 home runs, and 1,993 hits.

Horton later served as a coach for the Yankees and White Sox, after which he returned to the Tigers' in a front-office role, serving as community ambassador. He has been honored with a statue outside Comerica Park and by having his uniform number retired.

MICKEY STANLEY

The world champion 1968 Tigers were loaded with heroes. Mickey Lolich won three games in the World Series. Denny McLain notched 31 wins during the regular season. Willie Horton was among the league leaders with 36 homers. Jim Northrup topped the squad with 90 RBI and hit a grand-slam in the Series. Bill Freehan provided superb leadership behind the plate. But the most unsung hero was Mickey Stanley.

In a highly risky move, Tigers manager Mayo Smith moved Stanley, his gold-glove center fielder, to the unfamiliar position of shortstop in the World Series, in order to get the bats of outfielders Horton, Northrup and Al Kaline into the lineup. None of the Tigers' shortstops were good hitters, so the skipper took his chances on Stanley, who trained at shortstop in the season's final six games. The move paid off, as Detroit beat St. Louis in the World Series.

Tigers shortstop Ray Oyler defended the move, though it came at his expense. "Why shouldn't Mickey be a good shortstop? He has the range and the arm and coordination. Then add desire. All Mickey wants to do is play ball."

Stanley began his shortstop duty using his outfielder's mitt, but had trouble getting the ball out of the leather. He then borrowed an infielder's glove with shorter fingers from teammate Bob Christian. When asked what was wrong with the outfielder's glove, before Stanley could respond, teammate Norm Cash cracked, "It had cement in it."

Mickey spent his whole career in Detroit, from 1964 to 1978. He ranks 14th on the Tigers with 1,517 games played. Kaline and Denny McLain both have called Stanley the best athlete on all of his Tiger teams. His post-baseball endeavors included work as a manufacturers rep and real estate developer. Mickey recently was residing in Brighton, Michigan.

JIM NORTHRUP

On June 24, 1968, Tigers outfielder Jim Northrup belted grand-slam home runs in consecutive innings against Cleveland pitchers Eddie Fisher and Billy Rohr, matching a feat achieved earlier by only one player, Jim Gentile in 1961. Five days later, Northrup crushed another blast against Cisco Carlos of the White Sox to became the first major leaguer ever to hit three slams in a week. For good measure, he hit another in the World Series, as the Tigers bested the Cardinals in seven games.

Northrup was born and raised on a farm in Michigan, playing high school and college ball there before attending a tryout and signing with the Tigers for a $6,000 bonus. He remained a Tiger fan throughout his lifetime.

While often remembered for the grand slams, the best adjectives to describe Northrup were reliable, steady, and consistent. Beginning in 1966, when he won a regular job in the Tigers' outfield, until 1975, when he retired as a productive fourth outfielder for the Orioles, he put up consistently above-average numbers and fielded his position with grace and aplomb.

For most of his Tigers tenure, he was part of that memorable group with Al Kaline, Willie Horton, and Mickey Stanley. Pinch-hitting specialist Gates Brown rounded out the quintet that was together for more than a decade. He was called "Sweet Lips" by teammates because of his proclivity to offer caustic remarks.

Northrup set a career high for RBI in 1968 with 90, placing third in the AL. A year later in 1969, he registered his career-best home run total of 25 and was ninth in the loop in slugging percentage. His best batting average of .307 came in 1973. Defensively, he was often among the league leaders in outfield assists. For his career, Jim batted .267 with 153 home runs and 1,254 hits.

In a SABR profile written by Jim Sargent, Northrup commented on the managers for whom he played. He said that Mayo Smith, who managed the 1968 championship team, was a genial man who did not try to over-manage. He said, "Billy Martin put most of us in a frame of mind where he took the fun out of the game. And when there's no fun, it's not worth playing."

The Tigers shipped Jim to the Expos in 1974, and he recalled decades later in an interview on *Glory Days TV* that he dreaded playing for Montreal because they were managed by Gene

Mauch, who he tongue-in-cheek referred to as "God's gift to baseball." Only after general manager John McHale agreed to financial considerations and an airline ticket for his wife did Northrup agree to report.

Five weeks later, the Expos sold him to Baltimore, where he enjoyed playing for skipper Earl Weaver. The Orioles would fly him home to his family every Sunday night, and fly him back to the team on Tuesday, allowing him some time with his family every week.

Jim was still productive his final season and left the game on his own terms after the 1975 season, saying, "I quit because I'd had enough. I'd played 14 years." He then got a job as a manufacturers' rep from Bill Freehan's dad, and said he made more money doing that work than he ever made playing baseball. Drawing on his farm background, he also went into cattle herding.

To this day, Northrup holds the Tigers' team record for most RBI in a game with eight, a total he achieved not only in 1968, but again in 1973. He ranks among the top 20 Tigers of all-time in home runs, as well. He passed away in 2011 at the age of 71.

DAVE WICKERSHAM

Erie, Pennsylvania native Dave Wickersham hurled four no-hitters in American Legion ball, and signed with the Pirates in 1954. Branch Rickey explained that Dave was not enjoying his college classes, and was ready to play pro ball. But it was not until 1962 that he established himself as a big-leaguer. With an 11-4 record, he led the AL in winning percentage, despite missing two months with a broken rib. The weapon that helped him make the big leap forward? The screwball.

A's manager Ed Lopat helped Dave develop the weapon. As the pitcher related the following spring, "The screwball…helps me get the left-handers out and it sets up my other pitches. I don't know where I'd be without it."

The tall right-hander had a mediocre 1964 season, after which Kansas City swapped him to the Tigers. In those days, the A's had a bad habit of trading players right before their best seasons. It happened again here.

With plenty of run support, Dave posted a 19-12 mark in 1964. Only a questionable ejection by hot-tempered umpire Bill Valentine – who was later fired by the league president -- prevented him from recording 20 wins. Wick later said he harbored no resentment, though the arbiter expressed regret at costing the pitcher his 20th win.

Wickersham was nothing if not level-headed. A case in point came early in the 1964 season when he was trying to wrap up a victory over the Twins. His Tigers teammates committed two infield errors in the ninth inning to bring up Tony Oliva, but Dave got the final out. "You didn't see Wickersham kicking any dirt around after those errors," said pitching coach Frank Overmire. "He just pitched a little harder."

The pitcher's poise reflected his Christian faith. Even Tigers manager Charlie Dressen, normally insensitive to players' feelings, realized the importance of Wickersham's church attendance, and allowed him to pitch the second games of Sunday double-headers so he would have ample time to worship at church. One of Dave's favorite Bible verses was Romans 10:9-10.

With Detroit, he roomed with Don Demeter, another Christian believer. On one road trip to New York, the pair jumped into a taxi along with broadcaster Ernie Harwell and writer Watson Spoelstra to hear famed pastor Norman Vincent Peale preach at Marble Collegiate Church (founded in 1628). The topic of the sermon, according to Spoelstra's written account, was "Turning Gloom into Joy."

Not the league's hardest thrower, Wick compensated by studying hitters carefully. He and his wife kept records of his pitch selections and outcomes against each hitter. Although his record in 1965 dropped off to 9-14, at one point after his sixth straight loss, he received a telegram of encouraging words from Tigers owner John Fetzer. "I appreciate working for an owner like that," the pitcher noted.

He caught a second wind as a reliable Tigers relief pitcher in 1966 and 1967. Thereafter, in a straight-up swap of pitchers, the Tigers dispatched him to the Pirates for Dennis Ribant. Wick got into only 11 games for the 1968 Pirates, but the respect he had earned was evident. After Martin Luther King was assassinated in April and the Pirates voted 25-0 not to play for two days out of respect for Dr. King, the statement was issued jointly by Roberto Clemente and Wickersham.

Dave spent the autumn working at his father's apple farm in Pennsylvania and decided to retire from baseball. Then his wife called from their home in Overland Park, Kansas, indicating that the expansion Royals had invited him to pitch for their Omaha farm team. The hurler accepted the invitation and spent the rest of the winter getting into peak shape by running and throwing.

Sure enough, he impressed Royals pitching coach Mel Harder, made the parent club, and appeared in 34 games. In the very first Royals game, he hurled five innings of scoreless relief. He was one of four men to play for both Kansas City franchises.

Dave finished with a lifetime mark of 68-57, with a 3.66 ERA and five shutouts. His daughter, Carey, later became a news correspondent for the Fox affiliate in Kansas City. He was still living in Overland Park when he passed away in 2022.

TERRY FOX

Sixties baseball was replete with blue-chip prospects who commanded large signing bonuses. Conversely, reliever Terry Fox exemplified the athlete who completed high school without any offers yet became a productive major leaguer. Fox was a right-hander from suburban Chicago who spent most of his career with the Tigers.

Terry longed for a career in baseball while working part-time jobs as a cafeteria dishwasher and a fruit-auction stock boy. He traveled at his own expense to Chicago-area tryouts with the Braves, White Sox, Pirates and ultimately signed with the Atlanta Crackers, who had a working agreement with the Braves, for a few hundred bucks.

Fox pitched briefly for the 1960 Braves and joined the Tigers in 1961. He had stunning success that season with a 1.42 ERA in 39 outings, but one of his few bad outings was memorable. On September 17, 1961, Fox was pitching to Roger Maris of the Yankees. Maris stepped out of the batter's box as a line of noisy, honking geese flew over the stadium. Upon stepping back in, he nailed a Fox delivery for his 58th home run of the year. Because of the geese, baseball fans still talk about that home run.

Proving that his previous season was no fluke, Fox notched a 1.71 ERA with 16 saves in 1962. Only Dick Radatz and Marshall Bridges had more saves among AL firemen.

Fox had no trick pitches, just a fastball, curve and change-up. According to catcher Bill Freehan, who joined the Tigers in 1963, Fox was skilled in holding runners close and pickoff throws. Terry sustained an injury washing his car and required dozens of cortisone shots into the ulnar nerve but remained an effective Tigers reliever through 1965. He was sold to the Phillies in 1966 and finished with a minor-league season in 1967.

In an interview on the Baseball Almanac website, Fox observed a key difference between 1960s baseball and the modern game. He noted that once a reliever went in, he usually stayed in the whole game unless he was lifted for a pinch-hitter. There was less flipping back and forth between righties and lefties, or adhering to pitch counts, in those days.

He had a 29-19 lifetime record and a superb 2.99 ERA. Fox and his wife wound up making New Iberia, Louisiana their lifetime home. He worked in the oil patch for Texaco for many years before retiring.

RANDY HUNDLEY

This 14-year veteran changed the way the catcher position is played. Until Hundley, catchers used both hands to receive each pitch. Hundley began using a hinged glove that allowed him to catch with one hand and protect the throwing hand behind his back. Soon, Johnny Bench, Ray Fosse and other catchers adopted the new style of mitt and receiving.

Beginning in 1966, when he placed fourth in the NL rookie of the year voting, Hundley was a workhorse of a play-caller for the Cubs, something of a manager on the field who had the confidence of skipper Leo Durocher. He won a gold glove in 1967 and made the all-star team in 1969.

Beset by frequent injuries, he remained with the Cubs until 1973 and then played one season each with Minnesota and San Diego before returning to the Cubs. He was a .236 lifetime hitter with 82 shots into the seats. In his post-playing years, he managed in the minor leagues and pioneered the concept of baseball fantasy camps. The father of MLB catcher Todd Hundley, Randy continues to reside in Palatine, Illinois.

KEN RUDOLPH

The Cubs selected catcher Ken Rudolph in the second round of the first-ever amateur draft in 1965. It was a good selection. He caught for Chicago from 1969 to 1973, often backing up Randy Hundley, and then played for three other teams through 1977.

That rookie season, Ken mostly watched from the bench as the Cubs built a big lead in the NL East, only to be surpassed by the Miracle Mets. He roomed on road trips with outfielder Don Young or pitcher Ken Holtzman. Even when not in the lineup, he got a baseball education just observing the likes of Ernie Banks, Glenn Beckert, Ferguson Jenkins, Hank Aguirre, Bill Hands, Phil Regan and others on that talented team.

Ken recalls Banks as "a fabulous teammate who always was kind and supportive." Of the pitchers he caught, he says, "Fergie Jenkins always came to pitch. He was a true professional in every sense of the word. He had excellent control and was very smart." Rudolph says that Bill Hands "was a true competitor with a good assortment of pitches. He was a very hard worker who loved to pitch. Phil Regan was a dogged competitor. He had a great sinker and his motion made it difficult to pick up pitches. Hank Aguirre was a crafty lefthander whose tall frame and motion made him difficult to hit. There was lots of movement on his fastballs."

"I used a Rawlings one-hinge catcher's mitt and broke in a new glove every year by soaking it in water, let dry, and put shaving cream on it to keep it moist. During the winters, I always stayed in shape with other sports, weightlifting and conditioning," he recently recalled. The key to catching, he said, is to expect the unexpected, and never assume the pitch will be thrown where you call for it.

Born in the industrial town of Rockford, Illinois, near the Wisconsin border, Ken played high school ball at Cathedral High School in Los Angeles. He was playing at the University of

Nebraska at Lincoln when selected by the Cubs. His best season was 1974 when he hit .259 in 57 games for the Giants. Ken later became the head baseball coach at Arcadia High School in Phoenix.

ROLAND SHELDON

Less than a year after leaving the University of Connecticut campus and signing a contract offered by Yankees' scout Harry Hesse (who was a former minor-league teammate of Lou Gehrig), Rollie Sheldon became a key cog for the Yankees.

He got his first win in a May 31, 1961 game against Boston, in which both Mickey Mantle and Roger Maris went yard. Sheldon gave his club 163 solid innings as a long reliever and a starter on double-header days. Much of his bullpen work was in relief of Bud Daley, who had a rough season and kept getting knocked out of games. Sheldon capitalized on his opportunity, posting a record of 11-5. His best weapon was a nasty curve that was tough to hit when it was working. Yogi Berra and pitching coach Johnny Sain taught him to throw a change-up, which rounded out his repertoire.

Rookies in those days rode the back of the team bus, but on the night that Maris hit his 59th homer, the slugger brought a bunch of steamed crabs onto the bus and made a point of calling Sheldon up to the front to have some.

Rollie also provided the Yanks with an assist during the 1964 season, with a 5-2 record in 19 games. He later pitched for the A's and Red Sox and spent four more seasons in the minor leagues.

Sheldon, who also served four years in the air force, earned a physical education degree. He had a lifetime record of 38-36 with a 4.09 ERA and four career shutouts. After baseball, he worked in the insurance business. He resides in Lees Summit, Missouri.

RON HUNT

How was it possible for one player, Ron Hunt, to get hit by more pitches than any other NL player seven years in a row? Pitcher Bill Wakefield addressed that question in a SABR profile. He recalled, "Ron was, well, a kind of arrogant type of guy. He invited pitchers to throw at him. If you're going to crowd the plate, you're going to get hit by a lot of pitches, but Ron didn't care if other players didn't like him so much." Sounding a similar theme, historian Bill James wrote, "He was an arthritic second baseman with a poor arm. Hunt was not well liked by fans or by other players."

Hunt was a native of St. Louis who signed with the Braves. He played in MLB for 12 years for the Mets, Dodgers, Giants, Expos and his hometown Cardinals. Ron led the Mets in base hits in 1963 and represented them on the 1964 and 1966 NL all-star teams. After the 1966 season, he was swapped to the Dodgers in the Tommy Davis trade. He joined the Giants in 1969.

Hunt learned early on that he could get on base more often by leaning into inside pitches. He was a decent hitter with a lifetime .273 batting average, but between walks and hit by pitches, his career on-base percentage was a more impressive .368. He reached his apex in 1971 with Montreal when he became the first modern batter to get hit 50 times in a season. Even in his final season in 1974, he was hit more often than any other NL player. After retiring, he established a baseball-related foundation. He now resides in Wentzville, Missouri.

JIM LEFEBVRE

For eight years beginning in 1965, infielder Jim Lefebvre was one of the most visible faces of the Dodgers. He was a reliable fielder, despite having only average range, and an intense competitor. Handsome and personable, Lefebvre also made his mark in acting. Taking advantage of his proximity to Hollywood, he made guest appearances on Gilligan's Island, Batman, Alice, M*A*S*H, and other television shows.

Jim knew the Dodgers well. Even as a teen, he had been a bat boy, hanging out with players and picking up pointers. When he reported to spring training in 1965 as a non-roster invitee, he not only made the team, but went on to win the top NL rookie honors. It wasn't a surprise for Jim, who had enormous confidence, or for manager Walt Alston who loved the youngster's determination and intensity. He earned the NL's top rookie honors, though many fans felt it should have gone to Joe Morgan.

The switch-hitter's best season came a year later in 1966, when he led the team with 24 home runs and 74 RBI. The only disappointment was that the Dodgers' offense went flat in the World Series against Baltimore, where even Jim hit only .167, though he did connect for a home run.

Jim pulled a hamstring during May 1967 but still had a decent season, though Sandy Koufax's retirement left the Dodgers exposed as an eighth-place team. His lowlight for the season came during a game in April in which he committed three errors in one inning at the hot corner.

Buzzie Bavasi, the former Dodgers general manager, wrote that Lefebvre was the first player to ask to bring a financial advisor into a contract negotiation meeting. That led, he wrote, to players uniformly relying on agents. Bavasi believed the involvement of agents was a negative, in that it siphoned money away from teams and players alike.

Jim remained in the team's plans for several more seasons and produced 68 RBI in 1971. By 1972, the Dodgers had young infielders such as Lee Lacy, Dave Lopes, and Bobby Valentine forcing their way into the team's plans. Jim was released after the season, representing a major U-turn in his life. He was part of a business called Athletes Financial Services, which he co-owned with teammates Don Sutton, Willie Crawford, Joe Moeller, Alan Foster, Claude Osteen and Bill Singer, but was not ready to turn his back on baseball.

He went to Japan to play for four turbulent years from 1973 to 1976. He performed well his first season but fell short of his team manager's foolish prediction that he would win the triple crown. Things came to a head one day when he heaved his glove into the dugout out of frustration during a game. The manager, thinking it was aimed at him, became enraged and challenged Lefebvre to a fight. Lefebvre said bring it on, and it took a bevy of teammates to restore peace. The team imposed a large fine, which Lefebvre successfully contested, arguing that his glove was not aimed at his skipper.

After returning to the U.S., Lefebvre himself became a big-league manager for the Mariners, Cubs and Brewers. He later worked in China, helping to build baseball programs there. A lifetime .251 hitter, Lefebvre at last report was residing in Henderson, Nevada.

FRANK LINZY

Giants rookie Frank Linzy was arguably the NL's best reliever in 1965, throwing wicked sinkers and hard sliders. The right-hander posted a 9-3 record with 20 saves and a stunning 1.43 ERA. Only Ted Abernathy and Bill McCool saved more games, as Linzy placed third in the rookie of the year balloting behind Jim Lefebvre and Joe Morgan.

Linzy's sinking fastball, wrote columnist Bob Stevens, made "bat handles snap, splinters spray all over the diamond, and hitters glare evilly," generating "worm-killing" infield grounders that resulted in easy outs. Linzy happily embraced his relief-pitching role.

Giants pitching coach Larry Jansen explained, "Frank grips the ball with his middle and index fingers cradled in the valley between the seams. He doesn't come in contact with a seam at all. He just rolls the ball out of his hand and she does some funny things when it gets around the plate area."

Linzy grew up in rural Oklahoma in a house with no electricity, plumbing, or phone. When invitations came to play baseball, they were relayed from a neighbor who had a phone. The youngster made money on the side chopping cotton.

After inking an offer from Giants scout Bully McLean with no signing bonus, he began his career with the 1960 Salem Rebels in the Appalachian League as an outfielder. Salem manager Jodie Phipps – a former pitcher himself –advised him to switch to pitching.

Following his sterling NL rookie season, Linzy spent the winter quail hunting – which involved 15 to 30 miles of walking per day – as well as playing pick-up basketball and spending time with his wife, Elaine, and their infant daughters, Andrea and Beth.

After a mediocre 1966 season in which he battled back trouble and lost 11 games, he was back at the top of his game again in 1967 and 1968. Linzy's sinker began to drop less in 1969 and his ERA rose a bit, but he was still integral to the Giants' fortunes, posting a 14-9 record. All the while, the Giants were strong contenders, but unable to capture the pennant for the seventh straight season.

Linzy later pitched for the Cardinals, Brewers and Phillies through the 1974 season. He went to spring training in 1975 with the Padres, who cut him from the roster, and spent the rest of that summer pitching in Hawaii. Linzy retired with a lifetime mark of 62-57 with a 2.85 ERA and 110 saves.

In 1969, Linzy bought some land near his boyhood home, where he still lives today. In an article in the March 31, 2014 *Tulsa World,* Linzy said, "This is the best part of the country because you can go fishing and hunting anytime you want to go. I can shoot coyotes out of the window." Linzy said he has three televisions in his living room, to be able to watch the NCAA basketball tournament every March. He also enjoys watching *Gunsmoke* and MLB games.

BILL FAUL

Bill Faul, a side-arming right-hander, threw three shutouts for the 1965 Cubs, but he is better remembered for some unconventional off-the-field activity.

Faul, a University of Cincinnati standout who taught karate in the Air Force, came up with the Tigers. After throwing eight brilliant innings one day against the 1963 A's, he told reporters that the previous day he had undergone hypnosis, improving his vision, relaxation, and confidence. All hell broke loose. Writers ensured his hypnosis session became national news and the A's filed a protest of the game with the league president. Faul quickly became the talk of baseball, with teammates kidding him and opponents taunting him. Tigers Manager Bob Scheffing said, "The big thing about this kid is he listens, and he retains what he hears." Faul finished the season with a 5-6 record.

He was not the first pitcher to employ hypnotism; Don Newcombe tried it to help him overcome a fear of flying. Faul went further, taking courses and became a licensed hypnotist. But Chuck Dressen replaced Scheffing as the Tigers manager in 1964 and had no use for Faul, at one point calling him "Houdini," and the Tigers sold him to the Cubs.

Faul posted a 6-6 record for the 1965 Cubs, but things went south in 1966 after he clashed with new manager Leo Durocher leading to a demotion to the minors. Following the season, Faul worked on his slider and gave up cigarettes, coffee, alcohol, and candy. Yet, for the next three years, he pitched only at the minor-league level. His final turn in the majors was with the 1970 Giants; he retired for good with Midland, a Cubs' farm club, in 1973. His lifetime MLB record was 12-16.

In the minor leagues, his behavior became erratic. He reportedly ate live frogs and spat out the small bones, claiming the practice added some zip to his fastball. While playing for Omaha, he reportedly once was holding a parakeet that bit his hand. "That's it," Faul proclaimed as he bit the head off the parakeet and spat it to the ground.

When he passed away in Ohio in 2002, he still held the NCAA college record for the most strikeouts in a game. Despite the unusual behavior, he had made his mark as an athlete.

JOHNNY PODRES

When an interviewer asked former pitcher Stan Williams about being part of a Dodgers' rotation that included Sandy Koufax and Don Drysdale, Williams immediately proclaimed, "Please don't forget Johnny Podres!"

Indeed, Podres was a Dodgers' legend in his own right. He was so effective with his fiery fastball, sneaky curve, and solid change-up that he once set a record (later broken by Tom Seaver) with eight consecutive strikeouts. Podres led the NL in ERA and shutouts in 1957, was tops in winning percentage in 1961, and made the all-star team three times. With a 148-116 record, his lifetime winning percentage was a robust .561.

A native of New York's Adirondack Mountains, he was the son of a hardscrabble iron ore miner and listened to Dodgers' games on the radio as a kid. For all intents and purposes, he was still a kid when he made his debut at the tender age of 20 for one of the best teams of all time, the 1953 Dodgers, going 9-4 on the season.

He spent most of his career with the Dodgers, though he missed the 1956 season due to military service in the Navy. Not until 1966 was an aging Podres sent to the Tigers, for whom he pitched through the end of the 1967 season. After sitting out the 1968 campaign, he was back in uniform with the Padres in 1969, posting a 5-6 record.

Podres was also a tough out when he stepped up to the plate. His lifetime batting average was .190, superior to most of his fellow pitchers.

He was at his best in the post-season, collecting a 4-1 record and 2.11 ERA in World Series action. His biggest win came in game seven of the 1955 World Series. The lefty Podres was matched up against another southpaw, Tommy Byrnes of the Yankees. It was the game where Dodgers' outfielder Sandy Amoros made his spectacular catch, followed by a throw to first base to double off a base-runner. Podres went the distance against the Yankees to deliver Brooklyn's only world championship. He brashly promised his teammates he would hurl a shutout, and he did exactly that, as the Dodgers won the game, 2-0.

Catcher Roy Campanella raced to the mound after the final out and lifted him high off the ground, as his teammates rushed to join the celebration. The party continued at the Hotel Bossert in Brooklyn after the players had showered, and lasted for hours. Fans who had waited for decades for such a moment rejoiced.

Podres accompanied the Dodgers to their new western base in 1958, pacing the club with 13 wins, 11 of which came at home. In 1961, he posted an 18-5 record and tossed a couple of shutout innings in the second all-star game for good measure.

In 1963, when the Dodgers won the world championship representing Los Angeles, Podres was still going strong. He notched a 14-12 record and hurled 5 of his 24 regular-season career shutouts that season. Podres also won his only start in that year's World Series. Podres missed most of the 1964 season to injury, then went 7-6 for the world champion 1965 Dodgers.

When his pitching days came to a close, it was a foregone conclusion that he would stay in the game, sharing pitching knowledge. He was pitching coach for the Red Sox and Twins, a minor-league tutor for the Dodgers, and then pitching coach for the 1993 Phillies World Series squad. Several hurlers on that club credited Podres with helping them improve their craft and believe in themselves. Curt Schilling referred to him as a second father.

Along the way, Podres overcame alcoholism and battled constant health problems. In his spare time, he loved to bet on the horses at the race track, hunt, and spend time with his wife, Joan.

Decades later, a young writer named Benjamin Pomeranz interviewed him. Podres arrived for the interview in a car with a vanity license plate that read MVP-55. Smoking Camels, Podres told story after story with a wistful smile, saying, "I had good days and bad days, and hopefully the good outnumbered the bad. It was a great ride, and I stayed on as long as I could."

In 1996, Podres was the honorary team captain for the NL all-star team. Podres was honored by the Dodgers in 2005 as part of the 50th anniversary celebration of the 1955 World Series. The New York State Baseball Hall of Fame each year issues a lifetime achievement award given in Podres' name.

The Dodgers' legend passed away in 2008 in Glen Falls, New York, at the age of 75. He suffered from kidney and heart problems, as well as a leg infection. Duke Snider recalled him as "a pitcher who excelled at winning big games." Tom LaSorda called him "a great roomie, a great teammate, and a great friend."

WES PARKER

When Rawlings presented awards for the best fielders of the preceding 50 years in 2007, Wes Parker was selected as the first baseman. He was pleasantly surprised that anyone remembered his superb glove work.

Unlike many of his cohorts, Parker enjoyed a privileged upbringing, growing up in a wealthy family on a 2.5-acre estate in Brentwood. What even most of his teammates did not know at that time was that his parents were alcoholics whose constant verbal abuse shattered Wes's self-confidence. Even after he rose quickly through the minor leagues to the Dodgers' roster, he continued to have self-doubts and require therapy.

Wes gradually became a very good hitter, as well. In his finest season in 1970, he batted .319, led the NL in doubles with 47, and drove home 111 RBI. During one game in May 1970, he hit for the cycle, something no Dodger did again until Orlando Hudson 39 years later. Parker placed fifth in the MVP voting that season. He also had blazing speed on the basepaths, though he was not a prolific base thief.

Having personal wealth was an advantage. In 1966, when the Dodgers pressured players to make a trip to Japan after an exhausting pennant race, Parker politely – and repeatedly – told the front office he wouldn't make the trip, knowing that he was not dependent on the Dodgers for a livelihood if push came to shove. In the end, Parker, Sandy Koufax and Don Drysdale were the only ones to skip the trip.

Wes later conceded that after making the big leagues, he needed to muster more energy and concentration. "Baseball is a thinking man's game," Parker said during a public appearance. "Unless you play the game, or study the heck out of it, you never realize what a cerebral game it is."

He praises team owners Walter and Peter O'Malley for doing everything to put the team in a position to win. They purchased and outfitted a private jet, so the players would never have to walk through an airport. Luggage was automatically checked in and out. Parker was elected player rep, but he would not concur with a strike against the O'Malley family during the union walkout in 1972, and he stepped away from that role.

Overall, he was a lifetime .267 batter, with 64 home runs and 1,110 hits. After sitting out the 1973 season, he played a year in Japan in 1974, and batted .301 for Nankai. His teammates included two former major leaguers in outfielder Ron Lolich and pitcher Masanori Murakami.

After baseball, Parker split his time between acting, broadcasting and public speaking. He had a son in 1967 by his girlfriend, actress Patricia Randall. His name was occasionally confused with the similarly named Fess Parker (the Hollywood actor who starred as Daniel Boone for six years on a television show and operated a resort hotel in Santa Barbara). Wes continues to be part of the Dodgers speakers' bureau.

CLAUDE OSTEEN

After a dismal sixth-place finish in 1964, the Dodgers set about revamping their roster with a blockbuster trade. Los Angeles sent slugger Frank Howard, Ken McMullen, Dick Nen, Phil Ortega and Pete Richert to the Senators. For that bounty, the Dodgers received pitcher Claude Osteen, infielder John Kennedy and $100,000. The Dodgers never looked back, retaining Osteen for nine productive years.

At age 25 and coming off a 15-win season for Washington, the lefty was just what the Dodgers needed to round out their superb pitching corps. Although they missed Howard's bat, they nonetheless won the pennant in both 1965 and 1966.

Osteen won 147 games in his nine years in Los Angeles, while losing only 126. Capable of pitching deep into games, he hurled 34 of his 40 career shutouts in Dodger blue. To this day, he is still on baseball's top 50 all-time list for shutouts. He was a master at working the corners and he seldom hurt his own cause through walks.

Osteen explained, "Your legs would tell you if your control went astray. We ran, and ran some more, until our legs let us throw the ball exactly where we wanted to throw it," he said of Dodgers pitchers in his era. "We had great control, being conscious of not walking the leadoff hitter."

His biggest win may have been game three of the 1965 World Series. The Dodgers had dug a hole by losing the first two games to the Twins. He got them back into the series by tossing a shutout, and the Dodgers went on to win the world title.

Osteen twice was a 20-game winner. One year was in 1969, when he went 20-15 with a 2.66 ERA, while pitching 321 innings. Only Gaylord Perry shouldered a heavier workload in the NL. His other 20-win season, a bit of a surprise at age 32, came in 1972, when Osteen was 20-11 with a 2.64 ERA.

Claude finished up with two seasons with the Astros, Cardinals, and White Sox. His lifetime record was 196-195, diminished by some losing seasons at the start and end of his career. He fashioned an excellent 3.30 ERA over those 18 campaigns, and a 0.86 ERA in World Series action.

On a personal level, Claude learned the curve ball from his father, who ran a community merchandise store in Tennessee. "My dad was an amateur pitcher who taught me that I could get any hitter out," he noted. Claude finished his schooling at Reading High School, north of

Cincinnati, leading his school to the state title. Immersed in baseball, he was a Brooklyn fan, and his favorite players were Johnny Podres, Duke Snider, Don Newcombe, Pee Wee Reese and Junior Gilliam. But he was most impressed with Whitey Ford of the Yankees.

Right out of high school at age 17, he signed with the Reds, making his MLB debut in 1957, but spending most of the next two years in the minor leagues. He inked a contract with MacGregor to use their gloves. "They had a plant in Cincinnati and had followed me in high school," he explained.

It was a trade from the Reds to the Senators, who were losing 100 games a year in the early Sixties, that gave him the chance to pitch regularly, and refine his craft, at the MLB level. He made his home in University Park and Beltsville, a pair of suburbs in Maryland, while with the Senators. He later relocated to Brea, California during his Dodgers tenure.

Others who impacted his career were catcher Hobie Landrith, pitching coaches Jim Turner, Johnny Sain and Red Adams, as well as his first major league manager, Birdie Tebbetts. Through the years, Osteen enjoyed the camaraderie of rooming on the road with Ed Bailey, Ed Brinkman, Jay Hook, Jim Brewer, Ron Fairly and Ron Perranoski.

He later served as a pitching coach in the majors and minors, working for the Phillies, Cardinals, Rangers, and Dodgers organizations, and scouted for the Diamondbacks. Still remembered as an excellent hurler, he makes his home in Grand Prairie, Texas.

DON SUTTON

Don Sutton was an elite pitching prospect in Pensacola and in college, followed closely by scouts like Whitey Herzog of the A's. To the chagrin of other clubs, he ultimately signed with the Dodgers and needed only one season of minor-league work.

The right-hander made his debut on April 14, 1966, throwing seven solid innings against Houston. Serving as the Dodgers' fourth starter, he threw mostly fastballs and curves, posted a 12-12 record, and garnered the rookie pitcher of the year award. He missed the World Series with an arm strain.

A couple of things changed in 1967. With the retirement of Sandy Koufax, Sutton moved up in the rotation. He also tried getting fancy with auxiliary pitches and was less successful, winning only one of his first seven decisions. After manager Walt Alston and catcher Jeff Torborg admonished him to concentrate on his heater and curve, his fortunes improved, but he finished with only an 11-15 record. "I quit trying to be a finesse pitcher," he commented toward the end of the season. "I just tried to get good stuff on every pitch." He added, "Alston is to the Dodgers what corn bread is to the south."

Even at that early stage of his career, he soaked his elbow in an ice tub after every start, the same container that Koufax had used. The start to Sutton's 1968 season was delayed due to a six-month military stint at Fort Gordon, Georgia. Noting that the Army required lots of pushups, which tend to tighten the shoulder muscles, Don did stretching exercises to try to keep the shoulder loose.

Early on, Sutton became a close friend of teammates Torborg and Joe Moeller. As Christians, the three bonded naturally, and gathered for worship on Sunday mornings. Moeller credited both Sutton and Torborg with aiding his spiritual growth.

Sutton turned in another 11-15 season in 1968, but was more impressive, placing 13th in the NL in ERA. In 1969, busier than ever, he made 41 starts with a 17-18 record, despite missing two weeks for military duty. He and his wife Patti welcomed their first child and moved into a new home in the Los Angeles suburbs after the season. When not helping Patti tend to the little one that winter, Sutton ran three to five miles per day, lifted light weights, and played volleyball and basketball to stay in shape.

Don finally achieved the expected level of dominance in 1972, when he posted a 19-9 record with nine shutouts and a filthy 2.09 ERA. He remained a top pitcher throughout the decade, making four all-star teams. He won his first six post-season decisions, before going 0-3 in the 1978 playoffs and Series.

During the summer of 1980, Sutton declared himself the second-best NL pitcher after Steve Carlton. He left after the season as a free agent, and over the next eight years, he pitched for four other clubs, before closing out with the 1988 Dodgers.

When Sutton retired at age 43, he had a lifetime record of 324-256 with 58 shutouts and a 3.26 ERA. He later became an announcer for the Braves and the Nationals. In baseball history, only Cy Young and Nolan Ryan made more pitching starts, and no Dodger pitcher won more games than Sutton, who was inducted into the Hall of Fame in 1998. He died of cancer at age 75 in Rancho Mirage, California, in 2021.

WILLIE MCCOVEY

Former Giants pitcher Gaylord Perry called him "the most feared hitter of his time" and said "nobody hit the ball harder." Bob Bolin, another teammate, said, "He had the best swing you'd ever want to see."

Baseball fans quickly got an idea of the type of career Willie McCovey would enjoy. On July 30, 1959, he suited up for the first time and went four-for-four against Robin Roberts of the Phillies. A day later, the left-handed pull hitter had a game-winning hit against Pittsburgh. In his third game, he collected two doubles and a single. Then in his fourth contest, he hit the first of his 521 home runs. He finished that first half-season with a .354 batting average, 13 home runs, and during one stretch, a 22-game hitting streak. He copped the rookie of the year award.

Willie suffered from the sophomore jinx in 1960, as his batting average plunged 116 points, and at one point, he was returned to minor-league Tacoma. That was a disappointing year for San Francisco. Playing their third season on the west coast, the Giants underperformed, with Bill Rigney getting fired as manager mid-season, replaced on an interim basis by Tom Sheehan. Alvin Dark got the job on a long-term basis after the season.

The slugger from Mobile, Alabama got back on track in 1961 and again in 1962, the year the Giants captured the NL flag, playing part time. With both McCovey and Orlando Cepeda on the club, only one could play first base at a time. If the other started, it was in the outfield, and given the wicked winds at Candlestick Park, that could spell a treacherous situation.

It was not until 1963 that Willie played regularly again, and he responded with 44 home runs, the most in the senior circuit. The Giants were loaded with power hitters, as they also received 38 homers from Willie Mays, 34 from Cepeda, 21 from Ed Bailey, and 20 from Felipe Alou. Dark had been asking owner Horace Stoneham to trade one of the sluggers for pitching but Stoneham loved the fireworks and resisted such a move. The Giants drifted from first to third place that season.

The 1964 go-around was unsatisfying for McCovey and many of his teammates. Amidst high expectations, the team spent most of the year in third or fourth place, looking up at the Phillies and Cardinals. Then a New York scribe wrote an article accusing Dark of making a racially insensitive comment. A national controversy followed. McCovey, who hit only .220 that season with 18 homers, wondered aloud about how his manager felt about him. Although some players came to Dark's defense, the Giants finished fourth, and the skipper was fired during the final game of the season, replaced by coach Herman Franks. The Giants had more black and Latino players than most other clubs. McCovey most often roomed on the road with Jim Ray Hart. He also roomed at times with Mays, and was with Mays on his first date with his future second wife, Mae.

During the 1965 season, McCovey moved from left field back to first base, and responded with 39 jacks. Mays slugged 52 home runs, as the Giants placed second to the Dodgers, who had better pitching. Dark was of course gone, but his diagnosis of the Giants' lack of pitching depth was spot-on.

There would be no pennants over the next several years, but McCovey gradually became the clear fan favorite at Candlestick Park, especially among the legions of faithful in right field who awaited the lefty swinger's frequent home runs.

From 1968 to 1970, he was the NL's most fearsome slugger, hitting 120 home runs. He garnered the MVP award in 1969, despite the fact his team did not win its division. Pitchers got so tired of being burned that they walked McCovey 137 times in 1970. Despite being pitched around, he still drove in 126 runs, one of four 100-RBI seasons.

McCovey developed arthritic knees at an early age, yet continued to hustle and produce when others might have begged out of the lineup due to the pain. Cubs' hurler Dick Selma once threw McCovey 16 straight balls over four at bats. Mets' pitcher Gary Gentry said, "Just looking at him scares you." Teams sometimes employed a shift against McCovey, and he occasionally would drop a bunt down the third base line to keep opponents honest. Most often, he swung away and often delivered big hits despite the shift.

After the Giants won their division in 1971, during their unsuccessful NLCS against Pittsburgh, he did his part and then some, batting .429 with two homers in four games.

Despite injuries, he played until 1980 for the Giants, Padres, A's and back with San Francisco, and became one of those rare stars to play MLB in four decades. When he punched his ticket for the last time, he had 521 home runs, 1,555 RBI, 2,211 hits, and a.270 batting average. He was inducted into the Hall of Fame on the first ballot.

Willie was more than just a great slugger. Catcher Hobie Landrith recalled, "If he walked into a room and was smiling, everybody smiled. He electrified everyone." Outfielder Jose Cardenal recalled his rookie season saying, "Willie took care of me. He called me Junior. I didn't have any money so I carried his radio boombox from the airport to the hotel and he'd give me $20. That's how I was able to afford a steak."

In 1995, McCovey was convicted of tax evasion for failing to report about $70,000 in income from autograph sessions. He was sentenced to two years of probation and a $5,000 fine. President Barack Obama pardoned McCovey. In 2003, the Giants unveiled a statue bearing his likeness. More than 50 of his former teammates traveled to San Francisco to be there, including Masanori Murakami who made the trip from Japan.

ORLANDO CEPEDA

When prospect Orlando Cepeda played winter ball in Puerto Rico in 1957-1958, writer Ken Smith called him "a slasher of the Joe Medwick style." So, it was not a big surprise when Cepeda became the 1958 NL rookie of the year, helping the Giants improve their record by 11 wins over the previous year. MLB had just arrived in San Francisco and Orlando became tremendously popular. He often spent free evenings in the city's night spots, fostering a connection with the community and its fan base.

Cepeda made the all-star team annually from 1959 to 1964. His 1961 season saw him lead the NL with 46 homers and 142 RBI, placing second in the MVP vote count (behind Frank

Robinson). Yet, that season was a personal turning point in that he hurt his right knee in a collision at home plate and played with pain for the rest of his career.

Despite his production, Giants manager Alvin Dark, and later manager Herman Franks, grew frustrated with him not running out every ground ball. Cepeda blamed it on the knee. Things came to a head in 1965 when the pain became unbearable and Cepeda missed most of the campaign, eventually undergoing surgery.

With Willie McCovey by then firmly entrenched at first base, the Giants traded Cepeda to St. Louis early in the 1966 season. Playing loud Latino music and speaking Spanish while horsing around in the clubhouse had been viewed as objectionable in San Francisco but was accepted in St. Louis. He also got to play his favorite position, first base, rather than left field, as was often the case with the Giants.

Entering the 1967 season, the two things Cepeda had not accomplished were to win an MVP award and win a World Series. He checked both boxes in 1967. He led the NL in RBI and achieved a tremendous .923 OPS during the regular season. Although his bat went silent in the postseason, his Cardinals outlasted the Red Sox in seven games to win the championship.

Cepeda suffered through an off-season in 1968, though he did deliver a pair of home runs in the World Series, which the Cardinals lost to the Tigers. Following a trade to the Braves and another fair season in 1969, Cepeda's bat regained its explosiveness in 1970. He topped 100 RBI for the fifth and final time, while hitting .305. He was off to a fine start again in 1971 when he injured his previously healthy left knee. He played sparingly after the injury and had late-season surgery. Orlando saw even less action with the A's in 1972.

There was one more comeback to come. The AL adopted the DH rule in 1973, and the Red Sox tapped the veteran from Puerto Rico. He had a productive season, batting .286 with 20 home runs. Yet, the Red Sox were looking to go younger in 1974 and released him over the winter. He finally found a taker in Kansas City well into the 1974 season, but was unproductive, and retired with a .297 batting clip, 379 home runs and 2,351 hits.

Early on, Orlando's father had been a star in Puerto Rican winter ball, and Orlando had served as the bat boy during the winter of 1953-1954 for the Crabbers, a Santurce-based team whose roster included Willie Mays and Roberto Clemente. The youngster came to know the Santurce owner, Pedrin Zorrilla, who was involved in the signing of such talents as Clemente, Juan Pizarro, and others to MLB contracts. Zorrilla got Cepeda a Giants contract with a modest $500 bonus. Cepeda wound up spending most of the bonus on funeral expenses for his father, a municipal sewer worker, who died of malaria.

For a time, Cepeda's personal life after baseball was a mess. His first marriage had already ended due to his infidelity. He remarried but was arrested in 1975 for taking possession of 170 pounds of marijuana. He rechanneled his money to his legal defense, which led to him missing child-support payments. After serving 10 months in prison, he got a job as a minor-league hitting instructor, but lost the job evidently because of a sporadic attendance record.

He eventually remarried, settled down, and found steady work with the Giants, whose fans were happy to see him back with the franchise. He was elected to the Baseball Hall of Fame in 1999.

STEVE CARLTON

The list of left-handed pitchers with 300 or more wins is a short one. Warren Spahn leads the way with 363 triumphs. Steve Carlton is second with 329 wins. Rounding out the elite club are Eddie Plank (305), Tom Glavine (305), Randy Johnson (303) and Lefty Grove (300).

All six are enshrined in the Hall of Fame. Carlton actually pitched in Cooperstown before winning a major league game. He was with the Tulsa Oilers, a Cardinals farm club, when invited to pitch against the Twins in the annual Hall of Fame Game in 1966. (The Hall of Fame Game was an exhibition contest featuring major and minor league players, conducted at Doubleday Field annually from 1939 until 2008. It was replaced with the Hall of Fame Classic, featuring retired players, in 2009.) Carlton collected eight strikeouts in the game as the Cardinals won, 7-5.

Pitching through 1988, Steve struck out 4,136 hitters. His six one-hitters are an NL record (though Bob Feller threw 12 such gems in the AL and Nolan Ryan achieved the same total during his time in both leagues).

One of the anomalies of MLB over the years – with implications for Carlton – was the old "first-year player draft." In various forms, it was in effect from 1947 to 1950; from 1953 to 1957; and from 1959 to 1964. The primary purpose was to de-incentivize teams from paying big bonuses to amateur players. If a franchise could lose the player before he even had a chance to prove himself, the theory went, teams would be less likely to outbid one another for top talent and drive up player-personnel expenses. Critics said the rule penalized teams that were adept at signing and developing prospects.

In the case of Carlton, he posted a 15-5 record for three different Cardinals' farm clubs in 1964. He then became eligible to be snatched by another team in the first-year player draft. To make him ineligible to be drafted under the rules then in effect, the Cardinals carried him on their big-league roster for the entire 1965 season, even though he pitched only 25 innings. With plenty of time on his hands, he studied scouting reports and observed how pitchers approached the different hitters. He not surprisingly needed more minor-league experience, but that had to wait until 1966, when he was no longer at risk of being drafted.

Carlton himself was not a high-level bonus baby, having signed for just a $5,000 bonus. After he won his first game for St. Louis late in the 1966 season, Mets manager Wes Westrum said,

"The kid looked like he'd been around for 10 years. He was a cool cucumber and performed like a veteran."

Just 22 years old in 1967, the southpaw won 14 regular-season games and pitched six solid innings in game five of the World Series. In 1968, Steve won 13 contests and hurled five shutouts, including a one-hitter against the Cubs. During the World Series, he was used twice out of the bullpen, as manager Red Schoendienst preferred to go with a rotation of Bob Gibson, Nellie Briles and Ray Washburn. Detroit won the Series in seven contests.

By 1969, Carlton left little doubt that he should be near the top of the rotation. He won 17 games and his 2.17 ERA was second only to Juan Marichal in the NL. He was also the starting pitcher in the all-star game, allowing two runs in three innings of work. On September 15 of that year, he struck out 19 Mets, though he still lost the game.

Carlton endured a 10-19 season in 1970, then won 20 games for the first time in 1971. Amidst a contract dispute with owner August Busch, he was traded to the Phillies for hurler Rick Wise. Carlton turned in a historic season in his first year in Philadelphia, winning 27 games on a losing team.

The six-time 20-game winner actually was a better pitcher in the second half of his career. Three of his four Cy Young Awards came after his 30th birthday, as did three of his five strikeout titles.

As described in an article in *Baseball Digest,* Carlton was said to have had "a focus that bordered on robotic, a slider that bordered on unhittable, and a personality that bordered on bizarre." Starting in 1974, he refused to speak with reporters, a decision that framed the type of press coverage he would receive in the years to come.

Carlton later pitched for the Giants, White Sox, Indians and Twins and was inducted into the Hall of Fame in his first year of eligibility in 1994. Though born in Florida, at last report he was living in Colorado.

DAVEY JOHNSON

The same fiery competitiveness that made infielder Davey Johnson an admired teammate for the Orioles, Braves, Phillies and Cubs later made him one of the most successful managers of his generation.

He signed with the Orioles and spent three years in their farm system. Johnson initially gained as much notoriety for his voracious appetite as he did for his athletic skills. In the March 27, 1965 issue of *The Sporting News,* writer Doug Brown chronicled Johnson's habits as a "chow hound." Teammate Darold Knowles was quoted as saying, "At a smorgasbord one time, he went back for more so many times the hotel manager was giving him strange looks, like he was going to ban him or something. And then Dave went out and played that night." Catcher Larry Haney was quoted saying, "He eats like a young horse. If the two of us had a five-pound steak and five pounds of potatoes in front of us, I'd eat one pound of each and he'd eat the rest." Yet another teammate, Russ Snyder, offered, "Coming back from an exhibition game in Orlando last year, I watched Dave eat four chicken dinners and drink three or four cokes. The only reason he quit eating was because we ran out of food on the bus."

He made his major league debut late in the 1965 season, and then wrestled the starting second base job away from Jerry Adair in 1966. In that fall's World Series, he gained the distinction of collecting the last hit off Sandy Koufax.

By 1968, Johnson made the all-star team for the first of four times, and the following year he won the first of two gold glove awards. A picture of consistency, he compiled batting averages of .280, .281 and .282 in successive seasons under Earl Weaver. Baltimore won pennants each year. Despite that success and his love for playing the game, he grew to despise his annual contract hassles with the Orioles' front office, and before the 1970 season he even asked for a trade, before finally settling on terms.

After shoulder and back trouble led to an off-season in 1972, Johnson was dealt to the Braves. In one of the surprises of the 1973 season, Davey clubbed 43 home runs (his previous high was 17). He said being around Hank Aaron made him a better hitter.

In 1974, while his teammate Aaron was breaking the all-time home run record, Johnson added 15 more home runs of his own. In 1975 he was a teammate of Sadaharu Oh, the Japanese home run legend who had recently surpassed 714 home runs himself. Johnson returned to the States and spent two final years with the Phillies and Cubs. He retired after the 1978 season.

He went on to spend 17 years as a manager, working until age 70. His lifetime record as a skipper was 1372-1071 for a fantastic .562 winning percentage. In retirement, Johnson has been living in Winter Park, Florida.

DAROLD KNOWLES

One of the less-recognized aspects of being a major leaguer is dealing with sportswriters. In any era, there were always players who shunned that interaction. Reliever Darold Knowles was just the opposite. He knew the reporters had a job to do and did his best to give them insightful or amusing quotes to make their jobs a bit easier. "I always got along with them. They were very kind," he reflected in 2022.

Knowles pitched for seven teams between 1965 and 1980, armed with a superb sinker and adept at changing locations. He avoided throwing curves. Darold credits coach Harry Dunlop as well as teammates Charley Lau and Bob Saverine, with helping to make him a better pitcher.

While still a minor leaguer in the winter of 1963, Knowles took a winter job as a meat butcher. Orioles general manager Harry Dalton understandably became alarmed and steered the young man toward a sales job. Darold pitched in Rochester in 1964 and in Venezuela the next winter, serving notice that he was an elite prospect. He made his MLB debut with the Orioles in April 1965 and spent most of the season back at Triple-A Rochester with the Red Wings. While there, Phillies scouts Johnny Ogden and Dewey Griggs observed him and persuaded their team to acquire him.

Early in his career, Knowles pitched winter ball in Venezuela. "It was very different from today," he recalled. "We did lots of snorkeling and the food was good."

Philadelphia traded Darold to the Senators for outfielder Don Lock. By 1969, the lefty had become an elite reliever and an all-star, posting a 9-2 record and 2.24 ERA for the Senators. He enjoyed his situation so much that he purchased a home in nearby Suitland, Maryland. In 1970, his ERA was even better and he notched 27 saves, though through some bad breaks, he had only a 2-14 record.

Then from 1971 to 1974, he was an outstanding setup man with the A's. Darold's road roommates included catcher Jim French with Washington and hurler Catfish Hunter with Oakland.

A Missouri native, Knowles later settled in the Dunedin, Florida area, and worked as a pitching coach for many years. His 66-74 lifetime record was accompanied by an excellent 3.12 ERA and 143 saves.

FRED VALENTINE

In a 1966 *Washington Post* interview, Senators outfielder Fred Valentine said, "You know how education is for Negroes in the South. My dad was determined that I get a college education." With that in mind, Valentine spurned some modest bonus offers from pro teams when he finished high school and went on to become a baseball and football star at Tennessee Agricultural and Industrial College. He later earned a master's degree and a law degree as well.

His college years delayed his entry into pro ball, but race likely was a factor in keeping Fred at the Triple-A level for much of his career. He got to Triple-A Miami in 1959 yet was still playing at the same level in 1965 for Hawaii, where he ripped 25 homers and stole 68 bases. By this time, he was 30 years old, and had seen big-league action in only 38 games for Baltimore and 102 games for Washington. Both clubs seemed inclined to give playing time to white outfielders with modest track records during those years.

In 1966, Fred played regularly for the Senators and delivered a fine season with a .276 average, 16 homers and 22 steals. His 3.5 WAR rating paced the team and he placed 21st in MVP voting. The Senators placed a disappointing eighth, but Valentine and his wife Helena found they loved the nation's capital and made the area their lifetime home.

Fred was with the Nats until the 1968 trade deadline when he was swapped back to the Orioles. He spent 1969 at Rochester and played a year in Japan in 1970.

Valentine shared with the BlackCollegeNines website some memories from his days in 1958 with the Wilson Tobs. The white players stayed on one side of the railroad tracks and the black players lived in a house on the other side. In the stadium, there was a special grandstand reserved for African Americans. One day just before a game, the grandstand collapsed and team management asked Valentine for his advice on what to do. "One thing you can do, all these people are in and paid, you can just let them go up in the big grandstand, because you've got plenty of room up there. All these people in this small town know each other. Just let them sit wherever they want to." That led to the permanent integration of baseball seating in Wilson.

After baseball, Fred worked for Clark Construction in the nation's capital and was active in such charities as the Major League Players Alumni Association, Kiwanis, Knights of Columbus and the Cystic Fibrosis Society. A lifetime .247 hitter with 36 homers, he was 87 years old when he died the day after Christmas in 2022.

DICK LINES

Left-hander Dick Lines was a Senators' relief pitcher who notched a nifty 2.83 ERA his first two seasons, only to see his career sidetracked by a shoulder injury.

Lines was born in Canada and was 10 years old when his family moved to Virginia. The Pirates scouted him for three years in high school and signed him in 1957. That winter, the 19-year old enjoyed the freedom of adult life playing for Mazatlan in the Mexican Pacific Winter League. "I loved the experience," he recalled.

The Senators traded for him at the end of the 1965 training camp, and then promoted him to the major leagues for the 1966 and 1967 seasons. With Washington, he roomed on road trips with hurler Bob Humphreys. In 1967, the club had a surprisingly deep bullpen with Darold Knowles, Dave Baldwin, Casey Cox, Humphreys and Lines all having solid years.

Dick left baseball after the 1969 season. "I worked for Budweiser beer for a second career, and enjoyed it almost as much as playing baseball," he recently said. Like many players of his generation, he says the best part was simply competing against so many super players. These days, he lives in Lady Lake, Florida.

BOOG POWELL

Boog Powell is arguably one of the five greatest MLB players born in Florida. Steve Carlton, Andre Dawson and Chipper Jones would claim three of those spots. Powell and several other baseball legends would compete for the last two slots.

One of the top sluggers of his era, Powell's power constantly elicited awe. Indians manager Birdie Tebbetts said, "Every time he swings, I cringe." Teammate John Orsino said, "He does all his talking with his bat." Coach Gene Woodling said in 1964, "For a matter of six weeks, he was almost a one-man show for us."

That year, Powell led the AL in slugging percentage, calculated as at bats divided into total bases, while playing left field and hitting 39 home runs. He then spent the winter in Baltimore working for Churchill Ltd, a distributor of fine spirits. He didn't find the chilly winter to his liking.

Then came a 1965 season in which Powell took forever to get on track. Manager Hank Bauer attributed it to Boog's weight and challenged his slugger to get from 250 pounds back down to 240. Coincident or not, the home runs started coming again. But managing his weight was an enormous challenge for a guy standing six-foot-five with a large frame. Anything more than one meal a day would result in weight gain. Powell also spent that 1965 campaign shuttling between the outfield and first base, whereas he preferred to play one position or the other.

In 1966, Boog moved permanently to first base and while teammate Frank Robinson got the headlines with his triple crown, Powell had a tremendous season as well, hitting .287 with 34 circuit shots. That summer, he began using Robinson's bats, which were the same length and weight as his own. "The batch I had were soft, almost like balsa wood. They must have come from bad trees," he explained. He stayed with Robby's sticks until a new batch arrived for him. In the 1966 World Series against the Dodgers, Powell hit .356.

Reflecting at a SABR convention on the 1966 Orioles, Powell said, "It's really great coming to the ballpark every day knowing you're going to kick someone's ass….We played great defense and we didn't make any mistakes. We didn't beat ourselves. It was a lot of fun."

Powell endured an off-year in 1967, as his weight ballooned to 258 pounds. Following the season, Orioles executive Harry Dalton met him for lunch in Miami. The pair had a candid discussion, with Dalton laying down the law that Powell report to camp at 240 and maintain that level all season. That led to a winter of calisthenics at a fitness center and smaller portions at the dining table.

He reported to camp in 1969 in the best shape ever. Boog went on to hit .304 with a career-best 121 RBI and placed second in the 1969 MVP voting. He credited coach Charlie Lau with frequently reminding him not to lunge at pitches. The Orioles won the AL pennant but lost to the Mets in the World Series. Looking back, Powell said, "We had such a huge lead in the American League. I think we were flat. We weren't playing with all the emotion that we could have played with. Nothing went right." Boog was touched that several thousand O's fans were at the airport behind a fence to welcome the team home.

Powell then took the MVP award in 1970, when he helped the Birds to the world championship. His sterling production, with 35 homers and 114 RBI, was even more astounding considering how often opposing hurlers pitched around him.

Asked which of the pennant-winners was the best Orioles team (1966, 1969, 1970 or 1971), Boog said, "If I had to pick a year, the best team was in '69. We were really good. We just weren't good for five games."

The slugger remained with Baltimore through 1974 and then delivered one final high-impact season for Cleveland in 1975. By 1976, Boog was 34 years old and no longer productive. He got into 50 games for the 1977 Dodgers who released him on August 31 to open a spot on their 40-man roster for a younger player.

Powell's career numbers included a .266 batting average, 1,776 hits, and 339 home runs. The pitchers he victimized most were two of the best – Denny McLain and Luis Tiant – for nine home runs off each of them. He also victimized Catfish Hunter seven times.

Boog's early hobbies were skin diving and fishing, where his largest catch was a 140-pound jewelfish. He also has been a country music fan, claiming personal friendships with the likes of Roy Clark, Willie Nelson and Justin Tubb. At one point, there was talk of convening an Orioles country vocal group with teammates Powell, Eddie Fisher, Jerry Adair and Jackie Brandt, but nothing came of it.

For 28 years after his playing days were over, he and his son operated Boog's Barbecue restaurant at Orioles Park at Camden Yards, where he could be seen mingling with fans. Powell is a longtime member of the Orioles Hall of Fame.

WALLY BUNKER

When one thinks about great pitcher rookie seasons in the Sixties, Stan Bahnsen in 1968, Tom Seaver in 1967 and Wally Bunker in 1963 come to mind.

Bunker threw a sinker and relied less on strikeouts than some other hurlers. During his rookie season with the Orioles, Wally won 19 games as a 19-year-old rookie and led the league in winning percentage.

His story started at Capuchino High School in San Bruno, California, the school that produced Keith Hernandez a decade later. Bunker devastated opposing hitters and drew scouts galore to his games. Orioles scouts Don McShane and Fred Hoffman befriended Bunker when he was just 15 years old, so by the time he was old enough to go pro, he had a good feel for the Orioles organization. He signed for $75,000 in 1963, plunked down some cash on a Studebaker Avanti sports car (his dad invested the rest of the funds for him), and then ran off a 10-1 record for the Stockton Ports in the California League.

Bunker – just one year removed from high school -- began the 1964 season in the Orioles' bullpen, chiefly to prevent the other clubs from drafting him. But manager Hank Bauer moved him into the rotation in early May when starters Milt Pappas and Steve Barber were injured. He tossed a 99-pitch one-hitter against the Senators in his first 1964 start. The rest of the campaign was a dream ride for the young man, as he tamed enemy hitters to the tune of a 2.69 ERA. Among AL pitchers, only Dean Chance and Gary Peters notched more victories.

Being single, Bunker shared an apartment in Baltimore with teammate Chuck Estrada (Wally married his California-based fiancé Kathy Wild after the season.) The Birds were part of an exciting pennant race that year, ultimately finishing third with 97 wins. During the course of the season, the team took 33 flights (24 charters and nine commercial flights). In a patriotic gesture, team members wore Star Spangled Banner emblems on their sleeves all season in honor of the national anthem's 150th anniversary. The anthem was written by Francis Scott Key aboard a ship in the Baltimore harbor during the War of 1812.

After that sensational year, in which Bunker matched the record for most wins by a rookie, his arm was never again healthy. Shoulder pain caused him to change his arm slot and he began taking cortisone shots in May 1965. He won 10 games each in 1965 and 1966 but added a shutout against the Dodgers in the 1966 World Series, one of his career highlights. After the Orioles prevailed in the World Series, Bunker and his wife returned to his home town of San Bruno for a parade in his honor. Mayor Carney Berberian proclaimed Bunker "Mayor for a Day."

By 1967, though he was only 22 years old, the sore-shouldered hurler was pitching mostly out of the bullpen. In 1968, he spent part of the year in Triple-A Rochester, while getting into 18 games for Baltimore. As a diversion from his on-field struggles, he picked up an enjoyable hobby of playing the guitar.

The expansion draft offered Bunker a fresh beginning and in 1969, he started the first game in Royals history, made 31 starts, and registered a 12-11 record on a losing team. Bunker bought a home in Shawnee Mission, Missouri, and worked for the club in a public relations role during the off-season.

His comeback was impressive but short-lived. The shoulder pain was back in 1970 and his record plunged to 2-11. Accepting that his career was finished, he was with the Royals' Triple-A club in Omaha when he retired mid-season in 1971. His lifetime record was 60-52 with a 3.51 ERA. After baseball, he and his wife became entrepreneurs, artisans, manufacturers, and even co-authors of a book. Those endeavors made for an adventurous life for a pitcher whose baseball career had peaked by the age of 20. Bunker now lives in Bluffton, South Carolina.

MICKEY LOLICH

This affable lefty etched his name into MLB lore when he won three games in the 1968 World Series, including game seven, which he pitched on just two days of rest. That decisive contest was played in St. Louis, with Lolich and his Tigers prevailing over Bob Gibson and the Cardinals by a score of 4-1 to win the title. Writer Alan Halberstadt recently called Lolich "an absolute iron man with a rubber arm in an era when pitchers were not paid anywhere near the sinful amounts bestowed on the coddled arms of today."

For 12 straight seasons, Lolich logged 200 or more innings; four of those years, the workhorse topped 300 frames. During his peak, from 1964 to 1972, Lolich won 158 games while losing only 113. He placed first or second in the AL in strikeouts five times and was a three-time all-star. For many years, he held the AL record for most career strikeouts; CC Sabathia finally passed him in 2017. In five post-season starts, Mickey had a flawless 1.57 ERA.

Lolich, the grandson of Croatian immigrants, attended Lincoln High School in Portland, which also produced longtime infielder Johnny Pesky. He rooted for the Yankees as a child, and later wore uniform number 16 in honor of his favorite player, Whitey Ford.

Mickey is one of four pitchers to amass 200 wins as a Tiger, the others being Hooks Dauss, George Mullin and Hal Newhowser. He spent his whole career with Detroit, save for late-career stints with the Mets and Padres. He had the honor of being the team's opening day hurler seven times.

Part of what made those Tiger teams special was the personal closeness of the players. "We grew up together in the minor leagues, so…we had a bonding of knowing each other for many years" he told an interviewer.

Blessed with a fantastic sense of humor, Lolich recalled the home run he hit in the 1968 Series, saying he credited opposing pitcher Nellie Briles for hitting his bat. He shared amusing stories in his 2018 book, *Joy in Tigertown,* but he also addressed the role the Tigers played in unifying the Detroit community after the previous year's riots.

Lolich was affected more than most by the 1967 uprisings. One day after pitching, he traded his baseball uniform for his military reserve uniform for nearly two weeks of service. When he pitched his first game back in Detroit, he did so under death threats from the Black Panthers, with FBI agents stationed around the ballpark.

The lefty won 17 games for the 1968 Tigers during the regular season. After they won the World Series, the team was celebrating with champagne in the clubhouse, when Lolich noticed that owner John Fetzer was standing off to the side in his three-piece suit, seemingly excluded. Lolich and Bill Freehan picked the owner up, carried him to the next room, and threw him into the whirlpool. According to Lolich in a 2012 interview with Priscilla Massie, the owner thanked the players for involving him in the celebration.

One of the lower days of Mickey's career came on May 28, 1969, when both Cesar Tovar and Rod Carew stole home in the same inning. In fact, Carew stole his way around the diamond, with Lolich seemingly unfocused. Catcher Bill Freehan dourly stated, "You can't tag the runner if you don't have the ball in your hand." Yet, Lolich won 19 games that season for a Tigers club that drifted to second place.

After a 14-19 campaign in 1970, he enjoyed his best season the following year, in 1971. Mickey won 25 games, fanned 308 hitters, and placed second to Vida Blue in the Cy Young award voting. That spring, he finally mastered the cut fastball. "That pitch led me to 25 wins in 1971," he recalled.

Lolich says he was shocked when traded to the Mets after the 1975 season. As a player with 10 years of service and five years with the same team, he vetoed the trade. The Tigers general manager called back, berated Lolich mercilessly, and out of anger, Lolich agreed to report. Then after one year with the Mets, in which modest run support limited him to an 8-13 record, he stayed out of baseball for a year. That made him a free agent and he signed with San Diego where he pitched for two years.

After retiring, Lolich and his wife needed to decide where to live. She was originally from Florida, a state Lolich never liked. She had worked in his hometown of Portland but didn't like the frequent rain. They decided together that it made the most sense to remain in Michigan. Mickey explained years later, for players of his generation, there were often more business opportunities, noting "Your name helps open doors."

Lolich had a lifetime record of 217-191 with a 3.44 ERA. He hurled 41 shutouts and struck out 2,832 batters.

Jay Hook

Jay Hook was a lefty who had the misfortune of pitching for the Mets during their abysmal first two seasons. He already had an unsightly record of 17-28 (with the Redlegs) when he got to the Mets at age 25. Though he was the first Metropolitans pitcher to win a game, his two full seasons in New York were nothing but struggles, and when his career finished in 1964, his career record was 29-62. Importantly for Hook, he accumulated just enough service time to qualify for a pension.

The Chicago native planned ahead for his post-baseball days, spending winters studying at Northwestern University. He earned a bachelor's degree in engineering and took out a membership in the National Rocket Society. His scholarly pursuits earned him the nickname "Professor" during his days with the Mets. He later earned a master's degree in thermodynamics and enjoyed a rewarding career with Chrysler, Rockwell, and Masco. Jay now lives in Maple City, Michigan.

RON SWOBODA

The pride of Sparrows Point High School in Baltimore, Ron Swoboda played one year at the University of Maryland, then signed with Mets scout Pete Gebrian for a $35,000 incentive. Ron used the bonus to buy new cars for himself and his brother, and give $2,000 to his parents to pay off their house.

Ron made the 1965 opening day roster at the age of 21 and started fast by swatting home runs in two of his first four at bats. Despite some costly defensive misplays, he quickly became a fan favorite and clubbed 19 homers. As Til Ferdenzi wrote that June in *The Sporting News,* "He is fast becoming the box-office hotshot of the clients in Shea Stadium. When he's not playing, the customers miss him. Mention of Swoboda's name sends a buzz through the crowd, the same buzz given the big ones – Willie Mays, Mickey Mantle, Ted Williams, Stan Musial."

Manager Casey Stengel explained why Swoboda played only part-time, commenting "Swoboda's young and I'd like to put him in here and there where it will do us and him the most good." Like all players, Ron disliked being on the bench, but freely acknowledged his outfield skills needed improvement. He resented newspaper accounts saying he disliked practicing his glovework. After his rookie season, he reported to the Florida Instructional League, where he fielded hundreds of balls hit by coach Kerby Farrell. He also got married that off-season.

Over the next several years, Ron averaged about 55 RBI. Gradually, the Mets upgraded their outfield, but Swoboda was still a key contributor in 1969 when the Mets had their memorable year, contributing a .235 average, 9 homers and 52 RBI.

As many of this book's readers know, Swoboda's career highlight came in the ninth inning of game four of the 1969 World Series, when he made a diving catch of a Brooks Robinson line drive. That spectacular play kept the game in hand for Tom Seaver, and the Mets went on to win the contest and the Series. Video of the catch is still viewed by fans on YouTube. Swoboda contributed with the bat in the Series as well, hitting .400 and driving in the winning run in the final game.

Following the spirited championship celebrations, Swoboda sought a 50 percent pay raise. The Mets offered closer to 25 percent and Swoboda had little choice but to accept it. "There was no handshake when I signed," he lamented to reporters. "I thought they'd treat me fairer than they did. I'm sick over the whole thing. I never had a worse feeling inside in my whole life." Seeking to boost their income, Ron and teammate Ed Kranepool opened a restaurant together, called The Dugout, on Route 110 in Amityville, Long Island, in 1970.

Swoboda remained a Met until spring training 1971, when he was swapped to the Expos. Later that summer he was dealt to the Yankees, where he played for a couple of seasons. He went to spring training with the Braves in 1974 but failed to make the team and retired. Ron was a .242 lifetime hitter with 73 home runs. After his playing years, the affable Swoboda became a television analyst. He guest-starred in an episode of Everybody Loves Raymond, as well. He now resides in a more-than 100-year-old home in New Orleans.

TOM SEAVER

Right-hander Tom Seaver was a 21-year-old college pitcher when he signed with the Braves in February 1966, one month after the club drafted him. Because the college season had technically already started, MLB voided the contract and established a lottery for Seaver's services among any team willing to match the intended $52,000 bonus. Three clubs entered the sweepstakes – the Phillies, Indians and Mets. When the Mets won the lottery, it changed their franchise's trajectory.

By 1967, Seaver entered the Mets rotation, won 16 games, and made the first of 12 all-star teams. He followed up with 16 more wins in 1968, and only Juan Marichal, Bob Gibson and Steve Carlton had finer ERAs. Manager Gil Hodges called him "a young Whitey Ford with more stuff." By 1969, he was the league's best pitcher, posting a 25-7 record as the Mets went on to win an unlikely world championship.

Seaver threw both a rising fastball and a sinking fastball, as well as the slider. Midway through his career, he began throwing more curves, as well. He also had the ability to concentrate on his work and envision positive outcomes. Mets pitching instructor Frank Lary, a former Tigers ace, said what he liked most was that he never had to tell Seaver anything twice – Tom listened and acted on advice immediately. That power of concentration also allowed Seaver to locate pitches where he wanted them. Pitching coach Rube Walker said, "He's on the corners all the time. Just nibbling at the corners. You can't hit those pitches."

Another factor was his maturity off the field. A thoughtful young man committed to completing his college studies, Seaver went home to his wife immediately after every home game. He might visit some museums on road trips, but no energy was wasted on late nights out.

Early in the 1969 season, when the Mets were making a lot of mental mistakes to Hodges' consternation, Seaver spoke in Hodges' defense. "I get depressed when I make a mental mistake.

He's got to worry about an entire team and some of the things he's seen happen over and over again are too much."

Tom was an easy choice for the 1969 Cy Young award. He also became a national celebrity, on the cover of magazines, and promoting products like Vitalis after shave and Royal Crown Cola. So many invitations arrived for public appearances that he delayed his plans to complete his degree at USC that winter.

Seaver loved the challenge of pitching to the NL's toughest hitters, but also enjoyed fielding. He told writer Jack Lang, "Fielding my position is one of the most enjoyable parts of the game for me…handling balls back to the box, covering first, trying to figure the other team's strategy."

The hurler's exploits beyond the Sixties were equally impressive. He was a five-time 20-game winner, won five strikeout titles, and led the loop in ERA three times. As late as 1981, his 14-2 record for the Reds earned him the best NL winning percentage.

When he retired after the 1986 season, he had a lifetime record of 311-205 for a .603 percentage. His lifetime ERA was a sparkling 2.86 and his totals of 61 shutouts and 3,640 strikeouts placed him among the all-time greats.

As 1994 approached, there were ample marketing opportunities around the 25th anniversary of the 1969 Miracle Mets. Always a team leader, Seaver contacted his former teammates and proposed an approach that would allow all of the living members of the club to share in the revenue. That said a lot about the type of man that he was. A first-ballot Hall of Famer, Seaver was 75 years old when he passed away in California in 2020.

Tony Oliva

Minnesota fans celebrated in 2022 when Tony Oliva was elected to the Hall of Fame, 46 years after his career concluded. Oliva had some spectacular seasons, leading the AL in hits five years. But until 2022, his career had been considered too short to qualify for Cooperstown. Blame a 1971 knee injury for shortening his career.

Oliva possessed a great throwing arm, an ability to patrol the outfield, and a graceful swing that yielded a .304 lifetime batting average and 220 home runs. He was also a great ambassador for the game of baseball, during and after his playing career. When the Veterans Committee made its selections for 2022, Oliva finally got the long-awaited phone call, as did his longtime teammate, pitcher Jim Kaat.

Oliva often called himself "a little country boy" from Cuba. "I never played Little League or high school or amateur ball," he reflected recently. "We'd go to a tree and cut a branch to make a bat because we were a poor family. We lived in the country. We didn't have all of the beautiful equipment that we have today. We made our own. My love was to play ball."

His professional career began with no signing bonus. In fact, according to a 1966 article in *Baseball Digest,* he was not even under contract when he began playing minor-league ball. Del Norwood, his first manager, was not told what position Oliva played. Norwood observed the youngster for a bit, stationed him in right field, and Oliva played there nearly his entire career.

Oliva got a brief taste of major league pitching in 1962 and 1963. Then in 1964, the Twins inked him into their lineup and he proved more than ready, as he led the AL in total bases and walked off with the top-rookie award. Even as he proved himself in the sport, he expressed sheer joy at being paid to play ball. Speaking of New York, he later marveled, "I'll never forget my first home run here was over the head of Mickey Mantle."

When the Twins won the pennant in 1965, Tony hit a spectacular .321. His road roommate, fellow Cuban Sandy Valdespino, was an effective 10th man, getting into more than 100 games. After the 1967 season, Sandy was traded to the Braves. Tony, feeling comfortable about his status with the team, purchased Sandy's home on Portland Avenue. Tony later moved into the more affluent suburbs.

Although Oliva never won an MVP award, he placed second in the balloting twice. Once was in 1965 when teammate Zoilo Versalles won the trophy and the Twins won the pennant. The second time came in 1970 when Boog Powell won the award. Tony won his third and final batting title in 1971. Following his knee injury, he played designated hitter his last few seasons.

Kaat has said that although teammates Harmon Killebrew and Rod Carew got to the Hall of Fame sooner, Oliva was the hitter that opposing pitchers and catchers most feared.

Oliva was in the dugout for all three of Minnesota's pennants: As a player in 1965 and as a coach in 1987 and 1991. He has also served as a Twins broadcaster. At last check, he was residing in Bloomington, Minnesota.

GAYLORD PERRY

This Hall of Fame right-hander pitched all the way to 1983 but turned in some of his finest work in the Sixties. That included four consecutive seasons with an ERA below 3.00 from 1966 to 1969, during which the workhorse had a 71-54 record for the Giants.

Success was not immediate. The tall, gangling North Carolinian commanded broad fan interest from the get-go, since his older brother Jim was already a major-league star, but Gaylord's record was just 24-30 going into the 1966 campaign. Giants farm director Carl Hubbell later said, "At one point, we thought we signed the wrong guy."

In 1966, Giants pitching coach Larry Jansen began working with him. "He was dropping his arm just a little, enough to flatten out his curve and slider. It robbed his fastball of its effectiveness," Jansen told a writer. Making that type of adjustment is easier said then done, but Perry worked at it, and also picked up a new pitch from Jansen – a harder version of his slider.

It all came together and by the midpoint of that 1966 season, Perry was an all-star. He won 21 games, despite missing three weeks after injuring a foot sliding into second base on May 24. He had surgery on his other foot for a bone spur after the season.

In one remarkable game in 1967, Perry pitched 16 innings in a scoreless tie, and received a standing ovation from the opposing team's faithful at Cincinnati's Crosley Field when he left the diamond. In 1968, Gaylord hurled a no-hitter against the Cardinals, who returned the favor with a Ray Washburn no-no the next day. Catcher Dick Dietz said that Perry made only three bad pitches during his gem, getting away with all of them.

Gaylord gradually became known for doctored pitches. He said he first threw the wet stuff in a 23-inning game on May 31, 1964. Perry hurled 10 shutout innings of relief to earn the win.

Perry's reputation for throwing doctored pitches grew, giving hitters even more to think about at the plate. Curt Flood said Perry was a good enough pitcher that he didn't need the greaser. Managers sent umpires out to inspect Perry's glove, cap and uniform with increasing frequency. This continued into his time in the AL, including in 1972, when he won a career-high 24 games for Cleveland.

His reputation followed wherever he went. Gene Mauch said Perry's plaque at the Hall of Fame should have a tube of KY Jelly attached. Billy Martin said Perry smelled like a drugstore. Perry teased about the topic constantly, from his book, *Me and the Spitter,* to when he retired, commenting, "The league will be a little drier now, folks."

Perry also possessed an intense will to win. Teammates making mental or physical mistakes behind him often received an angry glare – or worse.

Perry had a long memory, as well. Once after Bill Grabarkewitz delivered a hit that knocked Perry out of the game, he told Bill as he walked past first base that he would never get another hit against him. Thereafter, Perry threw Bill nothing but spitballs.

When Perry won the Cy Young Award with the Padres in 1978, he became the first pitcher to win the award in both leagues.

Late in his career, he told *Sports Illustrated,* "I enjoy the game and I'd like to play as long as I can do well for a club. It's a pretty good half-year job. You meet some great people and you can always stay away from the wrong ones. Moving around is the hardest part." During the off-seasons, Perry returned to his 300-acre peanut farm.

Perry retired with a 314-265 record and a 3.11 ERA, along with 3,534 strikeouts and 53 shutouts. After he passed away in 2022 at the age of 84, Juan Marichal said, "He was smart, funny, and kind to everyone in the clubhouse. I will always remember Gaylord for his love and devotion to the game of baseball, his family, and his farm."

KEN ASPROMONTE

For one splendid season, Ken Aspromonte was one of the best second basemen in baseball. The year was 1960, and the Indians acquired him from the Senators as a stop-gap replacement for the injured Johnny Temple. Aspro hit so well that he stayed in the lineup even after Temple returned to health. Ken closed out the year with a .290 average and 10 homers. Only Harvey Kuenn and Tito Francona had better batting clips for Cleveland.

That winter, the new Senators franchise selected him in the expansion draft. Soon enough in 1961, the Indians reacquired him, but he never hit so well again. He later played for the Angels and Braves, and concluded his major-league playing career with the Cubs in 1963, finishing with a lifetime average of .249.

Along with his younger brother Bob, Ken grew up in Brooklyn at a time when many Italians and Jews lived in the borough and played baseball. He remembers playing as a youth against future New York Governor Mario Cuomo and the Torre brothers, as well as Whitey Ford. Sandy Koufax came through his high school (several years after Ken) as did singer Vic Damone, painter Peter Max, actress Rhea Perlman, convicted sex offender Michael Epstein, and talk-show host Larry King. Others from Lafayette High School included major leaguers Al Ferrara, Larry Yellen, Mike Fiore, Sal Campisi, Pete Falcone and John Franco.

Ken broke in with the Red Sox in 1957 and lockered next to Ted Williams. "His conversations always revolved around hitting," Ken told interviewer Lawrence Baldassaro. "He was very much to himself and didn't interact much with the other guys. He had a superstar status." Williams advised Ken, when in the on-deck circle, to look at the green grass, as the ball will be easier to see. Ken, who had led the Pacific Coast League in hitting, was traded to the original Senators early in 1958 and was disappointed that the Sox had given up on him so quickly.

Looking back, Aspro marvels at the big-league talent during his era. "I played in the years of Mickey Mantle, Roger Maris. Hank Aaron was a teammate with me in Milwaukee (in 1962) along with Warren Spahn. I played with more superstars than you've got hair on your head," he recalled. "It was unbelievable. It was a great era. Hank would hit home runs like I would hit singles."

After his time with the Cubs, he played three years in Japan. "It was different. What really struck me was there was no violence in their play. None whatsoever. It was like getting a group of guys from New York for a softball game together. They had a good time and they had a big pot of tea in their dugout. And they bowed to one another. Very rarely did they throw at anybody. Sliding into second base, there was no knocking anybody down." Aspro said that has changed over time, as more Japanese athletes have gotten instruction from Americans.

Ken managed the Indians from 1972 to 1974 and later worked in public relations in Las Vegas. He then teamed up with his brother Bob to buy and manage a lucrative Coors distributorship in Houston. Through the years, he also played in charity golf tournaments and served as an officer of the National Italian American Foundation. Both Ken and his brother Bob were inducted into the National Italian Sports Hall of Fame in 2012.

CATFISH HUNTER

Jim (Catfish) Hunter was only 22 years old when he hurled a perfect game against the Twins in Oakland on May 8, 1968. He fanned 11, including Harmon Killebrew three times. It was just the ninth perfect game in MLB history and the first AL perfecto in 46 years, played before a sparse crowd of less than 7,000 fans. Jim supported his own cause with three hits as the A's won, 4-0.

Hunter threw almost nothing but fastballs the entire contest. He said after the game that there was only one moment that concerned him, in the seventh inning when Rod Carew hit a sharp liner to left field. Joe Rudi was the left fielder, playing in his first big-league game, and he nervously chased it down. Owner Charlie Finley immediately gave Hunter a $5,000 raise. Jim Pagliaroni, who caught the game, received a $1,000 raise from the A's and an engraved gold watch from Hunter.

The achievement confirmed that Finley had made a good investment in 1964 when he signed the young farm boy. Hunter had asked for $75,000 plus a Ford Thunderbird. The A's said yes to the bonus and no to the car. Hunter inked the pact anyway. Upon signing, he went to Finley's farm in Indiana to relax before going to the Mayo Clinic to have some pellets (from a hunting accident) surgically removed from his right foot.

By the spring of 1965, he went directly to the A's big-league roster, without any minor-league seasoning, along with a handful of other youngsters. His road roommate that season was Skip Lockwood, then a third base prospect and later a successful pitcher, who wrote, "Reared in Hertford, North Carolina, he rolled every vowel he spoke….he was a character right out of a Mark Twain novel…Fish was a power pitcher, and his fastball had movement that made it hard to hit from both sides of the plate."

When the A's moved from Kansas City to Oakland after the 1967 season, Hunter commented, "All the players loved the city. The people were real nice and I found a place to go bass fishing." Needless to say, the move was a business decision and the players were not consulted. Hunter added that the players were none too fond of some of owner Charlie Finley's publicity stunts, like having his pitchers ride a mule into the game. "We resented riding that thing from the bullpen. He gave us 50 bucks but…." In addition to fishing Jim also hunted deer, geese, ducks, rabbits and quail.

Catfish's record in the Sixties was just 55-64 and he didn't enjoy a winning season until 1970. What got him to Cooperstown was his dominant five-year peak from 1971 to 1975, when he won 111 games and lost only 49. He was the number one starter on the A's clubs that won three World Series and received the Cy Young award in 1974.

After the A's owner failed to make payments on an annuity that was part of Catfish's contract, he was declared a free agent by arbitrator Peter Seitz. He signed with the Yankees ahead of the 1975 season and won 23 games his first season in New York. He pitched with the Yankees through 1979, though as a diabetic, he began needing insulin shots and his performance declined.

Tragically, Hunter lost his life to Lou Gehrig's disease in 1999 at the age of 53. An eight-time all-star, his lifetime record was 224-166 with a 3.26 ERA and 42 shutouts. Reflecting his excellence with both the A's and Yankees, his plaque in the Hall of Fame does not depict either club's logo.

MIKE HERSHBERGER

Massillon, Ohio is a steel town that has seen more than 20 of its natives reach the NFL, including legendary coach Paul Brown. It also produced some major league baseball players in outfielder Tommy Heinrich, pitcher Joe Sparma and outfielder Mike Hershberger.

Mike played both sports in high school, then went to the University of Cincinnati on a football scholarship. He signed with the White Sox a year later and spent 11 years in the major leagues with the White Sox, A's and Brewers. He was an excellent defensive player with a rifle of an arm and led the league in double plays in 1965. He was also a good contact hitter, with a lifetime average of .258. In his best season in 1963 for the ChiSox, he hit .279 with 26 doubles and 45 RBI. His final year in the big leagues was 1971. He went to camp with the Indians in the spring of 1972 as a local favorite but lost out to Adolpho Phillips for the final roster spot.

During his career, he stayed in shape by playing handball. After baseball, Hershberger remained active in sporting goods sales, serving at his church, coaching the teams of his three sons, and volunteering with community organizations. He passed away in Massillon in 2012 following a short illness.

ROLLIE FINGERS

One of just a handful of relievers in the Hall of Fame, Rollie Fingers made his mark as the ace closer for the A's clubs that won three straight world titles from 1972 to 1974. He later starred with the Padres and won the 1981 Cy Young and MVP awards as a Brewer.

The story begins years earlier. As Fingers told Kevin Neary in the 2013 book, *"Closer: Major League Players Reveal the Inside Pitch on Saving the Game,* "I grew up with baseball. When I was little, my dad played in the minor leagues in the St. Louis organization. He and Stan Musial were roommates. This is when Stan Musial was a pitcher…My father taught me everything about the game. Most of all, he taught me the proper mechanics of how to throw a baseball correctly. The biggest thing when you are a kid is to find someone who knows the proper way of throwing a baseball so you aren't hurting your arm."

Fingers signed with the A's, and in January 1965, owner Charles Finley invited several prospects, wearing suits and ties, to Chicago for three days of lectures and instruction in the fine points of baseball, delivered by general manager Ed Lopat. Several of those invitees went on to have big-league careers, including Fingers, pitcher Chuck Dobson, and catcher Ken Suarez. Most of the other names – Ronnie Kluch, Gordon Riese, Charlie MacDonald, Joe Bosworth, Rick Bicek, Greg Conger, and Melvin Grubka – are lost to minor-league history.

The A's envisioned Fingers as a starter, and from 1965 to 1968, he posted a 42-36 minor-league record. The 1969 A's were loaded with starting pitchers, so Fingers spent his rookie season in the bullpen, notching 12 saves. In 1970, after the A's traded starter Jim Nash, Fingers made 19 starts, with mixed results.

By 1971, he returned to the pen and became a premier reliever. If it was Fingers' success out of the pen that led to fortune, it was his trademark mustache that earned him fame. In 1972 Finley conceived the idea of a Mustache Day promotion to build interest in his team. Then as now, Oakland was not one of the top cities for attendance, and Finley was constantly trying out new ideas. As Mustache Day approached, all 25 players participated. This was during an era when some general managers fined players for facial hair displays. Fingers adopted his trademark waxed, curled mustache that became his calling card as much as his late-game entries from the bullpen.

Every year from 1971 to 1978, Fingers had an ERA below 3.00 while pitching no fewer than 107 innings. After the 1976 season, he signed a multi-year deal with the Padres as one of baseball's first free agents. He led the NL in saves twice for San Diego.

The seven-time all-star had a 114-118 record, a 2.90 ERA, and as of 2024 ranked 15th on the all-time save list with 341. Dan Quisenberry, a great reliever in his own right, said Fingers always threw the right pitch at the right time. Fingers was elected to the Hall of Fame in his second year on the ballot and went in wearing an A's cap.

REGGIE JACKSON

Early in the 1968 season, A's manager Bob Kennedy told an interviewer that his young team could win games despite not having anyone who could slug 30 or 40 home runs. "Don't get me wrong," he joked, "I'd take a guy like that if I could get one. But we don't need that to win."

He didn't have to wait long. By September, second-year outfielder Reggie Jackson had hit 29 home runs. Jackson was fourth in the league in homers and tied for eighth in RBI. Kennedy was fired at the end of the season – despite improving the A's record by 20 wins – but Jackson was just getting started.

In 1969, at age 23, he had an incredible first half, and newspapers began printing summaries comparing his home-run pace with that of Roger Maris in 1961 and Babe Ruth in 1927. Jackson cooled off a bit in the second half, but still wound up with 47 homers (good for third in the league) and placed fifth in MVP balloting. Pitchers intentionally walked him 20 times, more than anyone else in the circuit. In a conversation with slugger Frank Howard, he said, "They're starting to pitch around me, Frank." Howard responded, "Better get used to it."

Jackson was appropriately impressed by the presence of Joe DiMaggio as an A's coach. "He's such a symbol of greatness to a ballplayer," Jackson said in 1968, "something to strive for, someone to get approval from. It would be embarrassing not to hustle in front of such a man."

With his big swing, Reggie led the league in strikeouts every year from 1968 to 1971 (and again in 1982). But the 1969 season marked the first of 14 all-star selections for Jackson, who concluded his career with 563 home runs, 2,584 hits, a .262 lifetime batting average, and four home run titles.

Jackson also had superb range in the outfield with a strong arm in his early years. His roommate, pitcher Chuck Dobson, said in 1969, "He gets to the ball quick, catches everything and has a great arm." While his fielding became sloppier as he aged, early in his career he led right fielders in putouts five years and assists two seasons.

Jackson won the MVP award in 1973 and finished in the top five in MVP voting in four other years. He became known as Mister October for his World Series heroics with the A's and Yankees.

The star had a knack for attracting publicity and whipping up controversy. He called himself a 14-carat gold player and "the straw that stirs the drink." Tom Boswell wrote in 1977, "Perhaps more than any player of his generation, Jackson has learned how to sell himself…as an all-purpose celebrity." Asked whether Jackson was a hot dog, teammate Darold Knowles said there wasn't enough mustard in the world to cover him.

At times, Jackson may have gone too far in stoking controversy. His quarrels with Yankees owner George Steinbrenner and manager Billy Martin were epic. His relationship with team captain Thurman Munson was sometimes tense. In a book that Munson co-authored in 1978 with Marty Appel, he wrote, "Reggie's whole life is based on the unreal world of baseball. He has no stable family, no great business knowledge. His friends are those who tell him how great he is, and if they're celebrities, all the better." It is said that their relationship had improved before the plane crash that took Munson's life in 1979.

Jackson played all the way to age 41 and was elected to the Hall of Fame on the first ballot. He resides in California, still respected as a slugger for the ages.

REGGIE SMITH

It is unclear when the term "five-tool player" came into common use, but it certainly described outfielder Reggie Smith, who achieved the distinction of being selected to all-star teams in three different decades. A gifted athlete, he hit .287 with 314 home runs and 2,020 hits over the course of his MLB career, which began in 1966 and spanned 17 seasons.

Centennial High School in Compton produced Smith along with contemporary players Roy White and Don Wilson. He signed in 1963 and became a starter for the Red Sox in 1967, in time to help Boston win the pennant. In hitting .246 with 15 home runs, the switch-hitter placed second in the rookie of the year derby to Rod Carew of the Twins. Smith added two more home runs during the World Series against the Cardinals.

Reggie captured a gold glove in 1968 and made his first all-star squad in 1969. He led the AL in total bases and doubles in 1971.

The Red Sox owner then was Tom Yawkey. The owner had a track record of investing in his team, even if the club's record wasn't always stellar. In the mid-1950s, for example, it's said he offered one million dollars to the Indians for up-and-coming pitcher Herb Score.

In a political decision five decades after Reggie Smith's time with the Red Sox, the team removed the name "Yawkey Way" from the street outside Fenway Park because the Red Sox were the last team to integrate on July 21, 1959. (The Red Sox were not the only franchise that dragged its feet. The Phillies waited until 1957, and the Tigers until 1958, to desegregate.)

Smith told reporter Dan Shaughnessy that he opposed the change, saying, "Tom Yawkey treated me very fairly. I had conversations with him about the reputation that he had and the Red Sox had during the time I was there. He wanted to make sure that he had a good team and he wanted the best players he could possibly get, and if there was anything that I needed or any problems

Doug Kurkul

that I had to bring it to him and let him know. I was treated fairly and I know that when I left Boston, I was the highest-paid African-American player that he had, and I respect him for it.''

Smith continued to perform at a high level with the Cardinals, Dodgers and Giants. He played one final season in Japan, an unpleasant experience marked by arguments with umpires and verbal abuse from fans.

Off the field, Smith learned to play several musical instruments (including cello, flute, saxophone, clarinet and piano) and to pilot planes. He worked in the Dodgers' organization in 1990 and was coach of the 2000 U.S. Olympic gold-medal baseball team. He has also run a baseball clinic in California and devoted countless hours to fundraising for worthy causes. Smith currently lives in Encino, California.

CARL YASTRZEMSKI

Only once has the AL had triple-crown winners in consecutive years: Frank Robinson of the Orioles in 1966 and Carl Yastrzemski of the Red Sox in 1967. The other seven to win triple-crowns in the AL were Nap Lajoie, Ty Cobb, Jimmie Foxx, Lou Gehrig, Ted Williams (twice) and Mickey Mantle.

Carl's career combined a four-year period of pure dominance between 1967 and 1970 with remarkable staying power. As a 21-year-old rookie playing left field for Boston in 1961, he was the successor to Ted Williams. He was still a productive hitter when he hung up the spikes in 1983.

The 18-time all-star's stats reflect that longevity – a .285 batting average, 3,419 hits, and 452 home runs. His 1,844 RBI were 15th on the all-time list as of 2024. Pitcher Bob Humphreys of the Yankees and Senators spoke for many when he called Yaz the toughest hitter to get out. Carl was also an exceptional fielder, leading left fielders in assists eight times and snaring six gold gloves.

Yaz grew up on Long Island where his dad, uncles and brother were all ballplayers. Carl's first games were played in a clearing on his dad's potato farm, where he learned the value of hard work. One of his buddies was future Red Sox teammate and roommate Chuck Schilling. A Notre Dame student studying business, Carl received a $100,000 bonus when signing with Boston as a shortstop. He began his minor-league career as a second sacker but was moved to left field a year later. After joining the parent club, Carl and his wife bought a luxury home in Lynnfield, about 20 miles north of Fenway Park.

The Red Sox owner, Tom Yawkey, had no son of his own, just an adopted daughter. He developed a close relationship with certain players and Carl was one of them. This allowed the slugger to share his candid opinions with the owner and led to speculation over the years about Yaz's role in the termination of several managers.

Yaz won his first batting title in 1963, nine points better than runner-up Al Kaline, but all was not roses. At a speech in Norwood, Massachusetts, after the season, Carl said he was discouraged by his team's seventh place finish. Further, he expressed disgust that first-year Sox manager Johnny Pesky, without telling Carl first, related to reporters he would fine Yaz for one more baserunning miscue. "No one in authority ever spoke to me about it," he told the stunned audience at the rubber chicken event. "I resent a manager discussing discipline in public print."

Off-season banquets were common in the Sixties but criticizing a manager on the record wasn't. Columnist Hy Hurwitz called the whole situation "unhealthy," saying, "the plot against Pesky is possibly the most dangerous ever concocted in the 31 years that Yawkey has owned the Red Sox." Hurwitz elaborated, "It was reported that the conspirators include members of the press and radio as well as Red Sox personnel." Despite speculation, Pesky's contract was renewed for 1964.

Yaz spent the winter taking courses at Merrimack University and doing exercises designed to strengthen his back, arm and neck muscles. He hit his first grand-slam home run on May 3, 1964, helping Boston beat the Tigers, 11-7. He then went into a frustrating slump, commenting in June that "I just can't seem to tie together a few good days." Part of the problem was his penchant for trying to pull outside pitches.

In September, Pesky briefly benched Yaz for not running hard on an infield groundout. Carl told writer Larry Claflin, "If Pesky wants to call it loafing, let him call it that. I wasn't feeling well. I had a cold and I almost had to come out of the game in the second inning." He finished the year with decent statistics, but the club dropped to eighth place. Claflin reported that "Yastrzemski does not seem to be the same eager youth, full of desire to prove his ability, that he was a couple of years ago." Pesky was soon relieved of his duties.

For the 1965 season, with Billy Herman as manager, Yaz hit .312 and led the AL in slugging and on-base percentage as well as doubles. His personal success did not translate to the Sox, who lost 100 games. The story was much the same in 1966. Although Carl had a good year, the club lost 90 games and Herman was dismissed in September.

Carl's teammates elected him team captain but most were not personally close with him. They were happy to play cards with him during flights to reduce his flight anxiety, but as Hawk Harrelson later noted, Carl never seemed concerned about what anyone thought of him, including his teammates. "He didn't seek the spotlight, but he thrived in spite of it. He just wanted the team to win. He led by example."

Ahead of the 1967 season, Carl worked out with conditioning coach Gene Berde, who had trained Hungary's Olympic athletes. Carl arrived at spring training in incredible shape and Claflin wrote in June that his attitude had never been better. With new manager Dick Williams at the helm, Yaz seemed unfazed over having been relieved of his team captain duties. Carl started strong and finished the season on fire. His selection as MVP was a foregone conclusion.

The pennant was another matter. Heading into the season's final week, the Red Sox, Tigers, Twins and White Sox were still in contention. The Red Sox had just four games, all at home, remaining. On Tuesday, Carl slugged his 43rd homer against Luis Tiant, but Cleveland prevailed 6-3. On Wednesday, Carl had a hit and a walk, but Cleveland got to Jim Lonborg and won 6-0. That put Boston in second place, in a must-win situation against the Twins for the final two games. On Saturday, Carl blasted his 44th homer against Jim Merritt, and Boston won 6-4. In the season finale, Yaz went four-for-four and the Sox prevailed over Minnesota's Dean Chance, 5-3. The Red Sox won their first pennant in 21 years, a 100-to-one bet in Vegas.

With fans streaming madly onto the Fenway Park field, the entourage of players, coaches and writers made their way to the clubhouse. A tear-filled owner Tom Yawkey said, "Thank you for everything. This is the happiest day of my life."

Carl's 44 home runs were the second-highest in franchise history (trailing only Jimmie Foxx who hit 50 shots in 1938). His hot hitting continued during the World Series, as he batted .400 with three home runs, but the Cardinals prevailed in seven games.

Yaz won the batting title with a .300 average in 1968, hitting 23 home runs. He followed up with two more 40-homer seasons. By the time the Red Sox won the AL pennant in 1975, Carl was the regular first baseman and – along with Rico Petrocelli and briefly Tony Conigliaro – one of the few holdovers from the great 1967 team.

Carl continued to play at a high level until 1983, when he made the AL all-star team for one final time. Then in 2019, Carl enjoyed another personal highlight, seeing his grandson Mike become a star outfielder for the Giants. Watching the proud grandfather shake hands on the field with Mike, it was a reminder of Carl's incredible career during one of baseball's most memorable eras.

Appendix: The Leather

Most players from the Sixties signed contracts with glove manufacturers soon after turning pro. In exchange for promotional rights, they typically received two gloves and some baseball shoes every year during their minor and major league career. While most of the players never reached the major leagues, those who became top MLB stars sometimes appeared in magazine ads and catalogs for which they usually received special compensation from the glove-makers.

Four different sporting goods companies had the lion's share of the market. According to our research, the market was split roughly as follows: Rawlings with 38%; Wilson with 21%; Spalding with 20%; MacGregor with 15%; and other brands with about 6%. Some players used different brands at varying times during their career. Some also endorsed one brand while using a different one on the field.

Listed below are 350 players and gloves they are known to have used or endorsed. The list is believed to be accurate but is not comprehensive, as players may have used or endorsed other brands as well.

1. Hank Aaron - MacGregor
2. Tommie Aaron - Rawlings
3. Ted Abernathy - MacGregor and Hollander
4. Jerry Adair - Rawlings
5. Mike Adamson - Rawlings
6. Joe Adcock - Rawlings
7. Hank Aguirre - Rawlings
8. Bob Allison - Wilson
9. Matty Alou - Wilson
10. Jesus Alou - Spalding
11. Max Alvis - Wilson
12. Joe Amalfitano - Rawlings
13. Mike Andrews - Spalding
14. Luis Aparicio - Wilson
15. Gerry Arrigo - Wilson
16. Richie Ashburn - MacGregor
17. Bob Aspromonte - Spalding
18. Ken Aspromonte - Rawlings
19. Jack Baldschun - Spalding
20. Ernie Banks - Wilson
21. Steve Barber - Spalding
22. Earl Battey - Rawlings
23. Hank Bauer - Rawlings
24. Glenn Beckert - Wilson
25. Mark Belanger - Rawlings
26. Bo Belinsky - Rawlings, Grant's Pro Sports
27. Gary Bell - Wilson
28. Gus Bell - MacGregor
29. Johnny Bench - Rawlings
30. Dennis Bennett - Rawlings
31. Yogi Berra - Spalding
32. Ken Berry - Rawlings

33. Hal Bevan - Wilson
34. Curt Blefary - Rawlings
35. Paul Blair - Wilson
36. Don Blasingame - Wilson, JC Higgins/Sears
37. Steve Blass - Rawlings
38. John Boccabella - Rawlings
39. Bob Bolin - Wilson
40. Ed Bouchee - MacGregor
41. Jim Bouton - Spalding
42. Clete Boyer - Rawlings
43. Ken Boyer – Rawlings
44. Gene Brabender - MacGregor
45. Ron Brand - Rawlings
46. Jackie Brandt - used Wilson, endorsed Sonnett
47. Tom Brewer - Rawlings
48. Ed Brinkman - Wilson
49. Jim Britton - Rawlings
50. Ernie Broglio - MacGregor
51. Dick Brown - MacGregor
52. Bob Bruce - Rawlings
53. Jerry Buchek - Spalding
54. Don Buford - Sears
55. Bob Buhl - Wilson, Sears
56. Wally Bunker - Rawlings
57. Jim Bunning - Spalding and Reach
58. Bill Burbach - Rawlings
59. Lew Burdette - Rawlings
60. Johnny Callison - Spalding
61. Doug Camilli - Rawlings
62. Don Cardwell - Rawlings
63. Steve Carlton - Rawlings
64. Paul Casanova - Rawlings
65. Wayne Causey - Rawlings, Spalding, Wilson
66. Dean Chance - Hollander
67. Pete Charton - Spalding
68. Ossie Chavarria - Rawlings
69. Harry Chiti - Wilson
70. Galen Cisco - Rawlings
71. Roberto Clemente - Rawlings
72. Tony Cloninger - Rawlings

73. Jim Coker - MacGregor
74. Rocky Colavito - Spalding
75. Gordy Coleman - Rawlings
76. Joe Coleman - Wilson
77. Pat Corrales - MacGregor
78. Billy Cowan - MacGregor and Wilson
79. Del Crandall - MacGregor
80. Ray Culp - MacGregor
81. George Culver - Rawlings
82. Bruce Dal Canton - Rawlings
83. Vic Davalillo - MacGregor and Wilson
84. Jim Davenport - Wilson and Sonnett
85. Ted Davidson - MacGregor
86. Tommy Davis - Rawlings
87. Willie Davis - Wilson
88. Mike De La Hoz - Rawlings
89. Larry Dierker - Spalding
90. Dick Dietz - Rawlings
91. Pat Dobson - MacGregor
92. Dick Drago - Rawlings
93. Don Drysdale - Spalding
94. Ryne Duren - Wilson
95. Doc Edwards - Spalding
96. John Edwards - Rawlings
97. Tom Egan - Rawlings
98. Dock Ellis - Spalding
99. Sammy Ellis - MacGregor
100. Roy Face - Rawlings
101. Rollie Fingers - Rawlings
102. Hank Fischer - Rawlings
103. Eddie Fisher - Spalding
104. Jack Fisher - Wilson and Hollander
105. Curt Flood - Rawlings
106. Nellie Fox - Wilson
107. Terry Fox - MacGregor
108. Paul Foytack - Spalding
109. Earl Francis - Rawlings
110. Bill Freehan - Wilson
111. Jim Fregosi - Spalding
112. Bob Friend - Rawlings
113. Vern Fuller - Rowland – A 2001
114. Len Gabrielson - Spalding

115. John Gelnar - MacGregor
116. Joe Gibbon - Rawlings
117. Bob Gibson - Spalding
118. Russ Gibson - Spalding
119. Jim Gilliam - Rawlings
120. Dave Giusti - Rawlings
121. Jim Gosger - Wilson for first base, Spalding for outfield
122. Bill Grabarkewicz - Spalding
123. Dick Groat - Spalding
124. Harvey Haddix - Rawlings
125. Tom Haller - Spalding
126. Steve Hamilton - Wilson
127. Ken Hamlin - Rawlings
128. Bill Hands - Rawlings
129. Larry Haney - Rawlings
130. Ron Hansen - MacGregor and Spalding
131. Steve Hargan - Rawlings
132. Bud Harrelson - Rawlings and Spalding
133. Billy Harris (Cle-KC) - Rawlings
134. Gail Harris - MacGregor
135. Jim Ray Hart - MacGregor
136. Chuck Hartenstein - MacGregor
137. Bill Heath - Rawlings
138. Mike Hedlund - Spalding
139. Bob Heffner - Spalding
140. Woody Held - Sonnet
141. Bob Hendley - Rawlings
142. Phil Hennigan - Spalding
143. Bill Henry - Wilson
144. Ron Herbel - Wilson
145. Ray Herbert - Rawlings
146. Ed Herrmann - Rawlings
147. Mike Hershberger - used Wilson, endorsed Sonnett
148. Jack Hiatt - Rawlings, Wilson
149. Chuck Hiller - MacGregor
150. John Hiller - Wilson
151. Glen Hobbie - Sears
152. Gil Hodges - Wilson
153. Ken Holtzman - Rawlings
154. Joel Horlen - Spalding
155. Willie Horton - Wilson
156. Elston Howard - Rawlings and Hollander
157. Frank Howard - Hollander
158. Dick Howser - Rawlings
159. Dick Hughes - Spalding
160. Bob Humphreys - MacGregor
161. Randy Hundley - Spalding
162. Catfish Hunter - Wilson
163. Steve Huntz - Rawlings
164. Larry Jackson - Rawlings
165. Reggie Jackson - Rawlings
166. Sonny Jackson - Rawlings
167. Charlie James - Rawlings
168. Ray Jarvis - Rawlings
169. Larry Jaster - Rawlings
170. Julian Javier - Spalding
171. Tommy John - Wilson
172. Cleon Jones - Spalding
173. Al Kaline - Wilson
174. Eddie Kasko - Rawlings
175. Don Kessinger - Spalding
176. Mike Kilkenny - Rawlings
177. Harmon Killebrew - Wilson
178. Jerry Kindall - Wilson
179. Clay Kirby - Rawlings
180. Bobby Klaus - Spalding
181. Lou Klimchock - Spalding
182. Ted Kluszewski - MacGregor
183. Howie Koplitz - Rawlings
184. Joe Koppe - Wilson
185. Jack Kralick - Wilson
186. Tony Kubek - Rawlings
187. Harvey Kuenn - Wilson
188. Jack Lamabe - Wilson
189. Jim Landis - MacGregor
190. Don Larsen - Spalding
191. Tony LaRussa - Rawlings
192. Frank Lary - Wilson
193. Barry Latman - Spalding
194. Charlie Lau - Spalding
195. Vern Law - Rawlings

196. Denver Lemaster - MacGregor
197. Dave Leonhard - Spalding
198. Ted Lepcio - Rawlings
199. Dick Lines -Wilson
200. Phil Linz - Rawlings
201. Bobby Locke - Rawlings
202. Bob Locker - Spalding
203. Johnny Logan - Franklin
204. Mickey Lolich - Spalding
205. Sherm Lollar - Rawlings
206. Jeoff Long - Spalding
207. Marcelino Lopez - Spalding
208. Jerry Lynch - MacGregor
209. Art Mahaffey - Rawlings
210. Mickey Mantle - Rawlings, Sportcrest (Japan)
211. Juan Marichal - Wilson
212. Roger Maris - Spalding
213. JC Martin - Rawlings
214. Lee May - MacGregor
215. Willie Mays - MacGregor
216. Bill Mazeroski - MacGregor
217. Jim McAndrew - MacGregor
218. Al McBean - Spalding
219. Mike McCormick - MacGregor and Rawlings
220. Willie McCovey - Wilson
221. Tom McCraw - Rawlings
222. Lindy McDaniel - Rawlings
223. Sam McDowell - Wilson
224. Jim McGlothlin - Rawlings
225. Don McMahon - Rawlings
226. Roy McMillan - Wilson
227. Ken McMullen - Spalding
228. Dave McNally - Rawlings
229. Pete Mikkelsen - Rawlings
230. Felix Millan - Spalding
231. Joe Moeller - Spalding
232. Bill Monbouquette - Spalding
233. Walt Moryn - JC Higgins/Sears
234. Tom Murphy - Wilson
235. Stan Musial - Rawlings
236. Les Narum - Rawlings

237. Jim Nash - Wilson
238. Fred Newman - MacGregor
239. Phil Niekro - Wilson
240. Russ Nixon - MacGregor
241. Gary Nolan - Wilson and Rawlings
242. Joe Nossek - Wilson
243. Rich Nye - Wilson and Rawlings
244. Blue Moon Odom - Wilson
245. Tony Oliva - MacGregor
246. Gene Oliver - Rawlings
247. Nate Oliver - Rawlings
248. Claude Osteen - MacGregor
249. Jim O'Toole - Wilson
250. Jose Pagan - Spalding
251. Jim Pagliaroni - Spalding, Hollander
252. Jim Palmer - Spalding
253. Lowell Palmer - Rawlings
254. Milt Pappas - Wilson and Hollander
255. Wes Parker - Rawlings
256. Joe Pepitone - Spalding and Hollander
257. Tony Perez - MacGregor
258. Gaylord Perry - Wilson
259. Gary Peters - Spalding
260. Rico Petrocelli - Spalding
261. Tom Phoebus - Rawlings
262. Billy Pierce - JC Higgins/Sears
263. Jim Piersall - Wilson
264. Vada Pinson - Spalding
265. Juan Pizarro - MacGregor
266. Johnny Podres - Rawlings
267. Wally Post - Rawlings
268. Boog Powell - Rawlings
269. Vic Power - Spalding
270. Doug Rader - Wilson
271. Pedro Ramos - Spalding
272. Howie Reed - MacGregor
273. Phil Regan - Rawlings
274. Tom Reynolds - Wilson
275. Bobby Richardson - endorsed MacGregor, preferred Rawlings
276. Pete Richert - Rawlings
277. Steve Ridzik - Wilson

278. Robin Roberts - MacGregor
279. Brooks Robinson - Spalding
280. Frank Robinson - MacGregor
281. Cookie Rojas - Goodwin
282. Rich Rollins - Spalding
283. John Romano - Rawlings
284. Pete Rose - MacGregor
285. John Roseboro - MacGregor
286. Don Rudolph - Rawlings
287. Ken Rudolph - Rawlings
288. Pete Runnels - Wilson
289. Nolan Ryan - Spalding
290. Amado Samuel - Rawlings
291. Jack Sanford - Rawlings
292. Ron Santo - Wilson
293. Chuck Schilling - Rawlings
294. Dick Schofield - Rawlings
295. Herb Score - Rawlings and Barco Athletic
296. Diego Segui - Rawlings
297. Bob Shaw - Rawlings
298. Roland Sheldon - Spalding
299. Larry Sherry - Wilson
300. Bart Shirley - Rawlings
301. Bill Short - Wilson
302. Chris Short - Rawlings
303. Sonny Siebert - Spalding
304. Bill Singer - Spalding
305. Tommie Sisk - Spalding
306. Moose Skowron - MacGregor
307. Warren Spahn - Rawlings
308. Al Spangler - Wilson
309. Tracy Stallard - Spalding
310. Al Stanek - Spalding
311. Wes Stock - Wilson
312. George Stone - Rawlings
313. Ron Stone - Rawlings, Wilson
314. Ken Suarez - Spalding
315. Don Sutton - MacGregor
316. Fred Talbot - Spalding
317. Ron Taylor - Spalding
318. Johnny Temple - MacGregor
319. George Thomas - Wilson
320. Lee Thomas - MacGregor
321. Luis Tiant - Rawlings, MacGregor
322. Earl Torgeson - MacGregor
323. Frank Torre - MacGregor
324. Joe Torre - Spalding
325. Hector Torres - Rawlings
326. Tom Tresh - Rawlings
327. Jim Umbricht - MacGregor
328. Cecil Upshaw - Wilson
329. Zoilo Versalles - MacGregor
330. Dave Vineyard - Rawlings
331. Ozzie Virgil - Rawlings
332. Gary Wagner - Rawlings
333. Ray Washburn - Spalding
334. Gary Waslewski - Wilson
335. Dave Watkins - Rawlings
336. Eddie Watt - Rawlings
337. Mike Wegener - Spalding
338. Vic Wertz - Rawlings
339. Hoyt Wilhelm - Wilson
340. Billy Williams - Rawlings
341. Stan Williams - Rawlings
342. Ted Williams - Wilson and Sears
343. Don Wilson - MacGregor
344. Earl Wilson - Rawlings
345. Rick Wise - Wilson
346. Dooley Womack - Wilson
347. Wilbur Wood - Wilson
348. Gene Woodling - Rawlings
349. Al Worthington - Rawlings
350. John Wyatt - Rawlings
351. Early Wynn - Wilson
352. Chris Zachary - Spalding
353. Jerry Zimmerman - MacGregor

BIBLIOGRAPHY:
SUMMARY OF SOURCES

PLAYER REFLECTIONS

The author is grateful to the more than 40 former players (including 11 all-stars) and front-office administrators for sharing memories through telephone and in-person interviews, U.S. Mail and the exchange of email messages between 2006 and 2024:

Max Alvis, Bob Aspromonte, Ken Aspromonte, Steve Bailey, Ken Berry, Dick Bosman, Ted Bowsfield, Ron Brand, Jackie Brandt, Bruce Brubaker, Larry Burright, Dr. Pete Charton, George Culver, Johnny Edwards, Chuck Essegian, Eddie Fisher, James French, Esq., Vern Fuller, Jake Gibbs, Gus Gil, Pat Gillick, Tom Gramly, Billy Harris, Sonny Jackson, Charley James, Larry Jaster, Lou Klimchock, Darold Knowles, Don Lee, Jim Lonborg, Jeoff Long, Ken McBride, Tom McCraw, Sam McDowell, Jim Merritt, Joe Moeller, Joe Nossek, Dr. Rich Nye, Nate Oliver, Claude Osteen, Phil Regan, Merv Rettenmund, Tom Reynolds, Branch Rickey III, Ken Rudolph, Roland Sheldon, Bart Shirley, Sonny Siebert, Dick Simpson, Duke Sims, Al Spangler, Jack Spring, George Strickland, Ron Stone, Ken Suarez, Dick Tomanek, Del Unser, Dr. Dave Watkins, and Stan Williams.

BOOKS

A Pirate for Life, Steve Blass with Erik Sherman, Triumph Books, 2012.

Baseball Stars of 1971, edited by Ray Robinson, Pyramid Books, 1971.

Baseball's Best 1000, Derek Gentile, Black Dog & Leventhal, 2008.

Behind the Mask: An Inside Baseball Diary, Bill Freehan, edited by Steve Gelman and Dick Schaap, The World Publishing Company, 1970.

Birdie: Confessions of a Baseball Nomad, Birdie Tebbetts, Triumph Books, 2002.

Brooks: The Biography of Brooks Robinson, Doug Wilson, Thomas Dunne Books, 2014.

Cepeda: The Orlando Cepeda Story, Bruce Markusen, Arte Publico Press, 2001.

Closer: Major League Players Reveal the Inside Pitch on Saving the Game, Kevin Neary and Leigh A. Tobin, Running Press Book Publishers, 2013.

Crash: The Life and Times of Dick Allen, Dick Allen and Tim Whitaker, Ticknor & Fields, 1989.

Drama and Pride in the Gateway City: The 1964 Cardinals, Society for American Baseball Research, 2013.

Endless Seasons: Baseball in Southern California, Society for American Baseball Research, 2011.

Fairly at Bat: My 50 Years in Baseball, from the Batter's Box to the Broadcast Booth, Ron Fairly, Back Story Publishing, LLC, 2018.

From 33rd Street to Camden Yards: An Oral History of the Baltimore Orioles, John Eisenberg, Contemporary Books, 2001.

Gil Hodges: A Hall of Fame Life, Mort Zachter, University of Nebraska Press, 2015.

Good as Gold: My Eight Decades in Baseball, Jim Kaat with Douglas Lyons, Triumph Books, 2021.

Hawk: I Did it My Way, Ken Harrelson with Jeff Snook, Triumph Books, 2019.

Hustler: The Myths, Life and Lies of Pete Rose, Michael Y. Sokolove, Simon and Schuster, 1990.

Impact Player, Bobby Richardson with David Thomas, Tyndale House Publishing, 2012.

I Told You I Wasn't Perfect, Denny McLain and Eli Zaret, Triumph Books, 2007.

Insight Pitch: My Life as a Major League Closer, Skip Lockwood, Sports Publishing, 2018.

Joy in Mudville: The Big Book of Baseball Humor by Dick Schaap and Mort Gerberg, Doubleday Publishing, 1992.

Long Taters: A Biography of George (Boomer) Scott by Ron Anderson, McFarland Publishing, 2011.

Miracle Collapse: The 1969 Chicago Cubs, Doug Feldmann, University of Nebraska, 2006.

My 25 Years Covering Baseball's Heroes, Scandals, Triumphs, and Tragedies, Bill Madden, Sports Publishing LLC. 2004.

My Baseball Journey from the Negro Leagues to the Majors, George Altman and Lew Freedman, McFarland Publishing, 2013.

My Time at Bat: A Story of Perseverance, Chuck Hinton, Christian Living Books, 2002.

October 1964, David Halberstam, Villard Books, 1994.

Off the Record, Buzzie Bavasi with John Strege, Contemporary Books, 1987.

On the Run: The Never Dull, Often Shocking Life of Maury Wills, by Maury Wills and Mike Celizic, Carroll & Graf Publishers, 1991.

Snake Jazz, Dave Baldwin, 2009.

Son of Havana, Luis Tiant with Saul Visnia, Diversion Books, 2019.

Southern League: A True Story of Baseball, Civil Rights, and the Deep South's Most Compelling Pennant Race, Larry Colton, Grand Central Publishing, 2013.

Strike Three!: My Years in the 'Pen, Thomas A. Tomsick, MD, Jarndyce & Jarndyce Press, 2010.

The 1969 Cubs: Ferguson Jenkins with George Castle, Signature Strength Publishing, 2018.

The Anaheim Angels: A Complete History, by Ross Newhan, Hyperion Publishing, 2000.

The Kansas City Athletics: A Baseball History, 1954-1967, John E. Peterson, McFarland & Company, 2003.

The Last Innocents: The Collision of the Turbulent Sixties and the Los Angeles Dodgers, Michael Leahy, HarperCollins Publishers, 2016.

The Pride of Minnesota: The Twins in the Turbulent Sixties, Thom Henninger, University of Nebraska Press, 2021.

The Saga of Sudden Sam: The Rise, Fall, and Redemption of Sam McDowell, Sam McDowell and Martin Gitlin, Rowman & Littlefield, 2022.

The Willie Horton Story by Hal Butler, J. Messner Publishing, 1970.

The Yankees in the Early 1960s, William J. Ryczek, McFarland & Company, 2008.

Then Mickey Said to Roy: The Best Yankees Stories Ever Told, Roy White with Darrell Berger, Triumph Books, 2009.

This Side of Cooperstown: An Oral History of Major League Baseball in the 1950s, Larry Moffi, University of Iowa Press, 1996.

Toy Cannon: The Autobiography of Baseball's Jim Wynn, Jim Wynn with Bill McCurdy, McFarland & Company, 2010.

When in Doubt, Fire the Manager: My Life and Times in Baseball, Alvin Dark and John Underwood, E.P. Dutton, 1980.

When You Come to a Fork in the Road, Take It: Inspiration and Wisdom from One of Baseball's Great Heroes, Yogi Berra with Dave Kaplan, 2001.

NEWSPAPERS, MAGAZINES, WEBSITES

Akron Beacon Journal, Baltimore Sun, Baseball Digest magazine, *Baseball Italian Style, BlackCollegeNines.com, BaseballReference.com, Boston Courant, Cleveland Plain Dealer, Cleveland Press, CooperstownExpert.com, Lorain News Journal, Los Angeles Times, New York Times, Orange County Register, Orlando Sentinel, RedlegNation.com, Sport* magazine, SportingNews.com, *Sports Illustrated* magazine, *St. Louis* magazine, ThisGreatGame.com, The Sporting News.

ABOUT THE AUTHOR

Doug Kurkul is a public affairs, association management and strategic communications executive based in the Chicago suburbs. He is CEO of the American Foundry Society and past president of several business organizations in Texas and Nevada. He was also vice president of the National Association of Manufacturers in Washington, D.C.

A member of the Society for American Baseball Research, Kurkul also authored, *Portrait of a Franchise: An Intimate Look at the Cleveland Indians in the Rockin' Sixties.* In 2009, as President of the Reno-Sparks Chamber of Commerce, Kurkul worked with Pacific Coast League President Branch Rickey III, Aces manager Brett Butler and others to welcome the Reno Aces as the PCL's newest team.

Previously, he was Executive Editor of *Leadership for Manufacturers* magazine and Managing Editor of the award-winning book, *Manufacturing in America: A Legacy of Excellence.*

His writing has also been published in *The Austin Business Journal, Association Trends, Northern Nevada Business Weekly, Leadership for Manufacturers* magazine, *Reno-Gazette Journal, Ashland Times-Gazette, NAM Member Focus, Round Rock Leader,* and Statesman.com.

Made in the USA
Monee, IL
16 September 2024

65860600R00219